CONFLICT OF IDEALS

CHANGING
VALUES
IN
WESTERN
SOCIETY

Luther J. Binkley

CONFLICT OF IDEALS
Changing Values in Western Society

CONFLICT OF IDEALS
Changing Values
in Western Society

LUTHER J. BINKLEY

Professor and Chairman,
Department of Philosophy,
Franklin and Marshall College

VAN NOSTRAND · REINHOLD COMPANY

NEW YORK   *TORONTO*   *LONDON*   *MELBOURNE*

Van Nostrand Regional Offices: *New York, Chicago, San Francisco*

D. Van Nostrand Company, Ltd., *London*

D. Van Nostrand Company (Canada), Ltd., *Toronto*

D. Van Nostrand Australia Pty. Ltd., *Melbourne*

Library of Congress Catalog Card No. 69–11739

To Betty Jane

Preface

This book is concerned with the present conflict between opposing ideals in our Western world. Ours is indeed an age of revolutions—political, racial, ideological, and moral. Increasingly, people of all ages are questioning the traditional middle-class values of our culture—success, popularity, conformity, and status. While militants may be more outspoken than others, it is quite clear that they are by no means the only ones in quest of a human and humane way of life. "What is it to be a man? What life style should I choose? Are some values more basic than others? What should I do if my chosen values conflict with those of my society?" To help the reader answer these questions in his own reasoned way is a main purpose of this book.

If one is to satisfy his quest for values to which he could commit himself, he must have some understanding of the alternative ideals competing for his adherence. To provide a needed context for our search for viable ideals, the first chapter surveys the moral climate of this century. We shall see how the relativism and pragmatism of the early decades of this century have influenced contemporary morality. In our further inquiry we shall explore the changing values of Western society in the light of the insights of psychology and the social sciences, as well as of the humanities, philosophy and religion. The body of this book, therefore, explains in some detail the values defended by Marxism, Psychoanalytic Humanism, Existentialism, and the New Christian Morality. In the last chapter, I show how contemporary analytic philosophy is relevant, as an aid, to one in choosing between conflicting ideals of life.

This book can be used in many college courses which are concerned with the nature of man, the history of ideas, or contemporary Western civilization. Its orientation is appropriate for many courses in the humanities and the social sciences, as well as for the more traditional introductory courses in ethics or philosophy. This study, moreover, is equally directed to the general reader, whether student, adult, or inquiring "dropout." If it helps the reader, whoever he may be, to engage in a dialogue between proponents of competing values in Western society, its major objective will have been achieved.

This study of the changing values in Western society is intended as a guide to, rather than a substitute for, the works of the most important thinkers who have influenced the present search for a way of life. Each chapter expounds the basic philosophies of the writers considered and raises evaluative questions so that the reader can think through the issues for himself. The body of the text and the selections for further reading (found at the end of each chapter) refer the reader to significant first-hand sources so that he may explore in depth the value theories which interest him. If this book helps one understand the original sources, then it will have opened for him the wealth of insight which these writers can give to one seeking self-knowledge and a satisfactory way of life.

I am grateful to the following persons for their assistance in reading the manuscript in whole or in part and for making many valuable suggestions to me: Richard I. Evans, Professor of Psychology, University of Houston; Nicholas Fotion, Professor and Chairman, Department of Philosophy, New York State University College at Buffalo; Carl Meier, Assistant Professor of Philosophy, Franklin & Marshall College; John B. Noss, Professor Emeritus of Philosophy, Franklin & Marshall College; Paul Ramsey, Professor of Religion, Princeton University; Robert C. Solomon, Assistant Professor of Philosophy, University of Pennsylvania; Guy W. Stroh, Professor and Chairman, Department of Philosophy, Rider College; and Robert Tucker, Professor of Political Science, Princeton University.

I should like to express my gratitude to the Philosophy Department of Princeton University for their assistance during my stay as a Visiting Fellow in 1966–1967, and to Franklin & Marshall College for granting me a Sabbatical in order that I might complete this book. The counsel and good wishes of faculty and students at both institutions provided the stimulation for me to work productively.

There is one person, however, who deserves more thanks than anyone else. My wife, Betty Jane, not only typed the manuscript for the book, but served as my most helpful critic. In deep gratitude and affection, therefore, this book is appropriately dedicated to her.

LUTHER J. BINKLEY

Contents

Preface   vii
I. *The Moral Climate of Our Century*   1
   The Age of Relativism   2
   The Pragmatic Method   12
   The Search for a Way of Life   24

II. *Marxism and Communism*   44
   Marx and Engels: A Brief Biographical Sketch   45
   The Early Views of Marx: Alienated Man   48
   Classical Marxism: Historical Materialism   54
   From Classical Marxism to Russian Communism   63
   The Ideological Struggle Within Marxism   68
   Toward an Evaluation of Marxism   72

III. *Psychoanalytic Humanism: Freud and Fromm*   84
   Freud: The Structure of the Mind   85
   Freud: Implications of Psychoanalysis for Morality and Religion   94
   Toward an Evaluation of Freud   102
   Erich Fromm: Normative Humanism   106
   Non-Productive Character Orientations   111
   The Productive Character   116
   A Saner Society   119
   Toward an Evaluation of Fromm   121

IV. *The Origins of Existentialism: Kierkegaard and Nietzsche*   127
   Kierkegaard's Life   128
   The Three Stages of Life   130
   An Existential Choice—Becoming a Christian   136
   Toward an Evaluation of Kierkegaard   141
   Nietzsche: Man as the Creator of Values   144
   Nietzsche's Method: The Destruction of Idols   147
   The Two Moralities: Master and Slave   149
   The Death of God and the Overman   153
   Toward an Evaluation of Nietzsche   156

V. *Humanistic Existentialism: Jean-Paul Sartre*   162
    The Human Condition: Being and Nothingness   166
    Man: The Creator of Values   181
    Existential Humanism: An Ethic of Ambiguity   192
    Existential Marxism: The Critique of Dialectical Reason 204
    Toward an Evaluation of Humanistic Existentialism   213

VI. *Religious Existentialism, Radical Theology and the New Morality* 225
    Karl Barth: Neo-Orthodoxy   226
    Paul Tillich: God as the Unconditioned Being   228
    The Secular City and the Death of God   246
    Situation Ethics Versus Rule Ethics   251
    Toward an Evaluation of the New Theology
        and the New Morality   271

VII. *Meta-Ethics and Moral Decisions*   282
    The Meaning of Ethical Terms   287
    The Use of Moral Terms   292
    Toulmin's Good Reasons for Moral Judgments   298
    Hare's Analysis of a Moral Argument   303
    Toward an Evaluation of Meta-Ethics   312

    Epilogue—A Basis for Decision   325
    Acknowledgments   329
    Index   333

I

The Moral Climate of Our Century

One who is wide awake does not need to be told that the twentieth century has witnessed tremendous changes in almost all fields of human endeavor. In the realm of the physical sciences, Einstein heads the list of those who have produced a revolution in thought and method; everyone has heard of the theory of relativity, even if one is not quite sure what it is. The social sciences really have started to come into their own in this century, and many people are disturbed by the possibilities for the control of human behavior which have emerged as a result of the study of man by psychology and sociology. Even in the realm of religion, which has usually been considered to change very slowly, if at all, our century has seen the growth of historical studies of religion and the arrival of theologians who call for a new world-view in the light of the "death" of the traditional Hebraic-Christian God. The traditional values of Western civilization have been attacked not only by *avant-garde* artists, but also by many young people who have been disillusioned by our affluent society.

A hopeful aspect of our changing scene emerges in the new force which has been given to the very idea of one world. The sense of the possibility, even of the necessity, of one world has been heightened by the rapid developments in transportation and communication which our century has witnessed. But it does not seem necessary to elaborate or detail this theme, for we are all aware of the various changes due to the many technological innovations which have increased the pleasures of our existence, while at the same time adding to the tensions and anxieties of our lives. Many speakers and writers agree with Bertrand Russell who has pointed out in *Common Sense and Nuclear Warfare* that the enormous energy which man has now learned to use for destructive purposes

—the atom and hydrogen bombs—increases the urgency of learning to live together in peace with our fellow men. The important issue for all mankind today is, as Russell has put it:

> The awful prospect of the extermination of the human race, if not in the next war, then in the next but one or the next but two, is so sobering to any imagination which has seriously contemplated it as to demand very fundamental fresh thought on the whole subject not only of international relations but of human life and its capabilities.[1]

And yet, strange as it may seem, at the very time when we most need some basic agreement concerning values for the nuclear age we find radical disagreement not only between the various nations, but also among the political leaders, psychologists, philosophers and theologians of the Western world. This disagreement is not only a technological debate concerning the best means to achieve a more humane world, but more importantly it concerns the values themselves to which such a humane world might be committed. We shall explore in later chapters the various competing value systems which are viable options for our century, for it is our conviction that one cannot make an intelligent commitment to a way of life unless he understands various life-orientations from which he can choose.

The purpose of this chapter, however, is to sketch in a general way the moral climate of our time. It will prove to be very helpful in our inquiry to attempt to discover what some of the intellectual currents have been which have shaped our moral attitudes. What has happened to make this century one of relativism in morals? Are any new value orientations being proposed to replace the dead absolutes of the past? Let us now turn to an attempt to answer these questions.

The Age of Relativism   Our age has often been called an age of relativism. During the so-called Jazz Age of the Twenties Walter Lippmann observed that "the acids of modernity" had dissolved the religious certainties of the past. The influence of the scientific method and the growth of industrial and urban society were largely responsible, he believed, for the loss of faith in absolutes. Even in the realm of morals the codes we had inherited from the Hebrews of the Old Testament were beginning to dissolve in the spirit of a new age.[2] Lippmann's insights were confirmed by the findings of many social scientists who found in their studies that different cultures professed radically different values, thus suggesting that there was no justification for our traditional belief that our values were the only ones which sane men could adopt.

The most sustained treatment of relativism in ethics was by Edward Westermarck, whose studies show a blend of anthropological, sociological and philosophical interests. In the *Origin and Development of Moral Ideas* (1906) and *Ethical Relativity* (1932) he shows the great diversity among the moral judgments of different societies and individuals. Some of these differences in moral standards may be accounted for by differences in environment, in religion, and in beliefs, but many of them represented what he considered to be unresolvable moral differences. In providing examples of the latter type of moral differences, he referred to the various concepts held by different societies and by individuals as to how widely within or beyond the group the principles of morality apply, and what should be done when one's interests clash with those of others. These differences in moral judgment led Westermarck to conclude that ethics is based on emotional reactions in which there is a basic impulse to repay the good or evil that has been done to oneself. Westermarck held an individualistic theory of ethics to the extent that he maintained that what one calls good is that which arouses in him the emotion of approval, while that is considered bad which arouses the emotion of disapproval. He did point out, however, that no one can develop arbitrarily his own emotions of approval or disapproval. They are really conditioned to a great extent by the moral emotions held in the particular age and locality in which the person is living. Thus, moral standards were found to vary from age to age as well as from culture to culture.[3] Because Westermarck supported his conclusions with a wealth of historical data, his theory of moral relativism seemed to many minds convincing.

In addition to the monumental study of morals in various societies by Westermarck, several other scholars tended to support his findings. Emile Durkheim, who was primarily interested in sociology, in studying primitive societies suggested that the facts of human behavior were more important than ethical theories. One had first to understand how men did in fact act, before one could say anything meaningful about how they ought to act. Herein, he asserted, was one of the great mistakes made by most philosophers. They had pronounced their ideal ethical codes with little reference to the actual nature of man and his behavior. Durkheim stressed more than Westermarck did the role of society in forming one's moral standards. The feelings of approval or disapproval which characterize good and bad conduct, he suggested, are determined by the opinions of society as a unit rather than by the individuals of the society. For Durkheim the supreme authority concerning moral values is the particular society in which one happens to live. The peculiar urgency which attaches to moral commands is due to the fact that they originate in the society and not simply in individuals. But these commands are relativistic, on the basis of this kind of analysis, for they have no validity beyond the particular societies in which they appear.[4]

William Graham Sumner, the first significant American sociologist, also contributed to the belief that moral values are relative in maintaining that moral judgments were accurately described as non-rational manifestations of social forces. Moral values, according to him, are part of the folkways of a given society. Folkways are the customary ways by which man seeks to satisfy his basic needs. When folkways have a certain coerciveness about them, and when the implication is drawn that obeying them is good for the society which developed them, then they have become *mores.* That which we call good is, according to this view, only that to which we refer when we are expressing in forceful language the prevailing customs of our present society. But he also found that these customs varied from society to society, and that they tended to change within any given society from time to time. Philosophy and ethics then become nothing more than attempts to give some rational order to the prevailing folkways, and the reason for each age having its own distinctive philosophy is simply that each age attempts anew to rationalize its favorite customs, folkways and mores. No man can lift himself outside of the mores of his group, and Sumner insisted that the religious prophet or the social reformer was no exception to this rule. For Sumner morals are simply social customs which are more rigidly fixed and enforced than are such customs as styles in dress.[5]

Karl Mannheim has gone even further and has maintained that modes of thought are always conditioned by their social origins. All our ways of thinking are ideologies, according to Mannheim, even though we usually reserve the word to refer disparagingly to views with which we are in disagreement. As he puts it, the ethical system of any country at any time is simply an ideological expression by the prevailing group in power regarding the conduct it values as socially useful. All moral values and norms are then relative; an absolute standard is unobtainable. In fact, Mannheim maintained that even the very concepts of good and of right are purely ideological. It is true that he admitted that for a particular culture one ideology may be practicably more useful than another, but he found no way to stand apart from all ideologies so as to find a universal value.[6]

We might cite many more writers who have contributed to the prevailing relativistic climate in this century, but we have probably already made clear the converging lines of evidence from the social sciences which seem to suggest that "all values are relative." [7] We take for granted today that there are different patterns of culture; not all societies have adopted the same basic values as traditional Western civilization. What remains to be done, however, is to point out that there are conflicting judgments as to what relativism in morals implies.

One popular interpretation of the belief that all values are relative holds then that all values become equally arbitrary and irrational. According to this view, there is no rational justification for any act that an individual

does; to save a human life is as irrational as to commit murder. One author
has summarized this position as follows:

> It all depends on where you are,
> It all depends on when you are,
> It all depends on what you feel,
> It all depends on how you feel.
> It all depends on how you're raised,
> It all depends on what is praised,
> What's right today is wrong tomorrow,
> Joy in France, in England sorrow.
> It all depends on point of view,
> Australia or Timbuctoo,
> In Rome do as the Romans do.
> If tastes just happen to agree,
> Then you have morality.
> But where there are conflicting trends,
> It all depends, it all depends. . . .[8]

Sometimes, this interpretation of relativism is used to justify one's own
conduct, even if it harms other people. If all values are relative, and I
"get my kicks" in a different way than you, then it is claimed that you
have no right to object to my behavior. Thus, "All values are relative" is
often used as an emotive justification of any conduct whatsoever. As the
hero of John Barth's novel *The Floating Opera* puts it: "The reasons for
which people assign value to things are always ultimately (though not
necessarily immediately) arbitrary, irrational."[9]

The logical conclusion of this kind of an interpretation of relativism is
found in the contemporary Theatre of the Absurd. The plays of Samuel
Beckett, Eugène Ionesco, and Jean Genet reflect the breakdown of the
belief in rationality and in the traditional Hebraic-Christian values which
marked the recent past. The drama of the absurd not only deals with the
futility and uselessness of the ordinary activities of men, but also with the
emptiness in men's hearts resulting from the loss of the traditional values
of Western civilization. In Beckett's *Waiting for Godot* the main characters, Estragon and Vladimir, carry on meaningless conversations in order
to pass the time. Day after day they wait for Godot, who never arrives,
and yet they continue to wait, despite the absurdity of their behavior.
One day is like any other day, and there is no sense of purpose or meaning to their lives. They discuss separating from each other, hanging
themselves, moving to some other spot, but reject all these possibilities.
To do anything at all is absurd, and so they might just as well continue
in their senseless and eternal waiting. Their constant chatter and antics
seem to have only one justification:

VLADIMIR: That passed the time.
ESTRAGON: It would have passed in any case.
VLADIMIR: Yes, but not so rapidly.
              Pause.
ESTRAGON: What do we do now?
VLADIMIR: I don't know.
ESTRAGON: Let's go.
VLADIMIR: We can't.
ESTRAGON: Why not?
VLADIMIR: We're waiting for Godot.
ESTRAGON: (*despairingly*) Ah! [10]

Another aspect often present in the drama of the absurd stresses the overwhelming horror individuals face in having to cope with a vast world in the face of the impossibility of really having authentic communication with anyone else. In Ionesco's *The Chairs* an old married couple in their nineties await the arrival of a distinguished crowd of people who have been invited to hear the message which the old man will deliver at the end of his life. But since the old man is no orator, he has hired a professional orator to deliver his message. The guests arrive but are never seen or heard; instead the two old people fill the stage with chairs to seat them and carry on endless polite conversation with the empty chairs. The absurdity of attempting to communicate one's wisdom with other human beings is nicely satirized by the spectacle of the empty chairs on the stage. But the ending of the play portrays an even greater absurdity. The old man, convinced that the orator will deliver his message, jumps into the sea, followed by his wife. The professional orator faces the crowd of empty chairs, and prepares to speak. However, he is deaf and dumb and hence makes only an inarticulate gurgling noise. He then attempts to write something on a blackboard, but this is nothing more than a jumble of meaningless letters. Obviously, both in form and content, this play shows the ultimate meaninglessness and absurdity of man's existence.[11]

Jean Genet's plays attack the traditional values of Western civilization head on. All of us are portrayed as actors playing roles, and each role is shown to be empty, absurd, and meaningless. In *The Balcony* the scene is set in a fetishistic house of ill-repute, where people go in order to enact the roles which they really would prefer to play in the society in which they live. Despite a violent revolution being waged outside in the "real world" the clients, including the chief of police, continue to come to this establishment where they can act out whatever roles they desire. Ironically, the leader of the revolutionary band comes to the brothel to enact the role of chief of police. The mirrors in the house reflect the false images which men assume in their roles of fantasy, but Genet suggests that these images are not any more unreal than the roles most men actually perform in the outside world. Irma, proprietress of the house of illusions, makes this point in her speech to the audience at the end of the play: "You must now go home, where everything—you can be quite sure—will be even falser than here." [12]

The connection between the absurd and man's loss of belief in the traditional values of the past was clearly expressed by Albert Camus in *The Myth of Sisyphus:*

> A world that can be explained even with bad reasons is a familiar world. But, on the other hand, in a universe suddenly divested of illusions and lights, man feels an alien, a stranger. His exile is without remedy since he is deprived of the memory of a lost home or the hope of a promised land. This divorce between man and his life, the actor and his setting, is properly the feeling of absurdity. [13]

The theatre of the absurd is an attempt to portray the nature of human life when one comes to accept the belief that there are no values which are better than any others, that all life is therefore senseless and meaningless. It is an attempt to force man to confront his life with full awareness of the reality of arbitrary and irrational choices. If one is outraged and shocked by the themes and devices of the theatre of the absurd, one should recall that these dramatists believe that only by a new kind of play can we be awakened from our present conformism and moral insensibility. As Ionesco put it: "To tear ourselves away from the everyday, from habit, from mental laziness which hides from us the strangeness of reality, we must receive something like a real bludgeon blow." [14] The theatre of the absurd has sought to accomplish this mission; to reveal to the audience the absurdity of all value commitments if one believes that all values are equally irrational and arbitrary.

There is, however, a more justifiable interpretation of relativism than the one which we have discussed. This view maintains that moral judgments are relative to something or to some persons; they are not merely irrational and arbitrary whims. This kind of interpretation does not deny the findings of the social scientists for it recognizes that moral standards have in fact varied from culture to culture, from era to era, and even among the individuals in a particular society. In our own society, for example, it is clear that not all people hold the same moral judgments concerning euthanasia or birth control. But to maintain that moral evaluations are relative to our time in history and to the culture of which we are a part is not, according to this interpretation, to disparage morals but rather to help us to formulate more coherent and consistent basic principles for acting in our modern world. Just as science is relative to the age in which it is formulated, so quite naturally are our moral standards and judgments. Everyone knows that the physical sciences have changed radically in their basic principles since the time of their founding several centuries ago, and many scientists expect that similar changes are quite likely to occur in the future. What is not so often recognized is that no one argues that since science has changed so radically in several hundred years, any one is justified in holding arbitrary and irrational beliefs about scientific issues since all such beliefs are relative to the time in which they are formulated. Our understanding of human behavior and of the nature of man has also changed radically in the past several centuries, but this is no reason to maintain that therefore all values are equally absurd, arbitrary and irrational.

It is important that we do not mislead the reader to believe that this second interpretation of the significance of relativism rests on the assumption that moral values are exactly like scientific theories. Far from it, for while this kind of interpretation of relativism does call attention to the fact that scientific theories change and are in that sense relative to the age in which they are proclaimed, it also recognizes that there are crucial differences between believing in a scientific theory and committing oneself to a value judgment. The crucial tests for subscribing to a scientific theory depend upon the ability to explain observable events in terms of the theory, and to permit predictions of how similar events will occur in the future. A scientific theory concerning human behavior would attempt to explain man's actions in terms of a general theory, and then the theory would be accepted or rejected according to its success in predicting future behavior. We have no over-arching general scientific theory of human behavior as yet, although many social scientists claim that we know enough about man for some general explanations and predictions to be made. B. F. Skinner, the Harvard psychologist, has made some extremely penetrating generalizations about human behavior as a result of his experimentation with positive reinforcement as a factor in human conditioning.[15] But while this may tell us how man in fact behaves, and what techniques we can use to condition him to behave in other ways, this scientific study does not tell us how man *ought* to behave. Whenever we ask such questions as "What ought I to do?" we have gone beyond the facts and scientific theories and are asking for a value judgment.

To clarify the distinction we are drawing between facts and values let us consider an example from our own day. The mass media, such as television, have profited from the social scientists' study of human behavior. It is not by accident that television commercials seek to associate their products with the things which most men enjoy or desire. If we can be made to associate a particular brand of cigarettes with the virility of the cowboys of the old West, then we may be conditioned into not only smoking but also into purchasing that particular brand. Even more effective, however, will be to have the cowboy offer one of his cigarettes to a beautiful woman. The appeal will then be made to both the desire of males to be virile, strong he-men, and to the females to be feminine and beautiful. Advertising tries to find out what most people like, and then it seeks for ways by means of which it can associate the products of its clients with these human desires. The degree of success of these conditioning procedures can be determined by any one of you. Do you buy any cola beverage, any brand of aspirin? Or do you ask for a particular brand? If you ask for a particular brand, did you ever try to find out why? Does that brand of cola really taste better? Is that particular brand of aspirin any better than any other brand? Or have you been conditioned by the mass media to associate cola and aspirin with particular brands?

The reader will probably grant that the mass media do indeed condition us to behave in certain ways, but he might ask "Is it right for them to do so?" In the light of the evidence which suggests that there is a connection between the smoking of cigarettes and cancer, should not cigarette manufacturers discontinue their advertising campaigns? Is it right for them to continue to associate cigarette smoking with relaxation and pleasure, with really being a mature man? When questions such as these are raised we have entered the area of value judgments. Notice, however, that not every one would say that cigarette manufacturers should discontinue their advertising. An appeal could well be made for the right of the individual to make his own choice as to whether or not he wished to smoke. One might even argue that the states need the tax dollars which they get from the sale of cigarettes, or that the stockholders in the cigarette companies have a right to expect these companies to do everything they can to show a profit. Indeed, would not preventing cigarette companies from engaging in advertising campaigns be a violation of their rights in a free enterprise economy? This issue raises some very basic questions about values. Are economic values to be considered as more important than those of the health of the general populace? Is pleasure of the moment to be valued higher than a long life? Does a state have the right to prohibit its citizens from obtaining pleasure in the ways they choose, if some of their chosen behavior may be injurious to their health or welfare? Who is ultimately to make these decisions? The individual himself? The state, acting for the individual through the representatives he has elected to Congress?

It is possible to reply that a rational man who understands the techniques employed in advertising can resist the pressures brought to bear upon him to use certain products. Furthermore, there are many conflicting voices raised, and we have the opportunity to choose from among them the ones which we believe to be correct. And, of course, each one of us likes to think of himself as one of those rational individuals who makes his own decisions. Suppose, however, that we had been reared in a society like that described by Skinner in *Walden Two*. Frazier, the head of Walden Two, uses his knowledge of human conditioning to train all the inhabitants of this utopian community to cooperate with each other.

Competition is unheard of. All the frustrations and conflicts which we experience in our present world are eliminated. The conditioning process has been so thorough that none of the inhabitants raise any questions about the goals of this "ideal" community. Frazier invites some scholars from the outside world to his Walden Two so that they can observe how well he has succeeded. In a discussion with the philosopher in the group of visitors, Frazier proclaims:

> "This *is* the Good Life. We know it. It's a fact, not a theory. It has an experimental justification, not a rational one. As for your conflict of principles, that's an experimental question, too. We don't puzzle our little minds over the outcome of Love versus Duty. We simply arrange a world in which serious conflicts occur as seldom as possible or, with a little luck, not at all." [16]

But the philosopher's main reservation about Walden Two was not grasped by Frazier. Clearly it was a fact that he had conditioned the people in this community to respond in far more cooperative and peaceful ways than they do in our contemporary world. The philosopher, however, asked in effect, "Is this really the Good Life? Ought man to be conditioned into behaving docilely? Is the absence of all competition and conflict a good thing? How would it ever be possible for a genius or an exceptionally creative man to develop in Walden Two? Is not a genius, who rejects the values of his day, of more worth than thousands of conforming robot-like men? Why should Frazier determine the values to which the entire community would be conditioned to conform? What right did any man have to so completely determine the lives of others?" These were questions concerning values, not concerning facts and scientific theories.

The reader should now understand that to make a value judgment is to express a preference; it is to make an estimation of worth. We all make value judgments every day of our lives. In such a simple act as choosing to spend ten dollars to see a play, rather than to buy a book, one is expressing the belief that at that particular time seeing that particular play will be more worthwhile than buying that particular book. Furthermore, in such an act, we also can see what this second kind of interpretation of relativism maintains. One is not maintaining that it is always better to see a play than to buy a book; to do so would be to subscribe to an absolute value judgment. Rather, one's judgment is based upon the comparison of a particular play with a particular book at a particular time. If one had not recently bought a great many books, one might have chosen to buy a particular novel instead of going to the play. If one has been reading a great deal lately, and desires some form of relaxing entertainment, he might very well choose to see a particular musical comedy. Clearly, one would not maintain that everyone ought to make exactly the same choice as he made, but notice also that one's decision is not completely arbitrary, for reasons can be given for making the value judgment. Our concern here, however, will be with more basic and general value commitments, rather than with particular decisions. What do I most want out of Life? Is my personal integrity of greater value to me than success? Should I always be oriented so as to seek my own welfare, even if it is at the expense of others? Should my values not happen to agree with those generally held by my society, ought I to follow my own convictions anyway? These and many other questions like them raise general questions concerning one's basic values in terms of which many of one's everyday choices are made. This second interpretation of relativism, which we have been considering, reminds us that even these more basic commitments are related to specific persons who are living in a particular period of history. We must, therefore, not become the slaves of the principles of the past, but rather seek honestly for the most rationally defensible values which will assist in making our world a more humane one in which to live. Moral values then are not arbitrary; they are relative to man.

Relativism in moral theory need not, therefore, lead one into despair and absurdity; rather it may be seen as a liberating force requiring that each man make a serious effort to choose those values which he finds to be most meaningful for himself and society. John Barth has the hero of *The Floating Opera* reject the view he held earlier concerning the absurdity of values. After many years of thought and life, he realizes:

> If there are no absolutes, then a value is no less authentic, no less genuine, no less compelling, no less "real," for its being relative! It is one thing to say "Values are *only* relative"; quite another, and more thrilling, to remove the pejorative adverb and assert "There *are* relative values!" These, at least, we have, and if they are all we have, then *in no way whatsoever* are they inferior.[17]

We shall examine in later chapters the positions adopted concerning moral relativism by the proponents of different value orientations for our century. We shall find that some of these writers, such as Marx, Nietzsche and Freud, fully accept moral relativism as an inevitable fact in the modern world; while others, such as Kierkegaard and Fromm, attempt to defend a commitment to absolute or objective values. That we live in an age of pluralism will become quite apparent when we examine the views of contemporary theologians, some of whom frankly call for a new morality based on relativism. But we must not get ahead of our story. In addition to our century being called an age of relativism, we are often told that it is an age dominated by pragmatism. Let us see what this suggests about our contemporary moral climate.

The Pragmatic Method   It is often claimed that Americans are practical
                         people. They want to get things done; they
are more concerned with questions about the usefulness of an object or a
theory, than they are with more theoretical questions about the ultimate
meaning of life. Will an idea work? What is its "cash value"? Can we
really use a proposed theory to get some practical results? Questions
such as these reflect a down-to-earth concern with the actual problems
which people face in a modern technological society. Life is viewed in
terms of the next specific problem which must be solved, and not in
terms of ultimate values to which all men are asked to dedicate their lives.
Thus, for example, the popular pragmatism of Americans is expressed by
a concern to solve the problem of unemployment in one's own community. If one should ask, "What will men do when we have full employ-
ment? What are the ultimate goals which make life meaningful?" the
popular pragmatist would respond by shrugging his shoulders. He is not
interested in idle speculation about the nature of man; he wants to solve
the immediate pressing problem. After we have solved the most important of our immediate problems, there will be plenty of time to find some
new issues which will also require solution. Life is like traveling constantly on a train and never arriving; or, perhaps more accurately, one
arrives only when one dies. Then there are no more problems.

In the early part of the twentieth century, pragmatism was a philosophical movement which offered modern man an exhilarating program for
action. The pragmatic method, as developed by William James and
John Dewey, provided Americans with a philosophical justification of
their concern for practical deeds rather than for lofty ideals. Of even
greater importance, however, was the fact that the pragmatists accepted
the findings of the social sciences and admitted that values were indeed
relative. James and Dewey showed that modern man need not bog down
in helplessness when he admits the cultural relativity of his values. Instead, man might then for the first time really take seriously his task of
improving the particular situation in which he found himself. By actually
addressing oneself to the social wrongs which need to be corrected, one
could play his part in improving this world. Although many of the major
insights of the pragmatic philosophies of James and Dewey have been
distorted in our popular pragmatism of technological efficiency, we will
understand the present moral climate of our age much better if we examine their proposals and attempt to discover to what extent popular
pragmatism is a legitimate development from their philosophies.

William James (1842–1910) did much of his work in the nineteenth
century, but his thought represents clearly the open-mindedness, and scientific spirit of our present age. He is usually identified as the founder of
pragmatism, although his friend, Charles Sanders Peirce, was the first
person to use the term in describing a particular philosophical stance.

For William James pragmatism was not wholly novel; it was merely "a new name for some old ways of thinking." [18] Nevertheless, as James developed his own version of pragmatism he sounded like the philosopher of free enterprise, of individualism, of daring ventures, of practicality—in short, of progressive and changing America.

William James had been educated at Harvard Medical School, and taught psychology at Harvard before he turned to philosophy. His interest in the psychology of individuals, in how they think and react, runs through all of his writings. Much of his philosophy is concerned with the individual himself as he faces difficult moral choices. William James did not consider philosophy to be a detached, objective search for absolute truth; rather it was his own attempt to find a world-view which would give purpose and meaning to his life. Philosophy could not be divorced from the man who formed the philosophy. Of even greater importance was James' conviction that philosophy was for every man, and not merely for an aristocratic leisure class. He agreed with Gilbert K. Chesterton's remark that the most important thing about a man was his philosophy. In one of his lectures, James developed this theme as follows:

"There are some people—and I am one of them—who think that the most practical and important thing about a man is still his view of the universe. We think that for a landlady considering a lodger it is important to know his income, but still more important to know his philosophy. We think that for a general about to fight an enemy it is important to know the enemy's numbers, but still more important to know the enemy's philosophy". . . . I think with Mr. Chesterton in this matter. . . . For the philosophy which is so important in each of us is not a technical matter, it is our more or less dumb sense of what life honestly and deeply means. It is only partly got from books; it is our individual way of just seeing and feeling the total push and pressure of the cosmos. . . . It works in the minutest crannies and it opens out the widest vistas. It "bakes no bread," as has been said, but it can inspire our souls with courage; and repugnant as its manners, its doubting and challenging, its quibbling and dialectics, often are to common people, no one of us can get along without the far-flashing beams of light it sends over the world's perspectives. [19]

It is quite clear that, for William James, philosophy had one main practical purpose: to give meaning to one's life. In this sense, philosophy was of more importance to man than anything else, because it could deliver him from a totally senseless, absurd existence in what seemed to science to be a most indifferent, impersonal universe.

James was not at all content with any of the traditional philosophical approaches of the past as they had been presented. He distrusted the rationalists, who lost themselves in abstract first principles, and the skeptical empiricists, who were so devoted to what could be experienced in a particular case that they failed to draw any generalized conclusions whatsoever. He characteristically described these two philosophical attitudes as tender-minded (idealistic and optimistic outlook on life—rationalists) and tough-minded (scientific temper—"all I am after is the facts"). William James claimed to be firmly on the side of the empiricists, but in his development of pragmatism he clearly showed that he had a good deal of the tender-minded spirit about him also, especially in his dealing with religion. Pragmatism as applied by James became a doctrine of radical empiricism, a more open-ended empirical approach which did not confine itself to the facts of the sciences, but also took seriously any experience which any human being had. James described' this radical empiricist temper of pragmatism as follows:

> A pragmatist turns his back resolutely and once for all upon a lot of inveterate habits dear to professional philosophers. He turns away from abstraction and insufficiency, from verbal solutions, from bad *a priori* reasons, from fixed principles, closed systems, and pretended absolutes and origins. He turns towards concreteness and adequacy, towards facts, towards action and towards power. That means the empiricist temper regnant and the rationalist temper sincerely given up. It means the open air and possibilities of nature, as against dogma, artificiality, and the pretense of finality in truth.[20]

James here seemed to have caught the spirit of America as an open society in which each man was free to live his life as he saw fit. Pragmatism was a philosophy for concrete action in a world which still had many frontiers to be explored. Pragmatism was primarily a method of inquiry, and not a set of conclusions.

Concerning any beliefs about man or the world, the pragmatist always asks, "What difference will it make if I accept this belief rather than another one?" A belief is primarily a guide to action. James, therefore, did not hesitate to claim that a belief which made no difference in your life would not be true for you. However, a belief, which you rejected on pragmatic grounds, might well be accepted by someone else, if it really made a practical difference to him. Thus, in one of James' illustrations, he likened pragmatism to a hotel corridor which had numerous rooms opening out of it:

> In one you may find a man writing an atheistic volume; in the next some one on his knees praying for faith and strength; in a third a chemist investigating a body's properties. In a fourth a system of idealistic metaphysics is being excogitated; in a fifth the impossibility of metaphysics is being shown. But they all own the corridor, and all must pass through it if they want a practicable way of getting into or out of their respective rooms.[21]

Each of the men in his own way could find his own truth. James, in some of his writings, maintained that every man is free to judge the truth of any belief whatsoever in terms of practical consequences that are satisfactory to himself alone. He claimed that ideas *"become true just in so far as they help us to get into satisfactory relations with other parts of our experience."* [22] That is true which works, which actually makes a difference in the way one lives. But what is the nature of this difference which a belief makes to an individual? Is it wholly personal?

James drew a very important distinction between applying the pragmatic method in science or in matters of ultimate moral or religious concern. He claimed that in science we should wait for objective facts and the conclusive results of experimentation before we adopt an idea as true. Whenever the need of acting is not immediately paramount, as is usually the case in the sciences and in most matters of daily living, we ought to wait for sufficient evidence before we make up our minds. Thus, the test of the truth of a scientific assertion is its usefulness in meeting our expectations by predicting accurately future events. James was not proposing anything new with respect to how one ought to determine the truth of scientific claims. When one assumes a scientific posture, then James insisted:

> Decisions for the mere sake of deciding promptly and getting on to the next business would be wholly out of place. Throughout the breadth of physical nature facts are what they are quite independently of us, and seldom is there any such hurry about them that the risks of being duped by believing a premature theory need be faced. [23]

While this attitude of suspending belief until the facts are in is justified in the domain of science, James did not believe that science accounted for all the possible realms of truth.

In matters which are of vital personal importance to an individual, such as his moral and religious beliefs, James claimed that scientific evidence could not tip the truth scales one way or the other. He did not, however, justify one in withholding judgment on these matters because there was insufficient evidence. Instead, James insisted that each individual is forced to make decisions in the absence of conclusive evidence in all matters involving ultimate value commitments. Such commitments need not be completely arbitrary, however, for it was extremely important to James to show that in those areas of ultimate concern the pragmatic test of truth could be applied. One's commitment to a religious way of life, or to basic moral values, can be defended by showing that one's particular commitments actually make a practical difference in one's life. If it makes no difference in the life you lead if you accept a religious hypothesis as true rather than a naturalistic one, "then religious faith is a pure superfluity, better pruned away, and controversy about its legitimacy is a piece of idle trifling, unworthy of serious minds." [24] William James found that it made a great difference in his own life if he accepted the religious hypothesis as true. Let us see how he tried to justify his commitment on pragmatic grounds.

William James was convinced that our emotions and passions do influence what we believe. Few of us have actually conducted many scientific experiments, but we accept the authority of the authors of scientific textbooks for most of our scientific beliefs. We are, therefore, even in these scientific matters, often really affirming our faith in the reliability of the scientists, since we ourselves do not have the needed first-hand experience to verify their claims. But why do we put our faith in the scientists? We believe the scientists, according to James, because we have use for their theories. Might we not be justified in using faith in matters of morality and religion as well? If we are radical empiricists, can we dismiss the experiences of the religious mystics or of the great moral prophets? Should not all aspects of human experience be given a hearing? James wanted to insist that any man has the right to make his own decision concerning matters of faith which cannot be decided on objective grounds alone. In matters involving one's ultimate concerns, one may employ the will to believe:

> *Our passional nature not only lawfully may, but must, decide an option between propositions, whenever it is a genuine option that cannot by its nature be decided on intellectual grounds; for to say, under such circumstances, "Do not decide, but leave the question open," is itself a passional decision—just like deciding yes or no— and is attended with the same risk of losing the truth.*[25]

This justification of the will to believe is based upon what we today would call existential grounds. We shall see in later chapters that the contemporary existentialists also insist that if one is faced with making a basic moral decision that one must decide for oneself. Jean-Paul Sartre claims that if one chooses not to decide, or follows someone else's advice, one has still made a decision. This central theme of existentialism was already contained in William James' version of pragmatism. In many of the important matters of life, in choosing one's own life style, one must take a leap into the dark. Each person must choose and act as he thinks best, for here he has no appeal except to his own experience. James justified his own belief in God because it gave a meaning, a steadiness of moral purpose, to his life. The belief in God thus met his pragmatic test for truth: it worked, it made a practical difference in that it helped to fit together what had previously been isolated and unorganized aspects of his life.

We have seen that pragmatism in the hands of William James extolled the individual, not only the exceptional man of genius, but also the "common man." Philosophy was one's way of life, and, while it did not bake any bread, it determined the direction and meaning of one's efforts as a moral agent. In that sense, it was indeed practical and it had "cash value." James himself was concerned with the ultimate questions which men asked: Is there a God? Does man have free will? What ought I to do to become a better person and to make this a better world? These questions were not abstract or purely theoretical questions for James. These were extremely practical questions for him because he believed that how one would act in his everyday life depended upon how one answered these questions. Each man would have to answer these ultimate questions for himself; there were no public tests of truth to which he could appeal, as he could in the case of science. Thus, the grounds which one man gave to justify his ultimate commitment might be totally unjustified for another man.

There were many popular adaptations of William James' pragmatism which tried to show how the will to believe could achieve anything from financial success to religious peace of mind. Dale Carnegie's *How to Win Friends and Influence People*, first published in 1936, was one of the most popular of the books which provided information on how one could succeed in the business world by acting upon one's will to believe in oneself. Carnegie quoted from William James to reinforce his practical instructions for success in the business and social community. In the forties and fifties many popular religious books appeared which also adapted James' pragmatism to the purpose of aiding individuals to recover a sense of lost personal dignity and importance in a world becoming increasingly automated and complex. Fosdick's *On Being a Real Person*, published in 1943, allied William James to a liberal progessive theology, while Norman Vincent Peale's *The Power of Positive Thinking*, published in 1952, sought to provide specific techniques which one could employ in order to triumph over his inner feelings of insecurity so that one might become successful in his job and in his home life. Peale's book, which was at the top of the best seller lists for two years, was a popular exposition of the importance which should be placed on concentrating upon the means to achieving success, but it did not raise any serious question as to whether or not the goal of success itself was desirable. In this respect, it echoed the popular pragmatism of Americans, and gave it a kind of religious justification. Let's get the job done, and the ultimate ends will take care of themselves. The basic concern of William James with the ultimate questions concerning the meaning of life had been eliminated from the folk pragmatism of these popular books. That which works was given a much narrower interpretation than it had in any of the philosophical writings of the founders of pragmatism.

If William James may be considered the tender-minded pragmatist, in the sense that he extolled the right of the individual to choose his own ultimate beliefs, then John Dewey would represent the tough-minded pragmatist who reminded us that we live in a natural and social environment which conditions the individual's ways of responding. Although William James had pioneered in studying the psychology of individuals, he paid relatively little attention to the society in which an individual developed. John Dewey, the other great American pragmatist, although he too was interested in psychology, was more concerned with studying the processes of interaction between the individual and his natural and social environment. Moreover, unlike James, who maintained that not all questions which concerned man could be answered by science, John Dewey insisted that science ought to be applied to all of life. Even in matters of ultimate moral and religious concern, the use of the scientific method could produce concrete results which would be verifiable in the public world. It was Dewey's conviction that what a man believed was largely a reflection of his own culture. If the human condition were to be improved, then Dewey insisted one must first understand the nature of the social process in order that scientific control could be brought to bear upon those aspects of a society which were not conducive to the welfare of the human species. The popular folk belief which maintains that science can answer all man's questions derives therefore from John Dewey, rather than from William James.

John Dewey contended that man is a biological creature who can be understood only in terms of his behavior. He rejected thought for its own sake, because he claimed that thinking was a functional mechanism intended to provide for the survival of the human species. The individual human being is reared in a society which teaches him habitual ways of responding to the usual situations which he will meet in life. Most of our daily routine is made up of patterns of response which have become automatic to us. We do not think what to do while we are eating, nor while we are responding to other persons in the ways which were taught to us by our parents and teachers.

Dewey's whole conception of the nature of thought is that it is concerned with solving problems. But what is a problem? Sometimes, a man's habitual patterns of reaction are blocked, or some novel elements enter his concrete situation so that he has no fixed mode of response available. In such situations, man encounters a concrete problem which he must solve. Man is basically a creature of habit, and it is only when he needs to think in order to find a satisfactory solution to a new situation, that he thinks at all. Thus, Dewey preferred to call his philosophy instrumentalism rather than pragmatism, because this not only dissociated him from James' will to believe, but also it stressed that thinking is an instrument, a tool for survival, and not an end in itself.

It is extremely important to note that John Dewey was a humanist. He recognized that man lives in a precarious natural and social environment. It is man's capacity to think, however, which permits him to modify his environment so as to make it more stable and reliable. Dewey's basic moral commitment, in terms of which he proposed that society should be reconstructed, was to a democratic social order in which the dignity of every individual is respected. He therefore fervently believed that through rational cooperation, rather than through the use of force, our society could be transformed into one which would permit each person to realize his own growth as a person. When one reads Dewey's writings, one is immediately struck with the fact that Dewey's pragmatism would work only in a context of humanism.

Dewey believed that for the first time in history man now had a real opportunity to direct intelligently the course of social change. Science has the needed techniques which could be used to solve the major problems which man faces in nature and in society. While science had been used to change man's natural environment, it had not been seriously applied to the study of human behavior. Dewey, therefore, insisted that before any significant improvement could be brought about in the human condition, first of all, we would have to use the methods of the sciences in order to learn about the nature of man and society. Once we understand what man really is like, then we will be able to control scientifically the environment and the individual so as to bring about a maximum of well being for everyone. Dewey's whole philosophy was an attempt on his part to meet this great challenge. He proposed that what was needed was a reconstruction of philosophy, of morality, of society, and most important of all, of education.

While religion and philosophy had in past ages proposed ideals for human behavior, they had never seriously asked if man were the sort of creature who could ever reach these high ideals. Dewey was convinced that traditional religious beliefs, which encouraged men to prepare themselves for another life after death, actually interfered with men taking seriously the concrete problems they faced on earth. But now that man had the needed scientific techniques, it would be possible for him to improve this world. Modern man would not have to escape to a world described by religious imagination; instead, he could help to make this present world one in which he could dwell with more security than he had in the past.

Dewey's main thesis was that the scientific study of human nature should be united with a philosophical interest in values. Since man can think, he can change his social environment, and to an extent even his own nature. What was needed was for man, in the light of scientific information about his own nature, to set about solving the immediate problems in his society which interfered with progress. Of one thing Dewey was certain: man would never seriously attempt to change his social environment if he concentrated upon ideals which he could not achieve. We must forget about ultimate ends. There are no fixed goals or ends for man, according to Dewey, only specific ends-in-view which when they are achieved become means to other ends-in-view. We had not yet had any systematic reconstruction of society because we had not taken the means to social change seriously. Dewey insisted that we must really be concerned with the means, because unless we are, we shall never make any progress. In fact, until we realize that the next step we take is the most important one, we will never get very far in improving the human condition. Dewey illustrated his point by suggesting that the alcoholic, who wants to reform, will succeed only if he finds something else to take the place of his habitual dependence upon alcohol, and if he realizes that he must stop drinking now. He must turn down the first drink he is offered, for if he says, "I'll not count this one," he is not going to achieve his end-in-view. Dewey generalized this insight to apply to all concrete moral decisions:

> Until one takes intermediate acts seriously enough to treat them as ends, one wastes one's time in any effort at change of habits. Of the intermediate acts, the most important is the *next* one. The first or earliest means is the most important *end* to discover.[26]

With the development of an industrial society, Dewey recognized that old habitual ways of moral response would prove to be increasingly ineffective or irrelevant. His great interest in reforming education was based upon his conviction that it is through education that a society can best provide individuals with the abilities to respond effectively to the changing times the future would bring. In fact Dewey often claimed that the main task of philosophy in the modern world should be to provide a theoretical background for education. Philosophy and education should both be concerned primarily with the social and moral strifes of the present time. One of the main tasks of education should be to help people to use the scientific method in solving the concrete problems which were crucial at the moment. This in itself would not be sufficient, however, for we cannot foresee what the precise nature of the moral and social problems of the future will be. Education continued as long as one lived. Schools ought to make their pupils "capable of further education: more sensitive to conditions of growth and more able to take advantage of them. Acquisition of skill, possession of knowledge, attainment of culture are not ends: they are marks of growth and means to its continuing."[27] Formal education should help the child to become a problem-solver in the real world, but this can be done only if the child is encouraged to think for himself. Therefore, one of Dewey's most seminal insights was that education was not a preparation for life, but rather that education was life.

Dewey was convinced that most social change in the past had been haphazard. He was sure that changes would occur in the future, whether they were planned by man, or took place more or less by accident. The goal of his philosophy was to insure that social changes would be made intelligently and not instinctively, for only then would it be possible to "modulate the harshness of conflict, and turn the elements of disintegration into a constructive synthesis." [28] Dewey was here explaining a prevalent American belief in change becoming real progress if it were achieved by the cooperation of all the citizens of a democracy.

One popular misinterpretation of Dewey's philosophy claims that he was primarily concerned with adapting the individual to his environment, so that he is really a defender of conformism. It is true that, as we have already stressed, Dewey believed that the individual could only be understood as part of the culture in which he lived. But this is only one part of the picture. Instead of merely adapting an individual to an unsatisfactory society, Dewey was quite clear in proposing that the society which made life frustrating and boring to many of its citizens ought itself to be changed. We have stressed that his basic beliefs were humanistic. Therefore, Dewey proposed that we do not only change man to fit society, but we also change society to fit man. What he believed with great conviction was that the experimental method gave man a real possibility to direct social change, to control society and individuals, so that the harmonious welfare of all might be achieved.

We shall examine in a later chapter the humanism of Erich Fromm, a contemporary psychoanalyst, which updates Dewey's studies by showing how the scientific method can be applied to our present problems. Dewey was a pioneer in applying scientific insights to human conduct. His social and philosophical writings were direct attempts to help man improve the quality of his enjoyment of life. It was Dewey's conviction that only in a democracy could political institutions and the industrial community be so arranged as to contribute "to the all-around growth of every member of society." [29]

There is one more important respect in which Dewey's philosophy represented the climate of opinion of early twentieth-century America. He insisted that there are no absolute moral rules or principles; any particular moral rule is only an hypothesis to be tested time and time again. If a moral rule does not fit the new experiences we face, then we must make our own decisions as to the best course of conduct for these unique situations. Dewey's insistence upon the uniqueness of every moral situation is a point which, we shall show in later chapters, is defended by contemporary existentialists and the new morality of situation ethics.

Dewey clearly accepted the pragmatic view that the test of any particular thought is the specific action to which it leads. Unlike William James, however, he insisted that the model for pragmatic truth is science itself, so that the criteria for the workability of ideas must be social and public, rather than individual and private. Yet, we have certainly seen that Dewey was by no means indifferent to the individual human being. Far from that being the case, he stressed time and time again that the value of all social institutions was to be determined by the extent to which they helped provide the individual with more significant meaning for his life. If there is any candidate at all for an ultimate value in Dewey's philosophy it would be growth. Thus, his moral concern for the individual is clearly expressed in his statement concerning the real purpose of government, business, religion, art, and education:

> That purpose is to set free and to develop the capacities of human individuals without respect to race, sex, class or economic status. And this is all one with saying that the test of their value is the extent to which they educate every individual into the full stature of his possibility.[30]

This statement shows Dewey's own deep commitment to the goals of an open democratic society. It is quite clear that Dewey himself was not a crass pragmatist of expediency and opportunism, but rather a humanist deeply concerned with enriching the possibilities of experience for all men.

The popular interpretation of the pragmatic method as it is applied to the everyday problems which we face is several steps removed from the philosophies developed by William James and John Dewey. In our folk belief we tend to identify pragmatism with anything that is practical, with facing our problems one at a time, and with not being concerned about the goals of our specific activities. The everyday pragmatist is suspicious of ideas and theories, despite the fact that both James and Dewey insisted that ideas were very useful tools which could help to enrich the quality of life. Recently, some American theologians have rejoiced at this basic down-to-earth pragmatism which they find characterizes modern urban man. Harvey Cox in *The Secular City* describes contemporary pragmatic man as follows:

> He approaches problems by isolating them from irrelevant considerations, by bringing to bear the knowledge of different specialists, and by getting ready to grapple with a new series of problems when these have been provisionally solved. Life for him is a set of problems, not an unfathomable mystery. He brackets off the things that cannot be dealt with and deals with those that can. He wastes little time thinking about "ultimate" or "religious" questions. And he can live with highly provisional solutions.[31]

There can be little doubt that this pragmatic concern with limited social problems has permitted the cooperation of many people who might otherwise have been divided by their loyalties to conflicting basic ideals of life. Cox, and the "Death of God theologians," whose thought we shall examine in a later chapter, claim that even religion does not have any relevance to modern man if it insists that man ought to be concerned with ultimate questions such as the goals of life. One of the unique aspects of our century is the willingness on the part of many men to deal with their immediate problems and to put aside any questions concerning the ultimate ends toward which they are aiming. The pragmatic method has been of great help in delivering man from his bondage to the myths and dogmas of the past. What remains to be decided by history is whether or not man can successfully confine his attention to the immediate problems and completely ignore all doubts concerning the meaningfulness of his present activities. We shall see in later chapters that the existentialists, the humanists, and some theologians are not convinced that the pragmatic method can fulfill adequately all of man's basic human needs.

The pragmatic method, although it is more frequently questioned now than it was a few years ago, is still the major way in which Americans respond to problems. Charles Frankel maintains that this "unphilosophical pragmatism" is still characteristic of American life:

> Even today our economy is characterized by a passion for technology, our social science by a faith in methodology, and our approach to the world, as illustrated by our first ventures in foreign aid, by an apparent conviction that if men have the requisite know-how, and can solve their material problems, most of their other problems will fall into place.[32]

Unfortunately, it does not appear to be the case that all man's other problems are solved automatically if we deal only with our immediate material needs. In our present affluent society, some people have started to feel uneasy because, as we approach solving the basic economic problems of distribution, we seem to be creating new problems involving how man will use his leisure. Increasingly, many people are claiming that popular pragmatism is not enough. They should like to find some meaning for their lives over and above the sense of achievement they experience when they successfully solve their everyday practical problems. More and more people want to know where they are going, and why they ought to strive to get there. The rest of this book will be concerned with exploring alternative ideals of the preeminently best society and best man which have been proposed to answer our quest for values to which we could commit our lives.

Popular pragmatism has fallen on evil days, for it is not able to deal with problems in its desired technological way when there are conflicts of ideals or principles involved. When a society is not relatively stable, and when there is no general agreement on basic matters of moral principle, then the popular pragmatist is unable to supply a clear sense of direction. Those who are concerned only with efficiency, with improving the ways of doing things, turn out to be bewildered when they are faced with conflicts, not between ways of doing the job, but rather between goals concerning whether the specific task is worthy of being pursued.

Philosophical pragmatism as developed by James and Dewey also seems unable to answer man's quest for some final goal to which he could dedicate his life. James' will to believe seems to many to be too close to wishful thinking, while Dewey's frequent insistence that there are no ultimate ends but only ends-in-view does not seem to be much of an improvement over popular pragmatism's concern with efficiency. The reader should be very clear, however, on the basis of what we have already said, that these charges are only partially justified. We should not forget that James and Dewey were humanists. They were deeply committed to the values of an open democratic society in which the rights of each individual were respected. Ultimately, therefore, their own over-beliefs and moral ideals provided a rational context in which pragmatism could be used to enrich human experience.

The Search for a Way of Life There have been other factors, besides relativism and pragmatism, which have served to modify our approach toward values. The last decade or two has found modern man very concerned with finding something by which he could live. Many men have almost desperately sought for some values to which they could be fully devoted. This search for certainty has led many of our contemporaries back to the past in an attempt to recapture the lost radiance of the old ideals of bygone ages. In religion, this has resulted in many people finding certitude in Roman Catholicism or in Protestant Fundamentalism, where a revealed truth is made the rock upon which faith and morals rest. Others in quest of an absolute in religion have embraced Hinduism or Zen Buddhism or such adaptations of them as are found in theosophy and Christian Science.

But there have also been fresh attempts to find some bases in reality for a point of view or course of conduct never advocated before, or at least for one which has been radically adapted to the changing times of the present century.

Recently, loyalty to the business organization and seeking status in one's society have become the dominant goals of many Americans. William Whyte described this way of life in *The Organization Man*, while Vance Packard discussed a similar value orientation in *The Status Seekers*.[33] In loyalty to the organization, in loyalty to group thinking, in finding the organization to be a kind of protecting earthly father which helps one through difficulties, in conforming to the social customs which one's position in the organization demands, in allowing and even welcoming the organization taking over many functions of one's life, many people have found a new kind of secular religion, or at least a new institution in which they could find some feeling of certitude. It seems that an attitude which prevails rather widely in our society is that if you do your best for the organization, and do not question its inroads into your private life, the organization will take good care of you. Coupled with this loyalty to the organization, one also finds the search for status in choosing a certain profession or accepting a particular position with an important and large business.

Many critics have suggested that loyalty to an organization and seeking status in society are really just socially acceptable ways of "selling out," of refusing to be involved in choosing what acts one ought to take in the difficult world of the present. For some people, achieving security by complete loyalty to an organization represents an evasion of what it really means to be fully human. Becoming an organization man does not really solve that most difficult of all human problems: Who am I? Instead of finding an answer in terms of one's own internal values, one surrenders to simply performing the role which society seems to have provided for him. How unsatisfying and tragic this kind of an answer to a search for meaning in life can be is aptly illustrated by the life of the fictional Willy Loman in Arthur Miller's play, *Death of a Salesman*.[34]

One of the more recent movements which has attracted the interests of some people seeking a way of life is the Objectivism of Ayn Rand. Like the organization man, the ideal man represented by Ayn Rand finds his way of life in the business community, but rather than do so by becoming a "yes man" in the organizational structure, he is encouraged to become an individualist. Indeed, Ayn Rand attacks all forms of group thinking, of sacrifice of oneself for others, and of welfare legislation as forms of the mass evil of our time, collectivism. She blames American intellectuals for having defended the moral code of altruism and having attacked the one great economic system which extolled individualism, capitalism. While she extolls each individual developing his own code of values, she insists that this must be based on reason, rather than on arbitrary whim or desire. She agrees with the existentialists, whom we shall examine later on, that each man must choose his own values, but she disagrees with their insistence that there are no objective factors upon which man can rely in constructing his way of life. Indeed, she does not shrink from recognizing ultimate values upon which all other values depend:

> An *ultimate* value is that final goal or end to which all lesser goals are the means—and it sets the standard by which all lesser goals are *evaluated*. An organism's life is its *standard of value*: that which furthers its life is the *good*, that which threatens it is the *evil*. . . .

Ethics is *not* a mystic fantasy—nor a social convention—nor a dispensable, subjective luxury, to be switched or discarded in any emergency. Ethics is an *objective, metaphysical necessity of man's survival*—not by the grace of the supernatural nor of your neighbors nor of your whims, but by the grace of reality and the nature of life.[35]

The objective standard which Miss Rand proposes for ethics is the nature of human existence itself: "that which is required for man's survival *qua* man." [36] With Aristotle, she believes that the essential characteristic of man is his rationality; and with the defenders of laissez-faire capitalism, she proclaims that the only rational society is one in which the government pursues a hands-off policy both toward business and ideas. Every man should develop his intellectual powers in order that he can use them to achieve his greatest possible self-realization. Moreover, Miss Rand insists that each man should realize that his own life is an ultimate end in itself. In order to best fulfill his life, a rational man should make his own choices, and not be unduly influenced by others. In making these choices, however, he should be guided by the three values which she holds as basic to her Objectivist ethics: reason, purpose, and self-esteem. Each person should have the right to achieve his purposes, providing that they are rationally thought out; and society should grant each person the right to discuss his ideas in the free market-place. No man, however, is ever justified in trying to force others to accept his own ideas or values.

In order to stress the importance of each man's choosing his own life style, Miss Rand often refers to her ethic as the virtue of selfishness. We have already seen that she attacks all forms of altruism which, according to her interpretation, require the individual to sacrifice his own self-interest for others. Each man has a right to pursue his own happiness, only it should be a happiness purchased by reason and not by the arbitrary desires of the moment. One of her summary statements makes this aspect of her position very clear:

The Objectivist ethics holds that *human* good does not require human sacrifices and cannot be achieved by the sacrifice of anyone to anyone. It holds that the *rational* interests of men do not clash— that there is no conflict of interests among men who do not desire the unearned, who do not make sacrifices nor accept them, who deal with one another as *traders*, giving value for value.[37]

It is only fair to point out that Miss Rand does not deny the moral virtue of helping other people, providing that one's own interests are significantly enhanced thereby. A proper concern for and a willingness to aid the ones a person loves is therefore justified by an appeal to rational self-interest. Miss Rand explains:

Concern for the welfare of those one loves is a rational part of one's selfish interests. If a man who is passionately in love with his wife spends a fortune to cure her of a dangerous illness, it would be absurd to claim that he does it as a "sacrifice" for *her* sake, not his own, and that it makes no difference to *him* personally and selfishly, whether she lives or dies.

Any action that a man undertakes for the benefit of those he loves is *not a sacrifice* if, in the hierarchy of his values, in the total context of the choices open to him, it achieves that which is of greatest *personal* (and rational) importance to *him*. In the above example, his wife's survival is of greater value to the husband than anything else that his money could buy, it is of greatest importance to his own happiness and, therefore, his action is *not* a sacrifice.[38]

One owes no obligation to strangers, other than a generalized respect for them as fellow human beings. She therefore maintains that it is immoral to ask any man to sacrifice his time or his money to help the poor and needy in society. If one is trying to decide whether or not he ought to aid another man, Miss Rand proposes an almost mathematical model to determine what would be the right thing to do:

> The proper method of judging when or whether one should help another person is by reference to one's own rational self-interest and one's own hierarchy of values: the time, money or effort one gives or the risk one takes should be proportionate to the value of the person in relation to one's own happiness.[39]

It is imporant to note that Miss Rand stresses the rights of the individual as a rational human being, and maintains that we owe no duties to others, except to respect their basic individual rights. She specifies that by a "right" she means "a moral principle defining and sanctioning a man's freedom of action in a social context." [40] All rights stem from the one basic right of a man to his own life. Hence, every man ought to have the "freedom to act on his own judgment, for his own goals, by his own *voluntary, uncoerced* choice." [41] In order for a man to sustain his life in a society it is necessary for him to work, to produce, and Miss Rand insists that he has a moral right to use the money and the property he acquires as he sees fit. Property rights, therefore, are held to be basic to any moral society:

> The right to life is the source of all rights—and the right to property is their only implementation. Without property rights, no other rights are possible. Since man has to sustain his life by his own effort, the man who has no right to the product of his effort has no means to sustain his life. The man who produces while others dispose of his product, is a slave.[42]

Furthermore, since each man has the right to choose his own values and to pursue them, he has the rights to liberty and the pursuit of happiness.

The rights to life, liberty and the pursuit of happiness were the basic values proclaimed in the Declaration of Independence. The purpose of government was to secure these rights for all its citizens. Miss Rand maintains that this is the only moral justification for any government; no government has the right to force those who have achieved financial rewards for their labors to contribute by means of taxation to the support of those who have failed to earn enough to support themselves. "A right does not include the material implementation of that right by other men; it includes only the freedom to earn that implementation by one's own effort." [43] Even the right of free speech means only that every man has the right to utter his convictions without fear of government suppression. "It does *not* mean that others must provide him with a lecture hall, a radio station or a printing press through which to express his ideas." [44]

Miss Rand is very critical of the new welfare state which has replaced the old laissez-faire capitalism of the immediate past. There are no economic rights, she maintains, and the recent excursions of the government into legislation concerning open housing, medicare, and the war on poverty are specific symptoms which she cites of the break-down of the moral order upon which America was founded. A government should not be a "big brother," but should exist only to insure that no persons or groups will interfere with the rights of each individual to pursue his life in the way he has rationally chosen. The principle she puts forth is:

> The only proper, *moral* purpose of a government is to protect man's rights, which means: to protect him from physical violence—to protect his right to his own life, to his own liberty, to his own *property* and to the pursuit of his own happiness. Without property rights, no other rights are possible.[45]

It should be obvious to the reader that Ayn Rand's philosophy is firmly committed to laissez-faire capitalism as the best defender of the rights of man. But she finds capitalism to be even more important in her scheme of values, for she maintains that it is the only justifiable basis, not only for a political-economic system, but for any human relationship whatsoever. Its two great virtues, as she sees them, are its protection of property rights and its promotion of free trade. In a free capitalist economy one has the right to produce his goods, and then to sell them to anyone who is willing to pay the price which he asks. The consumer, in return, has the right to bargain over the price, or to refuse to buy the goods if he does not want them. Miss Rand extends this principle of free trade to cover all human relationships:

> The principle of *trade* is the only rational ethical principle for all human relationships, personal and social, private and public, spiritual and material. It is the principle of *justice*.[46]

Just as you choose those products which best fulfill your desires, so she maintains do you choose your friends. Furthermore, this is the only morally justifiable way of relating yourself to other people. What value does another person have to offer me? What will I get out of joining this organization? Here is a moral justification for selfish egoism. But notice, there is a reverse side of the coin as well. Just as you may reject a person who wishes to be your friend, so too other people are at liberty to reject you as well. If they find that you have little to offer them, then in the realm of "free trade" they are morally justified in having as little to do with you as possible. This is Miss Rand's principle of justice in operation.

Ayn Rand's Objectivism thus turns out to be a defense of rational self-interest and of unregulated capitalism, coupled with the hope that if all men are allowed to pursue their own rational interests, we shall be able to solve many of our perplexing social problems.

Despite the stress upon the rights of the individual, Ayn Rand's ideal man has striking similarities to the organization man. Both are dedicated to the business world as the hallmark of their values, and both are relatively indifferent to the plight of the unfortunate in our society. Perhaps the reason for many people rejecting these two approaches to seeking a way of life is that they are basically rooted in a selfish desire for one's own financial success. While some organization men might admit that their goal in life is to make money, Ayn Rand quite realistically has one of her spokesmen say in *Atlas Shrugged:* "Let me give you a tip on a clue to men's characters: the man who damns money has obtained it dishonorably; the man who respects it has earned it." [47]

It will prove interesting for the reader to examine Ayn Rand's philosophy in the light of the value systems we shall consider in later chapters of this book. Having some understanding of her viewpoint, we will be better prepared to evaluate the criticism of egoistic ethics and capitalism made by Karl Marx and Erich Fromm.

The stress upon the individual's right to happiness has taken a different turn in the *Playboy Philosophy* of Hugh Hefner. His magazine is best known for its celebration of the freedom that is now coming to the individual as a result of the sexual revolution, but in the articles he has written for the *Playboy Philosophy* the reader can discern many similarities in his over-all position and in Ayn Rand's. His attacks on the average man, on conformity, and on the traditional moral and religious values appear to be much the same as those of Miss Rand, with the exception that his articles are directed to a different audience. Hefner's summary statement of his philosophy sounds almost like the position defended by John Galt, the hero of *Atlas Shrugged:*

This, then, is the foundation of our philosophy—an emphasis on the importance of the individual and his freedom; the view that man's

personal self-interest is natural and good, and that it can be chan-
neled, through reason, to the benefit of the individual and his society;
the belief that morality should be based upon reason; the conviction
that society should exist as man's servant, not as his master; the idea
that the purpose in man's life should be found in the full living of
life itself and the individual pursuit of happiness.[48]

But there are other basic parallels as well. Hefner extolls capitalism and
in doing so indicates that like Ayn Rand he believes in selling ideas in
the market place:

> To some of us capitalism is almost a dirty word. It shouldn't be. It's
> time Americans stopped being embarrassed and almost ashamed of
> their form of government and their economy. It's the best two-horse
> parlay in the world and perhaps if we were more fully sold on it
> ourselves, we could do a better job of selling it to other countries.[49]

He also indicates that he fully approves of the American dream of success,
as he stresses that *Playboy* presents a total philosophy involving both
working hard at a job and expending one's energies in enjoyable use of
leisure time:

> Thus *PLAYBOY* exists, in part, as a motivation for men to expend
> greater effort in their work, develop their capabilities further and
> climb higher on the ladder of success. This is obviously desirable in
> our competitive, free enterprise system. . . .[50]

While Ayn Rand stresses the aspect of productive work in an industrial
economy, Hefner's *Playboy* is more concerned with the enjoyable use
of a man's leisure. Miss Rand is primarily concerned with the decline of
the individual in a collectivized society, while Hefner is more concerned
with freeing man from the traditional moral and religious convictions
which have hampered him in the free and enjoyable expression of his
sexuality. Yet, amazingly enough, their philosophies agree in stressing the
primacy of the individual's right to happiness, the supremacy of capitalism
to other economic systems, the belief that government should not interfere with the free circulation of any ideas, and the importance of each
man developing his own rational code of values.

But there are important differences to be found between the positions
of Ayn Rand and Hugh Hefner, especially concerning the nature and
degree of self-interest which each justifies. Ayn Rand, the reader will
recall, maintains that the individual ought not to be concerned with
others unless the others are of use to the individual; and even then, she
holds that it is immoral to sacrifice oneself for others. Hefner, on the
other hand, defends what he calls "enlightened self-interest" which "includes a concern for others. The individual should be willing to assist
those less fortunate, for a society—and each individual in it—benefits

from a concern for the welfare of all." [51] While many people have interpreted *Playboy* as sanctioning any form of sexual behavior from which
an individual would get pleasure, Hefner himself maintains that even in
sexual relationships he does not sanction selfishness:

> We are opposed to wholly selfish sex, but we are opposed to any
> human relationship that is entirely self-oriented—that takes all and
> gives nothing in return. We also believe that any such totally self-
> serving association is self-destructive.[52]

While it is true that Hefner recognizes that sex and love are not the same
thing, and that each can exist without the other, yet he maintains that
"the best sex, the most meaningful sex, is that which expresses the strong
emotional feeling we call love." [53]

Nevertheless, many of the features of *Playboy* seem to extoll sex as a
commodity to be enjoyed as other commodities in our affluent society.
For many people who do not read Hefner's *Playboy Philosophy*, but
glance at the playmates of the month and read the cartoons, John Crane's
analysis sums up the image of the ideal man conveyed:

> It is a universe for rather elegant and refined consumers, and girls are
> the grandest of all consumer goods. A girl is something, like a sports
> car or a bottle of Scotch or an Ivy League suit, that is meant to be
> used and enjoyed by men. But always with flair, with polish. There
> need be no entangling, no stifling alliances or obligations. Girls are
> playthings, and once enjoyed will have to be set aside and replaced
> with others new and fresh.[54]

Hugh Hefner in the first issue of *Playboy* sought to describe "What is
a Playboy?" in the sense in which he uses the term:

> He can be many things, providing he possesses a certain *point of view.*
> He must see life not as a vale of tears, but as a happy time; he must
> take joy in his work, without regarding it as the end and all of living;
> he must be an alert man, an aware man, a man of taste, a man sensitive
> to pleasure, a man who—without acquiring the stigma of the volup-
> tuary or dilettante—can live life to the hilt. This is the sort of man
> we mean when we use the word *playboy*.[55]

Playboy magazine has played a significant role in popularizing a new
attitude toward sex. We shall examine Freud's views in a later chapter,
for it was really Freud who brought a new approach to our understanding
of sex and its relationship to the rest of our lives. In addition to popularizing Freud, *Playboy* also refers approvingly to the Kinsey Reports on
male and female sexual behavior as helping to remove American sexual
hypocrisy. Largely because of the wide diversity of sexual practices which
Kinsey and his staff found in their study, *Playboy* has campaigned for the
repeal of the outmoded laws regulating sexual behavior between consent-

ing adults. Just as Ayn Rand objects to the interference of the state with the business of a corporation, so Hefner and his staff oppose society's attempts to force all individuals to conform to one sexual norm. Hefner maintains that "a man's morality, like his religion, is a personal affair best left to his own conscience." [56] In its attacks on our traditional puritanical laws and attitudes concerning sexual behavior *Playboy* has even won the support of many clergymen. Harvey Cox, an American theologian, who is very critical of *Playboy* in most respects, maintains that: "Moralistic criticisms of *Playboy* fail because its antimoralism is one of the few places in which *Playboy* is right." [57] We shall see, in a later chapter, that many Christian moralists agree with Hefner concerning the necessity for a more enlightened attitude toward sexual behavior, although they do not subscribe to the hedonistic way of life recommended by *Playboy*.

Hefner's philosophy and his magazine offer an individual pleasure and joy as a way of life; only one must be reasonably young, attractive and wealthy to enjoy it fully. His appeal to formulate a new morality "based upon honesty, understanding and reason rather than hypocrisy, superstition and ignorance" [58] is one that many people in our age would fully endorse. What many of these people would not be able to accept is the extolling of the individual's pleasure as the proper way of life in a world in which there are still persons who lack the basic necessities for life itself. To some of these individuals, no way of life is acceptable which does not place its primary concern upon helping others to achieve a decent standard of living. The *Playboy Philosophy* offers instead a modern version of hedonism, a justification for pursuing pleasure as the main goal of one's life. In a rather rhetorical passage Hefner justifies this way of life as fully consistent with the American dream:

> No conflict exists between the pleasure a modern American finds in material things and his struggle to discover a new scientific truth, or evolve a new philosophy, or create a work of art. The good life, the full life, encompasses all of these—and all of them satisfy and spur a man on to do more, see more, know more, experience more, accomplish more. This is the real meaning, the purpose, the point of life itself: the continuing, upward striving and searching for the ultimate truth and beauty. [59]

Hefner's *Playboy Philosophy* offers little of help to those concerned with eliminating racial injustice, poverty, and the lack of equal opportunity for all people in education, housing, and jobs. In fact, Hefner's defense of his philosophy as "an upward striving and searching for the ultimate truth and beauty" has a hollow ring. One would expect that a writer dedicated to showing that morality is relative to the individual, would also maintain that truth and beauty are in the same camp.

In the search for a satisfactory way of life many youth have been so disillusioned by the hypocrisy of our society that they have joined the ranks of what Kenneth Keniston calls "the uncommitted." These are the individuals who feel that they can not accept the cult of the organization man, of the rugged individualist, or of the pleasure-centered Playboy. But they are also unable to conform to the traditional Western value systems which are reinforced by organized religion. Some of these join the ranks of the alienated, and in a sense drop out of any sincere search for a way of life which they could accept. They become detached observers and while they are given to over-examining their own lives, they become more or less dedicated to the proposition that one ought not to commit himself to any values, movements or persons. Dr. Keniston finds that in our day it is not unusual to discover individuals choosing alienation as their way of life. Characteristically this kind of self-chosen alienation "takes the new form of rebellion without a cause, of rejection without a program, of refusal of what is without a vision of what should be." [60] One of the alienated students studied by Dr. Keniston summarized his reaction to "the American way of life" as follows: "I have no feeling of relationship to an over-all American society defined in terms of success and security. These are not ideals that give me any pleasure." [61]

The novels of J. D. Salinger are concerned with individuals who are not able to commit themselves to the traditional values of success and happiness. Holden Caulfield, who tells his story in *The Catcher in the Rye*, has become the prototype of many adolescents who see through the hypocrisy of their elders, but have not themselves found anything to which they could commit their lives. When Phoebe, his little sister, suggests to Holden that he might become a lawyer, he responds:

"Lawyers are all right, I guess—but it doesn't appeal to me," I said. "I mean they're all right if they go around saving innocent guys' lives all the time, and like that, but you don't *do* that kind of stuff if you're a lawyer. All you do is make a lot of dough and play golf and play bridge and buy cars and drink Martinis and look like a hot-shot. And besides. Even if you *did* go around saving guys' lives and all, how would you know if you did it because you really *wanted* to save guys' lives, or because you did it because what you *really* wanted to do was be a terrific lawyer, with everybody slapping you on the back and congratulating you in court when the goddam trial was over, the reporters and everybody. . . ? How would you know you weren't being a phony? The trouble is, you *wouldn't*." [62]

Holden Caulfield and most of Salinger's fictional characters are like the alienated students studied by Dr. Keniston. Although apparently blessed by reasonably wealthy and educated parents who have sent them to the best schools and colleges, they are given to excessive introspection concerning their own motivations and are often unable to find anything of value in American society. Like Holden Caulfield they cannot abide phonies, and above all else, they themselves do not want to become phonies.

Although much has been written in the last decade concerning the problem of alienation, we shall find in the next chapter that more than a hundred years ago Karl Marx maintained that man's alienation from his work, from his fellow men, and from himself constituted his greatest problem. It will be useful for the reader to form his own evaluation of the accuracy of Marx's analysis in the light of our present discussion of alienated youth. In later chapters we shall also discuss other writers who were disturbed by the "phony" values of their societies. The reader will find Kierkegaard and Nietzsche especially pertinent in this connection.

The ranks of the alienated and uncommitted are not large, but they are symptomatic of a conscious rejection of prevailing values, without a new vision for the future. Our society is not concerned with asking disturbing questions such as "Why do we stress conformity and success?" It is more concerned with getting the day-to-day problems solved. But increasingly many persons are again asking questions about our ultimate purposes, and are seeking for new values to which they can sincerely commit themselves. In evaluating his findings after his study of alienated college students at Harvard, Dr. Keniston remarked: "What is missing in the alienation of the youths we have studied, as in the little or big alienations of most other Americans, is any radical criticism of our society or any revolutionary alternative to the status quo." [63] But there are clearly signs that this is changing.

One of the most obvious movements we are witnessing today is the joining together of traditional Christians, humanists, and "the New Radicals" in the battle for racial equality. For over one hundred years after the emancipation of the slaves, little had been done to change our society so that Negroes would in fact have equal opportunity to achieve the benefits of an affluent economy. The myth of separate but equal education really served to disguise the inferiority of the schooling our society offered to the Negroes. They were clearly treated as second-class citizens who had to ride in the back of the bus, and who were denied service at "white" lunch counters in the South. However, our ideals professed freedom, justice, and the dignity of the individual. In the 1960's many Americans decided to attempt to achieve these ideals, to stop closing their eyes to the plight of the Negro, and the civil rights movement was born. The sit-ins at segregated lunch counters, the protest march on Washington, and numerous local campaigns to help make the equality of all citizens a reality, instead of a pious dream, have shown a real commitment to brotherhood. These efforts have achieved only token equality for the Negro, however, and many sensitive people have become discouraged with the slow process of peaceful change in fully integrating all citizens into one society. Riots and violence in the ghettos have served to dramatize the plight of many Negroes in a society which was only theoretically dedicated to justice and brotherhood for all.

The *Report of the National Advisory Commission on Civil Disorders* stressed that one of the major underlying causes of the riots in the cities was the failure of white, moderate, middle-class Americans to treat the Negro citizens fairly. This commission stressed that unless the ideals of equality and justice were actually implemented by concrete programs by both government and private enterprise, we would "make permanent the division of our country into two societies; one, largely Negro and poor, located in the central cities; the other, predominantly white and affluent, located in the suburbs and in outlying areas." [64] Clearly, much remains to be done before equality is fully achieved for all citizens. Nevertheless, the beginning which has been made has served to encourage those who reject the present image of our society to unite in trying to achieve a better one.

The extremists in the movements for civil rights, for peace, and for free speech have been labeled "the New Radicals." They have suffered imprisonment, abuse, and in some cases, even the loss of their lives, in their attempts to change our society. To sit on the sidelines, to behave decently, not to question the values of our society, would be the height of immorality to the New Radicals. To refuse to protest in the name of human values against the status quo would be to become as guilty as those Germans who decently obeyed their orders to execute people in the concentration camps. The New Radicals do not want to be like one of the accused in the play *The Investigation:*

> Personally
> I always behaved decently
> Anyway what could I do
> Orders are orders
> And now just because I obeyed
> I've got this trial hung on my neck [65]

Those who tacitly acquiesce in the injustices of our present society are, in the eyes of the New Radicals, just as immoral as those who actively persecute their fellow men. Not to work for human equality, is to tacitly accept inequality. To be fully human, requires that one plays his part in changing our present society so that the ideals of justice and fairness become a reality.

This new generation of American radicals has organized groups dedicated to achieving their alternate vision for society: SNCC (Student Non-violent Coordinating Committee), SDS (Students for a Democratic Society), FSM (the Berkeley Free Speech Movement), etc. Whether their protest is against the intimidation of the Negro, or against the draft policy, or in favor of the right of students to political activism on the campus, there are three general value commitments which undergird their specific activities.

That human' freedom and participation should be extended. That every individual is noble. That a new society based on love and trust must be created.[66]

Their protest is against a society which has failed to achieve these values, and which in their eyes is becoming increasingly corrupt. But at the deepest level, Jack Newfield, who has studied these movements, believes that the New Radicals are rebelling against a purely pragmatic technological civilization that is increasingly dehumanizing man.

They feel powerless and unreal beneath the unfeeling instruments that control their lives. They comprehend the essentially undemocratic nature of the military-industrial complex; the Power Elite; the multiversity with its IBM course cards; urban renewal by technocrats; canned television laughter; wire taps; automation; computer marriages and artificial insemination; and, finally the mysterious button somewhere that can trigger the nuclear holocaust.[67]

Unlike the uncommitted youth, however, the New Radicals are actively trying to change the world. They are trying "to create a world in which love is more possible." [68] Despite the growth of technocracy, they believe that they can establish a social climate in which human brotherhood will become a reality. That the New Radicals have a vision for the future in addition to their rejection of the prevailing American values can be discovered in the following excerpts from a speech by one of the leaders of the Berkeley Free Speech Movement, Mario Savio:

The most crucial problems facing the United States today are the problem of automation and the problem of racial injustice. . . . The university is the place where people begin seriously to question the conditions of their existence and raise the issue of whether they can be committed to the society they have been born into. After a long period of apathy during the fifties, students have begun not only to question but, having arrived at answers, to act on those answers. This is part of a growing understanding among many people in America that history has not ended, that a better society is possible, and that it is worthy dying for. . . .

American society in the standard conception it has of itself is simply no longer exciting. The most exciting things going on in America today are movements to change America. America is becoming ever more the utopia of sterilized, automated contentment. . . . This chrome-plated consumers' paradise would have us grow up to be well-behaved children. But an important minority of men and women coming to the front today have shown that they will die rather than be standardized, replaceable, and irrelevant.[69]

While many people applaud the concern of the New Radicals for the rights of all human beings, there have been serious criticisms made of their organized movements. They have been accused of being politically naive in believing that mass protest marchers proudly bearing placards proclaiming, "Make Love Not War" would actually result in any change in American foreign policy. Even some of their defenders find that their refusal to trust anyone over thirty years of age may cut them off from some needed guidance and wisdom. In short, while their protests have brought home to all of us the failure of our society to measure up to its professed ideals, they have not come forth with a consistent program for organized action to change our society. But then, perhaps, their mission has been accomplished by alerting us to the hypocrisy of our society and by calling upon us to actually practice the virtues which we profess.

The age of relativism did much to destroy man's hopes for finding ultimate values to which he could commit himself firmly and unequivocally. We have seen that some people have interpreted relativism to mean that all values are on an equal footing, that they are all irrational, arbitrary, and perhaps even absurd. On the other hand, others have rejoiced that they now have the opportunity to create their own values, to find some principles which would make sense to them, and to which they could dedicate their lives. We have examined some of the alternative value orientations which are offered to us today by the Organization Man, by Ayn Rand, by Hugh Hefner, and by the New Radicals. It does not appear that we shall be able to come up with values upon which all people can agree. A closer scrutiny of the popular philosophies of our own day, however, does reveal that each one of them is searching for some common basic human values. They all seem to agree on the importance and dignity of each individual, but they do not agree on what the relationship of the individual should be to society. There is, however, hope that we may be able to find, or create, a theoretical basis for values which will give us at least some guidance for making the specific value decisions which each one of us is called upon to make every day of our lives. As Professor Edel has put it:

> Today the demand for such a theoretical footing is a modest one. It is not a quest for absolutes, not simply a fear of the dark, not a demand for a security that relieves us of decision. It is simply the hope that the great issues of the modern world can be faced with the confidence that there are solutions available to reason and experience. Modern man does not ask for a complete morality. He is used to living with problems, and even to feeling that he may have to struggle against ignorance and intransigence. He knows also that

theoretical answers are not easy. But with the tremendous growth and spread of knowledge may he not find some assurance that there are a few firm posts to which a common-human morality can be moored? He does not ask for a detailed map, but he must at least have a compass to guide his ethical course.[70]

We have seen that there are hopeful signs that men are again becoming concerned with basic human values. Many young people, not only the New Radicals, are engaged in an attempt to find significant values to which they can dedicate their lives. We have examined the moral climate of our century in order to provide the background against which this study of alternative value systems is written. The search for a way of life is not purely an intellectual exercise, for while it is worthwhile in and of itself to gain knowledge of the alternative ethical viewpoints which are live options in our century, it is even more a matter of personal significance to each person that he consciously develop his own system of values. If he does not commit himself to his own value choices, he will become an automatic "Yea sayer" to the prevailing values of his society. Socrates' motto that an unexamined life is not worth living is still true today. Let us turn then to those thinkers of the nineteenth and twentieth centuries whose writings appear to be the most relevant to our choice of a way of life.

NOTES FOR CHAPTER I

1 Bertrand Russell, *Common Sense and Nuclear Warfare* (London: George Allen & Unwin, Ltd., 1959), p. 91.
2 Walter Lippmann, *A Preface to Morals* (New York: The Macmillan Co., 1929), *passim.*
3 Edward Westermarck, *Ethical Relativity* (Paterson, N. J.: Littlefield, Adams & Co., 1960), *passim.*
4 Emile Durkheim, *The Elementary Forms of the Religious Life,* trans. by Joseph Ward Swain (New York: Collier Books, 1961), *passim.*
5 William Graham Sumner, *Folkways: A Study of the Sociological Importance of Usages, Manners, Customs, Mores, and Morals* (New York: The New American Library of World Literature, Inc., 1960).
6 Karl Mannheim, *Ideology and Utopia: An Introduction to the Sociology of Knowledge,* trans. by Louis Wirth and Edward Shils (New York: A Harvest Book, Harcourt, Brace & World, Inc., 1936).
7 Among works which have appeared recently, the reader might be interested in referring to Ruth Benedict, *Patterns of Culture* (Boston: Houghton Mifflin Co., 1934), and the numerous anthropological writings of Margaret Mead.
8 Quoted in Abraham Edel, *Ethical Judgment: The Use of Science in Ethics* (New York: The Free Press, A Division of The Macmillan Co., 1955), p. 16. Edel himself does not subscribe to this kind of an interpretation of ethical relativity; in fact his book is an excellent attempt to find a common human basis for morality.

9   John Barth, *The Floating Opera* (New York: An Avon Library Book, 1956), p. 216.

10 Samuel Beckett, *Waiting for Godot: A Tragicomedy in Two Acts* (New York: Grove Press, Inc., 1954), pp. 31–32.

11 Eugène Ionesco, *Four Plays: The Bald Soprano, The Lesson, Jack or the Submission, The Chairs*, trans. by Donald M. Allen (New York: Grove Press, Inc., 1958).

12 Jean Genet, *The Balcony*, trans. by Bernard Frechtman (New York: Grove Press, Inc., 1958), p. 115.

13 Albert Camus, *The Myth of Sisyphus and Other Essays*, trans. by Justin O'Brien (New York: Vintage Books, Inc., Random House, 1959), p. 5.

14 Eugène Ionesco, "Discovering the Theatre," in *Theatre in the Twentieth Century*, ed. by Robert W. Corrigan (New York: Grove Press, Inc., 1965), p. 86.

15 B. F. Skinner, *Science and Human Behavior* (New York: The Free Press, A Division of The Macmillan Co., 1965), *passim*.

16 B. F. Skinner, *Walden Two* (New York: The Macmillan Co., 1962), p. 161.

17 Barth, *The Floating Opera*, p. 271.

18 This was the subtitle of William James, *Pragmatism*, originally published in 1907.

19 William James, *Pragmatism and Four Essays from The Meaning of Truth*, ed. by Ralph Barton Perry (New York: Meridian Books, 1955), pp. 17–19.

20 *Ibid.*, p. 45.

21 *Ibid.*, p. 47.

22 *Ibid.*, p. 49.

23 William James, "The Will to Believe," in *Essays in Pragmatism*, ed. and introd. by Alburey Castell (New York: Hafner Publishing Co., Inc., 1962), p. 101.

24 *Ibid.*, p. 108 (footnote).

25 *Ibid.*, p. 95.

26 John Dewey, *Human Nature and Conduct: An Introduction to Social Psychology*, introd. by John Dewey (New York: The Modern Library, 1930), p. 35.

27 John Dewey, *Reconstruction in Philosophy* (Boston: Beacon Press, 1957), p. 185.

28 Dewey, *Human Nature and Conduct: An Introduction to Social Psychology*, p. 129.

29 Dewey, *Reconstruction in Philosophy*, p. 186.

30 *Ibid.*, p. 186.

31 Harvey Cox, *The Secular City: Secularization and Urbanization in Theological Perspective* (Rev. ed.; New York: The Macmillan Co., 1966), p. 55.

32 Charles Frankel, "Unphilosophical Pragmatism," in *The Love of Anxiety and Other Essays* (New York: Dell Publishing Co., Inc., 1967), p. 143.

33 William H. Whyte, Jr., *The Organization Man* (Garden City, N. Y.: Anchor Books, Doubleday & Co., Inc., 1957), *passim*; Vance Packard, *The Status Seekers* (New York: Pocket Books, Inc., 1961), *passim*.

34 Arthur Miller, *Death of a Salesman* (New York: Bantam Books, Inc., 1951).

35 Ayn Rand, "The Objectivist Ethics," in *The Virtue of Selfishness: A New*

Concept of Egoism (New York: The New American Library of World Literature, Inc., 1964), pp. 17, 23.

36 *Ibid.,* p. 23.
37 *Ibid.,* p. 31.
38 Rand, "The Ethics of Emergencies," in *The Virtue of Selfishness,* pp. 44–45.
39 *Ibid.,* p. 45.
40 Rand, "Man's Rights," in *The Virtue of Selfishness,* p. 93.
41 *Ibid.,* p. 94.
42 *Ibid.,* p. 94.
43 *Ibid.,* pp. 96–97.
44 *Ibid.,* p. 97.
45 Rand, "The Objectivist Ethics," in *The Virtue of Selfishness,* p. 33.
46 *Ibid.,* p. 31.
47 Ayn Rand, *Atlas Shrugged* in *For the New Intellectual: The Philosophy of Ayn Rand* (New York: The New American Library of World Literature, Inc., 1961), p. 91.
48 Hugh M. Hefner, *The Playboy Philosophy: Parts I, II, III,* and *IV* (Chicago: H M H Publishing Co., Inc., 1962–1965), p. 107.
49 *Ibid.,* p. 14.
50 *Ibid.,* p. 13.
51 *Ibid.,* p. 100.
52 *Ibid.,* p. 51.
53 *Ibid.,* p. 179.
54 John Crane, "Philosophy and Phantasy in Playboy Magazine and What This Suggests About Us," quoted in *ibid.,* p. 7.
55 Hefner, *Playboy Philosophy,* p. 3.
56 *Ibid.,* p. 19.
57 Cox, *The Secular City,* p. 178.
58 Hefner, *Playboy Philosophy,* p. 162.
59 *Ibid.,* p. 17.
60 Kenneth Keniston, *The Uncommitted: Alienated Youth in American Society* (New York: Dell Publishing Co., Inc., 1967), p. 6.
61 *Ibid.,* p. 59.
62 J. D. Salinger, *The Catcher in the Rye* (New York: The New American Library of World Literature, Inc., 1960), p. 155.
63 Keniston, *The Uncommitted,* p. 419.
64 *Report of the National Advisory Commission on Civil Disorders* (New York: Bantam Books, Inc., 1968), p. 22.
65 Peter Weiss, *The Investigation (A Play),* English version by Jon Swan and Ulu Grosbard (New York: Atheneum Publishers, 1966), p. 19.
66 Jack Newfield, *A Prophetic Minority* (New York: The New American Library of World Literature, Inc., 1967), p. 144.
67 *Ibid.,* p. 23.
68 *Ibid.,* p. 19.
69 Mario Savio, "An End to History," in *The New Radicals: A Report with Documents,* ed. by Paul Jacobs and Saul Landau (New York: Vintage Books, Inc., Random House, 1966), pp. 231–232, 234.
70 Edel, *Ethical Judgment,* pp. 18–19.

SELECTED READINGS

Available in paperback edition.

The moral climate of our age can readily be discovered by reading contemporary literature, as well as by studying the works of non-fiction devoted specifically to moral and cultural problems. The works of fiction listed are not necessarily examples of great literature, but they do present interesting interpretations of life in the twentieth century.

CONTEMPORARY NOVELS AND SHORT STORIES

* Barth, John. *The Floating Opera.* New York: An Avon Library Book, 1956.
* Ellison, Ralph. *Invisible Man.* New York: The New American Library of World Literature, Inc., 1953.
* Huxley, Aldous. *Brave New World.* New York: Bantam Books, Inc., 1946.
* Marquand, John P. *Point of No Return.* New York: Bantam Books, Inc., 1961.
* Orwell, George. *Animal Farm.* New York: The New American Library of World Literature, Inc., 1957.
* ———. *1984.* New York: The New American Library of World Literature, Inc., 1952.
* Rand, Ayn. *Atlas Shrugged.* New York: The New American Library of World Literature, Inc., 1959.
* ———. *The Fountainhead.* New York: The New American Library of World Literature, Inc., 1943.
* Salinger, J. D. *The Catcher in the Rye.* New York: The New American Library of World Literature, Inc., 1960.
* ———. *Nine Stories.* New York: The New American Library of World Literature, Inc., 1954.
* Skinner, B. F. *Walden Two.* New York: The Macmillian Co., 1962.

CONTEMPORARY PLAYS

* Beckett, Samuel. *Waiting for Godot: A Tragicomedy in Two Acts.* New York: Grove Press, Inc., 1954.
* Genet, Jean. *The Balcony.* Translated by Bernard Frechtman. New York: Grove Press, Inc., 1958.
* Ionesco, Eugène. *Four Plays: The Bald Soprano, The Lesson, Jack or the Submission, The Chairs.* Translated by Donald M. Allen. New York: Grove Press, Inc., 1958.
* Miller, Arthur. *Death of a Salesman.* New York: Bantam Books, Inc., 1951.
* Weiss, Peter. *The Investigation (A Play).* English version by Jon Swan and Ulu Grosbard. New York: Atheneum Publishers, 1966.

PRIMARY SOURCES

* Benedict, Ruth. *Patterns of Culture.* Boston: Houghton Mifflin Co., 1934.
* Dewey, John. *Human Nature and Conduct: An Introduction to Social Psychology.* New York: The Modern Library, 1930.
* ———. *Reconstruction in Philosophy.* Boston: Beacon Press, 1957.

42 *Conflict of Ideals*

* Durkheim, Emile. *The Elementary Forms of the Religious Life*. Translated
by Joseph Ward Swain. New York: Collier Books, 1961.
* Edel, Abraham. *Ethical Judgment: The Use of Science in Ethics*. New York:
The Free Press, A Division of The Macmillan Co., 1955.
* Frankel, Charles. *The Love of Anxiety and Other Essays*. New York: Dell
Publishing Co., Inc., 1967.
* Hefner, Hugh M. *The Playboy Philosophy: Parts I, II, III, and IV*. Chicago:
H M H Publishing Co., Inc., 1962–1965.
* Jacobs, Paul and Saul Landau, eds. *The New Radicals: A Report with Docu-
ments*. New York: Vintage Books, Inc., Random House, 1966.
* James, William. *Essays in Pragmatism*. Edited and introduction by Alburey
Castell. New York: Hafner Publishing Co., Inc., 1962.
* ———. *Pragmatism and Four Essays from The Meaning of Truth*. Edited
by Ralph Barton Perry. New York: Meridian Books, 1955.
* Keniston, Kenneth. *The Uncommitted: Alienated Youth in American
Society*. New York: Dell Publishing Co., Inc., 1967.
* McLuhan, Marshall. *Understanding Media: The Extensions of Man*. New
York: McGraw-Hill Book Co., 1965.
* ——— and Quentin Fiore. *The Medium Is the Massage*. New York:
Bantam Books, Inc., 1967.
* Mannheim, Karl. *Ideology and Utopia: An Introduction to the Sociology of
Knowledge*. Translated by Louis Wirth and Edward Shils. New
York: A Harvest Book, Harcourt, Brace & World, Inc., 1936.
* Marcuse, Herbert. *One Dimensional Man: Studies in the Ideology of Ad-
vanced Industrial Society*. Boston: Beacon Press, 1964.
* May, Rollo. *Psychology and the Human Dilemma*. Princeton, N. J.: D. Van
Nostrand Co., Inc., 1967.
* Mead, Margaret. *And Keep Your Powder Dry: An Anthropologist Looks
at America*. New York: William Morrow and Co., 1965.
* Newfield, Jack. *A Prophetic Minority*. New York: The New American
Library of World Literature, Inc., 1967.
*Packard, Vance. *The Hidden Persuaders*. New York: Pocket Books, Inc.,
1957.
* ———. *The Status Seekers*. New York: Pocket Books, Inc., 1961.
* Rand, Ayn. *For the New Intellectual: The Philosophy of Ayn Rand*. New
York: The New American Library of World Literature, Inc.,
1961.
* ———. *The Virtue of Selfishness: A New Concept of Egoism*. New York:
The New American Library of World Literature, Inc., 1964.
* *Report of the National Advisory Commission on Civil Disorders*. New York:
Bantam Books, Inc., 1968.
* Rorty, Amelie, ed. *Pragmatic Philosophy: An Anthology*. Garden City, N. Y.:
Anchor Books, Doubleday & Co., Inc., 1966. The best anthology
on pragmatism. Includes recent neo-pragmatic writers, as well as
James and Dewey.
* Russell, Bertrand. *Common Sense and Nuclear Warfare*. London: George
Allen & Unwin, Ltd., 1959.
* Skinner, B. F. *Science and Human Behavior*. New York: The Free Press,
A Division of The Macmillan Co., 1965.
* Sumner, William Graham. *Folkways: A Study of the Sociological Importance
of Usages, Manners, Customs, Mores, and Morals*. New York:

Mentor Books, The New American Library of World Literature, Inc., 1960.

* Westermarck, Edward. *Ethical Relativity*. Paterson, N. J.: Littlefield, Adams & Co., 1960.

* Whyte, William H. Jr. *The Organization Man*. Garden City, N. Y.: Anchor Books, Doubleday & Co., Inc., 1957.

II

Marxism and Communism

The basic ideal of Marxism is humanistic, both in the sense that it concentrates its attention upon man in this world, and in its vision of an ultimately classless society in which all individuals will for the first time achieve their full freedom as men. The writings of Karl Marx and Friedrich Engels, whose works constitute the corpus of Marxist literature, are exerting much more influence today than they did a decade ago. Not only in officially Communist countries, such as Russia and China, but in the underdeveloped nations of Southeast Asia and Africa, as well as in Europe, England and the United States, Marxism is exerting a powerful influence upon those people who are seriously seeking for a way of life which will give each human being a greater sense of dignity and worth than he now appears to have in this age of cold wars and ideological struggles.

Part of the reason for the renewed interest in Marxism is political. Russia has since the time of the Revolution of 1917 officially endorsed Marxism as its basic philosophy, despite the fact that the writings of Marx and Engels have had to be continuously reinterpreted and modified in order to meet the pragmatic needs of the U.S.S.R. Russia's gigantic strides in catching up with the Western capitalist nations in technology, production and science have been a source of inspiration to the underdeveloped peoples of Southeast Asia and Africa, who also must begin from primitive economic circumstances in their bid to become independent world powers. Communist China also serves as a model for many of these underdeveloped nations which are seeking methods to bring their peoples of age in the modern world.

The main reason for the renewed interest in Marxism in the United States, England and Europe does not seem to be political, but rather philosophical or moralistic. In fact, many of the leaders of the emerging African nations, as well as the leaders in the Iron Curtain countries of Europe, look toward Marxism as a promise of a better way of life for their people. The ethical aspects of the teachings of Marx have come to the forefront, largely as a result of the recent publication of the early philosophical writings of Karl Marx. In these early writings, written before the publication of the *Communist Manifesto* in 1848, Marx's main concern is with the problem of man's alienation, a problem that is currently analyzed by many contemporary writers. These early philosophical writings of Marx were until recently viewed as the productions of an immature schoolboy who was still trying to fight his way out of the mystic obscurantism of Hegelianism. Marx's fame was thus centered on his great opus *Capital* which was interpreted as an outdated treatise on economics. Recent scholarship by Robert C. Tucker, Erich Fromm, and the various contributions to the international symposium *Socialist Humanism* have shown that Marx's later writings cannot be effectively interpreted unless they are seen as a development of, rather than a revulsion from, the earlier more philosophical writings.[1] As a result current interest in the Western world centers on Marx's view of man, his analysis of alienated man, and his proposals for a more humane society in which each man would be free from exploitation in order that he could develop to the fullest *all* of his human capabilities. Hence, while it may still be true to say that Marx's opus *Capital* was not a scientific study, in that he used only the facts which would support his preconceived view of the inevitable collapse of capitalism, it becomes more likely that the significance of Marx for the future will be based not on Marx as an economist but on Marx as a philosopher and a prophet.

Marx and Engels: A Brief Biographical Sketch   Before examining in some
detail the basic methodology and doctrines of Marx and Engels it will be helpful to have some understanding of their lives, especially since their writings are almost always directed at some specific problem of concern to their age of history.[2]

Karl Marx (1818–1883) was born in Treves in the Rhineland. His parents were Jewish (on both his mother's and father's side of the house there had been rabbis), but when Karl was six years old his father had the whole family baptized as Protestant Christians. Karl's father was a lawyer who intellectually was influenced by the eighteenth-century enlightenment. Karl's prophetic zeal (reminiscent of the eighth-century Hebrew prophets) and his belief in the inevitable arrival of a socialist society were probably aspects which he acquired early in life from his father.

Karl went from the private schools of Trier to the universities of Bonn and Berlin. He was much impressed by the young left-wing Hegelians in Berlin, and his early philosophical writing was largely an attempt to expand upon their criticism of religion by devising a dialectical method which could be used to criticize all the institutions and beliefs of the nineteenth-century German world. Although he received a doctorate from the University of Jena, he was considered to be too radical for an academic appointment. Marx thus turned to socialistic journalism, becoming editor of the *Rheinische Zeitung* in 1842. Upon the suppression of Marx's newspaper by the German authorities in 1843, he went to Paris where he could study socialism at first hand in its very center of influence.

The years Marx spent in Paris from 1843 to 1845 are considered to have been decisive for his future career. It was in Paris that he met Friedrich Engels in 1844; this was the beginning of a lifelong career of cooperation and collaboration between the two men. Engels (1820–1895), the son of a wealthy German textile manufacturer, had independently arrived at a position very similar to Marx's. Marx had arrived at his analysis of society and his advocacy of Communism largely as a result of his own philosophical critique of Hegel; Engels, on the other hand, had worked in his father's factories in Manchester and hence had observed at first hand the actual conditions under which the working class in England lived and labored. Marx was able to give Engels the comprehensive historical-philosophical framework for his ideas, while Engels was able to provide Marx with a wealth of concrete data in support of his philosophical thesis of historical materialism.

Marx's ideas as published in a German newspaper edited in Paris appeared to become more radical and objectionable to the Prussian authorities, who prevailed upon France to expel Marx in 1845. Marx went to Brussels where he was soon joined by Engels who arrived from England in order to work with Marx. It was in Brussels that Marx found himself for the first time at the command of a truly revolutionary Communist party organization. From this time on, Marx's career (and Engels') was involved with many details of party organization, revolutionary activity, and with the practical attempt of trying to put his ideas into practice in the world. "As soon as he [Marx] concluded that the establishment of communism could only be achieved by a rising of the proletariat, his entire existence turned into an attempt to organize and discipline it for its task." [3] The London center of the Communist League asked Marx to write a definitive statement of its aims and beliefs. Marx and Engels collaborated on this task, and the result, as is well known, was the famous *Communist Manifesto* of 1848.

The year of abortive revolutions in Europe was 1848, and Marx and Engels were directly involved in most of them. When the revolution broke out in Germany, Marx hurried to Cologne where he edited a radical daily newspaper, the *Neue Rheinische Zeitung*, which was effectively addressed to the members of the working class. When Marx called upon his readers not to pay their taxes, the German authorities had him arrested on the charge of treason. Marx had himself studied law as a youth, and thus used the occasion of his trial not only to defend himself, but to lecture the jury on the political and social state of Germany and other countries. Marx was not only acquitted, but the foreman of the jury thanked Marx for the instructive lecture he had delivered to them. The Prussian government could not annul this verdict of acquittal, but it did succeed in having Marx again expelled from Germany. Marx returned to Paris, but found that he was unwelcome there also. Thus, in 1849, he emigrated to London, where he was to remain for the rest of his life.

Perhaps Marx's participation in the abortive revolutions of 1848 had sobered his enthusiasm by suggesting that a more detailed theoretical structure would be required before there could be a successful proletarian revolution. At any rate, he kept relatively free of the squabbles among the competitive socialist groups of the German workers in London, and concentrated his efforts upon daily reading and writing in the library of the British Museum. The product of his research was *Capital*, the first volume of which was published in 1867. The remaining notes for future volumes were later edited and published by Engels. During the years 1851 to 1862 Marx supported himself by writing as a European correspondent for Horace Greeley's *New York Tribune*. Engels also contributed to the support of the Marx family by the income he received from again working in his father's factory in Manchester.

Marx did, however, emerge on to the active political scene once more. This time he became the leader of the General Council of the First International (called the International Workingmen's Association) which was organized in 1864. Marx gave the Inaugural Address for the First International, and eloquently called for the workingmen of the world to unite for only in solidarity could they become free of the oppression of capitalism. Until 1872, when splits and expulsions had greatly weakened the International, it was a force to be reckoned with in Europe and its leader, Karl Marx, had become a world-renowned figure.

Upon Marx's death in 1883, Engels edited the surviving manuscripts of Marx and wrote extensively himself in order to expound more fully the views of historical materialism and Communism. It is time now to turn directly to the leading "revolutionary" ideas of Karl Marx, for perhaps then we shall be able to understand what Engels meant when he said: "We are what we are because of him: without him we should still be sunk in a slough of confusion." [4]

The Early Views of Marx: Alienated Man   Karl Marx listed his favorite
                                           maxim as "I believe nothing
human to be alien to me," and his favorite motto as "Of all one must
doubt." [5] In a significant sense these aphorisms give us a basic insight
into his conception of man, as well as the method which he sought to
employ in his attempt to remove the obstacles to full human development by all men. Too often Marx's main contribution to Western thought
has been viewed as a vulgar creed of economic determinism which reduces the individual person to nothing more than a pawn in the hands
of forces over which he has no control. We shall examine this charge
against Marx's theory later on. At this stage, however, it will be more
helpful for us to begin with the view of man which Marx developed
in his early writings, a position which he never abandoned despite the
fact that he was occupied with more particular economic and political
problems in his later writings.[6]

   Much of the latent content of Marx's early writings, as well as his
method, owes much to Hegel. Marx as a student had become thoroughly
grounded in Hegelianism, and was especially attracted to the interpretations and revisions of Hegel by the left-wing Hegelians such as Feuerbach.
Hegel had held that all of nature and history were but an attempt by the
Absolute Spirit (the ultimate reality, Hegel's "philosophical God") to
realize itself. This was a gigantic metaphysical position which Hegel
sought to develop by showing that there was a general developmental
process on-going in the entire universe. With respect to history he tried
to show that in the ancient world only one man was free—the Absolute
Ruler, but that by a process of conflict and evolution history was ap-
proaching the stage of the modern or German world in which all men
would be free. But this historical process was really for Hegel also the
way in which God becomes fully God, for nature and history were
actually God, Spirit, the whole of Reality. Nature is unconscious of itself
as spirit, but man is spirit becoming more and more conscious of itself
as spirit by means of knowledge. As long as something appears as an
external object to the knowing spirit the object is alienated from the
knower. Hegel referred to this as the self-alienation of spirit. But when
the philosopher overcomes this externality of the object which he finds
confronting him by realizing that the object is actually a part of the
totality of the knowing self who transcends the object by his knowing of
it, then the self-alienation of man is also overcome. But, for Hegel, this
process actually involves God returning to himself and being delivered
from the state of alienation or separation; for man knowing totally is
really God's fully becoming conscious of Himself. Hegel's philosophical
man thus is the Absolute Spirit or God becoming fully aware of its own
nature and thus restoring the "at-one-ness" of nature, man and God.

   The left-wing Hegelians believed that Hegel had discovered the truth, but that he had covered it with a veil of mystical and idealistic obscurantism, largely because he was under the belief that a philosophically purified religion expressed the ultimate truth of the universe. What their reading of Hegel revealed to them was that man was actually God, but man not as the absolute knower of Hegel, but rather as the ordinary empirical man of everyday life. These young Hegelians recognized that much had to be done to change the world so that man could realize that he was the only "God" there was, and therefore they called for programs to educate man so that he could live without the illusions of religion.

The left-wing Hegelian Feuerbach had more influence upon the early Marx than any other thinker. Feuerbach's *Essence of Christianity* (1841) showed Marx that henceforward his concern should be with the real man, viewed naturalistically as a part of the material world and not as an alien spiritual being. While Feuerbach devoted his energies to the criticism of religion and philosophical theology in order that man might be liberated from the spell of religion, Marx enlarged this critical method to attack the entire sphere of political, economic and social life which shackled individual men.

Marx's awareness of the extent to which a man's ideas and ideals are shaped by the nature of the society in which he dwells, as well as his aspirations for the real freedom of all men, are already clearly evident in *On the Jewish Question*, written in 1843. This essay was a reply to the views of another left-wing Hegelian, Bruno Bauer, who had argued for the political emancipation of the Jews in Germany. Marx suggests that Bauer's treatment was too narrowly confined to the German nation, and should instead have dealt with the more general question, "What is the relation between *complete* political emancipation and religion?" [7] He finds that religion is actually a sign of secular narrowness, and that political emancipation of any man or group of men "is the *emancipation* of the state from Judaism, Christianity, and *religion* in general." [8] What Marx suggests here is that Jews might be given the political rights of citizens, a kind of political emancipation, and yet they would not achieve complete human emancipation itself. Marx saw that a governmental guarantee of the right to vote does not automatically confer this right in fact unless all men are freed from their egoistic concerns and prejudices. At this stage of his career Marx differentiated between the species-life of man (the social essence of each man as belonging to humanity) and the material egoistic life of individual men. As rights were conferred upon men by the political state the individual men were not liberated into human freedom, but rather they acquired only the specific liberties of egoistic individuals in a capitalistic society. The natural man is then conceived to be the individual in his immediate practical egoistic existence, while political man is regarded as an allegorical abstract moral person. Hence, political emancipation, while it is a goal along the way, is not the final emancipation of man. Marx's conclusion to this early essay sounds the utopian call for freedom of the individual and the solidarity of the group for which he was to become famous in the *Communist Manifesto:*

> Human emancipation will only be complete when the real, individual man has absorbed into himself the abstract citizen; when as an individual man, in his everyday life, in his work, and in his relationships, he has become a *species-being;* and when he has recognized and organized his own powers (*forces propres*) as *social* powers so that he no longer separates this social power from himself as *political* power.[9]

While many of Marx's early writings were written in a rather pedantic philosophical vocabulary, nevertheless, his clear apprehension of the alienation of man in society is expressed in almost prophetic imagery. Marx inverted Hegel's view of the self-alienation of God in nature and history, and found instead that man was alienated from nature, from his fellow human beings, and even from himself. An alien is a stranger, a foreigner, one who is not at home where he lives. For Marx man should be a creative, productive person but instead man found that he had to struggle constantly in order to eke out a mere existence, with no time or energy left for cultivating his full capacities. Religion, furthermore, contributes to man's alienation by maintaining that he will find things better in another world. Feuerbach had made a great contribution, Marx stated, in showing that religion itself was an illusion. What now remained to be done was "to establish the *truth of this world*. The immediate *task of philosophy*, which is in the service of history, is to unmask human self-alienation in its *secular form* now that it has been unmasked in its *sacred form*." [10]

But it would not be enough simply to show the forms of alienation by means of philosophy or critical thought, for Marx insisted that the existing situation, once it was correctly understood, had to be changed forcibly. Marx in his early writings stressed the necessity of action, of philosophy changing the world and not merely thinking about it, a theme which recurs throughout his entire career:

> Material force can only be overthrown by material force; but theory itself becomes a material force when it has seized the masses. Theory is capable of seizing the masses when it demonstrates *ad hominem*, and it demonstrates *ad hominem* as soon as it becomes radical. To be radical is to grasp things by the root. But for man the root is man himself. . . . The criticism of religion ends with the doctrine that *man is the supreme being for man*. It ends, therefore, with the *categorical imperative to overthrow all those conditions* in which man is an abased, enslaved, abandoned, contemptible being—conditions which can hardly be better described than in the exclamation

of a Frenchman on the occasion of a proposed tax upon dogs: "Wretched dogs! They want to treat you like men!" [11]

Marx's description of alienation in his early *Philosophical and Economic Manuscripts* was one which he was to transpose into social alienation resulting from the division of labor in *Capital*. However, a common thread runs through the early writings and *Capital:* the workingman by means of his labor has created an objective world of things which now hold him in bondage. All labor up to now, according to Marx, has been alienated labor, whether it has been menial physical labor or mental activity. Marx summarized his findings in his essay *Alienated Labor:*

> From political economy itself, in its own words, we have shown that the worker sinks to the level of a commodity, and to a most miserable commodity; that the misery of the worker increases with the power and volume of his production; that the necessary result of competition is the accumulation of capital in a few hands, and thus a restoration of monopoly in a more terrible form; and finally that the distinction between capitalist and landlord, and between agricultural labourer and industrial worker, must disappear, and the whole of society divide into two classes of property *owners* and *propertyless* workers.[12]

Marx is here enunciating a thesis he developed at great lengths later on. The worker sells his skill to the owner of the factory; he is in turn treated like a thing by the employer who tries to purchase the worker's labor power at the lowest possible wage. It is not surprising then that even the worker begins to think of himself as merely an object which can be taken up and discarded as needed by the employer. The all-consuming urge of capitalists is to make a profit, and in their pursuit of this it does not matter to them that they are dehumanizing the workers whom they employ. But for Marx this process of dehumanization effects the entire society, for "the *devaluation* of the human world increases in direct relation with the *increase in value* of the world of things." [13]

The objects created by the worker become opposed to him, alienated from him, not merely because they are sold on the market by men other than the workers who produce them, but mainly because even the process of production itself involves self-alienation of the worker. Marx forcibly presents his analysis of the plight of the worker in the following passage:

> What constitutes the alienation of labour? First, that the work is *external* to the worker, that it is not part of his nature; and that, consequently, he does not fulfil himself in his work but denies himself, has a feeling of misery rather than well-being, does not develop freely his mental and physical energies but is physically exhausted

and mentally debased. The worker, therefore, feels himself at home only during his leisure time, whereas at work he feels homeless. His work is not voluntary, but imposed, *forced labour*. It is not the satisfaction of a need, but only a *means* for satisfying other needs. Its alien character is clearly shown by the fact that as soon as there is no physical or other compulsion it is avoided like the plague. . . . Finally, the external character of work for the worker is shown by the fact that it is not his own work but work for someone else, that in work he does not belong to himself but to another person.[14]

But labor not only alienated man from the objects he produces and from himself, but also it alienated him from his fellow men. Not only does the individual worker lose all sense of spontaneity in his work, but he loses the sense of human solidarity which is basic to the essence of man. The alienated worker notices that what he produces is for another man, the employer, so that what is a source of misery to the worker becomes a means of enjoyment for the employer. He is although not literally a slave, actually in bondage to another man, his employer.

The real God of the capitalist world, suggests Marx, is money. The urge to possess, to have money, becomes all dominant and all values are expressed in monetary terms. The worker, as well as the capitalist, wants more money, but the worker is still in bondage to uncreative labor even if he gets a raise in wages. Again Marx reminds one of the eighth-century Hebrew prophets as he writes:

Money is the jealous God of Israel, beside which no other god may exist. Money abases all the gods of mankind and changes them into commodities. Money is the universal and self-sufficient *value* of all things. It has, therefore, deprived the whole world, both the human world and nature, of their own proper value. Money is the alienated essence of man's work and existence; this essence dominates him and he worships it.[15]

Marx finds that the artificial need for money is the only need created by the modern industrialist system, which operates so that money can buy anything from beauty to fame to a vocation; only not for the worker, who is to have just enough money so that he can sustain his life at the level of subsistence. The man-made products which money can buy become desirable for the wealthy, and there is always a great increase in these unneeded luxuries. But meanwhile the poor worker is reduced to survival in residences even worse than early man's cave dwellings, while the modern factory assembly lines are but a refinement of the old Roman treadmills.

What is even worse, according to Marx, is that this entire capitalistic system is given a moral justification by its encouraging the accumulation of savings, and advocating an ascetic miserly life:

Its principal thesis is the renunciation of life and of human needs. The less you eat, drink, buy books, go to the theatre or to balls, or to the public house, and the less you think, love, theorize, sing, paint, fence, etc. the more you will be able to save and the *greater* will become your treasure which neither moth nor rust will corrupt—your *capital.* The less you *are,* the less you express your life, the more you *have,* the greater is your *alienated* life and the greater is the saving of your alienated being. Everything which the economist takes from you in the way of life and humanity, he restores to you in the form of *money* and *wealth.*[16]

But, as Marx continues, this is a rather dubious morality for "how can I be virtuous if I am not alive and how can I have a good conscience if I am not aware of anything?"[17] Thus, both for the worker, who has no home of his own but must inhabit the dwelling of another man who can evict him for nonpayment of rent, and for the capitalist, whose life is filled with the avaricious search for more wealth, life becomes a matter of *not having* or *having.* But for Marx the real nature of man consists in that which *he is* and not in what *he has.* Money permits man to buy anything, if he has the money; even virtue and vice have their prices. Marx the moralist calls this capitalistic ethic an inversion of the real nature of man which has reduced man to an object and estranged him from his essential humanity.

Let us not fail to note, however, that Marx has a positive ideal of what man should be like, an ideal which he often professed would be reached only after a complete proletarian revolution. It is an ideal which is humanistic and stresses the aesthetic aspect of all creative work and activity:

Let us assume *man* to be *man,* and his relation to the world to be a human one. Then love can only be exchanged for love, trust for trust, etc. If you wish to enjoy art you must be an artistically cultivated person; if you wish to influence other people you must be a person who really has a stimulating and encouraging effect upon others. Every one of your relations to man and to nature must be a *specific expression,* corresponding to the object of your will, of your *real individual* life.[18]

Marx did not share the beliefs of the Utopian Socialists of his day that understanding would of itself overcome the debasement of human existence, for he tended to view man's alienation more and more in the dramatic terms of two classes of men opposing each other in preparation for a gigantic epic battle. The self-alienation of man thus becomes in effect the social alienation of two different groups of men, the workers (proletariat) and the non-workers (capitalists). Neither of these classes represents a complete image of humanity, but the proletariat is the only group which may through a heroic revolution establish a classless society in which each man may be fully creative and human. In this ultimate Communism all men will work, but none will engage in alienated labor, for their work will be done freely and with joy; their work will be productive and creative and they will have the time and leisure to develop fully their manifold capacities for art, science, hunting, fishing, and all kinds of enjoyable human activities. There will no longer be an estrangement of man from nature and from his fellow men; man will be rich in a new way—in a fully human way so that the beauty and joy of life will abound for all men as they cooperatively live and love in a fully humanized world. The reader may no doubt recognize that this ultimate Communism of Karl Marx may with justice be called a Paradise on Earth, a dream which has many affinities with the visions of prophets in both the Old and New Testaments. Marx was dreaming and yearning for a day when no man would find anything human alien to him.

It is time now to turn to an investigation of the *Communist Manifesto*—that historic document in which "classical Marxism" in terms of a materialistic philosophy of history was first clearly formulated.

Classical Marxism: Historical Materialism   The average reader is probably familiar with Marx's view as expressed in the *Communist Manifesto*, or more unfortunately he may have heard at second-hand that Marx is a believer in materialism and economic determinism. At the outset it will be important to clarify that when materialism is used with reference to Marx it is philosophical materialism that is meant, and not the usual everyday use of the word to designate a predominant interest in the accumulation of money and possessions. As we have already seen, Marx was anything but a "materialist" in this ordinary sense of the word. When he characterized his philosophy as materialism, he did so in order to contrast it with Hegelian philosophical idealism. For Hegel reality consisted in an ultimate Mind or Spirit, while the natural material universe was but a derivative of this ultimate Mind. Marx, when he called his world-view materialism, tried to suggest that his philosophy was scientific; it was a way of beginning with the concrete reality of the world which discovered that all ideas were deeply rooted in man's actual material existence in a natural and historical world. As Marx stated, "Life is not determined by consciousness, but consciousness by life." [19] According to this view, man cannot think at all unless his material needs are satisfied, and then what he does think will be dependent upon the material mode of production of the society in which he lives.

Historical materialism, for Marx, represented the basic theory and method which he used in his study of history to demonstrate the truth of his prediction of an inevitable class war between the proletariat and the capitalists. As he put it:

The mode of production in material life determines the general character of the social, political and spiritual processes of life. It is not the consciousness of men that determine their existence, but, on the contrary, their social existence determines their consciousness.[20]

This method is sometimes called dialectical materialism, for this shows the relationship of Marx's procedure to that of Hegel. Hegel had maintained that all of nature and history is filled with a strife of opposing forces; this is the strife of thesis with antithesis, each claiming to be true but neither representing the complete truth. What results in time is that a synthesis emerges in which the truths of the thesis and the antithesis are reconciled and fused, while their errors are abandoned. This synthesis becomes a new thesis, to which a new antithesis appears; in time there is a reconciliation in a new synthesis, and the process continues on and on. That Marx and Engels both made use of this dialectical method can be readily discovered in the theory of history as class struggles which they presented in the *Communist Manifesto:*

The history of all hitherto existing society is the history of class struggles.

Freeman and slave, patrician and plebeian, lord and serf, guild-master and journeyman, in a word, oppressor and oppressed, stood in constant opposition to one another, carried on an uninterrupted, now hidden, now open fight, a fight that each time ended, either in a revolutionary reconstitution of society at large, or in the common ruin of the contending classes.[21]

What made the situation of the nineteenth century different in their eyes was that the struggle in history was being simplified into two great hostile classes: the bourgeoisie and the proletariat. The struggle between these two classes was interpreted as the last fight between the haves and the have-nots before the arrival of a classless society, which would be the final and ultimate synthesis of opposing forces in history. In oratorical prose the *Communist Manifesto* echoes Marx's theme of the alienation of the worker which, as we have seen, was one of the leitmotifs in his early writings. We are now told that the machine has introduced a dehumanizing element that has added new horrors to the situation of the working-man. The capitalistic manufacturing system with its "subjection of nature's forces to man and machinery; the application of chemistry to industry and agriculture; [the development of] steam-navigation, railways and electric telegraphs; the clearing of whole continents for cultivation," and so on, has "put an end to all feudal, patriarchal, idyllic relations." Personal worth has been converted into exchange value in the market place of Free Trade. With the sole exception of the owners of the means of production, all men are wage laborers—even the educated men in the formerly hallowed professions; while even the executives of the modern

State constitute "but a committee for managing the common affairs of the whole bourgeoisie." The intimate family relation itself has been reduced to merely a money relation. "In a word, for exploitation, veiled by religious and political illusions, it [the bourgeoisie] has substituted naked, shameless, direct, brutal exploitation." [22]

The *Manifesto* continues that this dehumanizing process is becoming world-wide; all nations "even the most barbarian," are forced, "on pain of extinction" to accept so-called "civilization"—that is, they are obliged to become bourgeois themselves.[23]

The bourgeoisie are not to have all things their own way, however, for their very successes confront them with new and complex difficulties. In vivid imagery the *Manifesto* tells us that the bourgeois society is "like the sorcerer, who is no longer able to control the powers of the nether world whom he has called up by his spells." The expansion of modern production becomes so rapid that the capitalists are no longer able to control the forces let loose into society: in their urge to get larger profits, capitalists tend to force out their smaller competitors; there is over-production and labor unrest; there will be an end to the discovery of new markets which can absorb the goods of over-production; and the workers, who form the bulk of the armies of the world, will get tired of fighting wars for their capitalist overlords. It is crises such as these which the *Communist Manifesto* states "by their periodic return put on its trial, each time more threateningly, the existence of the entire bourgeois society." [24]

Meanwhile, the bourgeois industrial system has called into existence a distressed class which is fated to bring death to bourgeois society—this class is the proletariat. This ever-growing class is composed of laborers who, possessing no means of production, have nothing to sell but their labor power, and who can live only as long as they can find work. In capitalist society the workers are treated as a commodity, much like the raw materials and the machines which are also essential for production. Not only is there a competition among all male laborers in the free market place for jobs, but women and children are also seeking work. Hence, the capitalist always has readily at hand a source of cheap labor. But this is still not the worst plight of the workingman. Because the use of machinery has led to an increasingly greater division of labor, his work has lost all individual character and joy; he is a mere dehumanized appendage of the machine. The workingman is thus not only exploited by the capitalist who makes him work long hours for barely subsistence wages, but also his work becomes so mechanical that he is virtually an objective machine himself. Here again we find Marx developing the theme of alienation which was so central in his early writings.

The proletariat in the beginning is a very unorganized collection of workers, each one of whom competes against every other worker for the jobs which are available. As the industrial system becomes more complex and more highly organized, the working class is joined by the lower strata of the middle class—small tradesmen, handicraftsmen, small farmers, and ultimately even by a growing number of former capitalists who have lost out in the industrial struggle. Its ranks are also swelled by an increasing number of liberals and intellectuals who reject their bourgeois heritage and embrace the cause of the proletariat. The recruits from the ranks of the educated, and former capitalists, will provide the leadership which the proletariat needs in order to become an organized class. Now all things have been arranged on the stage of history, according to the *Communist Manifesto*, for the epic battle between the proletariat and the bourgeoisie. Once the workers have become organized they will succeed for they have right on their side. The *Manifesto* clearly states: "The proletarian movement is the self-conscious, independent movement of the immense majority, in the interests of the immense majority." The capitalists have thus in producing this proletarian class really produced their "own gravediggers." [25]

The early Marx, you may recall, stressed that theory was not enough— action was needed. In the *Communist Manifesto* we have above all a clarion call to action, and a specific program of stages to be undertaken in achieving the victory of an ultimately classless society. First of all, the proletariat is to become the ruling class, it is "to win the battle of democracy." Once the proletariat has become politically supreme, by winning the revolution against the capitalists, it will have to take the means of production and centralize them in the hands of the proletarian state. There will not be a romantic return to small towns and cottage industry, for the more efficient capitalist method of production will be used, but it will now be controlled by the very workers who formerly were subjugated by it. Marx and Engels recognized that despotic measures would be required to carry out these changes. While the exact nature of these measures will vary from nation to nation, they believed that in the most advanced industrialized countries the following specific changes would generally be applicable: (1) abolition of property in land, (2) a heavy graduated income tax, (3) abolition of all right of inheritance, (4) confiscation of the property of all emigrants and rebels, (5) centralization of credit in the hands of a national bank, (6) centralization of the means of communication and transport in the hands of the State, (7) extension of factories and all productive forces by the State, (8) equal liability of all to labor, (9) combination of agriculture with manufacturing industry, and a more equitable distribution of the population between town and country, (10) free education for all children in public schools, together with the abolition of child labor. [26]

In a frequently quoted passage which follows the above specific proposals, we find reference to the ultimate society which will appear after the first phase of Communism:

When, in the course of development, class distinctions have disappeared and all production has been concentrated in the hands of a
vast association of the whole nation, the public power will lose its
political character. Political power, properly so called, is merely the
organized power of one class for oppressing another. If the proletariat
during its contest with the bourgeoisie is compelled, by the force of
circumstances, to organize itself as a class, if, by means of a revolution, it makes itself the ruling class and as such sweeps away by force
the old conditions of production, then it will have swept away, along
with these conditions, the conditions for the existence of class
antagonisms and classes generally and will thereby have abolished
its own supremacy as a class.

In place of the old bourgeois society, with its classes and class
antagonisms, we shall have an association in which the free development of each is the condition for the free development of all.[27]

This passage has been quoted in full because it has had much normative
significance for Marxists and Communists; despite the fact that twenty-
five years after it was written Marx and Engels remarked of it in the
preface to the 1872 German edition of the *Manifesto:*

That passage would, in many respects, be very differently worded
today. In view of the gigantic strides of Modern Industry in the
last twenty-five years, and of the accompanying improved and
extended party organization of the working class, in view of the
practical experience gained, first in the February Revolution, and
then, still more, in the Paris Commune, where the proletariat for the
first time held political power for two whole months, this programme
has in some details become antiquated. One thing especially was
proved by the Commune, *viz.*, that "the working class cannot simply
lay hold of the ready-made State machinery, and wield it for its own
purposes." [28]

What Marx and Engels advocated in their later years was that in the
transition between the capitalist and the Communist society, the old
governmental machinery of oppression and of self-perpetuating political
groups of the capitalist state must at first be replaced by an interim
"dictatorship of the proletariat." Marx mentioned the dictatorship of the
proletariat only a few times in his later writings, but he had already
indicated in his writings of 1844 that there would be a first crude phase
of "raw Communism" before the arrival of the higher phase of the classless society.

In Marx's *Critique of the Gotha Program* of 1875 we find his classical
formulation of the interim and higher phases of Communism, an analysis
which Lenin was to use as one of the main justifications for his Russian
experiment. Marx in opposing the unity platform of Gotha, which was
designed to bring non-Marxists into the same party, stated that the initial

emergence of Communism from capitalistic society will inevitably have defects in it which it will have inherited from capitalism. It will be a society which will bear in every respect, economic, moral, and intellectual, "the birthmarks of the old society from whose womb it emerges." For example, the worker will continue to think of being rewarded for his labor in terms of "bourgeois right." He will accordingly receive from the newly emerging society a certificate signifying that he has supplied so much labor ("after deducting his labor for the common funds"), and with this certificate he will draw "from the social stock of means of consumption as much as costs the same amount of labor." But this defect is inevitable at the start of the new society for "right can never be higher than the economic structure of society and the cultural development conditioned by it." This phase of revolutionary transformation from capitalism to the ultimate Communist society, Marx stressed "can be nothing but *the revolutionary dictatorship of the proletariat*." [29]

But Marx did not hesitate to again put forth his vision of the promised land, only it shall not appear immediately after the workers have gained political control of the state. The millennium has been postponed, and his requirements for the higher phase of Communism to appear seem so radically different from present society, that one suspects that Marx was dreaming of another world.

In a higher phase of communist society, after the enslaving subordination of the individual to the division of labor, and therewith also the antithesis between mental and physical labor, has vanished; after labor has become not only a means of life but life's prime want; after the productive forces have also increased with the all-round development of the individual, and all the springs of cooperative wealth flow more abundantly—only then can the narrow horizon of bourgeois right be crossed in its entirety and society inscribe on its banners: "From each according to his ability, to each according to his needs!" [30]

Marx as the humanist, although a realistic and sobered one, again comes to the foreground. He did not believe that human brotherhood was possible until some time after the proletarian revolution. He did hope, however, that out of the forceful overthrow of capitalist society, with plenty of hatred for the capitalist class to motivate it, and after the dictatorship of the proletariat had changed the conditions of economic activity, a peaceful and humane society would emerge, in which each individual would be able to make the most of himself. He hoped and believed that the interim oppressive state would "wither away." Then, and only then, would everybody be respected, and would everybody be free. Greed and selfishness, inherited from the bourgeois state, would disappear; the willingness to work for the good of all would take their place. Self-alienation, now the lot of the worker who is a mere appendage of the machine, a mere cog in the machinery, would be known no more; individual "human totality" would be restored. The division of labor would no longer assign a man to some definite tedious circumscribed sphere of activity from which he could not escape without losing his means of subsistence. Marx's dream for human freedom in a utopian Communism is expressed in *The German Ideology* (completed by 1846):

> In communist society, where nobody has one exclusive sphere of activity but each can become accomplished in any branch he wishes, society regulates the general production and thus makes it possible for me to do one thing to-day and another to-morrow, to hunt in the morning, fish in the afternoon, rear cattle in the evening, criticize after dinner, just as I have a mind, without ever becoming hunter, fisherman, shepherd or critic.[31]

In short, the new economic situation brought into being by the abolition of private property and the distribution of goods according to human need will bring, as Marx believed, moral and spiritual freedom to the individual in a community so arranged that he can become an integrated man and develop his artistic and scientific talents to his heart's content.

The position which we have considered above is usually interpreted as the classical Marxist philosophy of history or historical materialism. We should recall that while clearly its main stress is upon the historical inevitability of a class struggle between the bourgeoisie and the proletariat, a struggle in which the proletariat will win since they will represent the majority of the people in the vanguard of the new social movement, that there is also an emphasis upon the active role which man can play in assisting the inevitable course of history. Marxian determinism is largely a cause-effect determinism, which fervently maintains that if certain events occur in the objective history of society, then inevitably certain results will follow—just as striking a match against an abrasive surface produces a flame. Nevertheless, there is a difference between the cause and effect relationship in the simple example of striking a match and the historical determinism which for classical Marxism undergirds the development of human societies. The essential difference is that in history man plays an active, and not a passive, role. While both Marx and Engels placed great stress upon their belief that each man's thoughts and position in history are determined by the economic development of his society, and the part which he plays in the productive process of that society; nevertheless, they did not forget that part of the dialectical process involves man's reacting with or against his natural and economic environment. In fact it was this interplay between the objective forces of nature and history and man's reactions to these forces which Marx stressed in defending his position against the crude materialists, on the one hand, and the idealists, on the other. The crude materialists maintained that man was completely shaped by natural events over which he had no control at all, while the idealists maintained that by thought alone man could change his world. Marx tried to steer a course between these two extremes, but in doing so it is correct to note that he often overstressed the materialistic or deterministic elements to the neglect of the active role played by man's thoughts and deeds.

Engels recognized that both Marx and he had tended to overstress the importance of the economic aspect of history. In *Anti-Dühring*, first published in 1880, Engels wrote:

> The forces operating in society work exactly like the forces operating in Nature: blindly, violently, destructively, so long as we do not understand them and fail to take them into account. But when once we have recognized them and understood how they work, their direction and their effects, the gradual subjection of them to our will and the use of them for the attainment of our aims depends entirely upon ourselves.[32]

Engels continued by explaining that the difference is like the difference between the forces of electricity in a thunder storm, and the tamed forces of electricity placed in the service of man. Man's understanding will make a difference in history, for he will be able by social planning to replace the recurrent crises of the capitalistic system by a conscious "regulation of production in accordance with the needs both of society as a whole and of each individual." [33]

It is a point of some importance to recall that Engels is not retracting historical materialism; he is rather more clearly explaining that in the early development of the view both Marx and he had tended to overemphasize the inevitability of the fall of capitalism to the neglect of the part which man could play in this process. Thus, in the *German Ideology*, written by both Marx and Engels before the *Communist Manifesto*, they stressed that the ruling class of an epoch determines the prevailing ideas and ideals of the society, and that therefore the world-view of a society is merely an intellectual expression "of the dominant material relationships." [34] In *Anti-Dühring* Engels reiterated this theme with no variation as he insisted that there is no eternal morality, since all men derive their moral codes "from the practical relations on which their class position is based—from the economic relations in which they carry on production and exchange." [35] Specifically, he suggested that with regard to the moral command "Thou shalt not steal" we have an illustration of a moral rule which makes sense only in a society where there is private property.

> In a society in which the motive for stealing has been done away with, in which therefore at the very most only lunatics would ever steal, how the teacher of morals would be laughed at who tried solemnly to proclaim the eternal truth: Thou shalt not steal! [36]

Both Marx and Engels, nevertheless, believed that things would become quite different when the ultimate Communist society would be achieved. Again in the early *German Ideology* Marx and Engels not only called for men to intervene actively in the course of history in order to establish freedom for everyone, but they also suggested that in the ultimate classless society the conditions will be changed so radically that man will control, and not be controlled by, history:

> The transformation, through the division of labour, of personal powers (relationships) into material powers, cannot be dispelled by dismissing the general idea of it from one's mind, but only *by the action of individuals* in again subjecting these material powers to themselves and abolishing the division of labour. This is not possible without the community. Only in community with others has each individual the means of cultivating his gifts in all directions; only in the community, therefore, is personal freedom possible.[37]

To show that this theme continued throughout the writings of Marx and Engels, let us again look at Engels' *Anti-Dühring*, where in a summary passage he again stressed that in a classless society man will for the first time really become the master of his destiny:

> The seizure of the means of production by society puts an end to commodity production, and therewith to the domination of the product over the producer. Anarchy in social production is replaced by conscious organisation on a planned basis. The struggle for individual existence comes to an end. And at this point, in a certain sense, man finally cuts himself off from the animal world, leaves the conditions of animal existence behind him and enters conditions which are really human. The conditions of existence forming man's environment, which up to now have dominated man, at this point pass under the domination and control of man, who now for the first time becomes the real conscious master of Nature, because and in so far as he has become master of his own social organisation. . . . The objective, external forces which have hitherto dominated history, will then pass under the control of men themselves. It is only from this point that men, with full consciousness, will fashion their own history. . . . It is humanity's leap from the realm of necessity into the realm of freedom.[38]

As we have previously noted, in the ultimate classless society alienated labor will cease, and productive activity will become a joy for all men. It was for this purpose that Marxists called upon all the workingmen of the world to unite. That the union of all workingmen did not occur, that the lot of the worker improved in the nations which were most advanced technologically, that the predicted class struggle did not result in worldwide revolution is too well known to need more than a casual mention here. We should, however, in order to understand the prevalence of

Marxism as a viable world-view look at the changes and developments of Marxism as it became the official doctrine of Russia under Lenin and Stalin.

From Classical Marxism to Russian Communism   It is difficult to predict the future, and Marx fared little better at this task than do other men. Marx's detailed analysis of capitalism in England in the nineteenth century clearly disclosed the injustices from which the average workingman was suffering, as well as the recurrent crises which unregulated capitalism experienced in its constant desire for larger profits. But the "inevitable revolt" by the workers against the capitalistic system which Marx had predicted did not occur. Ironically, one of the reasons for the revolution not occurring may have been the writings of Marx which played some part, along with those of Jeremy Bentham, in the adoption by the advanced capitalist states of social legislation which controlled the "greedy capitalists" and guaranteed fairer wages and better working conditions to the laborers. At any rate, Engels in his later writings recognized that history was not going according to the expectations he had shared with Marx, since the working class was getting a progressively higher standard of living which tended to make the workers content with society.

In Engels' preface of 1895 to Marx's *The Class Struggles in France 1848–1850*, he admitted that the events of the last fifty years had proved them wrong in their expectation of a violent proletarian revolution. In fact, he suggested that conditions had changed so radically that: "The time of surprise attacks, of revolutions carried through by small conscious minorities at the head of unconscious masses, is past." [39] He now believed that the real shock troops of the new society were found in the political parties of the workingmen which have won many victories at the ballot boxes. Just as Marx had inverted Hegel, so in 1895 Engels honestly confessed:

> The irony of world history turns everything upside down. We, the "revolutionists," the "overthrowers"—we are thriving far better on legal methods than on illegal methods and overthrow. The parties of Order, as they call themselves, are perishing under the legal conditions created by themselves . . . whereas we, under this legality, get firm muscles and rosy cheeks and look like life eternal.[40]

Of course, Engels did not abandon the belief that there will eventually be a knock-down battle with capitalism, but it is clear that this belief was given much less importance than it had in the early days of the Communist movement.

Engels realized that a good part of the program of the *Communist Manifesto* had been achieved by peaceful means. Legislation for the welfare of the worker, legislation limiting monopolies and trusts, graduated income taxes, free public education for all children—all of these we now take for granted as part of our democratic heritage. Yet, we should recall that they were parts of the Communist program of 1848. What had happened in the advanced capitalist countries of Germany, England and the United States was exactly what Engels noted—ballots had won for the workingman, and hence bullets seemed unnecessary. But Marxism, thanks to the voluminous writings of Marx and Engels, could be interpreted in conformity with a peaceful victory of the working class, though less readily. The result was that "revisionists" appeared—and are still appearing!

Eduard Bernstein, the leader of the Communist movement in Germany, despite the fact that he had been a close friend of Engels, frankly called for an *Evolutionary Socialism* in his revision of Marxism. For Bernstein, socialism was the fulfillment of political democracy in which all men were to be equally free; hence, he not only objected to a revolution but also to the idea of a dictatorship of the proletariat. Bernstein gave up the dream of a classless utopia at the end of history, and frankly admitted that some of his views were not in harmony with those of Marx-Engels. How could they be, he claimed, since history had showed that Marx-Engels were wrong. His stress was placed upon "the struggle for the political rights of the working man, on the political activity of working men in town and country for the interests of their class, as well as on the work of the industrial organisation of the workers. . . . My thoughts and efforts are concerned with the duties of the present and the nearest future. . . ."[41] When Bernstein's book appeared in 1899, it looked as though the revolutionary aspects of Marxian philosophy might not survive into the twentieth century.

Revolutionary Marxism has not only survived, however, but it has become the ideology of one of the great world powers—Russia. However, the orthodox Marxists of Russia have also modified the original theories of classical Marxism, as well they had to for Marx never expected a revolution to be successful in such a backward non-capitalistic country as Russia was at the time Lenin won power in 1917. Marx and Engels always stressed that the proletarian revolution would take place only as a result of the uprising of the working class during a particularly severe crisis brought on by capitalist overproduction. Russia under the tsars was still largely a feudal economy; the peasants were the large exploited class, while capitalism was only beginning to make inroads into the traditional small manufacturing system. Many orthodox young Russian Marxists in the 1890's eagerly sought to aid the advance of bourgeois capitalism on the grounds that until this development had been accomplished the country would not be ripe for a Communist revolution. "Revisionist" Russian Marxists of the same period argued that by a gradual development of society the lot of the working class and the peasants could be improved. Against the background of this ideological battle, Lenin emerged as the leader who was destined to become the first head of a Communist state.

Lenin, for his revolutionary agitation, had spent five years in exile in Siberia (1895–1900). During this time he formulated the ideas he expressed in a pamphlet published in 1902, *What Is To Be Done?* He honestly admitted that the situation in Russia was not that envisioned by Marx as ripe for a Communist revolution; nevertheless, he took pains to stress that he was merely interpreting and adding to the doctrine of orthodox Marxism, rather than "revising" it. Orthodox Marxists had for some time referred to "revisionists" with as much disdain as the orthodox Christian had shown toward heretics. While Lenin was in reality changing Marxist doctrine in important respects, he wanted to avoid the stigma of "revisionist" in order that he might have the support of the orthodox Marxists in other countries. His claiming not to be a "revisionist" was not merely a verbal sleight of hand, for he believed it extremely important to be considered "orthodox" for reasons of strategy. Lenin's main concern was to bring the Communists to power in Russia as soon as possible; therefore, he showed in his later writings that he was unwilling to wait for the maturation of bourgeois capitalism in feudal Russia.

What would bring about a Communist revolution in Russia? Lenin obviously could not appeal to a spontaneous uprising of the working class, since Russia had few workers in comparison to the immense number of its peasants. Of greater significance was the fact that neither the workers nor the peasants were educated and organized. Lenin asked his readers to recall that neither Marx nor Engels were themselves members of the proletariat. The original Communist doctrine expressed in the *Manifesto* was itself the outgrowth of two bourgeois minds, Marx and Engels. Therefore, Lenin concluded it was not at all unorthodox to maintain that revolutionary Communism in Russia must start with the activities of an intellectual elite. The members of the working class, he maintained, would not attain their class consciousness by themselves; they needed leaders who would tell them what to do and see to it that they did it. Lenin proposed to recruit these leaders from the ranks of professional revolutionaries.

One of the main tasks of the professional revolutionaries would be to recruit and train workers to become agitators, propagandists and organizers for the Communist Party. Lenin clearly intended to fight against what he called "spontaneity" which would lead the workers to rest content with a mild redress of their grievances through Trade Unions. He sided with Karl Kautsky, one of the leaders of German Marxism at the time, in maintaining that the ideology for the class struggle had to be instilled into the workers from without by professional leaders. Lenin proposed to accomplish this task by means of a highly organized and tightly disciplined Communist Party. Party leaders would issue orders to the worker agitators, coordinate the revolution, and enlist other segments of the society to support their cause. Lenin had already predicted in his early writings that:

> When we shall have detachments of specially trained working-class revolutionists who have gone through long years of preparation (and, of course, revolutionists "of all arms") no political police in the world will be able to contend against them, for these detachments will consist of men absolutely devoted and loyal to the revolution, and will themselves enjoy the absolute confidence and devotion of the broad masses of the workers.[42]

Even more significant for the development of Communism in Russia was Lenin's later proposal for a rigid system of control within the ranks of the Communist Party itself. Until the revolution had been won, Lenin realized that the Communist Party would have to function underground. He therefore insisted that the Party would have to be self-disciplining and self-perpetuating in order for it to maintain a consistent course toward victory. Party leaders were to be given extraordinary powers to purge members who failed to carry out orders or who seemed to vacillate in their enthusiasm for the cause. Lenin maintained that the leaders need not justify their actions to the populace, since after all only the leaders of the Party know what is best for the masses in whose name they are acting.

We should also stress that Lenin did try to remain faithful to what he considered the basic ideas of Marx. In *State and Revolution*, written a few months before Lenin came to power in 1917, he argued that a Communist revolution must do away with the bourgeois state, and put in its place a dictatorship of the proletariat. His point here was to reject the German evolutionary socialist position which maintained that the bourgeois state itself would gradually wither away, as the workers' lot continued to improve. No, shouted Lenin, true Marxism maintains that there must be a violent overthrow of the bourgeois state. The heirs to this state will constitute what he called a "half-state" under the dictatorship of the proletariat. Since any workingman can be trained to perform the simple tasks of administration within this "half-state" the dictatorship of the proletariat will gradually wither away. Lenin did not attempt to predict how long it would take for the dictatorship of the proletariat to wither away, but he did suggest what conditions would have to be fulfilled for all vestiges of state control to disappear. When the workers learn to run the forces of production for themselves, when there are no threats of capitalist reaction to the new society, when the habits of the new order have become deeply ingrained in all of the people, then, and not before, will the state wither away. Lenin thus reaffirmed the faith of Marx in a classless society at the end of the interim dictatorship:

> It will become possible for the state to wither away completely when society adopts the rule: "From each according to his ability, to each according to his needs," i.e., when people have become so accustomed to observing the fundamental rules of social intercourse and when their labor becomes so productive that they will voluntarily work *according to their ability.*[43]

What has happened in Russia since Lenin's rise to power in 1917 is well known. Lenin waged a successful revolution in a non-capitalistic country, fully expecting that this would be a vanguard of Communist revolutions throughout the imperialist world. These other revolutions were not forthcoming, so that Lenin was forced to make many concessions to Marxist theory in developing heavy industry in Russia, in pacifying the peasants with more consumer goods, in remaining in power during a Civil War, and in developing a loyal party to support his policies. Tactical retreats from even the dreams of a first phase of Communism were always justified by a text from Marx or by "historical necessity."

Stalin as Lenin's successor appealed to Lenin's doctrines as the ones he was implementing. In *The Foundations of Leninism* (1924) Stalin stressed the importance of strengthening the dictatorship of the proletariat in Russia in order that Russia might aid conspiracy toward revolution in both the developed and underdeveloped countries of the world. Russia's task as Stalin viewed it was to destroy international imperialism, but in terms of his actions he was primarily interested in strategy and tactics for day-to-day strengthening of his Party. No deviation in thought or action was to be tolerated.

After the tremendous success of Communism in Russia, why was the state not withering away? Stalin boldly attempted to justify the growing power of the Russian State by a reinterpretation of Marxist theory. In his Report to the Eighteenth Party Congress in 1939, he explained that the belief of Marx-Engels that the state's power would wither away was predicated on the assumption that socialism was already victorious in the majority of countries. Then socialist lands would no longer be under the danger of foreign attack. However, instead of a socialist encirclement there is a capitalist encirclement of one socialist country, Russia. While he admitted that the state would continue to change its form and function in the future, he firmly insisted that it cannot wither away as long as there is a capitalist encirclement which poses the danger of possible foreign attacks. This modification of Marxist theory he justified by claiming that Lenin himself had found it quite orthodox to change the theory of Communism at those points where it had not anticipated what has happened in the course of history.

Since the death of Stalin in 1956, Russia seems to have moved toward "revisionism" itself. At least the stress upon peaceful co-existence, and the section on morality in the revised program of the Soviet Communist Party drafted in 1961 reflect a retreat toward bourgeois ideals. Among the principles of Communist morality affirmed in this "new manifesto" there are of course loyalty to the Communist cause, and "conscientious labor for the good of society." But also some of the old bourgeois values are now listed as Communist ones: "Honesty and truthfulness, moral purity, modesty and guilelessness in social and private life; mutual respect in the family, and concern for the upbringing of children." [44] At any rate, Russian Communism never has been, and does not seem to be now, an exemplification in history of the ultimate society of freedom about which Marx dreamed and for which he labored.

We can learn an instructive lesson from this brief sketch of some of the major changes which have occurred to Marx's ideal in the process of its being incorporated into institutional Russian Communism. Ideals are never really fully realized in the actual political-social systems that brandish them. Thus, Soviet Communism is no more an actualization of Marx's dream than was the Holy Roman Empire an actual embodiment of the teachings of the New Testament. Our own society professes the ideal of individual freedom, but, in many respects, we too have modified this ideal as we have had to face the realistic problems of life in a huge technological society. This is not to say that ideals in themselves are valueless, but is rather to provide us with the sobering reminder that while an ideal provides a target at which a society may aim, no society ever hits the target dead-center.

The Ideological Struggle Within Marxism   We are primarily interested in Marxism as one of the competing value systems in our present world; hence, a brief survey of what has happened to Marxism in this century outside the Soviet Union may help us to understand its attractiveness to such diverse groups as American intellectuals, the youth of China, and the leaders of developing African and Asian nations. We have already noted that Lenin and Stalin modified Marxism, or extended it, as they were prone to say, in order to accommodate the classical theories of Marxism to a country which was by no means experiencing a proletarian revolution. We should also bear in mind, however, that Lenin and Stalin took pains to justify their "advances" upon classical Marxism either by finding some passage in Marx or Engels to which they could appeal in a secular exegesis, or else by claiming that since Marx and Engels had not lived to see imperialism as the last stage of capitalism, the Marxian theories had to be reinterpreted in order to meet the actual facts of history. In the light of Russia's claiming to be a country based upon the Marxist ideology, it is not surprising to find that other Communist leaders in other lands have felt fully justified in adapting Marxism to their countries' needs. In the course of this adaptation of Marxism the changes are sometimes so radical that little of the original humanism of Karl Marx has survived, while in other lands, it is precisely Marx's humanism as expounded in his early writings which is extolled as "pure Marxism." Let us look briefly at some of the changes in the Marxist ideology which have occurred outside Russia.

In China Mao Tse-tung, in the early days of the Communist revolution, insisted that Marx-Leninism is the arrow but that it must be aimed at the target of the actual problems of China. Mao thus interpreted Marx-Leninism as a guide to action and not as a dogma; nevertheless, he found it desirable to go to great pains to show that the development in China was really in accordance with the underlying principles of Marx-Leninism. In 1945 he firmly came out in opposition to a dictatorship of the proletariat and a one-party system such as that in Russia. Marx-Leninism as he interpreted it for China allowed cooperation with all other parties which did not oppose his plans. As he put it:

Chinese history will create the Chinese system. A special type, a New Democratic type of state with a union of several democratic classes will be produced, which will be *entirely necessary and rational* to us and different from the Russian system.[45]

The reader can detect for himself that this emphasis upon the Chinese development being "entirely necessary and rational" is obviously a justificatory reference to the Marxian philosophy of historical determinism.

The old saying that "nothing succeeds like success," can clearly be applied to the results of the Communist revolution in China. The Chinese are now also a world power; they have been able to challenge the Russian Communists with being revisionists for taking an approach of peaceful co-existence; and some of the smaller Asian and African countries look more to Chinese Communism for a model for their own national development than they do to Russia. It is surely clear, if we refer to the adaptation of Marx's view to the Russian and the Chinese revolutions, that we have two different examples of "institutional Communism," each claiming to be essentially true to Marx and yet each of which has departed from his views in precisely those aspects of his thought which did not seem to fit the pragmatic requirements of their individual countries. The ideological aspects of "institutional Communism" in both Russia and China require an acknowledgment, on the one hand, that Marx did discover the laws which govern history, while, on the other hand, stretching these laws far from their original meaning in defense of actions undertaken in order to acquire and maintain power in a modern political state. In this tension of ideological loyalty to Marx while also adjusting to the particular problems of day-to-day government, it is not surprising if the teachings of Karl Marx are often overlooked, if not consciously disobeyed.

Some experts on current African affairs go so far as to suggest that Afro-Communism has very little in common with the teachings of Karl Marx, not even in the form in which they were adapted for the use of Russia or China. The stress upon Pan-Africanism, racialism and nationalism surely is not something defended in the *Communist Manifesto*, nor, for that matter, in the writings of Lenin. One scholar has characterized Afro-Communism as "above all a means of gaining political power for a small group of intellectuals." [46] The main concern seems to be with establishing the African nations as a third power bloc in the world, and the Communist leaders of these nations are not overly influenced by the necessity of loyalty to the ideas of Marx or Lenin. "They regard themselves as the founding members of a new third group, the African ex-Colonial International; 'People of the Colonies Unite,' Kwame Nkrumah wrote in one of his articles. . . ." [47] Other intellectual leaders among the African Communists find that Marx's analysis does not apply to their society, because they maintain that since money and industrial production have not alienated the Africans, they still have a firm basis of humane values upon which a new nationalism can be built in their economically backward countries.

The ideological struggle concerning the interpretation of Marxism for today's world is not confined to Russia, China and Africa. The reader may recall the "revisionist" voices raised a decade ago in the central European satellite nations, such as Czechoslovakia, Hungary and Poland. Here the leading objections were to the deviation from classical Marxism with its humanistic qualities by the establishment of an iron-clad rule of the Russian Communist Party.

The Yugoslavian Milovan Djilas in *The New Class* sought to demonstrate that Russian Communism had not moved toward a classless society, but instead had established an autocratic political bureaucracy which has become a new class tyrannizing over the workers even more than the bourgeois capitalist class ever did. Djilas maintained that the Communist Party was the core of this new class but not identical with it: "The new class may be said to be made up of those who have special privileges and economic preference because of the administrative monopoly they hold." [48] The bureaucrats in a Communist state become entrenched in their exclusive power over the use of collectively owned state property, they accord themselves large financial rewards, and exist as parasites upon the working class in whose name they are supposedly working. Djilas in one sentence dramatically summed up the change which he found had occurred in Communism as it passed from Marx through Lenin to Stalin:

Marx died a poor emigrant in London, but was valued by learned men and valued in the movement; Lenin died as the leader of one of the greatest revolutions, but died as a dictator about whom a cult had already begun to form; when Stalin died, he had already transformed himself into a god.[49]

While the capitalist owners knew their position in society, the new Communist class deludes itself into thinking it is acting for the people, while actually all of its actions are predicated upon strengthening its position in the new society. "All changes initiated by the communist chiefs are dictated first of all by the interests and aspirations of the new class, which, like every social group, lives and reacts, defends itself and advances, with the aim of increasing its power." [50] Thus, the dictatorship of the proletariat has become a monster which actually controls all the property. It is only a myth that state property belongs to all the people in the state; in reality, it belongs to those who administer it—the new class. Djilas claimed that this new class in Communist lands has gained more power over man than any class previously known in history. He admitted, however, that at the beginning this new class played a creative role in achieving industrialization of a backward land, but "the new class can now do nothing more than strengthen its brute force and pillage the people." [51] Djilas did not believe that "the new class" could maintain its power indefinitely:

> While the revolution can be considered an epochal accomplishment of the new class, its methods of rule fill some of the most shameful pages in history. Men will marvel at the grandiose ventures it accomplished and will be ashamed of the means it used.

> When the new class leaves the historical scene—and this must happen—there will be less sorrow over its passing than there was for any other class before it. Smothering everything except what suited its ego, it has condemned itself to failure and shameful ruin.[52]

The numerous Communist writings of the last decade against the Stalin cult clearly show an attempt to dissociate Communism from the tactics of this dictator. Of even greater importance, however, is the rebirth of interest in the writings of Karl Marx himself. We might say that the cry is "back to the source" and away from the secondary and tertiary interpretations of Lenin, Stalin and Mao Tse-tung. The recent publication in English of Marx's early writings has spurred a renewed interest by scholars into the entire corpus of Marx's work. Many readers of Marx now believe that he should be viewed as a humanist, as a philosopher, or as a religious prophet, rather than as an economist. More important for our purposes, however, is the discovery by many people that Marx may still have something of value to say to us today, especially in his concept of alienation and in his classical humanistic ideal of freedom for all mankind.

Socialist Humanism, a recent anthology edited by the psychoanalyst Erich Fromm, brings together articles by Communists and non-Communists from the East and the West on such themes as alienation, freedom, man, and humanism. While most of the papers in this volume cite Marx, they do so largely to stress his humanistic values, or to show how Marx's views have been falsified in history. So perhaps we have come full circle. We began with the writings of the early Marx, moved to his revolutionary program as expressed in the *Communist Manifesto* and his later writings, and then have noted what happened to his ideas when they became institutionalized in Russia and China. The concern of recent writers with the complete philosophy of Karl Marx and its relevance as a point of reference for humanistic action in today's world is helping to restore him to his rightful position as a prophet who protested against man's inhumanity to man and called forth for a new age in which all men would be free.

Toward an Evaluation of Marxism   We shall concentrate primarily here upon the classical Marxism as formulated by Marx and Engels, for it is this view which even the institutional Communists refer to as their basic value system. Our main concern is with competing value systems in our world, and it is in this context that we shall make some comments toward an evaluation of Marxism.

Few people can read the writings of Marx without being forcibly struck by his sincere sympathy with the lot of the unfortunate workingman of the nineteenth century. Here was a man who was so disturbed by the injustices of the then existing capitalist society, that he not only called for a better day of freedom and justice, but also proposed a program to implement the fulfilling of his ideals for mankind. Marx was no idle dreamer, who looked for "a new heaven and a new earth" to appear miraculously, but rather he was more like the prophet Amos in the Old Testament in telling men what they must do in order to become really free. Marx saw that knowledge and action, ideas and the social system in which they were developed, moral values and the economic basis of a society were inseparably intertwined. In one respect, we may view him as one of the first social scientists since he attempted to study society in order to discover the dynamics which motivated its behavior. But he was not only a social scientist, for he also saw the necessity of active involvement by men if the world were to be made better. A theme running through his entire life was expressed in his *Theses on Feuerbach:* "The philosophers have only *interpreted* the world differently, the point is, to *change* it." [53] Marx's study of the economic basis of capitalist England in the nineteenth century, and his attempt to organize the working class in the hope of realizing through them a better society were but two sides of the same program for Marx. There could be, for him, no real knowledge which did not issue in action; and there could be no efficacious action unless it was based upon a detailed knowledge of the course of history.

If Marx is to be classified as a social scientist, however, we must recognize that he was one on a philosophical basis. His theory of class struggle, of historical materialism, was developed by him long before he began the careful study of documents in the British Museum which led to his opus, *Capital*. His conclusions were really arrived at first, and only later did he seek the facts to document them.

As a philosopher, as a prophet or founder of a new secular religion, or even as a "value legislator" (to borrow Nietzsche's term) we may be better able to come to grips with the significance of Marx. His economic theories have been surpassed by Keynes; his predictions of the disappearance of a middle class, of the inevitable class warfare between the bourgeoisie and the proletariat, to say nothing of the new Communist society to arrive at the end of history—these have been falsified by the on-going course of the very history whose inevitable laws he thought he had discovered. Marx, like many theorists who clearly see the dependence of their opponents' views, or the views of people who lived in previous historical epochs, upon their position in history at a particular time and in a particular place, believed erroneously that his own views were "objective" and "necessary." But as anyone soon realizes, Marx's analysis, while it fitted the capitalistic system of England in the middle of the nineteenth century, has little direct applicability to today's welfare states and planned economies. Léopold Senghor clearly and succinctly summarizes five respects in which Marx's specific theory about the demise of capitalism was wrong:

1. The "class struggle" is much more complex than Marx thought. In fact, the working class is not a simple reality. Moreover, it is diminishing, while the several categories of salaried workers with dissimilar interests are increasing.

2. The peasants, whom Marx considered more or less impervious to revolutionary ferment and dedicated "to the stupidity of rural life," have, in underdeveloped countries, belied his judgment.

3. The theory of capitalist concentration has not been borne out by the facts. On the contrary, the number of small and medium-sized businesses continues to grow in Western European countries.

4. Though periodic economic crises have not ceased, they are becoming rarer, and we cannot reasonably foresee a general cataclysm ending the capitalist system, which is adjusting to economic and social evolution.

5. "Socialism" has not triumphed in the industrial nations of Western Europe as Marx predicted it would, but in the underdeveloped nations of Eastern Europe and Asia.[54]

One might go even further, and suggest that an explanation of societies in terms of classes is far too simple; one needs to think only of the many roles which contemporary sociologists remind us we play, to see how overly simple and incorrect it is to resort to two or three classes for an accurate description in a behavioral analysis of a complex society. Our interests may be influenced more by the clubs we belong to, the games we play, the friends we have, the books we read, and the television programs we watch than by the fact that we work in a factory and are therefore "wage laborers."

All of these specific objections to Marx's teachings can be summed up by his most glaring error—his belief that he had discovered laws of history which were as well grounded as, and acted in the same deterministic manner as, laws of nature. The reader will recall that this is the aspect of Marx's thought called "historical materialism." Engels in 1885 called this "discovery" of the law of historical development the great achievement of Marx.

> It was precisely Marx who had first discovered the great law of motion of history, the law according to which all historical struggles, whether they proceed in the political, religious, philosophical or some other ideological domain, are in fact only the more or less clear expression of struggles of social classes, and that the existence and thereby the collisions, too, between these classes are in turn conditioned by the degree of development of their economic position, by the mode of their production and of their exchange determined by it. This law, . . . has the same significance for history as the law of the transformation of energy has for natural science. . . .[55]

Engels tried desperately to drive home his analogy of the "laws" of history with the laws of natural science.

Karl Popper has criticized this view as "economic historicism" which he claims arises because of "the confusion between *scientific prediction*, as we know it from physics or astronomy, and *large-scale historical prophecy*, which foretells in broad lines the main tendencies of the future development of society. These two kinds of prediction are very different and the scientific character of the first is no argument in favour of the scientific character of the second."[56] In the natural sciences a law is used to predict future events, such as Newton's well known law of gravity which can be used to predict that if you throw a stone up into the air, it must fall to the ground. Repeated experiments with all sorts of objects confirm Newton's law; if we met a number of events which did not accord with the law, we would set to work to find a new law or revise this one to take account of our new experiences. However, there are a number of crucial differences between events occurring in the natural world which are studied by physics, and the complex interactions of human beings which we refer to as history. Popper does not want to deny that there can be theories of history, but he does insist that they are not scientific and not law-like. History deals with understanding specific events which are not repeatable in the way in which experiments can be repeated in a chemistry laboratory. What Marx was really engaged in was, according to Popper, historical prophecy based on a theory that economic considerations were the basic determinants of what happened in history. This theory in itself is oversimplified, but aside from that, it clearly is not a scientific law. If it were put forth seriously as a scientific law by Marxists, then it should now be abandoned because the course of history itself has falsified this apparent law; the breakdown of capitalism and the dawning of a new classless society has not occurred. Marx's so-called natural law of history was really not a scientific law, but rather his philosophy of history, based on his inversion of the Hegelian dialectic.

We have reached a point of crucial importance in our attempt to provide an evaluation of the thought of Marx. Clearly, if we view him primarily as a social scientist who claimed to have "discovered" the natural law of historical development, he was simply mistaken. We are all aware of the complexities of history, and few of us are willing to settle for such a simple explanation of history as "class struggle" which will inevitably result in the triumphs of the de-classed proletarians. Marx's emphasis upon the part which the economic and sociological factors of a society play in the course of the development of a society has helped to eliminate the naive acceptance of Carlyle's view that history is made by heroes, by great men. Thanks to Marx, we would more modestly suggest that history is the product of the interaction of great men, and little men, with their social and natural environment. But this seems to be a truism, and like most truisms it tells us very little. Certainly it does not give us the laws of historical development so that we can predict the future; but, it does suggest how difficult it is, in the light of the complex interaction of men with the economic, social, political, ethical, religious, scientific, and technological aspects of the contemporary world, to predict with any degree of exactitude what the future will bring. In this respect, Marx's failure has taught us a great lesson.

The Western world, however, does not view Marx as primarily an economist or as a philosopher of history. Increasingly, we are coming to look upon Marx as a moralist, and perhaps even as a religious moralist. At first glance this would seem to be a blatant contradiction for did not Marx himself in the *Communist Manifesto* protest against petty bourgeois morality? And did he not also say that "religion was the opiate of the people?" How then can we be justified in looking at Marx as a moralist, or as a religious prophet?

It is important to note, first of all, that all those men whom we today revere as great moralists were attacking the traditionally held moral codes of their own day. Plato, Jesus, Bentham, John Stuart Mill, to name but a few from our own Western tradition, objected to the slavish following of rules which turned morality into blind legalism. Even a casual reading of the writings of Marx should make one aware that he too was protesting against the industrial society of his day which had imposed a moral code upon the workingmen which placed more value upon objects than upon men. Marx found the society of his day so evil that it deserved to be destroyed in order that man might, for the first time, become fully human and free. His condemnation of capitalism, we must recall, was based largely on his sympathy with the workingman who suffered under this system. Thus, Marx's condemnation of petty bourgeois morality was a condemnation of a specific moral code which was inhumane; in his eyes an economic system which forced through education and law an immoral "moral code" upon the people deserved to die at the hands of the people who were oppressed economically and morally by it. In this respect, Marx surely stands as one of the great moralists of the recent past. Thus the contemporary philosopher Sidney Hook says of Marx: "Marx was a democratic socialist, a secular humanist, and a fighter for human freedom." [57] Hook explains that Marx chose to be called a "Communist" in his own day in order to differentiate himself from the utopian socialists who merely dreamed about a better society, but did not actively involve themselves in working to get that society. However, Hook maintains that:

> Were he [Marx] alive today, confronted by the grotesque and terrible caricature of his social ideals in countries which call themselves "people's democracies" and "communist" societies, he would undoubtedly have characterized himself differently. He would have done this not only in protest against the semantic outrage but to draw the most emphatic line of differentiation between his own ideals of a socialist society, in which the free development of each is the condition for the free development of all, and current Communist practices in which the individual, especially the critical individual with a sense of the value of human dignity, is ruthlessly destroyed.[58]

Marx's insight into man's alienation is held by many to be his major contribution to a better understanding of human nature. Erich Fromm, Robert Tucker, and many of the writers in the international symposium *Socialist Humanism*, maintain that it is Marx's views on alienation which confer modernity upon Marx's moral insights. In his analysis of the human scene, Marx saw that in the course of history man had not only developed more control over the forces of nature, but also that he had become increasingly alienated. As we have already noticed the process of alienation for Marx involved three aspects: (a) man as the subject was alienated from the products which he produced, (b) man was alienated from himself because he did not find his fulfillment in his work, and (c) man was alienated from other men, especially from those men for whom he produced material goods. Fromm has suggested that the concept of alienation is the secular equivalent of sin, since alienation suggests that man is not what he ought to be.[59] Marx was not only concerned with the fact that the workingman did not get a fair share of the profits from his labor. Rather, like Kierkegaard, whom we shall consider later on, he was concerned with the "salvation" of the individual human being. Marx's main objection to capitalism was that it did not permit the full development of man's creative powers, but instead enslaved all men—workers and capitalists alike—to a system which was primarily motivated by the worship of things. The capitalist system values a man for what he has, not for what he is. The result is that money becomes the great god of capitalism, and all other values, moral and spiritual, are perverted into its service. Marx believed that the workingman was the most alienated in a capitalist society since all that he had was his labor power which he had to sell to the capitalist.

Erich Fromm and Mathilde Niel extend Marx's view of alienation by applying it to all men in our present technological society. As Fromm puts it:

Marx did not foresee the extent to which alienation was to become the fate of the vast majority of people, especially of the ever-increasing segment of the population which manipulate symbols and men, rather than machines. If anything, the clerk, the salesman, the executive, are even more alienated today than the skilled manual worker. The latter's functioning still depends on the expression of certain personal qualities like skill, reliability, etc., and he is not forced to sell his "personality," his smile, his opinions in the bargain; the symbol manipulators are hired not only for their skill, but for all those personality qualities which make them "attractive personality packages," easy to handle and to manipulate.[60]

The subtle manipulation which all of us undergo by means of the mass media increases our sense of alienation from our humanity.

Mathilde Niel, even more clearly than Fromm, suggests that the problem of alienation in our present technological society is the most serious problem of our age. She finds that, on the one hand, technology holds out the possibility for all men to become more creative, because it increasingly frees us from useless toil and brings the promise of a decent living standard to all of us. On the other hand, however, it has become an end in itself, and we are virtually paralyzed for creativity by technology's preoccupation with useful research, and with quantity and efficiency in production and distribution. Instead of ushering in an age for individual development and productivity, technology tries to substitute an equalitarian notion of consumption as the good life. "The acquisition of a new car, a new gadget, a new object has become the religion, the goal of life of the majority of individuals in the rich nations." [61] Technology thus makes man's alienation more blatant; "machinery and technology have a natural tendency to enslave man, and they are likely to become just as dangerous enemies as the most inhuman type of capitalism." [62] While analyses such as this go far beyond Marx's interpretation, we should recall that the first significant analysis of alienation in a particular period of history was made by Marx. It was Marx who showed modern man that he was not at home in the world, that he was separated from nature and his fellow men, but, even worse, he was alienated from the real core of his potentially creative human personality.

Christianity suggests how man can be saved from sin; Marx also suggested a way of salvation for man from alienation. For Marx man could be saved by socialism, by the arrival at the end of this historical epoch of a classless society in which creative work would replace alienated labor, a society in which all would be free to develop their intellectual and spiritual talents in a community of brotherhood. In the final phase of Communism, man would again become at-one with himself, with his fellow men and with nature. It is a vulgarization of Marx's thought which suggests that all he was interested in was well-fed workers who would be paid sufficient wages so that they could amuse themselves in any way they wished. The "welfare state" is not what Marx's apocalyptic vision was all about. Socialism was, for him, the necessary condition for a society in which each man could fully realize himself in freedom and creativity. Marx had, in his early writings, said that he wished to destroy man's illusions in order that man might learn to live without illusion. A welfare state which provides the worker with the money for beer, television sets, and keeping up with the Joneses, is as far removed from the dream of Marx as the capitalistic state which he attacked. It was not the satisfaction of the artificially produced needs of a mass media culture which Marx looked forward to as the society in which man would find his redemption on this earth. Rather in the ultimate stage of a Communist society Marx believed that man would be free to fulfill his essence as a human being; he would then be free to realize his higher spiritual nature, because he would live in a world "where nothing human would be alien to him."

It should be obvious to the reader that Marx's thought has many affinities with the Hebraic-Christian religion. In fact, Marxism has often been characterized as a humanistic version of Christianity, and his dream of a classless society has been called "the kingdom of God" without God. Marx's objection to the religion of his day was derived from the same reasons he gave for rejecting bourgeois morality—religion alienated man from his true essence by encouraging him to accept his subservient position on this earth in the hopes of achieving a reward in the hereafter. But like Hegel before him, some scholars claim that what Marx really did was to construct a humanistic religion, a religion centered in and for man. Robert Tucker in his book, *Philosophy and Myth in Karl Marx*, maintains that Marx was a religious moralist, and that Marxism clearly shows at least four structural similarities to a religious system: (1) It is an all-inclusive unified world-view. (2) Like Christianity, man's fall and redemption are worked out in a philosophy of history. (3) Christianity calls for man to be born again if he is to be saved, while Marx recognizes that a new type of regenerated man must arise for the ideal of "from each according to his ability, and to each according to his need" to be realized. (4) A union of thought and action permeated Christianity and the teaching of Marx—the Christian is to perform good works because of his beliefs, while for Marx man is to engage actively in the struggle to overthrow the present society in the light of the doctrines about capitalism presented in his philosophy. In addition, Tucker's interpretation of Marx is centered on his belief that Marx unconsciously developed a myth as he transformed the inner subjective forces of self-alienation within an individual man into an historical drama between My Lord Capital and the Collective Worker. Hence, Marx in *Capital* was presenting his revelation, his vision of the present evilness of the world and his dream of a future unclouded day.[63]

Marx's teaching viewed as a kind of religious moralism poses difficulties, nevertheless. While Marx correctly saw that all previous moralities were based on the state of development of the society in which they were put forth, he clearly regarded his vision as an ultimate one, the final synthesis from which there would be no more basic advancement. But, as we have already noted, society has changed radically from the time of Marx so that in place of an unregulated capitalism, we are faced with states in which social planning has mitigated, if not entirely eliminated, the objectionable aspects of nineteenth-century capitalism. The millennium of the classless society in which all men are free has still not dawned, and for the interim Marx gives us little guidance. Even his analysis of alienation needs to be reinterpreted, as Fromm and Niel admit, in order to deal with our mass technological society in which the rest of the population are even more alienated from their essential humanity than are the workers.

The basic difficulty in Marx's view, however, stems from his naive expectation that a change in economic production and distribution would bring about a radical change in man's nature. It is true that Marx recognized that there is a creative interaction between man and his environment, but the stress is almost always placed upon the environment determining man's mode of thought, his morality and his religion. Thus, after a relatively brief period of a dictatorship of the proletariat after the overthrow of capitalism, he expected the coerciveness of the state to wither away. Man would in a generation or so be re-educated to cooperate with his fellows, to put forth his best efforts in labor for the common storehouse, and to unselfishly be content with those goods which he actually needed. The miracle would be accomplished by the abolition of private property, and the centralization of the means of production in the hands of the workers themselves. Marx did recognize that there will be a few freaks in this society, but they will be easily dealt with in humane ways. Basically, the new man, the reborn man, will be brought forth by a change in the economic system. There is no denying Marx's great insight that our ideas and ideals are conditioned largely by the kind of society in which we live, but it is one thing to be conditioned by the values of one's society, and another thing to be completely determined by them so that all concern by the self for rights which are opposed to those of others will be eliminated. Egoists cannot be remade into selfless dedicated members of the ideal society that easily. In short, Marx may justly be accused of having had too pessimistic a view of man in capitalist society, and too optimistic a view of man in his dream of the ultimate classless society.

The course of history itself, since the death of Marx, has shown that the predicted revolution did not occur. Social lubricants, such as social security, unemployment compensation, shorter working hours, and better working conditions have reduced the friction between the owners of production and the workers. By evolution, through the ballot box, and even by appeal to bourgeois values such as justice and fairness, the lot of the average man has been improving in the more economically developed nations of the Western world.

The appeal of Marx to our day is thus that of a moral prophet, and one will remain true to him if one attempts to read the facts of our present society in the light of humane values, and then act in the light of one's findings so as to make our world a place where all men can become more creative and free. Karl Popper, the great defender of a democratic open society, who rejects Marx's historicism, finds that Marx's real contribution is to be found in his moral radicalism which he emphatically says we should keep alive. In Popper's summary statement of the value of Marx we are told:

> It cannot be doubted that the secret of his religious influence was in its moral appeal, that his criticism of capitalism was effective mainly as a moral criticism. Marx showed that a social system can as such be unjust; that if the system is bad, then all the righteousness of the individuals who profit from it is a mere sham righteousness, is mere hypocrisy. For our responsibility extends to the system, to the institutions which we allow to persist.[64]

It is then Marx the prophet who survives as an influence in our choice of world-views; while Marx the economist and prognosticator of the inevitable course of history has passed into the limbo of merely historical interest.

NOTES FOR CHAPTER II

1 Robert C. Tucker, *Philosophy and Myth in Karl Marx* (Cambridge, England: Cambridge University Press, 1961); Erich Fromm, *Marx's Concept of Man* (New York: Frederick Ungar Publishing Co., 1961); Erich Fromm, *Beyond the Chains of Illusion—My Encounter with Marx and Freud* (New York: Pocket Books, Inc., 1962); Erich Fromm, ed., *Socialist Humanism—An International Symposium* (New York: Anchor Books, Doubleday & Co., Inc., 1966).
2 See Isaiah Berlin, *Karl Marx—His Life and Environment* (New York: Oxford University Press, 1963); and Frederick Engels, *Karl Marx* (1877) in Karl Marx and Frederick Engels, *Selected Works* (2 vols.; Moscow: Foreign Languages Publishing House, 1962), II, 156–166.
3 Berlin, *Karl Marx—His Life and Environment*, p. 160.
4 Quoted from Engels in *ibid.*, p. 236.
5 Marx, *Confession* in Fromm, *Marx's Concept of Man*, p. 257.
6 I am indebted for the interpretation presented throughout this section to Tucker, *Philosophy and Myth in Karl Marx*.
7 Karl Marx, *Early Writings*, trans. and ed. by T. B. Bottomore (New York: McGraw-Hill Book Co., 1964), p. 9.
8 *Ibid.*, p. 10.
9 *Ibid.*, p. 31.
10 *Ibid.*, p. 44.
11 *Ibid.*, p. 52.
12 *Ibid.*, p. 120.
13 *Ibid.*, p. 121.
14 *Ibid.*, pp. 124–125.
15 *Ibid.*, p. 37.
16 *Ibid.*, p. 171.
17 *Ibid.*, p. 173.
18 *Ibid.*, pp. 193–194.
19 Karl Marx and Friedrich Engels, *The German Ideology, Parts I and III*, ed. and introd. by R. Pascal (New York: International Publishers Co., Inc., 1963), p. 15.
20 Karl Marx, *A Contribution to the Critique of Political Economy* (Chicago: Charles H. Kerr, 1904), pp. 11–12.
21 Karl Marx and Friedrich Engels, *The Communist Manifesto* in *Essential Works of Marxism*, ed. by Arthur P. Mendel (New York: Bantam Books, Inc., 1965), p. 13 (Section I). Henceforth, references to *The Communist Manifesto* will be to sections within it so that any edition of this work may be consulted.
22 *Ibid.*, Section I.
23 *Ibid.*, Section I.
24 *Ibid.*, Section I.
25 *Ibid.*, Section I.

26 *Ibid.*, Section II.
27 *Ibid.*, Section II.
28 Marx and Engels, *Selected Works*, I, 22.
29 Karl Marx, *Critique of the Gotha Program* in Karl Marx and Friedrich Engels, *Basic Writings on Politics and Philosophy*, ed. by Lewis S. Feuer (New York: Anchor Books, Doubleday & Co., Inc., 1959), pp. 115 ff.
30 *Ibid.*, p. 119.
31 Marx and Engels, *The German Ideology*, p. 22.
32 Frederick Engels, *Herr Eugen Dühring's Revolution in Science (Anti-Dühring)* (New York: International Publishers Co., Inc., 1966), p. 305.
33 *Ibid.*, p. 306.
34 Marx and Engels, *The German Ideology*, p. 39.
35 Engels, *Anti-Dühring*, p. 104.
36 *Ibid.*, p. 104.
37 Marx and Engels, *The German Ideology*, p. 74 (my italics).
38 Engels, *Anti-Dühring*, pp. 309–310.
39 Marx and Engels, *Selected Works*, I, 134.
40 *Ibid.*, I, 136.
41 Eduard Bernstein, *Evolutionary Socialism* (New York: Schocken Books, 1961), p. xxix.
42 V. I. Lenin, *What Is To Be Done? Burning Questions of Our Movement* (New York: International Publishers Co., Inc., 1929), p. 124.
43 V. I. Lenin, *State and Revolution* in *Essential Works of Marxism*, p. 178.
44 *The New Program of the Communist Party of the Soviet Union* in *Essential Works of Marxism*, p. 467.
45 Mao Tse-tung, "On Coalition Government," in *Dictatorship and Totalitarianism: Selected Readings*, ed. and introd. by Betty B. Burch (Princeton, N. J.: D. Van Nostrand Co., Inc., 1964), p. 107 (my italics).
46 Walter Z. Laqueur, "Communism and Nationalism in Tropical Africa," in *Dictatorship and Totalitarianism*, p. 121.
47 *Ibid.*, p. 123.
48 Milovan Djilas, "The New Class," in *Essential Works of Marxism*, p. 321.
49 *Ibid.*, p. 328.
50 *Ibid.*, p. 341.
51 *Ibid.*, p. 345.
52 *Ibid.*, pp. 345–346.
53 Marx and Engels, *The German Ideology*, p. 199.
54 Léopold Senghor, "Socialism is a Humanism," in *Socialist Humanism*, pp. 59–60.
55 Marx and Engels, *Selected Works*, I, 246.
56 Karl R. Popper, *The Open Society and Its Enemies* (2 vols; New York: Harper Torchbooks, 1963), II, 85–86.
57 Sidney Hook, *From Hegel to Marx: Studies in the Intellectual Development of Karl Marx* (Ann Arbor: University of Michigan Press, 1962), p. 2.
58 *Ibid.*, p. 2.
59 Fromm, *Marx's Concept of Man*, pp. 46 ff.
60 *Ibid.*, pp. 56–57.
61 Mathilde Niel, "The Phenomenon of Technology: Liberation or Alienation of Man?" in *Socialist Humanism*, p. 340.
62 *Ibid.*, p. 345.

63 Tucker, *Philosophy and Myth in Karl Marx*, pp. 21–27; 218–232.
64 Popper, *The Open Society and Its Enemies*, II, 211.

SELECTED READINGS

Available in paperback edition.

* Berlin, Isaiah. *Karl Marx: His Life and Environment.* New York: Oxford University Press, 1963.
* Burch, Betty B., ed. *Dictatorship and Totalitarianism: Selected Readings.* Princeton, N. J.: D. Van Nostrand Co., Inc., 1964.
* Crossman, Richard, ed. *The God That Failed.* New York: Bantam Books, Inc., 1964. Andre Gide, Louis Fischer, Arthur Koestler, Ignazio Silone, Stephen Spender, and Richard Wright describe why they changed their minds about Communism.
* Engels, Frederick. *Herr Eugen Dühring's Revolution in Science (Anti-Dühring).* New York: International Publishers Co., Inc., 1966.
* Fromm, Erich. *Beyond the Chains of Illusion: My Encounter with Marx and Freud.* New York: Pocket Books, Inc., 1962.
* ———. *Marx's Concept of Man.* New York: Frederick Ungar Publishing Co., 1961.
* ———, ed. *Socialist Humanism: An International Symposium.* Garden City, N. Y.: Anchor Books, Doubleday & Co., Inc., 1966.
* Hook, Sidney. *From Hegel to Marx: Studies in the Intellectual Development of Karl Marx.* Ann Arbor: The University of Michigan Press, 1962.
* Lenin, V. I. *What Is To Be Done? Burning Questions of Our Movement.* New York: International Publishers Co., Inc., 1929.
* Marcuse, Herbert. *Reason and Revolution: Hegel and the Rise of Social Theory.* Boston: Beacon Press, 1966.
* Marx, Karl. *Early Writings (On the Jewish Question; Contribution to the Critique of Hegel's Philosophy of Right; Economic and Philosophical Manuscripts).* Translated and edited by T. B. Bottomore. New York: McGraw-Hill Co., 1964.
* ——— and Friedrich Engels. *Basic Writings on Politics and Philosophy.* Edited by Lewis S. Feuer. Garden City, N. Y.: Anchor Books, Doubleday & Co., Inc., 1959. An excellent anthology.
* ———. *The German Ideology, Parts I and III.* Edited and introduction by R. Pascal. New York: International Publishers Co., Inc., 1966.
* ———. *Selected Works.* 2 vols. Moscow: Foreign Languages Publishing House, 1962. The best source for complete unabridged texts.
* Mendel, Arthur P., ed. *Essential Works of Marxism.* New York: Bantam Books, Inc., 1965. Includes Marx and Engels, *The Communist Manifesto;* Engels, *Socialism: Utopian and Scientific;* Lenin, *State and Revolution;* Stalin, *The Foundation of Leninism; The New Program of the Communist Party of the Soviet Union;* and selections from the writings of Kolakowski, Mao Tse-tung and Djilas.
* Popper, Karl R. *The Open Society and Its Enemies.* Vol. II *(The High Tide of Prophecy: Hegel, Marx, and the Aftermath).* New York: Harper Torchbooks, 1963.
* Tucker, Robert C. *Philosophy and Myth in Karl Marx.* Cambridge, England: Cambridge University Press, 1965.

III

Psychoanalytic Humanism:
Freud and Fromm

Freud is one of the great pioneers of our century. His theories concerning the power which the unconscious aspects of our mental lives hold over us have played a great part in modifying our traditional notion that man is a predominantly rational being. Freud is, of course, best known for his practice of psychoanalysis by which he was able to help many maladjusted and neurotic persons to achieve a more successful adaptation to their world. He claimed to be using the methods of science in his investigation of the mental life of his patients, and he proposed hypotheses to explain what had gone wrong in their development. Freud came to believe that the mentally ill person differed only in degree from the normal man, so that an intensive study of mental illness could shed light upon the mental processes of all men. At work in all of us he found the sex instincts, the drive toward aggression, the repressing of unacceptable memories or wishes, and the sublimation of primitive impulses. His popular image is usually that of an advocate of a freer sexuality; although, as we shall see, Freud himself was far from being an advocate of sexual license. There can be little doubt, however, that our moral climate today has a distinctly Freudian overtone in its more liberal attitude toward sexual relations, and in its greater tolerance of individuals who depart from the "normal" conventions of society.

Sigmund Freud (1856–1939) was a young physician practicing in Vienna when he came to the conclusion that many of his patients were not suffering from physical disorders but rather from mental disturbances. After studying the hypnotic methods of therapy used by the Frenchman

Charcot, he attempted to employ these methods in treating his own patients. He discovered, however, that while the symptoms of the mental disorder were sometimes removed successfully under hypnosis, his patients frequently developed new symptoms and had to be treated again. Freud then successfully used a method for which he has become famous: free association. He found that this method, without the use of hypnosis, was just as fruitful without having any of the attendant disadvantages. His technique consisted of getting his patients to relax and talk freely about anything which occurred to them, no matter how illogical or offensive this material might appear to be. Freud used this method in interpreting the dreams of his patients in order to uncover the psychic mechanism which although hidden from them was causing their neuroses. When the patient himself discovered the repressed wishes or memories, he would then be able to master them consciously and be freed from their domination.

Freud's success in curing many neurotics led other physicians to come to Vienna to work with him. Freud became an international figure, eagerly defended by some, violently attacked by others. His attackers claimed that he was unscientific, especially in his treatment of sexuality. In 1910 the International Psycho-Analytic Association was established, and Freud devoted much of his time to the development of the movement. Also about this time he began to write on the broader implications of psychoanalysis for morality, religion, art, and civilization. In fact, Freud himself said that he at first had no great desire to be a physician, and was therefore glad to return to the problems of culture and civilization which had always fascinated him. Let us now turn to an investigation of those views of Freud with which anyone in the modern world must come to terms in his attempt to construct a world-view for himself.

Freud: The Structure of the Mind   Freud often remarked that the basic discovery of psychoanalysis was the unconscious. Although Freud used the word "unconscious" in many different ways during his career, one underlying meaning does run through his writings. The unconscious is that vast stream of basic impulses and drives, as well as forgotten experiences, which shapes the behavior of man without his consciousness being aware of it. What we experience as conscious thinking and awareness is really only a very small part of our mental lives. Freud used an interesting analogy to bring home his point. The conscious part of our minds is like the small top of the iceberg which is above the surface of the ocean, while the unconscious is like the huge block of ice which is beneath the surface of the ocean and out of sight. Freud found this analogy to be a rather reliable description of the mind, and did not hesitate to call himself a "depth psychologist;" that is, one who plunges beneath the surface of our conscious experience to find what is really going on in the depths of our being.

Freud's theory of the unconscious did not just maintain that this was the region where our memories were stored. Of even greater importance for man was that the unconscious was the source of his dynamic impulses, instincts, drives, motivations, racial inheritances, and unresolved conflicts. The latter were extremely crucial, Freud maintained, for most of them were unresolved sexual conflicts which were carried over from childhood. The little child had powerful sexual impulses and wishes which it was forced to deny because they conflicted with the parental standards of what was right behavior. Furthermore, the child was made to feel guilty or ashamed for even having such desires, so that they were repressed so deeply into the unconscious that most of us have completely forgotten them. Our unconscious has not forgotten these primitive sexual impulses, however, for there they remain as dynamic and bent upon satisfaction as ever. Sometimes, in our dreams these unconscious wishes escape from our conscious control, but even then they are usually disguised so that we do not clearly understand what they are.

In his earlier writings Freud distinguished the unconscious from the pre-conscious. The unconscious included all those impulses and desires which were denied admission to consciousness, while the pre-conscious referred to those memories and desires which were temporarily outside the stream of consciousness, but which could gain admittance without resistance. He used the analogy of a doorkeeper or a censor to help explain his position. Memories which are not distasteful to us, and desires which we could consider acceptable, can be admitted into the polite society of consciousness by the vigilant doorkeeper or censor. Thus, we can usually recall names of friends and events from our recent past with little difficulty. But, sometimes, our attempts at recall fail although we say, "I know his name as well as my own." Freud in *Psychopathology of Everyday Life* and some of his other more general works tried to show that there was always a reason for the individual's not being able to recall the name which he claimed he knew so well. The name had been repressed into the unconscious, perhaps because although you professed to like the person who bore this name, you really considered him a threat and hated him. But, only a lengthy investigation of the circumstances and of your own mental history could give the actual reason. At any rate, Freud assured us, nothing happened by chance in the mental life; everything in this domain was caused, even if we were unconscious of the truly dynamic factors at work.

Freud's explanatory hypothesis of the unconscious and the pre-conscious was based not only upon his therapeutic sessions with his neurotic patients, but also upon his own self-analysis and observation of the behavior of so-called normal people. The pre-conscious materials were simply not present to consciousness at the moment, but a redirection of attention could quickly bring them forth. You are probably not conscious at the moment of what you had for dinner last night, but it should not take too much effort for you to recall it to your present consciousness. With the unconscious materials, however, it is not all that easy. If our unpleasant wishes and experiences could simply, once for all time, be forgotten completely, then they would no longer exert any dynamic influence upon our lives. Freud maintained, however, that no desire or experience which we have ever had is ever really forgotten. To this belief he often coupled his conviction that each individual in his infancy recapitulated the mental history of the human race. The conscious ego surely cannot allow impulses toward incest, murder, or cannibalism to come forth into direct action in our present civilized world. Its only recourse is to repress these impulses below the threshold of consciousness itself. Freud at times did not hesitate to picture the unconscious as though it were a seething cauldron seeking to boil over into the world. If all of us are still subject to these horrible dynamic impulses, how is it that any of us can remain sane or civilized?

Fortunately, each one of us has an escape valve, as it were, by which these primitive impulses and wishes can occasionally gain enough entrance into the conscious world to prevent their completely destroying us. Dreams are the mechanism by which our repressed wishes and experiences are disguised by symbolism so as to permit their passing the conscious censor. Freud found all dreams to be wish-fulfillments. In most dreams, the latent material (the actual disturbing wish) is so well disguised in the manifest content (the dream itself) that sleep is not interrupted and we are not forced to reason about "the absurd or silly" dream. A dream then is a compromise between the demands of the repressed impulse and the conscious resistance of the censoring ego. Usually, dreams are able to relieve the inner tensions seething within us without disturbing our sleep; but sometimes, as in a nightmare, the dream comes altogether too close to the real hidden impulse behind it, so that the sleeper is forced to wake up in order to keep the painful reality away from his conscious awareness. Freud concluded that his study of dreams had proved that, *"what is suppressed continues to exist in normal people as well as abnormal, and remains capable of psychical functioning."* [1]

In the early 1920's, Freud formulated a revised theory concerning the nature of the mind in order to make even clearer that his interpretation of mental activity was dynamic, and not structural. He now distinguished within the organization of the personality an *id*, an *ego*, and a *super-ego*.

The *id* was the name Freud gave to the oldest of the mental agencies: "It contains everything that is inherited, that is present at birth, that is fixed in the constitution—above all, therefore, the instincts. . . ." [2] After an individual is born, he comes into contact with the external world.

A portion of the id now becomes separated from it, the *ego*, and acts henceforward as the intermediary between the id and the external world. The id represents man's primitive passions and instincts which clamor for expression, while the ego represents man's common sense and reason which seeks to conform the desires of the id to the requirements of the external world. The ego tends to repress those demands of the id which it finds too primitive and irrational, but it must often allow at least a modified form of satisfaction to these drives, for after all the dynamic energy of life itself is in the id. The id is thus the source of the Freudian libido, the energy or driving force behind the instinctive impulses, as well as being that huge part of the self which is repressed and hidden from consciousness. The irrational id is always impatient with the reality considerations of the ego and seeks immediate gratification regardless of the unfitness of its desires. Freud maintained that the id was ruled, therefore, by the "pleasure principle," and was accordingly amoral, not aware of "right" or "wrong."

The *ego* is that aspect of the personality which was partly formed in early childhood by parental training and its dealings with the external world. It has had to face up to the facts, conform to social requirements, and act in terms of common sense, reason and logic. Freud characterized it as following a "reality principle." The ego, when affairs can be well managed, is able to redirect the blind passions of the id into socially acceptable channels by aim-inhibition or sublimation. The healthy ego, always aware of its own origins in the id, must seek to serve the id, at the same time that it must give full credence to the restricting factors presented to it by other people and the external world. Rarely, however, can affairs be managed so ideally. The ego often represses the impulses from the id when it is unable to restrain and control them. Its main function is self-preservation, but it can never forget that its origin was in the id:

> The ego must on the whole carry out the id's intentions, it fulfils its task by finding out the circumstances in which those intentions can best be achieved. The ego's relation to the id might be compared with that of a rider to his horse. The horse supplies the locomotive energy, while the rider has the privilege of deciding on the goal and of guiding the powerful animal's movement. But only too often there arises between the ego and the id the not precisely ideal situation of the rider being obliged to guide the horse along the path by which it itself wants to go.[3]

The *super-ego*, the third aspect of the personality, is partly unconscious in origin and partly the product of the emotional bond of the child with its parents and other ego-ideals. The small child is unable of itself to control the impulses of the id, and so easily comes under the authority of the parents, school teachers, and others with whom it is closely associated. In their loving care, the parents frequently are quite severe in restricting the behavior of the infantile ego; while, the child, who is extremely dependent at the time, tends to identify himself with his parents in their disciplinary action. The parent's moral code thus is internalized in the child so that he adopts their standards as to when the id impulses should be repressed or expressed. Because these attitudes are fixed early, they tend to persist, with only slight modifications, throughout life. These internalized attitudes constitute the super-ego, a stern guardian of behavior, who has all the force of parental authority and sanctions behind it. The higher ethical ideals of mankind are reinforced in the individual by the super-ego which constantly punishes one by means of guilt feelings and a bad conscience for failing to live up to the ideal. In this respect it functions quite as irrationally as the id, for it will not accept extenuating circumstances and tends to punish evil thoughts with as great zeal as it does actual misdeeds. It is true, for Freud, that as a person grows older and matures he incorporates his own ideals for himself, as well as the ideals which his society accepts, into his super-ego. Often, however, this simply means that the super-ego is besieged by conflicting ideals, making even more complicated the battle to preserve one's mental health. Like the id, it has the power to master the ego as it stands apart and criticizes it:

> It is a memorial of the former weakness and dependence of the ego, and the mature ego remains subject to its domination. As the child was once under a compulsion to obey its parents, so the ego submits to the categorical imperative of the super-ego.[4]

We see, then, that the ego, which is the rational part of the personality, is in constant difficulty. It is pressed from below by the irrational id, which urges it to live by the pleasure principle and seek immediate gratification for its impulses; but it is also sternly censored from above by the irrationally intolerant super-ego, which will not hear of any modification of its ideals of perfection. Freud commented on its uneasy role:

> We are warned by a proverb against serving two masters at the same time. The poor ego has things even worse: it serves three severe masters and does what it can to bring their claims and demands into harmony with one another. These claims are always divergent and often seem incompatible. No wonder that the ego so often fails in its task. Its three tyrannical masters are the external world, the super-ego and the id. . . . It feels hemmed in on three sides, threatened by three kinds of danger, to which, if it is hard pressed, it reacts by generating anxiety. Owing to its origin from the experiences of the perceptual system, it is earmarked for representing the demands of the external world, but it strives too to be a loyal servant of the id, to remain on good terms with it. . . . On the other hand it is ob-

served at every step it takes by the strict super-ego, which lays down definite standards for its conduct, without taking any account of its difficulties from the direction of the id and the external world, and which, if those standards are not obeyed, punishes it with tense feelings of inferiority and of guilt. Thus the ego, driven by the id, confined by the super-ego, repulsed by reality, struggles to master its economic task of bringing about harmony among the forces and influences working in and upon it; and we can understand how it is that so often we cannot suppress a cry: 'Life is not easy!' [5]

In addition to Freud's great emphasis upon the unconscious, he is probably best known for his discussion of man's basic instincts or drives. In his earlier writings he referred to two basic kinds of instincts: the sexual and the self-preservative. After the First World War he was so greatly impressed by man's tendencies toward aggression and destructiveness that he referred to the two basic instincts as Eros (love) and Thanatos (death). Let us examine his earlier classification in order to see if his later view, for which he is best known, is in harmony with it or not.

The self-preservative instincts, which he sometimes called the ego-instincts, were pliable and easily adaptable to the demands of external necessity. Indeed if we did not learn how to adapt ourselves to our food supply and our environment, we would not survive at all. These instincts, therefore, usually respond to the reality principle of the ego, and do not cause neuroses. Things are not so simple with the sexual instincts, however, for they crave satisfaction even at the price of self-preservation.

Freud's contribution to our knowledge of the sexual impulse is probably the most publicized aspect of his investigations, and it is also very frequently misunderstood. Even in his early writings, Freud gave a much larger connotation to "sexual" than is customary in our culture. For example, the life of a little child seemed to him full of incestuous desire for the parent of the opposite sex; even the attraction between brothers and sisters was sexual; in short, all turning of male to female, or vice versa, in any form whatsoever, was rooted in the sexual instinct. Furthermore, any pleasure derived from touching, fondling, pushing, and other physical contacts, including pleasure in handling one's own body, was delightful for the same reasons as kissing and other more directly sexual actions are. "Sexual" therefore has the broadest connotations in Freud's writings. Even the bonds between a leader and his followers, a teacher and his students, the psychoanalyst and his patients, were characterized in some of his writings as primarily sexual in nature. Of course, these latter illustrations represent aim-inhibited or sublimated sexuality in the services of civilization, but Freud wished to show that their origins were really in the basic undirected sexual impulses which were at the very core of human personality.

The undifferentiated sexual impulses quickly assumed definite forms in a child, Freud maintained. The earliest stage of sexuality he called the oral phase, in which the child at first found its greatest delight in being fed. As the child began to be toilet trained, he went through an anal phase, in which his main pleasure was found in the control he exercised over defecation. Only later as the child progressed toward adolescence did his interest shift directly to the genitals. This ideal pattern of transition is rarely found in its pure state, however, for Freud maintained that even "normal" men have holdovers from the oral and anal stages in their character. Of course, in most adults these pregenital stages are reflected in activities not directly related to their origin, so that, for example, the miser is a representative of the anal-retentive personality because he holds on to his money. One should never forget that Freud recognized that there were many transitional stages, as well as differences in the ways in which various individuals responded to their environments, so that it would be a gross oversimplification to look for these three stages of sexuality in their pure forms. What Freud attempted to do was to describe a typical pattern for the development of human sexuality from the pregenital stages to the genital stage.

The development of a mature genital sexuality is rarely easy, Freud maintained. Many of the sexual impulses which the id desires to carry out are strictly forbidden by the super-ego, with the result that they are repressed in childhood and become unconscious urges. Freud's most famous example of this kind is the Oedipus complex, a psychological attitude named from the play by Sophocles in which Oedipus, without knowing it, kills his father and marries his mother. In girls, a matching attitude is called the Electra complex, after the daughter of King Agamemnon, who avenged her beloved father by plotting the death of her mother. Freud explained:

> The son, when quite a little child, already begins to develop a peculiar tenderness toward his mother, whom he looks upon as his own property, regarding his father in the light of a rival who disputes this sole possession of his; similarly the little daughter sees in her mother someone who disturbs her tender relation to her father and occupies a place which she feels she herself could very well fill. . . . Moreover, the parents themselves frequently stimulate the children to react with an Oedipus complex, for parents are often guided in their preferences by the difference in sex of their children, so that the father favours the daughter and the mother the son; or else, where conjugal love has grown cold, the child may be taken as a substitute for the love-object which has ceased to attract.[6]

The failure of individuals to resolve the Oedipus complex was at the root of many neuroses and sexual perversions. Freud shocked many people by suggesting that the desire for incest is a quite natural desire since the first object choice is always the person with whom the child has formed the strongest emotional bond. Hence, the stringent legal and moral prohibition against incest is required "to prevent this sustained infantile tendency from being carried into effect." [7] In normal persons the Oedipus complex is successfully repressed, thus freeing these persons to pursue love objects elsewhere. In these cases, the new emotional attachment with a member of the opposite sex supplants the primitive infantile desires; to all intents and purposes, the Oedipus complex has then been overcome. However, even in these more successful cases, there is often an unconscious compensation toward the parents so that the super-ego's self-identification with the standards of the parents is greatly intensified. In effect, it is as though one now says that he will never do anything which his parents would not approve. Rarely did Freud think that one could control the basic sexual impulses with complete rationality. As Freud put it:

> From the time of puberty onward the human individual must devote himself to the great task of *freeing himself from the parents;* and only after this detachment is accomplished can he cease to be a child and so become a member of the social community. . . . These tasks are laid down for every man; it is noteworthy how seldom they are carried through ideally, that is, how seldom they are solved in a manner psychologically as well as socially satisfactory. [8]

Some men faced an even greater task than overcoming parental dominance. They had to overcome their own extreme self-love. Freud's later investigations suggested to him that the child's first object of affection may be its own body. It achieves great pleasure from observing itself, from playing with itself, and so begins to love itself. Freud, with his fondness for Greek mythology, referred to this as narcissism, named for the Narcissus of the Greek myth who fell in love with his own image when he saw it reflected in a pool of water. In some adults their inability to relate satisfactorily with others is caused by their still being in love with themselves, either as they are now or with some ideal which they hold forth for their achievement. Most normal men have left this stage of vanity behind as they seek their satisfaction with other people, but even here a fondness for one's self-image may reflect narcissism still at work in the unconscious.

As Freud grew older, he tended to emphasize the destructive impulses in the personality and in society, and he combined the self-preservative impulses with the sexual instinct. In his later writings he therefore contrasts the aggressive instincts, whose aim is destruction, with the sexual instincts or Eros, whose aim is to combine more and more substances into unities. In fact Freud thought that the ancient Greek Empedocles had correctly described the entire cosmos as caught in an eternal struggle between love (Eros) and hate (Thanatos). The tendencies toward cruelty (sadism) and toward the desire to be hurt (masochism) which he found in so many of his patients, coupled with the irrational destructiveness of the First World War, convinced him that these impulses of vicious aggressiveness and of self-destruction were signs of a basic unconscious death wish in all men. It seemed to him that in their experiences of the conflict of love and death men subconsciously know that death will be the inevitable victor; life and love are only for a time triumphant. Although when men are strong and vigorous, and their desires are on the way toward fulfillment in love, they are in love with life itself; nevertheless, as men grow weary in the ceaseless struggle of life, they long to return to the inorganic state from which they came. Freud was in essence developing a philosophical view to explain the Hamlet in all of us; consciously or unconsciously we are propounding the alternative of being or non-being, secretly wishing to die, while at the same time feeling fearful of what this may entail. The later Freud, like many of the contemporary existentialists, believed that one had to live one's life in full awareness that the goal of life was death. Furthermore, on the social scene he found that the aggressive instincts, much more than the sexual ones, "make human communal life difficult and threaten its survival." [9] We shall see a little later what some of the moral implications were which Freud drew from this belief.

What we have seen of the mind's structure as Freud described it reveals the mind to be the battleground of competing impulses and desires struggling against a recalcitrant super-ego. The poor little ego has a hard time of it in its effort to keep a balance in the mental life. In fact, it frequently loses many skirmishes, if not the entire war. Let us glance briefly at some of the difficult problems with which the ego must deal. Neuroses are irrepressible eruptions of the id in the form of behavior that eases the anxiety issuing from conflicts within the personality. Essentially, neuroses are "escape mechanisms." The id demands an outlet for its irrational aims, and the super-ego modifies the behavior to make it more acceptable to society than it would be in its natural state. Examples of neurotic ways of escape are: the ego's adoption of symptoms of disease as a disguise for unresolved mental conflicts; compulsive acts that symbolize the repressed impulse, such as obsessive hand-washing that unconsciously reveals a deep-seated guilt feeling; and forms of insanity that represent the ego's surrender to a world of fantasy as a substitute for the intolerable realities of the actual world. On the borderline of the neurotic are the rationalizations and projections by which the ego attempts to give logical form to irrational material.

Freud through psychoanalysis attempted to reveal the nature of these escape mechanisms so that his patients would be freed to face reality. However, he in general approved of one type of escape mechanism. This

was *sublimation.* In this case, a form of behavior is adopted which con-
forms to the high ideals of the super-ego (and of society) and yet allows
the id to be satisfied. In sublimation, Freud maintained that sexual and
destructive energy can be redirected so as to be expended in socially
useful ways. Thus, a maiden school teacher may satisfy her desire to be
a mother by love of her pupils, who are in effect her children; a priest
may unconsciously forestall the sexual difficulties inherent in celibacy by
serving Mother Church and being a "father" to the "children" of his
parish; poets and artists may give socially approved expression to their
exhibitionist tendencies through their created works of art; surgeons
may satisfy their sadistic tendencies through a beneficial use of the knife,
and so on. Sublimation opens up a substitute channel for the flow of the
id impulses and thus gives them a satisfactory outlet. Freud did not
hesitate to claim that the progress of civilization was purchased at the
price of repression and sublimation; of the two, only sublimation, if not
engaged in too frequently, could help preserve the mental health of the
individual.

Freud: Implications of Psychoanalysis   Freud often claimed that he was
for Morality and Religion   not interested in constructing a
                                           philosophy of life, and that the
only road to truth was to be found in a strict pursuit of the scientific
method. Nevertheless, it becomes very clear to one who reads the books
which Freud wrote after the First World War that he was dealing with
the big questions of morality, religion, civilization, war and peace in a
way which could not be construed as a rigid adherence to purely the
methods of the sciences. It is true that he often will insert long paragraphs
which rhetorically ask if he should continue his investigation into the
phenomena of morality and religion on a huge cultural scale. He sometimes will admit that he is not an expert in these fields, but then he
quotes those whom he considers as experts, and merrily goes on his way
to present his own conclusions. While one may often find that Freud is
on rather shaky ground in presenting evidence for his theories concerning
the origins of morality and religion, one cannot help but find his speculations at least as likely as those offered by the philosophers of the past.

   In *Totem and Taboo,* published in 1913, he attempted to discover the
origins of both morality and religion in the prehistorical life of primitive
man. He drew heavily upon the writings of the anthropologists of his day,
such as James Frazer and W. Robertson Smith, and tried to correlate
their findings with his own discoveries concerning the infantile memories
of his neurotic patients. We have already noted that Freud subscribed
to the belief of racial memory and claimed that each man recapitulated
in his childhood the entire cultural history of humanity. Neurotics were
possessed by infantile fixations, and a study of their regressions, Freud

believed, would give us insight into the mental life of the human race in its infancy. Conversely, he claimed that a study of the lives of primitive mankind would also shed light upon the behavior of fixated neurotics in our own culture.

Freud was in at least one respect a dutiful child of early twentieth-century philosophy. He was a positivist. In *Totem and Taboo* Freud clearly adopts the positivistic view that mankind has evolved through three stages. He characterizes these stages as (1) the animistic stage, during which man believed that everything whatsoever was alive; (2) the religious stage, during which man believed that a Father God controlled nature and his destiny; and (3) the scientific stage into which modern man is emerging as he seeks for rational explanations of specific happenings in nature and history. But if each individual recapitulates the history of the human race, then each one of us must pass through these three stages in our own development. Freud proposed the following parallel:

> We find that the animistic phase corresponds in time as well as in content with narcism, the religious phase corresponds to that stage of object finding which is characterized by dependence on the parents, while the scientific stage has its full counterpart in the individual's state of maturity where, having renounced the pleasure principle and having adapted himself to reality, he seeks his object in the outer world.[10]

Now Freud had the presuppositions from which he could construct his scientific myth concerning the origin of morality and religion.

Freud proposed that the origins of morality and religion were to be found in prehistoric totemism, which venerated a particular animal as the ancestor of the tribe. On sacred feast days this animal would be killed and eaten by the tribe, but it was protected by taboos on all other occasions. Freud claimed that psychoanalysis could reconstruct what really was behind this custom:

> Psychoanalysis has revealed to us that the totem animal is really a substitute for the father, and this really explains the contradiction that it is usually forbidden to kill the totem animal, that the killing of it results in a holiday and that the animal is killed and yet mourned. The ambivalent emotional attitude which today still marks the father complex in our children and so often continues into adult life also extended to the father substitute of the totem animal.[11]

But Freud goes even further and reconstructs what must have happened in a "primitive horde" long before totemism appeared upon the scene. A powerful father must have ruled, at first, over the "primitive horde." He was an autocratic authority and brooked no opposition to his commands. This primeval father kept the women of the tribe for himself. His sons, who hated and at the same time loved and admired their father (ambivalence), became old enough to want the women whom the father refused to share with them. One by one, the father expelled rebellious sons from the horde. But, one day, the expelled brothers joined together, killed the father and ate him. Together they were able to accomplish what none of them could do alone. Nevertheless, they admired the father and "accomplished their identification with him by devouring him and each acquired a part of his strength." [12] But afterwards, the hatred of their father having been fully satisfied, love and admiration for him reasserted itself. They began to have guilt feelings for their destruction of their father. Their remorse led them to prohibit by law what the father had before simply prevented by his strong power. "They undid their deed by declaring that the killing of the father substitute, the totem, was not allowed, and renounced the fruits of their deed by denying themselves the liberated women." [13] Thus, Freud found a likely prehistoric origin of the two crimes of which mankind has such great fear: murder and incest.

Freud admitted that no such primitive society has ever been observed, but he believed that his myth is plausible nonetheless since it fits in perfectly with the Oedipus complex of all men. Now we know, he suggested, why infants repress with such severity their desires to kill their fathers and marry their mothers—it is because they recall what their primitive ancestors once did in reality! What was once a reality, thus persists in the fantasy life of all men.

One ought not to conclude that Freud was ridiculing morality and religion. Far from it, for he recognized that without moral prohibitions and religious beliefs mankind would have perished long ago. Religion had given man a unified view of life, while morality had tamed his passions and directed them into socially useful channels. Freud believed that man's aggressive instincts would soon annihilate the human race if we ever returned to a state of original nature. Religion has performed the function of making this world a more tolerable one in which man could live. If a personal God watches over and guides the destiny of man and nature, then good must eventually win out, if not in this world, then in the next. Morality, in the religious view, has the universe on its side and this tends to help man renounce his primitive instinctual drives for his own direct satisfaction in the hope of winning greater happiness in the end. Freud maintained that "religious ideas have sprung from the same need as all the other achievements of culture: from the necessity for defending itself against the crushing supremacy of nature." [14] While Freud acknowledged the contribution of religion to the development of man, he claimed that modern scientific man could no longer accept its dogmas. As men began to see that science was the only road to truth, religion would no longer be able to maintain its hold over them.

Religion, Freud claimed, is now seen to be an illusion—an illusion based on the "terrifying effect of infantile helplessness" which originally turned to the father for protection and now turns to a Father in the sky who is still more powerful. As individuals mature, they reject their childish illusions; as the human race matures, it will recognize that its religious beliefs are cultural illusions which also must be abandoned. Even on the pragmatic side Freud maintained that religion had not accomplished very much if one considers the many thousands of years during which it has ruled over man. The more that science deals with particular human problems in a successful way, the less will people continue to believe in religion.

Freud continued his penchant for comparing social phenomena to observations he had made in his neurotic patients. Religion thus became the "universal obsessional neurosis of humanity." [15] The true believer is thus spared having an individual neurosis of his very own for he shares the cultural neurosis of his society. But the time was now at hand, claimed Freud, to cure men of the cultural neurosis of religion and to replace it by conscious rational effort to improve their lives.

Against objections that the removal of the power of religion to control men would lower morality, Freud argued that it was debatable as to whether or not religion had ever really supported a high view of morals. Sin could always be excused after the proper acts of penance and contrition; moreover, "by making these great concessions to human instincts" sometimes religion has actually supported immorality.[16] Morals, Freud claimed, would likely improve if religion were abolished. Religion keeps man in a state of neurotic dependence on a protective power; but this is to remain in a state of childishness. "Man cannot remain a child forever; he must venture at last into the hostile world." [17] He must face reality without illusions.

What would it mean, according to Freud, for man to mature and face reality? In *Civilization and Its Discontents* he admitted that most men found a purpose for life in terms of the religious system which they accepted. Freud proposed to turn away from what men said their purpose in life was, such as to glorify God or to advance the coming of the kingdom of heaven, and to look instead at the actual behavior of men. If one looks at the way men act, then, Freud believed, one could no longer be in doubt concerning what men really wanted from life: "They strive after happiness; they want to become happy and to remain so." [18] By happiness Freud had in mind an absence of pain and the presence of strong feelings of pleasure. Obviously no man can completely eliminate pain from his life, and even his intense moments of pleasure are few and far between. Freud suggested that facing up to reality involved the realization that man cannot achieve his primary goal of happiness, because man faces pain and suffering from three different directions: "from our own body, which is doomed to decay and dissolution and which cannot even do without pain and anxiety as warning signals; from the external world, which may rage against us with overwhelming and merciless forces of destruction; and finally from our relations to other men." [19] In short, facing the reality principle requires one to first of all give up any hopes one may entertain for achieving unmitigated happiness.

Despite man's victories over the forces of nature by means of his science, he tends to feel even more uncomfortable and unhappy in his social relationships. Freud maintained that some men blamed civilization itself for their discontents; civilization imposed unrealistic limitations upon the basic instinctual life of man and hence made it impossible for man to find happiness. While it is true that Freud had a certain provisional sympathy with this complaint, especially when discussing the overly restrictive sexual mores of his own culture, he certainly never advocated overthrowing civilization and returning to the original state of nature. Rousseau in the eighteenth century had claimed that man in his original state of nature was basically good, and that it was civilization which had corrupted him. Freud did not by any means share the belief that man originally lived in a golden age of perfection. Instead, he claimed, it was the taming and redirecting of man's basic instincts by civilization which differentiated man from the animals. Without civilization there would be no art, no beauty, no knowledge, no science. Yet despite the high premium which civilization places upon man's higher intellectual activities, it has failed to come forth with a satisfactory method of regulating man's relationships with his fellow men. The essence of a civilization is found, for Freud, in placing the power of the community over that of the individual so that "the members of the community restrict themselves in their possibilities of satisfaction." [20] The difficulty which any civilization faces is that individuals are not easily persuaded to give up their instinctual cravings for their own pleasure. The best that can be done is to attempt to find an "expedient accommodation . . . between this claim of the individual and the cultural claims of the group." [21]

Freud's objection to what he called the cultural super-ego, the prevailing morality of his day, was very similar to his complaint against the individual's super-ego: it was irrational both in what it sternly prohibited and in what it ardently required of man. One ought not to hate, be aggressive or despise other men; in fact, one ought to love one's neighbor and one's enemy. If one were not able to live up to this ideal, and no one could, then one was made to feel guilty, sinful, or evil. The ethical demands of the cultural super-ego are made without asking whether the individual can carry them out or not. No attention is paid to the differences in the mental lives, desires, and hopes of individuals. "On the contrary, it [the cultural super-ego] assumes that a man's ego is psychologically capable of anything that is required of it, that his ego has unlimited mastery over his id." [22] But, even in "normal" people only so much can be demanded in the way of control over the id. There must be some direct outlet for both the sexual passions and the aggressive impulses (Eros and Thanatos) for sublimation and aim-inhibited conduct cannot completely replace the original goals of the instincts.

The Christian ethic with its emphasis upon love for one's neighbor and even for one's enemy comes in for particular attack by Freud. Eros, for him, in both its more directly sexual acts and in its aim-inhibited conduct, is always concerned with the worthwhileness of the person loved. As Freud put it: "My love is something valuable to me which I ought not to throw away without reflection. . . . If I love someone, he must deserve it in some way." [23] Now my neighbor rarely deserves my love, but he often merits my hostility because of the way he treats me. If my neighbor does show consideration toward me, then Freud admitted I will naturally be inclined to treat him with respect. But if I show love toward all men without regard to their merits, I spread my affection so widely that it will do little good, and I place myself at a disadvantage in that other men will use me and exploit me for their own satisfactions. Freud suggested that this cultural ideal would have been much more realistic if it had been put: " 'Love thy neighbour as thy neighbour loves thee.' " [24] Furthermore, the impossible ideal requiring me to love all my neighbors inevitably fills me with feelings of guilt since it is impossible for any man to fulfill the command.

Eros has been able to enlarge human communities through aim-inhibited love so that affection can be centered upon a nation, but there has always been an out-group toward which one could vent his hatred, hostility and aggression. The necessity for an opposing group as Freud saw it, was the presence of the aggressive drive in man. Man's aggressive drive needs an outlet, but civilization has prevented man from giving direct expression to his hostility, just as it has inhibited direct expression of his erotic drives. In fact, unless the aggressive instincts were redirected by the forces of civilization, man would still be a prehistoric animal. Thus, men are allowed by their culture to vent their hatred and hostility upon the outsiders, the strangers, the foreigners, or the enemies. Freud recognized that the greatest problem facing modern civilization was whether or not the aggressive instincts could be tamed. No moralist ever posed the problem of modern civilization better than did Freud:

> The fateful question for the human species seems to me to be whether and to what extent their cultural development will succeed in mastering the disturbance of their communal life by the human instinct of aggression and self-destruction. . . . Men have gained control over the forces of nature to such an extent that with their help they would have no difficulty in exterminating one another to the last man. They know this, and hence comes a large part of their current unrest, their unhappiness and their mood of anxiety.[25]

50 x 46

Freud wrote the above comment in 1930, before the discovery of nuclear weapons. As he saw it, the question could be expressed symbolically by asking whether Heavenly Eros would be able to defeat Thanatos. The old religions, and the irrational cultural super-ego would not be adequate to this task—of that he was sure.

Freud was more than a critic of society, for he did offer some positive suggestions toward constructing a more realistic morality. His ideal for humanity was expressed in his formula: "Where id was, there ego shall be." [26] After all of Freud's analyses which revealed how much men tended to rationalize their conduct, while their actions were really controlled by unconscious forces over which their reason had no control, the reader may be somewhat surprised to find that Freud's goal for mankind is to develop the life of reason. We should recall, however, that reason never was totally powerless in Freud's view, for when one learned to understand what the deep unconscious forces were which motivated him, he could then learn to control and direct them through aim-inhibition or sublimation in ways relatively satisfactory to his culture. Man's first step toward maturity would require his learning to recognize the illusions under which he had been living. His next step, and the one which he had not yet taken, would be to attempt to build a world-view based upon science and reason.

Freud believed that reason was one of the strongest unifying bonds among men. The methods of the sciences should be applied to the relations of men in society as well as to the study of the mental life of individuals. When this had been done, then it was Freud's faith that we might be able to construct a world-view which eliminated the illusions of religion and the irrational demands of the cultural super-ego. What would replace the old illusions would be a less comforting faith, with no guarantee of success, in men using the tools of reason and science to solve the particular problems which they faced in living on this earth. As Freud put it:

> Our best hope for the future is that intellect—the scientific spirit, reason—may in process of time establish a dictatorship in the mental life of man. The nature of reason is a guarantee that afterwards it will not fail to give man's emotional impulses and what is determined by them the position they deserve. But the common compulsion exercised by such a dominance of reason will prove to be the strongest uniting bond among men and lead the way to further unions. [27]

Reason had an additional advantage over previous ways of dealing with man's problems—it was self-corrective and could be applied to whatever problems the future might bring.

The radical experiment of seeking to control man by reason rather than by irrational morality and religion would be a dangerous one. Freud fully admitted that if the average man became convinced that there was no God to enforce morality, he might go on an endless spree of irrational assaults and killings. Nevertheless, Freud thought that the experiment was worth attempting. Clearly many of the culturally enforced prohibitions against various kinds of sexual conduct would have to be done away with, and here again there would be great risk to the stability and security of civilization. Should the experiment of a rational morality fail then Freud admitted that "I am ready to give up the reform and to return to the earlier, purely descriptive judgement: man is a creature of weak intelligence who is governed by his instinctual wishes." [28] Whatever else Freud advocated, it is clear that he was hoping for "an ethic of honesty" in which men would be delivered from their illusions, recognize their instinctual equipment, and do the best that they could to make this earth a more hospitable place in which to dwell. [29]

Freud considered his task to be an analytical one—both with respect to individuals and societies. He did not claim to be a moral prophet who had a new vision for humanity, and he refused to offer specific suggestions on many ethical issues on the grounds that to do so would take him outside his area of competence. He did, however, make some positive suggestions concerning the education of children, because he believed that by applying psychoanalytic insight to education we might be able to rear a generation which would be less prone to neurosis.

Freud did not advocate a non-restrictive nor a child-directed education. He admitted that the first task of any educational system was to teach the child to control his instincts. If a child were allowed to express all his instincts directly without control, life would be intolerable for the parents and the child would be seriously damaged for living in society later on. A new education based on the knowledge gained through psychoanalysis must seek for an optimum of control and expression, which will damage the child the least and provide the greatest benefit for society at large. Education should, according to Freud, "be a matter of deciding how much to forbid, at what times and by what means." [30] Furthermore, the educators must realize that individuals are not exactly alike, and allowances must be made for their constitutional differences. Freud believed that the best way to educate a child is to combine the right amount of love with effective rational authority. But to do this will require intelligent educators who will be willing to experiment with their methods. At any rate, the aim should not be to produce a generation of rebels, but to prepare individuals to be as healthy and efficient as possible.

Freud's brief remarks on education reflect his general attitude toward the place of the individual in society. It is a gross misinterpretation of Freud which advocates the overthrowing of all cultural rules in behalf of an unrestricted free sexuality. It is true to say that Freud considered the sexual norms of his "middle class" culture to be overly repressive, but he also realized that without some rational control of the sexual impulses civilization would collapse. What he advocated was a norm of mental health, both for individuals and for civilization itself. The first step along the way to achieving this goal would be to recognize and understand the great powerfulness of our unconscious impulses. His faith in reason exemplified his conviction that if man understood what he was really like, he would then be able to direct his impulses toward satisfaction in ways helpful to his fellow men. For Freud, as for Socrates, an adequate morality could be built only upon man's self-knowledge. When we recognize the complexities in our own nature, we will be more inclined to be charitable toward other men. It might then prove possible for all men to work together using the methods of science and reason to achieve a world in which each individual could gain a greater amount of happiness while still contributing to the cultural group to which he belongs. Reason, in Freud's view, could reinforce Eros in its battle with Thanatos so that it at least wins some important battles, even if it is doomed to lose the war.

Toward an Evaluation of Freud Freud is one of the most influential writers of our time. His method of psychoanalysis has been adopted, in whole or in part, by physicians in their treatment of the mentally ill. Of even greater importance, however, he stands as the scientist who made us aware of the deep-seated drives within us. If Marx made us aware of how much of our thinking was conditioned by the role we played in a capitalist society, Freud made us aware that much of our thinking was but rationalization, that is, finding socially acceptable excuses for our actions. According to Freud, our deep-seated sexual and aggressive drives found expression in one way or another, although civilization had done its best to repress or sublimate them. Any one who reads Freud will find it difficult to maintain an extremely optimistic opinion concerning the role which reason can play in his own life, although it is possible for one to exert more rational control over these irrational forces if one learns to recognize them.

It cannot be doubted that Freud's investigation of the sexual basis of the neuroses of many of his patients and his theories concerning the harmful effects of sexual repression have played a large part in helping to liberalize the sexual attitudes of most people in our society. At least, sexual matters are considered fit subjects for discussion, and increasingly people are becoming more understanding of those who indulge in sexual practices which are still often legally prohibited. The sexual revolution is undoubtedly one effect of the popularization of Freud. The reader should recall, however, that it is a vulgarization of Freud's views which sanctions complete sexual freedom. Freud took pains to point out that civilization can progress only at the price of some restrictions upon one's sexual life. What he was after was a more rational handling of sexual matters, rather than a complete libertinism.

One of the criticisms frequently leveled at Freud's work by psychologists is that he was not truly scientific in his methods. He relied, it is often charged, on the insights he obtained in treating his patients for a theory concerning human nature. These patients were abnormal; they had failed in one way or another to realize themselves as complete men and women. Should one take seriously Freud's application of his studies of abnormal people to the psychology of normal people? This objection is usually met by psychoanalysts with the comment that abnormality is a matter of degree and that even the so-called normal person has mental quirks which are at least partially neurotic. The claim is that by studying the mentally sick man, in whom his eccentricities are heightened to the point where he has difficulty in adjusting to others in his society, we may learn about our own irrational drives and motives and, thus, be better able to achieve mental stability in our own lives. Nevertheless, it remains an open question as to the degree of distortion which Freud's theory involves because of its great reliance upon the study of abnormal persons.

The objection that Freud tended to generalize on the basis of insufficient evidence gains greater force when one investigates his writings on religion, morality and civilization. His explanations of the origin of morality and religion, which we have examined, are most charitably described as "scientific myths." Contemporary anthropologists, such as Ruth Benedict and Margaret Mead, do not find that the Oedipus complex is universal, but rather that it appears only in cultures which are predominantly patriarchal. Even more damaging to Freud's theories was his reliance upon racial memory in each child, an assumption which has been discredited by most social scientists. In fairness to Freud, one should point out that he did at times stress that he was only constructing a likely story to account for the origins of morality and religion. Nevertheless, Freud tended to proceed as though his likely story had become a proved scientific theory which discredited religion as an infantile regression.

Another weakness which many critics have found in Freud's theories consists in his too-ready reliance upon innate biological instincts to account for human behavior. The Neo-Freudians, who acknowledge that Freud was basically correct in his stress upon the unconscious motivations of human behavior, reject the idea of innate instincts in favor of basic drives which are modified by the culture in which the individual is reared. In fact, many writers reject Freud's description of mental behavior in terms of the id, ego and super-ego as an account which has more affinities to biological structure than to mental activity. Although Freud claimed that he was presenting a dynamic theory of the mind, it is difficult in terms of his theory not to think of the mind as a three-storied structure. To the layman, however, the terms id, ego, and super-ego have become part of his vocabulary with which he interprets the actions of others, if not always of himself. In justness to Freud, he himself asked that this description not be taken too literally, but rather be used as an explanatory device to account for the apparently irrational conflicts in all men.

A general criticism against Freud's position usually claims that he paid too little attention to the social environment in his study of man. He failed to see that man is a plastic creature who can be modified by his culture, rather than a biological being with fixed instinctual drives which can at best be sublimated or repressed by culture. Freud had himself suffered because he was a Jew in a predominantly hostile gentile environment, and because he dared to discuss man as a sexual animal in an age which had chosen to ignore this aspect of human nature. His own description of man's lack of love for his neighbors and of his inherent aggressiveness presents a good case for the kind of inhumane treatment that Freud himself had to put up with. The neighbor, he said, is:

> Someone who tempts them to satisfy their aggressiveness on him, to exploit his capacity for work without compensation, to use him sexually without his consent, to seize his possessions, to humiliate him, to cause him pain, to torture and to kill him. *Homo homini lupus.* [Man is a wolf to man.] Who, in the face of all his experience of life and of history, will have the courage to dispute this assertion? [31]

Neo-Freudians, as well as Christian moralists, have disputed this assertion. They have not denied that frequently men have treated each other as though they were acting like wolves, but they have also stressed that man has, if rarely, risen to the heights of love and human kindness to his fellows. Erich Fromm, among others, unhesitatingly rejects Freud's belief in an innate aggressive instinct. Fromm claims that contemporary Western man has been culturally conditioned to be aggressive since the ideal of his society is to get ahead by triumphing over others. For Fromm, the drive to destructiveness is not part of the inherent psychological make-up of man, but is a cultural trait which can be changed.

Many of the adverse criticisms against Freud claim that he tried to do too much. He should have remained, it is claimed, a psychoanalyst dealing with his own patients and trying to refine this method of therapy for the mentally ill. As we have seen, however, Freud claimed that after the First World War he returned to the problems which were his greatest concern, the problems of society. He tried to apply the insights he had acquired from psychoanalysis onto the broad arena of man in Western civilization. While his theories concerning morality, religion and culture often go beyond the facts, nevertheless, Freud stands as a human being who was concerned about the basic issues of his day. Anyone who deals with the "big issues" cannot help going beyond his technical sphere of competence. Instead of simply rejecting Freud's conclusions concerning morality and religion, it would be far better to see in him a moralist who was honestly trying to come to grips with the issues of life or death, peace or war. He was a seeker after wisdom who was not willing to be restricted by a narrowly circumscribed sphere within his medical specialty. Freud belongs in the tradition of those humanists who have maintained that self-knowledge is basic to human betterment. Despite his own protests to the contrary, Freud was a philosopher seeking to construct a coherent world-view for contemporary man.

The most significant criticisms of Freud's theories came from within the psychoanalytic movement itself. Freud attempted in an authoritarian manner to keep the movement orthodox, with the result that two of his early associates who disagreed with him formed their own schools of psychoanalysis. Alfred Adler, as early as 1910, objected to Freud's emphasis upon sexuality as the basis of neuroses and proposed instead that all men were motivated by a drive for power. Individuals developed inferiority complexes when they found that they could not fulfill their desires for superiority over others. Adler described the attitudes which a child developed in its struggle for power as a "life style" which became determinative for his actions when he became an adult. Thus, for Adler, it was not sexual conflicts but inadequate life styles which caused neuroses. As a consequence, Adler placed far more emphasis upon the ego in his system than did Freud, for it was the ego which had to wage a successful battle to recover its needed sense of superiority.

Carl Jung, another of the early colleagues of Freud, also departed from Freud by playing down the role of sexual conflicts and childhood experiences in favor of studying the present conflicts of the patient. Jung is best known by the layman for his division of men into introverts and extroverts. Even more than Freud, he relied upon racial memory and constructed elaborate theories to account for a collective unconscious in which the individual is related to the entire history of the human race. An unequal development of the various conscious and unconscious psychic aspects of a man are the cause of neurosis in Jung's theory.

The deviations of Adler and Jung from Freud were basically concerning the theoretical causes of mental illness. The Neo-Freudians, as they are usually called, while acknowledging the great significance of Freud's findings, point out that his theories described the nature of man in only one kind of society. Man's behavior, they held, was more determined by social factors than by his biological nature. Otto Rank, Erich Fromm, Karen Horney, Abram Kardiner, and H. S. Sullivan all turned to the investigation of the individual in the particular society in which he lived. For these psychoanalysts a study of the prevailing culture and its influence upon the disturbed individual was the key to mental health which Freud had failed to use.

Most of the Neo-Freudians, however, did not question the wisdom of adjusting the individual to live more peacefully with his fellow men; they did not ask whether or not society itself should be changed. Herbert Marcuse in *Eros and Civilization* has pointed out a fundamental discrepency between Freudian theory and therapy: "while psychoanalytic theory recognizes that the sickness of the individual is ultimately caused and sustained by the sickness of his civilization, psychoanalytic therapy aims at curing the individual so that he can continue to function as part of a sick civilization without surrendering to it altogether." [32] Freud himself had suggested in *Civilization and Its Discontents* that whole cultures might in the course of development have become neurotic. He recognized the difficulty of making such a diagnosis from within a particular culture, but stated that "we may expect that one day someone will venture to embark upon a pathology of cultural communities." [33] Erich Fromm has accepted this challenge, and in the next section we shall examine in some detail his criticisms of our "sick society" as well as his proposals for a better way of life for mankind.

Erich Fromm: Normative Humanism   Fromm, although he is sometimes called a Neo-Freudian, really represents a "third force" within the ranks of psychoanalysts. A significant number of contemporary psychologists, such as Gordon Allport, Rollo May, Carl Rogers, and Abraham Maslow, have presented plausible alternatives to the traditional Freudian psychology. We shall examine Fromm's position as an example of the attempts which have been made by some behavioral scientists to pass beyond the neutrality of cultural relativism to a basic normative commitment to the "humaneness" of man. Fromm will prove to be a good exemplar of this new approach, especially since he acknowledges that he is as indebted to the teachings of Karl Marx as he is to those of Sigmund Freud. Before we look at his specific worldview, which he calls normative humanism, it may help us to gain perspective if we indicate his basic disagreements with Freud.

Fromm agrees with the other "third force" psychologists in rejecting Freud's instinct theories. An example will show to what extent he has done so. Freud's view that the libido is a quantity of force led him to say that when an individual is in love he loses libido by his attachment to another person; hence some men justify themselves in retaining their strength by loving only themselves (narcissism). In opposition to this view Fromm holds that one is enriched rather than exhausted by loving another, and actually that one cannot love himself if he is incapable of loving others. Love is inexhaustible for Fromm, and not, as for Freud, a fixed biological quantity which can be easily depleted.

One of the principal criticisms that Fromm makes of Freud is that the strivings of man cannot be adequately explained in terms of the sex and death instincts. Nor does he agree with Freud that man is fundamentally antisocial. He accuses Freud of overstating the case for the destructive aspects of man's nature. As a matter of fact Fromm claims that the opposite phenomenon is at work in his patients. He is impressed by the creative and productive impulses in man, and finds tremendous strivings for happiness and health in all of his patients. To cure a patient is to remove the barriers which block the effectiveness of these healthful strivings. Neurosis, on the other hand, is due to the irrational pressures exerted upon an individual by our prevailing non-productive culture.

We should recall that the Neo-Freudians all reacted against Freud's exclusive emphasis upon biological instincts as a falsification of the relationship of man to his society. Fromm agrees with the Neo-Freudians that although hunger and sex are common human needs growing out of physiological demands, man's characteristics, his thoughts, acts and personality are products of culture, starting with the interaction of child and parent in a home situation set largely by society. Many of the Neo-Freudians, such as Kardiner and Sullivan, regard man as molded by the family and other social institutions. Fromm, however, tends to stress the individual's response to his society as one in which individuals can change society rather than be molded by it. We shall see that in his view our present society is sick, so that to adjust one to this society, would not really be restoring him to mental health. Fromm does not shrink from making value judgments, for to him the real business of psychology is to show man how he ought to live in order to realize his basic human nature.

Fromm's first popular book was *Escape from Freedom* (published in 1941), in which he tried to diagnose the plight of modern man in both democratic and totalitarian lands. He tried to show how man had emerged in history from a necessary dependence upon the group for survival to his ambiguous freedom in the contemporary world. The freedom which modern man finds available to him is startling and unnerving in so far as he is compelled to act for himself, to think, to regard himself as a person separate from nature and his social group, and is faced with the threat of loneliness, helplessness and insecurity. Modern man is therefore tempted to escape from freedom, either in obedience to some authoritarian power or by "automaton conformity" to the customs of his democratic social group. The sense of responsibility for making one's own decisions is avoided by following the leader, or by conforming with whatever "one does" in a crowd.

In his later books Fromm has sought to give positive suggestions for

helping modern man come of age in our world. His best book in presenting a humanistic world-view is *Man for Himself* (published in 1947).
We shall examine the position which he presents in this book in some
detail, and indicate changes or developments in his position which he has
presented in his later writings.

Two things should be said about Fromm's position before we examine
it in detail. In the first place, he attempts to set forth an ethics that is
truly humanistic—it seeks to show man how he can be *for* himself.
Here again the difference between Freud and Fromm appears. Where
Freud emphasized the id, Fromm stresses the ego. That is to say, Fromm
asserts that man's life is not necessarily controlled by irrational impulses,
but is capable, rather, of rational direction. This, Fromm reminds us,
was the great insight of all humanistic systems of ethics in the past. Plato,
Aristotle, Spinoza, and more recently, John Dewey have all insisted that
man can use reason to guide his impulses in the directions in which they
can be most usefully satisfied. Fromm agrees with the classical humanists
that man has a basic essence, a basic nature, which can best be described
as rational. In the second place, Fromm aims to discover valid norms for
human behavior. He does not shrink from speaking of his search for a
normative ethics based on a knowledge of man's nature. Clearly, Fromm
does not want to be mistaken for a relativist.

Let us see now in some detail how Fromm proposes to set up an
objective ethics which will do justice both to the classical systems of
humanistic ethics and to the insights of modern psychoanalysis.

Modern man is full of pride, and justifiably so, for he has created a
unique state of material well-being, while at the same time conquering
many of those aspects of nature which are dangerous to him. Yet, man
is uneasy. He feels powerless as an individual in a vast society; he has
become the slave of the machines which he has created; and he is ignorant
with respect to the meaning and nature of his life here on earth. He has
gained "freedom from" but as a rule not "freedom to" develop as
an individual. Instead of facing squarely up to these problems modern
man has retreated to the belief that he is incapable of finding solutions
to them because he is insignificant in the universe. And with man's
retreat from these problems he has accepted relativism: the belief that
all value judgments are a matter of taste, and therefore quite as arbitrary
as a decision regarding whether to eat steak or chicken.

It is usually thought by modern man that he must choose between an
arbitrary subjective relativism or an objective authoritarian system of
values. Since many men want something affirmative in which they can
believe, they tend to seek refuge in one authoritarian system or another,
whether it be that of a church or of a political group. This may seem
to be an easy solution to man's dilemma, for now all he must do is obey
the authority. If he does as the authority says, then he is rewarded, while
if he disobeys the authority he is punished. But this, as Fromm sees it, is

to act like a child in the presence of its parents; it is not fully mature. The vicious aspect of most authoritarian systems, Fromm points out, is that they are devoted to their own interests and are not primarily concerned with the welfare of their subjects. The authority is all powerful; and if not all-knowing, it at least claims to know more than any of its subjects. The main virtue stressed in any authoritarian system is obedience, while the great vice is disobedience to the authority. Perhaps the reason for the return to authoritarianism in the modern world (whether it be to the authoritarian churches or to totalitarian theories of government) is that the authority compensates for the individual's feeling of weakness and inferiority.

On the other hand, Fromm finds that a subjective relativism is deeply dissatisfying to its adherents. Man craves for some meaning in life beyond his own tastes of the moment. There is still another way out, however; it is a third way, the one which Fromm expounds, the way of a humanistic ethics. Humanism maintains that man himself can determine the criteria for virtue and vice. It is not what the authority desires that is actually good, but rather what is good for man. Conversely, what is detrimental to man is evil. Fromm's humanism agrees with that advocated by the classical philosophers who maintained that there is nothing higher than human existence. However, the point which Fromm wishes to stress is that normative humanism is not just another form of subjectivism, but rather it is actually an objective morality. Just as the art of painting is an application of the sciences of painting, so Fromm maintains that the art of living can be based upon the scientific study of man.

> Humanistic ethics, for which "good" is synonymous with good for man and "bad" with bad for man, proposes that in order to know *what* is good for man we have to know his nature. *Humanistic ethics is the applied science of the "art of living" based upon the theoretical "science of man."* [34]

Unfortunately, man has studied very carefully all of the sciences and techniques except those connected with living a productive life. Before an applied science of ethics is possible a theoretical science of man is a necessity. At this point Fromm is in complete agreement with John Dewey, who maintained that before we can determine with accuracy what man's ideals ought to be, we must first know what man is.

We should emphasize again that Fromm does not maintain that man's ethical conflicts can satisfactorily be resolved by a mere adjustment to our prevailing culture, for this might cripple man rather than help him to realize himself. If a particular cultural pattern interferes with man, as he is and can be, then the pattern should be changed.

> He [man] can adapt himself to almost any culture pattern, but in so far as these are contradictory to his nature he develops mental

and emotional disturbances which force him eventually to change these conditions since he can not change his nature.[35]

Human Nature which is the subject of the science of man, for Fromm, is actually a theoretical construction based upon the observation of the behavior of individuals in specific social settings. Fortunately he finds that there are two main types of sources available for this inquiry into man's nature: (1) the findings of the biological and social sciences, and (2) the classics of literature and philosophy which portray human nature through the writers' understanding of life. In fact, Fromm finds that in many respects the great writers of the past correctly understood human nature; contemporary social science is really not adding much that is new to this understanding, but it is placing it upon a secure empirical basis.

Fromm tries to dissociate his view of humanism from that of the naive optimism of the nineteenth-century humanists by his insistence that the human condition always contains some ambiguities which cannot be overcome by historical change. Man is the only creature who can be bored and discontented. Man's search for new solutions to his problems is not the result of an innate drive toward progress; it is true of him rather, that "having lost paradise, the unity with nature, he has become the eternal wanderer (Odysseus, Oedipus, Abraham, Faust); he is impelled to go forward and with everlasting effort to make the unknown known by filling in with answers the blank spaces of his knowledge." [36]

Some of these basic problems of man are rooted in the nature of human existence; it is these which Fromm calls "existential dichotomies." These contradictions man can not eliminate, but he can react to them in various ways. The most fundamental existential dichotomies are: (1) the conflict between life and death; (2) the conflict between man's long-range visions and his short life; and (3) the realization that he is alone (he is an individual) and yet he must be related to others (he must dwell in society). All of man's religions, his ideologies, his philosophies, have sought to come to grips with these basic problems of human existence. Man's mind seeks answers to these contradictions.

> He [man] can appease his mind by soothing and harmonizing ideologies. He can try to escape from his inner restlessness by ceaseless activity in pleasure or business. He can try to abrogate his freedom and to turn himself into an instrument of powers outside himself, submerging his self in them. But he remains dissatisfied, anxious, and restless.[37]

It is at this point that Fromm introduces the solution of humanism to this basic perplexity of man.

> There is only one solution to his [man's] problem: to face the truth, to acknowledge his fundamental aloneness and solitude in a universe indifferent to his fate, to recognize that there is no power transcend-

ing him which can solve his problem for him. . . . If he faces the truth without panic he will recognize that *there is no meaning to life except the meaning man gives his life by the unfolding of his powers, by living productively.*[38]

Fromm stresses that this need of man to account for his existence, to find meaning in life, cannot be explained purely in mechanistic terms. Man attempts to construct a world-view (a philosophy) from which, as a frame of reference, "he can derive an answer to the question of where he stands and what he ought to do." [39] An intellectual solution is never enough; he must also become devoted to the aims and ideals suggested by such a solution, so that he will act creatively. Since man's craving for meaning in his life requires an emotional as well as an intellectual commitment, Fromm describes man's search as for a "frame of orientation and devotion." [40]

Acknowledging that each man must have a "frame of orientation and devotion," the question remains, "Which frame?" There are numerous competing ideologies, some of which are theistic and some of which are non-theistic. The mature person, in choosing between competing ideologies, will choose one which permits him to be "mature, productive and rational." [41] In this sense, all men are idealists, and they differ only in the nature of the ideals to which they give themselves. The Marxist gives his life to the "classless society" with as much devotion as a Christian gives his life to God. In judging between these systems, Fromm suggests that we must decide with respect to (a) their truth, (b) the extent to which they unfold man's powers, and (c) the degree to which they answer man's need for meaning.

Although the existential dichotomies are insoluble, the historical dichotomies which plague man are not eternal; as man-made problems, they are capable of solution. Quite often people have confused existential with historical dichotomies, so that in times past some men refused to strive for the abolition of slavery on the grounds that this institution was based on an eternal law of nature. Today the contradiction between the abundance of technical advances and the incapacity to use these for the peace and welfare of people is soluble. This problem is based on man's lack of wisdom and is not rooted in the nature of human existence. For Fromm, therefore, one must be careful not to mistake a problem which can be solved in history with those growing out of eternal characteristics of human nature.

Non-Productive Character Orientations   Character provides a basis for ethical judgment, according to Fromm; and one of his unique accomplishments is to sketch the various character types of Western civilization. He finds that there are five *non-productive* types of character orientation as follows: (1) the receptive,

(2) the exploitative, (3) the hoarding, (4) the marketing, and (5) the necrophilic. Admitting that few persons are of any one pure type, he does find that under certain cultural conditions individuals tend to be dominated by one of these non-productive types; or, if they are healthy, mature individuals, by the *productive* type. Let us look more closely at each of these character types.

(1) The receptive orientation is characterized primarily by a feeling on the individual's part that everything of value comes from outside himself, and therefore he is the receiver of whatever these values may be—love, pleasure, knowledge, or some material object. In religion people with the receptive orientation seek for a "magic helper" in their problems, and they are dependent upon people in general for support. When they are alone, they feel lost, because they cannot do anything without help.

Although we have said that Fromm departs from Freud in his characterology, he does find that this receptive group closely approximates the group which Freud called the "oral" personalities. They tend to overcome their anxieties by eating or drinking. In general, these receptive people are optimistic and friendly, but they become anxious if their "source of supply" is threatened.

In his more recent writings Fromm has noted that a great many people in contemporary America seem to fit in with a receptive orientation. Especially in his use of leisure time does Fromm find that modern man is completely passive and receptive. As Fromm puts it: "He [modern man] is the eternal consumer; he 'takes in' drink, food, cigarettes, lectures, sights, books, movies; all are consumed, swallowed. The world is one great object for his appetite: a big bottle, a big apple, a big breast." [42]

(2) In the exploitative orientation the individual also feels that all things of value come from outside the self, but instead of being content to receive these things as gifts he tends to take them away from others by cunning or force. Those objects which another person possesses are to him the most desirable. His motto is " 'Stolen fruits are sweetest.' " [43]

This character orientation also has certain similarities to Freud's oral personalities, for they are characterized by the biting mouth. They often make sarcastic remarks about others; they are filled with envy, jealousy and suspicion.

Above all, people who are dominated by an exploitative character orientation are as unproductive as those dominated by the receptive orientation. The big difference between the two types is that while the receptive are willing to be passive receivers from others, the exploitative believe that others will not give to them and that therefore they must take what they want.

(3) The person with the hoarding orientation finds his security in keeping what he already possesses. He finds little new which he wants

outside of himself, and he is reluctant to spend what he has. The miser perfectly represents this attitude, since he seeks to store away his savings in some safe place where no one can possibly get at them. In their relations with others people with this orientation possess the other person, so that even love becomes a relationship in which the beloved is securely possessed by the lover.

The hoarding orientation resembles to some extent Freud's "anal" personality, whose aim is to retain all things within the person. These people have tight-lipped mouths; they are orderly to the point of being ridiculous, and are extremely conscious of the importance of punctuality. They seem to feel that they have only limited amounts of energy and are reluctant to expend it lest it be too rapidly diminished. They tend to be suspicious of outsiders, and consider intimacy a threat to their security.

Nineteenth-century capitalism tended to encourage the development of hoarding personalities with its emphasis upon the virtues of saving money and of keeping for oneself whatever profits one could acquire in free enterprise. Today Fromm finds that this character type tends to be predominant only among members of the lower middle-class, more so in Europe than in America. The growth of twentieth-century American capitalism has made virtues of debt, of consumer loans, of time-payment plans, and of sociability, so that little comfort is given in our society to individuals with a hoarding orientation.

(4) Fromm considers the marketing orientation as the prevailing one in the mid-twentieth century. It is a relatively new one in history, and therefore has no definite affinity with Freud's characterology. Fromm recognizes, however, that this type of life orientation is very similar to Marx's description of alienation in a capitalist society. In the first markets, the purchaser knew the man from whom he was buying, so that retailing involved a personal relationship built on honesty and faithfulness. Today, the entire industrial system, as well as the marketing system, is impersonal. One produces for a market, and not for a particular person. Naturally, when the concept of value as exchange value (a thing is worth what it can command in the market) grew, persons began to be valued for their exchange utility. It became important to have the kind of "personality" which others would hire. One is hired because he can sell himself in the market. He does the right things, belongs to the right clubs, and has his children in the right private schools. The fashions change in the personality market, and one must change with the fashions if he wishes to be in demand. The valuable person thus becomes the person who is successful, in the sense that he has persuaded those who hire him that he is just right for the job because he possesses the needed "personality" and has the desired "contacts."

The reader, if he desires a good illustration of Fromm's point, may recall that the marketing personality, although it is not called that, dominates Willy Loman in Arthur Miller's *Death of a Salesman*. There was a time when Willy was a successful salesman; he knew all the buyers and they liked him and bought from him. But now at middle age his exchange value has diminished; he can no longer make the sales which he used to make. His life reaches a dead end. His favorite son, Biff, did not succeed in athletics and school. Moreover, Willy is fired from a job he held for many years because "times have changed" and he is no longer "in demand" as a salesman. The implication of the play seems to be that he has sold his personality and become simply an article which the sales market discards when it is outmoded.

Another illustration of this marketing orientation is presented in John Marquand's novel *The Point of No Return*. The hero in this work is more successful than Willy Loman, for he does become vice-president of the bank. The price which he pays, however, is giving up life in the little country town in which he was born for a life of social climbing in order that he can make more and more money. He has a house in the country, he throws cocktail parties, his children are in private schools, he drives a "big" car—but, and this is the point, he has become so enmeshed in the pursuit of success that he doesn't really enjoy any of these things. He wants to live as a creative individual, but the tragedy is that he has reached the point of no return.

Fromm suggests, indeed, that the marketing orientation has invaded the colleges, insofar as students are interested only in specialized knowledge, because this type of knowledge is in demand, and do not show much interest in courses which are not immediately useful.

> Knowledge of man himself, psychology, which in the great tradition of Western thought was held to be the condition for virtue, for right living, for happiness, has degenerated into an instrument to be used for better manipulation of others and oneself, in market research, in political propaganda, in advertising, and so on.[44]

> Students are supposed to learn so many things that they have hardly time and energy left to *think*. Not the interest in the subjects taught or in knowledge and insight as such, but the enhanced exchange value knowledge gives is the main incentive for wanting more and better education.[45]

Actually, the marketing orientation differs from the other three nonproductive orientations in the sense that while each of the latter represents some one quality of character as dominant, the marketing orientation represents no one particular quality but rather an emptiness that can be filled by whatever the market demands at the moment. If respectability is desired by the market, one seeks to *look* respectable, and whether he actually *is* respectable is not considered any one's concern.

The premise of the marketing orientation is emptiness, the lack of any specific quality which could not be subject to change, since any persistent trait of character might conflict some day with the requirements of the market.[46]

The marketing personality is in Marx's terms alienated from the products of his labor, from his fellow men and from himself as a real human being. Fromm suggests that this type of man is in danger of losing his uniqueness as an individual and becoming a mere robot.

(5) During the last few years Fromm has proposed a fifth nonproductive type of character orientation: the necrophilic. This orientation is present in those people who love death more than life, who are fascinated by the mechanical rather than by the organic, and who secretly long to return to the original inorganic state from which they emerged when they were born. Fromm has in terms of this character orientation made his peace with Freud's death wish. He now agrees with Freud that the most fundamental polarity in man is between the desire for life and the desire for death, but he denies that both are biologically given tendencies in man. Instead, Fromm considers necrophilia to be a pathological phenomenon, the only real perversion, arising in contemporary men whose strivings for life fulfillment have been blocked.

It is clear that Fromm has become more concerned with the threat of nuclear annihilation of the human race, and disturbed by the failure of man to do anything really constructive to prevent its occurrence. Those of us who gaily go about our business seeking more and better gadgets, while also treating our fellow human beings as things, are already partly in the grips of necrophilia, according to Fromm. Likewise an excessive concern with law and order, with using force, with justice which pays no attention to the persons involved, are further traits of this nonproductive orientation. These individuals believe that a button can be pushed to turn on love, happiness, and even the destruction of their enemies. These persons have fallen in love with the opposite of life and have been seduced by the mechanical, the inorganic, the inhumane—they are necrophilic.

As exemplars of the pure type of necrophilic orientation Fromm cites Hitler, Stalin and Eichmann. His description of Eichmann may help the reader to form a clearer picture of this character orientation in its extreme phase:

Eichmann was fascinated by order and death. His supreme values were obedience and the proper functioning of the organization. He transported Jews as he would have transported coal. That they were human beings was hardly within the field of his vision; hence, even the problem of his having hated or not hated his victims is irrelevant. He was the perfect bureaucrat who had transformed all life into the administration of things.[47]

The Productive Character   A sixth kind of orientation Fromm considers
                              radically different from the preceding types,
for it is, in contrast to the others, a productive orientation. To go back
to Freud for a moment, the mature personality is in Freud's terminology
the genital character, but Freud neglected to describe it beyond saying
that this character structure was one which permitted the individual
to function well socially and sexually. Fromm is concerned with defining
carefully the traits of a mature productive personality.

The productive man, Fromm says, realizes his potentialities and becomes a creator instead of being a mere automaton who submits to
authority, or a creature ruled by his irrational passions. The truly productive man creates himself, in a very real way. There is nothing new in this
idea; the existentialists make it their cardinal principle; but many centuries
ago Aristotle was also interested in the self-realization of man, that is,
in man's developing those potentialities which mark him off as more than
an animal. Fromm refers to the classics of literature for illustrations of
the productive character. Thus, Goethe's *Faust* makes its central character
the symbol of man's search for meaning in life. As Mephistopheles introduces the aging professor of philosophy, Faust, to the pleasures of
the senses, the latter is as disillusioned by these as he was previously
cynical about the possibilities of knowledge. Faust is saved at the end of
Part II by becoming productive, a change which is symbolized by his
winning back tillable land from the sea. Faust has learned the lesson that
*"He only earns his freedom and existence, Who daily conquers them
anew."* [48] Faust is thus redeemed—he is not any longer an unproductive
individual.

The productive character as described by Fromm is marked by productive love and thinking. Genuine love is characterized by care, responsibility, respect, and knowledge. One must labor for that which he loves,
so that actions and the attitude of love are actually inseparable. Really to
love a person is to care for him, to respect his potentialities and himself,
and to feel responsible for his growth especially in the self-realization of
his powers. The other basic pole of the mature character is the ability to
use intelligence in objective reasoning. The productive person uses intelligence as a tool for attaining his goals in life. He is able to see objects
as they actually are, and not as he would wish them to be. Furthermore,
he has the ability to see the totality of a situation and to penetrate beneath
the surface to the heart of the matter.

Actually the mature person is able to find a balance between being
alone and being with others, between thinking and doing, between loving
and being loved, between work and worship. If any one of these elements
is stressed to the neglect of the other, maturity is not reached. One must
be active but he must also be able to profit by moments of quiet. In
short, the productive character strikes a proper balance between work,

love, and reason, neither over-stressing nor neglecting any one of these components of mature living. Such a person is not selfishly interested in accumulating possessions; he is interested, rather, in realizing his potentialities, at the same time that he is striving for the harmonious development of others. The joys of life for him far outweigh any desire to be destructive.

The degree to which a man has achieved a productive orientation toward life will be reflected, according to Fromm, in his conscience. If he is still under the control of an authoritarian conscience which punishes him with guilt feelings for disobeying the internalized voice of authority, he has not achieved a productive existence. In his analysis of the typical authoritarian conscience Fromm is in essential agreement with Freud. He views it as an irrational internalized acceptance of what his society tells him he ought to do in order to be acceptable to it. The productive man, however, is not a man without a conscience, but rather is a person who is possessed of a humanistic conscience which evaluates actions as good which tend toward the unfolding of human personality, while it condemns as bad any actions which are injurious to human personality. Fromm describes the humanistic conscience as follows:

> Humanistic conscience is the reaction of our total personality to its proper functioning or dysfunctioning. . . . Conscience judges our functioning as human beings; it is (as the root of the word *con-scientia* indicates) *knowledge within oneself*, knowledge of our respective success or failure in the art of living.[49]

Conscience, in its humanistic sense, is the voice of our true selves calling us to live productive lives.

Modern man rarely hears his humanistic conscience for the simple reason that he does not allow himself the time to be alone with himself. It has to operate, therefore, in indirect fashion through vague feelings of anxiety and fear. In agreement with Freud, Fromm also recognizes that the dream may be the only outlet for our humanistic conscience, but unfortunately when we wake up we get so busy that we do not attempt to understand what the dream was trying to tell us.

Our discussion has perhaps overlooked one significant point which Fromm stresses, namely, that each person's conscience is somewhat of a unique mixture of authoritarian and humanistic elements. Indeed, the specific norms recommended by the authoritarian and humanistic consciences may be the same, the difference lying in their source. The moral commands not to kill, not to hate, and not to steal are norms of both authoritarian and humanistic ethics. Fromm agrees with Julian Huxley that in our culture the authoritarian conscience precedes the development of the humanistic conscience, just as babyhood precedes maturity, but he expresses his opinion that this need not necessarily be the case. Although admitting he cannot prove it, he believes that in a non-authoritarian society it would not be necessary for an authoritarian conscience to exist as a precondition for the formation of a humanistic conscience.

The humanistic conscience, although the voice of our true selves evaluating our lives, is not free from cultural influences. We appropriate the humanistic norms which have been developed by the great moralists of the past and on this basis seek to determine the degree to which we are achieving our potentialities for human fulfillment. The essential difference between a humanistic and an authoritarian conscience is that the former does not accept irrational authority of any sort, whether it be religious, political or social. Man, as Fromm stresses over and over again, must be responsible for himself.

Fromm does attempt to give a more specific criterion for determining one's success in achieving a productive life than we have so far stated. It is happiness. One should note with care that happiness is not the goal of life, for Fromm, but rather that it is the most reliable by-product of a creative and productive life. In fact, he differentiates between subjective and objective happiness. The former consists in the subject's individual feelings of satisfaction, while the latter is rooted in objective conditions which have been met in pursuing the art of living. Many neurotic persons believe that they have found pleasure and happiness in their compulsive behavior, but this certainly cannot be considered productive living. Actually neurosis is a moral problem (and here again notice how Fromm has departed from the convictions of Freud), for a neurotic person is one who finds pleasure in that which is actually harmful to him. True objective happiness, on the other hand, is associated with an increase in productive thinking and loving, and with creativity. Happiness in this sense is the main indication that man has found an adequate answer to the problem of his existence. He is full of joy because he has realized to the greatest extent his potentialities, and in so doing has found his true relationship with the world. *"Happiness is the criterion of excellence in the art of living, of virtue in the meaning it has in humanistic ethics."* [50]

With Fromm's constant emphasis upon man being for himself, independently of any authority, it may come as something of a surprise to discover that he stresses faith as an essential character trait of a productive man. The lack of faith he finds to be symptomatic of relativism, of emptiness, and of uncertainty. By one's faith he understands "a character trait which pervades all his experiences, which enables a man to face reality without illusions and yet to live by his faith." [51] No man can avoid having faith of some kind; the question is whether or not he has an adequate, realistic and rational faith. Fromm even finds that the Hebraic-Christian religion has provided an adequate faith for modern man if it is interpreted humanistically. Dogmatic faith in authoritarian figures, however, cannot help but be crippling to man; dogmatic faith is in terms of Fromm's analysis analogous to the authoritarian conscience. Neither are really concerned with man's development of a meaningful concern for his own existence.

The type of faith which Fromm recommends is rational faith based on productive intellectual and emotional activity. This faith must be rooted in one's own experience and in one's confidence to observe and judge its validity. He finds that science itself provides a good model for a rational faith:

> At every step from the conception of a rational vision to the formulation of a theory, *faith* is necessary: faith in the vision as a rationally valid aim to pursue, faith in the hypothesis as a likely and plausible proposition, and faith in the final theory, at least until a general consensus about its validity has been reached. This faith is rooted in one's own experience, in the confidence in one's power of thought, observation, and judgment.[52]

It is not in science alone that faith is needed; faith is needed even more in the realm of personal relationships. Fromm stresses that friendship and love are based upon faith rather than upon facts. But one must also have faith in oneself, if one is not to become a pawn of others. The object of faith, however, cannot reasonably transcend human experience; faith in mankind is therefore the ultimate pinnacle of the kind of faith Fromm recommends. It is this which he means by *Man for Himself.*

A Saner Society Fromm is not only concerned with the development of a theory of humanistic ethics; he also makes significant suggestions for improving the lot of mankind in today's world. As we have already noted, Fromm believes that it is society which is sick, rather than the individuals within it. Or perhaps more accurately, he believes that our present super-capitalist society produces persons who are pressured into adopting marketing and necrophilic life orientations. In fact only if our society is changed so as to encourage creative and productive individuals will modern man be able to find joy and human fulfillment in his own life.

According to Fromm, our insanity is nationalism. Modern man finds his identity within a nation, and looks at members of other nations as strangers. To belong to the biggest and best nation, to have the largest stock pile of atomic weapons, to be the first to reach the moon—these and many other nationalistic desires prevent modern man from becoming devoted to the universal cause of human welfare. As Fromm states it, "Just as love for one individual which excludes the love for others is not love, love for one's country which is not part of one's love for humanity is not love, but idolatrous worship." [53]

What Fromm finds most distressing about man's condition in the modern world is that most men are not even aware of how subtly they are being conditioned into becoming more like robots than like men. Twentieth-century capitalism can thrive only if new commodities are produced and markets found for these products. As consumers we are manipulated even more than we are as workers. We are made to believe that we are free and independent, but the forces of the mass media play upon our desires not to be different, to be in fashion, to conform with a socially respectable image. The rhythm of daily life in our society is: "Produce, consume, enjoy together, in step, without asking questions." [54]

Our very preoccupation with security from the cradle to the grave in a welfare state reveals our fear of individuality. Fromm, like the existentialists, reminds us that life is never ultimately secure and that we cannot have absolute certainty about the future. An individual who dares to think seriously about life will not seek for security, but *"to be able to tolerate insecurity, without panic and undue fear."* [55]

The gap between man's technical use of intelligence to create new weapons and his lack of the human wisdom with which to create satisfactorily an international community is likely to lead to an atomic war. Fromm, like many other contemporary writers, wants to remind us that the stakes in our present crisis may well be the extinction of human civilization. But tinkering reforms will not help. Fromm calls for massive changes which should occur simultaneously in the economic, political, moral and cultural spheres if we are to create a sane society. It would go beyond our purposes here to detail his suggestions. The interested reader will find his program in *The Sane Society*. In general, Fromm recommends that individual men again come to their sense of dignity and importance and use their reason to modify society. In the economic and political systems he advocates providing for greater participation by the workers and the voters in the actual decisions of management and government. His program is an attempt to create a society in which man will no longer be alienated but will be free to become a fully responsible person. Fromm's program is in many respects an American revision of the suggestions of the early Marx, who also sought for a society in which each individual would have an opportunity to become fully human. Only a society which provides for the complete development of individual personality in a community which is pervaded by moral and spiritual values deserves to be called sane. But of more importance for Fromm, only in such a sane society can man really achieve mental health and self-fulfillment.

While Fromm is not overly optimistic that man will come to his senses in time to avert a nuclear holocaust, he does believe that if man learns to be *for himself* in the sense of developing his potentialities, the outcome may be a more productive race of men. As he puts it, the outcome for man is not foreordained; either the salvation or destruction of mankind may be the result.

The decision rests with man. It rests upon his ability to take himself, his life and happiness seriously; on his willingness to face his and his society's moral problem. It rests upon his courage to be himself and to be for himself.[56]

One thing is clear to Fromm. Only if people become more important than things in our society will we be saved from becoming robots or from being destroyed in a nuclear war.

Toward an Evaluation of Fromm There have been other voices in our century saying much the same kind of thing as Fromm. David Riesman, a sociologist, in *The Lonely Crowd* contrasts the other-directed person with the autonomous person in a way which is similar to Fromm's differentiation between the marketing personality and the productive man. William Whyte's *The Organization Man*, Vance Packard's *The Hidden Persuaders*, and Herbert Marcuse's *One-Dimensional Man* all reinforce Fromm's position that modern man is becoming a robot manipulated by mass media. Existential psychiatrists, such as Rollo May and Ludwick Binswanger, reinforce from a perspective of existentialism Fromm's stress upon the importance of the individual person achieving a sense of creative meaningfulness in his life. There seems to be little doubt that Fromm has correctly diagnosed the plight of many people in modern society who seem to be caught up in the pattern of automaton conformity.

Fromm's view concerning the influence of society upon the life values of the individual is generally regarded as a more adequate analysis than Freud's view of the purely repressive function of society. Furthermore, Fromm's rejection of the basic instincts in favor of individual human patterns of adaptation to the environment also seems to be an advance upon Freud's views.

Our evaluation will concentrate upon that aspect of Fromm's thought which he calls normative humanism, because this is his basic position concerning our quest for a value orientation. Most people would gladly accept Fromm's belief that people are to be valued more highly than things, but many would question basing this judgment upon the supposed findings of the social sciences. What is often suggested is that Fromm actually begins with his set of normative presuppositions about what man ought to be like, and then tries to support these judgments by appeal to literary and philosophical classics and the findings of the social sciences.[57] Philosophers have generally maintained that "ought" cannot be derived from "is." That is, a value judgment cannot be derived solely from the facts concerning how human beings behave but must also involve some judgment that this kind of conduct is desirable. Fromm, according to this charge, has not fully realized that he is proposing norms for human behavior, that he is expressing a preference which cannot be derived logically from a study of the facts.[58]

Fromm, at times, deliberately calls his position "normative humanism"; thus implying that he knows that he is proposing a standard for man which is not based merely upon a study of human behavior, but which also maintains that man ought to be the central consideration in any moral decision. It is in this respect that Fromm's view is closely related to classical humanist positions of the past. Not everyone will agree, however, with humanism as a basic value orientation which all men should follow. The religious man, for example, may agree with the stress which Fromm places upon the importance of the individual human being achieving a sense of meaning in his life, while maintaining that humanism itself needs the support of a belief in God if it is to command one's allegiance. The existentialist finds that while the type of position presented by Fromm seems to extoll the individual who must achieve his own self-realization, that indeed the opposite is what results from this kind of humanism. According to the existentialist Fromm errs by proposing a universal norm for all men; if we realize fully the uniqueness of each person we shall then understand that there can be no universal norm for all men.

Fromm's ethical position seems to be a more sophisticated version of the old Greek ideal of a sound mind in a sound body. He holds that all men are alike in their basic human needs, and that by becoming fully productive in all of their relationships men can realize their basic human natures. While it is true that he recognizes that some men will excel more in one area of life than in others, nevertheless, Fromm extolls each person fully developing all aspects of his physical, mental and spiritual nature. But might not this result in a new cult of conformity and mediocrity? Is it not the case that some men, who have made outstanding contributions to Western culture were one-sided, did not fulfill adequately all aspects of their potentialities? Freud, Marx, Van Gogh, Nietzsche and Kierkegaard are not exemplars of the completely productive man in all the aspects which Fromm considers. Yet, in the light of the great contributions which these men made to our culture, who can say that these men ought to have lived differently? The reader no doubt has his own opinions on questions such as these, but the point clearly is that if these questions can be asked sincerely, then Fromm's humanistic ethics does not rest on as secure a foundation as he maintains.

Fromm is at his best in his diagnosis of the plight of modern man. No one can fail to recognize the importance of his attempt to restore more dignity to human life in our complex modern world. In many respects he, as did Marx, sounds like an Old Testament prophet calling man away from the worship of idols. Unfortunately, his proposals for the new man and the new world sound extremely utopian. Only if all aspects of our culture are changed simultaneously, he tells us, can modern man find the possibility of living an independent and meaningful existence. Is it not rather the case that change has proceeded more rapidly in one area of society, with a resultant cultural lag in the other areas? Would not an improvement in our moral attitude toward people bring about political and economic changes later on? Must all these changes occur all at once? Like Marx, Fromm looks forward to a new period of history in which man will leave behind his alienated past. But if he is correct that we are becoming robots, one may ask whether it is possible for robots to rebel. Who will create the new society?

Perhaps our criticisms of Fromm are wide of the mark. He does suggest that very few men, if any, will ever achieve complete productivity in all the aspects of their lives. What his view offers to us is an ideal toward which we can strive. We can seek to become more creative and more humane in our treatment of others. If we do not achieve perfection, at least we are more aware of the dehumanizing tendencies of our society than we were before our study of Fromm. But more than this can be said. Fromm's ideal of a productive person is one which we can seek to fulfill in as many aspects of our lives as possible. For many individuals who cannot accept a traditional authoritarian ethic, Fromm's normative humanism has much to be said for it as a basic value orientation.

NOTES FOR CHAPTER III

1 Sigmund Freud, *The Interpretation of Dreams*, trans. and ed. by James Strachey (New York: Science Editions, John Wiley and Sons, Inc., 1961), p. 608.
2 Sigmund Freud, *An Outline of Psychoanalysis*, trans. and ed. by James Strachey (New York: W. W. Norton & Co., Inc., 1963), p. 14.
3 Sigmund Freud, *New Introductory Lectures on Psychoanalysis*, trans. and ed. by James Strachey (New York: W. W. Norton & Co., Inc., 1965), p. 77.
4 Sigmund Freud, *The Ego and the Id*, trans. by Joan Riviere, rev. and ed. by James Strachey (New York: W. W. Norton & Co., Inc., 1962), p. 38.
5 Freud, *New Introductory Lectures on Psychoanalysis*, pp. 77–78.
6 Sigmund Freud, *A General Introduction to Psychoanalysis*, trans. and ed. by Joan Riviere (New York: Washington Square Press, Inc., 1952), pp. 217–218.
7 *Ibid.*, p. 344.
8 *Ibid.*, pp. 345–346.
9 Freud, *New Introductory Lectures on Psychoanalysis*, p. 110.
10 Sigmund Freud, *Totem and Taboo* in *The Basic Writings of Sigmund Freud*, trans. and ed. by A. A. Brill (New York: The Modern Library, 1938), pp. 876–877.

11 *Ibid.*, p. 915.
12 *Ibid.*, p. 916.
13 *Ibid.*, p. 917.
14 Sigmund Freud, *The Future of an Illusion*, trans. by W. D. Robson-Scott (Garden City, N. Y.: Anchor Books, Doubleday & Co., Inc., 1957), p. 34.
15 *Ibid.*, pp. 77–78.
16 *Ibid.*, pp. 67–68.
17 *Ibid.*, p. 88.
18 Sigmund Freud, *Civilization and Its Discontents*, trans. and ed. by James Strachey (New York: W. W. Norton & Co., Inc., 1962), p. 23.
19 *Ibid.*, p. 24.
20 *Ibid.*, p. 42.
21 *Ibid.*, p. 43.
22 *Ibid.*, p. 90.
23 *Ibid.*, p. 56.
24 *Ibid.*, p. 57.
25 *Ibid.*, p. 92.
26 Freud, *New Introductory Lectures on Psychoanalysis*, p. 80.
27 *Ibid.*, p. 171.
28 Freud, *The Future of an Illusion*, p. 87.
29 Philip Rieff, *Freud: The Mind of the Moralist* (Garden City, N. Y.: Anchor Books, Doubleday & Co., Inc., 1961), ch. IX.
30 Freud, *New Introductory Lectures on Psychoanalysis*, p. 149.
31 Freud, *Civilization and Its Discontents*, p. 58.
32 Herbert Marcuse, *Eros and Civilization: A Philosophical Inquiry into Freud* (New York: Vintage Books, Inc., Random House, 1955), p. 224.
33 Freud, *Civilization and Its Discontents*, p. 91.
34 Erich Fromm, *Man For Himself: An Inquiry into the Psychology of Ethics* (Greenwich, Conn.: Fawcett World Library, 1967), p. 27.
35 *Ibid.*, p. 32.
36 *Ibid.*, p. 50.
37 *Ibid.*, p. 53.
38 *Ibid.*, p. 53.
39 *Ibid.*, p. 55.
40 *Ibid.*, p. 56ff.
41 *Ibid.*, p. 57.
42 Erich Fromm, *The Dogma of Christ and Other Essays on Religion, Psychology and Culture* (New York: Holt, Rinehart & Winston, Inc., 1963), p. 96.
43 Fromm, *Man for Himself*, p. 72.
44 *Ibid.*, p. 83.
45 *Ibid.*, pp. 83–84.
46 *Ibid.*, p. 85.
47 Erich Fromm, "Creators and Destroyers," *Saturday Review*, January 4, 1964, pp. 22–25.
48 Quoted from Goethe's *Faust* in Fromm, *Man for Himself*, p. 100.
49 Fromm, *Man for Himself*, p. 162.
50 *Ibid.*, p. 192.
51 *Ibid.*, p. 201.
52 *Ibid.*, pp. 207–208.
53 Erich Fromm, *The Sane Society* (Greenwich, Conn.: Fawcett World Library, 1965), p. 60.

54 *Ibid.*, p. 102.
55 *Ibid.*, p. 174.
56 Fromm, *Man for Himself*, p. 251.
57 *Cf.* Joseph Margolis, *Psychotherapy and Morality: A Study of Two Concepts* (New York: Random House, 1966), ch. 3.
58 For a more detailed treatment of the naturalistic fallacy see Luther J. Binkley, *Contemporary Ethical Theories* (New York: Philosophical Library, Inc., 1961), pp. 1–25, 132–159; G. E. Moore, *Principia Ethica* (Cambridge, England: Cambridge University Press, 1959), pp. 1–141; R. M. Hare, *The Language of Morals* (Oxford: Clarendon Press, 1952), pp. 79–93, 111–150.

SELECTED READINGS

Available in paperback edition.

*Erikson, Erik H. *Insight and Responsibility: Lectures on the Ethical Implications of Psychoanalytic Insight.* New York: W. W. Norton & Co., Inc., 1964.
Evans, Richard I. *Dialogue with Erich Fromm.* New York: Harper & Row, Publishers, 1966.
Freud, Sigmund. *The Basic Writings of Sigmund Freud: Psychopathology of Everyday Life, The Interpretation of Dreams, Three Contributions to the Theory of Sex, Wit and Its Relation to the Unconscious, Totem and Taboo,* and *The History of the Psychoanalytic Movement.* Translated and edited by A. A. Brill. New York: The Modern Library, 1938.
*———. *Civilization and Its Discontents.* Translated and edited by James Strachey. New York: W. W. Norton & Co., Inc., 1962.
*———. *The Future of an Illusion.* Translated by W. D. Robson-Scott. Revised and edited by James Strachey. Garden City, N. Y.: Anchor Books, Doubleday & Co., Inc., 1957.
*———. *New Introductory Lectures on Psychoanalysis.* Translated and edited by James Strachey. New York: W. W. Norton & Co., Inc., 1965.
*———. *An Outline of Psychoanalysis.* Translated and edited by James Strachey. New York: W. W. Norton & Co., Inc., 1963.
*———. *Psychopathology of Everyday Life.* Translated by A. A. Brill. New York: The New American Library of World Literature, Inc., 1951.
*Fromm, Erich. *The Art of Loving.* New York: Bantam Books, Inc., 1956.
*———. *Escape from Freedom.* New York: An Avon Library Book, 1965.
*———. *The Heart of Man: Its Genius for Good and Evil.* New York: Harper & Row, Publishers, 1964.
*———. *Man for Himself: An Inquiry into the Psychology of Ethics.* Greenwich, Conn.: Fawcett World Library, 1967.
*———. *Psychoanalysis and Religion.* New Haven: Yale University Press, 1950.
*———. *The Sane Society.* Greenwich, Conn.: Fawcett World Library, 1965.

* Marcuse, Herbert. *Eros and Civilization: A Philosophical Inquiry into Freud.* New York: Vintage Books, Inc., Random House, 1955.
* Margolis, Joseph. *Psychotherapy and Morality: A Study of Two Concepts.* New York: Random House, Inc., 1966.
* Rieff, Philip. *Freud: The Mind of the Moralist.* Garden City, N. Y.: Anchor Books, Doubleday & Co., Inc., 1961.
* Schaar, John H. *Escape from Authority: The Perspectives of Erich Fromm.* New York: Harper Torchbooks, 1961.

IV

The Origins of Existentialism: Kierkegaard and Nietzsche

All of the writers whose views we have so far examined agree that there is a basic human nature, although they disagree on precisely what it is. The existentialists, however, maintain that there is no such thing as a basic human nature or essence; each individual is unique and must choose for himself what he wishes to make out of his life. Contrary to the prevailing attitude of British and American philosophers, the existentialists maintain that scientific objectivity is a falsification of human existence. The truth, they claim, lies in subjectivity. The existentialists agree on the importance of inwardness and of individual freedom. Apart from this basic attitude, however, the existentialists are far from being in agreement. Some of them are deeply religious, while others are atheists, or at least naturalists. While they have exerted little influence upon British and American philosophers, they have attracted much interest from theologians and literary figures.

In our age which tends to stress impersonality, science, and the supremacy of the masses, existentialism has had a peculiar fascination, for it asserts, against the prevailing trends, the value of the individual, who must moment by moment make his own decisions in the course of life. This stress upon the inner private values and experiences of the individual as the ultimate reality of human experience was first clearly sounded in the writings of Søren Kierkegaard and Friedrich Nietzsche. While Kierkegaard and Nietzsche are poles apart on many of their ideas, as we shall see, they do agree on the primacy of the individual. It was these two nineteenth-century philosophers who read the signs of their age which pointed toward herd conformity, and protested against it in favor of free choice for the individual. As we examine their philosophies, we shall be amazed at how modern they sound.

Kierkegaard's Life   The founder of existentialism was the Danish writer Søren Kierkegaard (1813–1855). It is somewhat ironical that although Kierkegaard's influence was limited to his native land during his lifetime, he has become a world figure in the twentieth century. Contemporary existentialism, while it often departs from his views, would be almost inconceivable without the pioneering work of Kierkegaard. He addressed his writings to the individual, and much of what he says was meant to create an offense, to irritate the reader into serious reconsideration of his own life. While one may not always agree with Kierkegaard's observations, one ought to be familiar with his position, for clearly he is one of the most influential minds of the modern era. Kierkegaard's philosophy was so closely intertwined with his own life that it will prove helpful for us to look at his life before we examine his philosophy.

Søren Kierkegaard had a rather unusual home life.[1] His mother was his father's second wife. She had been his father's housekeeper for some years before they were married. Although his father was 56 when Søren was born, and completely dominated the child, the boy worshipped him, and was little influenced by the mother. The father, a wealthy retired wool merchant in Copenhagen, had rather orthodox religious views and was sternly pietistic. As Søren grew up he never completely escaped from his father's influence. Clearly his relationship with his father strongly colored his own mature religious position.

Inclined to melancholy, Søren had a secret dread which haunted him all his life. His biographers usually link this secret dread with his concern for his father, who thought that he had committed as a child the unpardonable sin of cursing God. It may be that this fear was communicated to young Søren by his father, although there is some evidence to suggest that something even more shocking occurred to the boy. Some think that Søren caught his father in the act of adultery. For a young man who had worshipped the very ground on which his father walked, this would have' been an earthshaking discovery. Perhaps it was this which Søren referred to in his *Journals* as the Great Earthquake.[2] At any rate, he was afflicted with melancholy and tended to regard life as more a realm of suffering and sin rather than as a place of joy and pleasure.

Søren entered the University of Copenhagen with the intention of preparing for the ministry. He was, however, so annoyed with the subservience to dogma and the superficial rationalistic solutions of preachers and professors that he rebelled at this career. He always reacted violently to sham and shallowness. He turned thereafter to literature, and found quite a career as an author of aesthetic and religious works.

Probably the most important event in his life, and also the one which is the most difficult to understand, was his affair with Regina Olsen, the daughter of a government official in Denmark. Apparently the two were in love with each other; at least, their engagement was announced. But a year after the announcement was made Kierkegaard broke the engagement. This caused much gossip in Copenhagen, most of it critical of Kierkegaard's action. In many of his writings, including *Either/Or*, he refers to the agonizing nature of his decision to break off with the woman whom he still loved. Kierkegaard tells us that he was confronted with the choice of either happiness on earth or godliness, either Regina or God, and after some very serious thinking he decided to choose God. He continued to hope, however, that somehow in an unexpected way God would see fit to restore Regina to him. In this hope he remained a bachelor to the end of his life, although Regina married somebody else.

There were some other incidents of importance in his life. Kierkegaard deliberately provoked the newspaper *Corsair* to attack him. This paper had a thriving circulation due to its policy of publishing rumors and scandals dealing with public figures in Denmark. Kierkegaard did not like being totally ignored by the *Corsair*, but he did not expect the attack he provoked to last so long or to have the effect which it did upon the common people of Copenhagen. He wrote bitter replies to the hints at scandal in his life and the caricatures of his philosophy which appeared in the *Corsair*. He clearly was not pleased with the treatment he began to receive from the public, for he became so well known that even the little children yelled "Either/Or" after him when they saw him in the streets. As far as most of the citizens of Copenhagen were concerned, he was a first-rate scoundrel. Partly because of the harsh treatment accorded him by the newspapers and those who read them, Kierkegaard developed more and more contempt for society. Mass opinion, mass meetings, reminded him of the deer in the deer park (a recreational area on the outskirts of Copenhagen) which stupidly followed whichever one led off.

As Kierkegaard grew older he became increasingly concerned with Christianity. He differentiated between the religion of the Church, which he condemned and ridiculed, and the religion of Christ, which he tried to advocate and follow. The religion of Christ was difficult and, moreover, an extremely private affair, while the official religion of the Danish Church was comfortable, pleasing and public. In airing this thinking Kierkegaard's outspokenness got him into trouble. He could not resist attacking Professor Martensen's eulogy of Bishop Mynster, and in numerous published articles maintained that whatever the dead bishop had been, he was clearly not a witness to the truth of Christ. Mynster had been the pastor of the Kierkegaard family, and Kierkegaard had himself heard many of his sermons. To have said that the late bishop had accommodated Christianity to the materialistic and secular desires of the people, that he had compromised the harsh truths of Christ by means of a suave rationalism—that would have been a true eulogy. But to extoll the bishop as a real follower of the Christ who knew not where to lay his head—that was more than Kierkegaard could stand. For him, to become a real Christian was the most difficult thing in the world, while the Danish Church was falsely making Christianity appear to be easy so that it would be socially acceptable for everybody.

The attack on the church was only part of Kierkegaard's general condemnation of his age. He thoroughly loathed Hegelian philosophy which had constructed a system to explain everything, but which had completely forgotten the personal subjective nature of the individual human being. His life as well as his philosophy was an attempt to stress the primacy of the individual over the masses, to emphasize existence (life as immediately experienced) rather than essence (the characteristics of objects as they appear in cognitive experience).

The existential character of all his writings grew out of his life-long attempt to answer the problem he set for himself in his *Journal* entry of August 1, 1835:

> What I really lack is to be clear in my mind *what I am to do*, not what I am to know, except in so far as a certain understanding must precede every action. The thing is to understand myself, to see what God really wishes *me* to do; the thing is to find a truth which is true *for me*, to find *the idea for which I can live and die*.[3]

Let us turn now to an examination of his writings themselves, for it was in his writings that he explored the alternatives which proposed themselves to him as possible candidates for his own life style.

The Three Stages of Life   One of the most interesting contributions of Kierkegaard was his description of three distinguishable types of life which a man could choose to live. Unfortunately, as he often pointed out, most men fail to choose at all and live only that kind of life which their age tells them is appropriate. Once an individual assumes responsibility for his own life, however, Kierkegaard held that there were at least three main possibilities open to him. He referred to them as "stages on life's way," although he by no means maintained that everyone would finally arrive at the last stage he described. *Either/Or* and *Stages On Life's Way* are the works in which he depicts these three stages as (1) the aesthetic stage, (2) the ethical stage, and (3) the religious stage.

(1) The Aesthetic Stage—While we have come to identify the aesthetic

with beauty and fine art, Kierkegaard used the term in its more basic sense of that which appeals directly and immediately to the senses. In the aesthetic stage of life, then, a man adopts his life strategy so as to find immediate pleasure. The young man "A" with whom much of the first part of *Either/Or* is concerned is just such a man. Appropriately enough, "A" refers to Don Juan as an ideal fictional exemplar of the aesthetic life. Don Juan craved the maximum of pleasure in his relationship with women, and sought to avoid the responsibilities which would come to him if he ever married. But Don Juan is fictional, and "A" seems to realize the difficulties of achieving immediate pleasure in life, although he does find that he can achieve great pleasure in listening to Mozart's *Don Juan.* "A" attempts therefore to turn his life into an art whereby he will be able to have the maximum of enjoyment while minimizing boredom. In order to achieve this goal he must adopt no commitments to others or to principles; he must live for the joy of the moment. He must, as Kierkegaard humorously puts it, practice "the rotation method" by varying his pleasures in much the same way as a wise farmer rotates his crops.

The immediate pleasures and freedom inherent in the aesthetic way of life may satisfy one for awhile, but Kierkegaard fails to find that it can be ultimately satisfying. The sensory pleasures prove to be momentary. The aesthetic man experiences at one time frustration, at another satiety; boredom sets in at last, when all the goods of the pleasurable life have turned to ashes in the mouth. The man who skips lightly from one amusement to another knows nothing of life's depths, and never really penetrates into the ethical or religious aspects of life. The short-sightedness of the aesthetic man excludes from his view the true dimensions of tragedy and morality. One who lives only for the present cannot comprehend the eternal. The aesthetic man, furthermore, is a victim of external circumstances; he is in a sense in the hands of fate. He must be entertained by other things or persons; he does not penetrate into inward subjective experiences. He believes he can be happy if he gets this or that thing, this woman or that gadget, but after achieving it he finds that he is not nearly as happy as he thought he would be. Most of the objects he seeks are fleeting and transitory; even the beautiful young girl turns old and fat. Kierkegaard describes himself as having gone through the aesthetic stage. He knew from his own experience that his pleasures had been momentary, and that the aesthetic man has only a superficial view of life.

At the end of his discussion of the aesthetic stage in *Either/Or* Kierkegaard inserts the "Diary of the Seducer," supposedly the private journal of Johannes, a friend of "A." This Diary reveals the depths of unconcern for other persons to which the aesthetic life can sink, and is largely responsible for "A" beginning to reflect himself out of a purely aesthetic mode of existence. Unlike Don Juan, who took great sensual delight in his exploits with women, Johannes the Seducer takes delight in the art of seduction itself. Johannes describes his method, which took a long time, to captivate so artfully the young girl's mind and personality that in the end she thinks she seduced him. After the seduction, he abandons the girl, for his joy was in the technique not in the sensual conquest. Kierkegaard has here presented the menace of the aesthetic way of life— life itself is lost for the sake of the technique of an art. Here the aesthetic life has been pushed to its extreme limit, and few there are who would not recoil from the cold, calculating inhumanity of Johannes the Seducer.

(2) The Ethical Stage—The ethical man realizes that the search for happiness through entertainment, through beauty, and through external things is doomed to failure. He has become more inward and soul-searching than the aesthetic man, and he gives himself wholly to that which he believes to be right.

Kierkegaard did not believe that reasons could be given which would conclusively show the superiority of the ethical way of life to the aesthetic way. One would have to make a choice without knowing in advance that the ethical would be more ultimately satisfying to one than the aesthetic life. In *Either/Or* the persona "A" is tempted to repudiate the aesthetic because of his despair at finding happiness through immediate pleasurable experiences. Kierkegaard uses a married judge who writes letters to "A" as his prime example of the ethical stage of life. The judge's letters seek to show "A" the far better way, but "A" must in the last analysis choose whether or not he shall attempt to change his mode of living.

The judge seeks to convert "A," the younger aesthetic man, to a life in which he will accept responsibilities to others, a life represented in the judge's case by a stable marriage, as well as by the very office of the judge who must decide difficult cases of law. The categories of good and bad, right and wrong, are held forward as more important for human life than pleasure and pain.

The ethical man, as Kierkegaard described him, is the sort of man Kant would have admired—a man who does his duty according to the principle of acting so that he can will his conduct to become universal. The ethical man stresses the virtues of kindness, honesty, moderation, and love; he realizes that without these virtues life is superficial, cruel, and without meaning. Unlike the aesthetic man who lives from moment to moment, the ethical man realizes that he must make decisions. In dealing with others the ethical man always falls back upon the norms to which he has committed his life and attempts to apply them honestly to the specific circumstances with which he is confronted.

The judge in his advice to "A" encourages him to despair of the life of immediate enjoyment in order that he may be open to the imperative of an ethical life. To make the transition from the aesthetic to the ethical life one must freely repent of his past life and freely choose to seek to do one's duty toward his fellow men in the future. The choice here is not between good and evil, but is more basically the choice to adopt a new set of values—the values of good and evil. To become ethical is to choose a new way of being a man, to accept duties toward others, and to abandon one's selfish preoccupation with one's own immediate gratification. The judge clearly admonishes "A" in this fashion:

> My either/or does not in the first instance denote the choice be-
> tween good and evil; it denotes the choice whereby one chooses good
> *and* evil/or excludes them. Here the question is under what de-
> terminants one would contemplate the whole of existence and would
> himself live. That the man who chooses good and evil chooses the
> good is indeed true, but this becomes evident only afterwards; for
> the aesthetical is not the evil but neutrality, and that is the reason why
> I affirmed that it is the ethical which constitutes the choice.[4]

It is important to bear in mind that Kierkegaard is not listing a specific set of duties which when obeyed constitute the ethical man; for him, that too often constituted the life of the anonymous man lost in the crowd of conformity. Rather, to be an ethical man is to choose to live by the categories of good and evil, to become serious about one's relationships with others, and then in the specific circumstances of one's life to attempt to act in such a way that one's conduct could be universalized. For Kierkegaard, "The ethical is concerned with particular human beings, and with each and every one of them by himself." [5]

Becoming a serious man, that is making one's decisions in terms of good and evil, does not mean that one's life loses all enjoyment. Kierke-gaard remarked that the aesthetical was "dethroned" but not eliminated completely from one's life. In fact, one becomes more or less indifferent to those external factors which were previously so important in the aesthetic stage. It is in this sense that the judge tells "A" that the ethical redeems the aesthetic aspects of life by putting them in their proper place. The ethical man becomes master of himself, thereby achieving a selfhood which had been denied him in the aesthetic stage.

(3) The Religious Stage—There can be no doubt that Kierkegaard con-sidered the religious way of life to be the best way of all. Only by be-coming truly religious can an individual become a full human being. We should stress, however, that Kierkegaard was describing three different kinds of existence, and not at all suggesting that everyone must move through the aesthetic to the ethical and thence to the religious stage. Even more clearly, his descriptions are not meant to represent youth, middle age, and old age. As is the case in all of his writings he is writing for his own edification, as well as for that of his reader. These three

stages of life were possibilities, but in actual existence Kierkegaard did not hesitate to admit that they overlapped. In the first of the three discourses which he published at the same time as *Stages On Life's Way* he proclaimed: "There are many ways which lead to the same truth, and each man takes his own." [6] Of course, the truth to which he was referring was the ultimate truth of becoming a Christian, but he was always careful to point out that there were many ways to arrive at this truth.

Either/Or is concerned largely with contrasting the aesthetic with the ethical way of life. Almost as an after-thought, at the very end of the long book, he has the judge insert a sermon which he had received from a minister in Jutland. This sermon shows the inadequacies of the judge's ethical stage of life, just as the judge had tried to show "A" the inadequacies of the aesthetic life. All the judge's advice about moral responsibility, about choosing to be a moral man, is questioned by the very title of the sermon: "The Edification Implied in the Thought That As Against God We Are Always in the Wrong." [7]

When Kierkegaard returned to the same problem in *Stages On Life's Way* he devoted more than two-thirds of the book to a discussion of the religious way of life. He wanted to make it clear that the highest choice a man could make for a way of life was not the ethical but the religious. In the *Concluding Unscientific Postscript* he explained what he had tried to do:

> There are three stages: an aesthetic, an ethical, and a religious. But these are not distinguished abstractly, as the immediate, the mediate and the synthesis of the two [this would have been the way of the Hegelian philosophers], but rather concretely, in existential determinations, as enjoyment-perdition; action-victory; suffering. But in spite of this triple division the book is nevertheless an either-or. The ethical and the religious stages have in fact an essential relationship to one another. The difficulty with *Either-Or* is that it was rounded out to a conclusion ethically. . . . In the *Stages* this is clarified, and the religious is thus assigned to its proper place.[8]

The third stage, as Kierkegaard indicated above, is marked by suffering. Far more than the man who is devoted to morality as his highest goal, the truly religious man is aware of suffering, guilt and pathos.

Just as frustration and boredom were likely to drive the aesthetic man to make the leap toward the ethical way of life, so the inability of the moral man to carry out his duties perfectly could drive him toward the religious leap of faith. The moral man becomes filled with despair because he is unable to always do what he ought because he is also a sinner. He begins to realize that the ethical task is so gigantic as to be hopeless, and that furthermore man is by nature tragically separated from God. The ethical man can speak with knowledge on morality and immorality, on good and bad, which are humanistic categories, but the religious man judges life in accordance with the religious categories of sin, guilt, redemption, and salvation. Even the ethical man is convicted of sin and guilt. But—and this is the tragic aspect of his situation—his sense of guilt does not wholly arise from any wrongdoing he may have done, but rather from a sense of his own inadequacy as a man. The sense of sin is man's despair of himself as man and indicates in realistic experience the limitations man feels when confronted by the infinite transcendent God. This despair, this tragic sense of sin, is what Kierkegaard referred to as "the sickness unto death." [9]

The more moral a man is, the more aware he becomes of his own guilt. He too faces a choice. Either he can continue in his ethical way of life, seek to do the relatively right act for the occasion, and submit to his feelings of inadequacy and guilt; or he can choose to make the leap of faith into the unseen arms of the forgiving God. He can choose to become a Christian and accept the paradox of the God-man; in making this choice he will not be made ethically better than he is, but he will discover his true self as a man fully dependent upon the transcendent God. He will then know himself as completely in debt to God, his creator, before whom, he himself is insignificant.

At this point we come upon one of the most startling of Kierkegaard's convictions. He maintained that because religion is man's absolute task, while ethics is only his relative task, there can be a teleological suspension of ethics. In *Fear and Trembling* Kierkegaard asserted that the true Christian must leave the people around him, renounce his former ways and sacrifice even that which he regards as the good. The true Christian must believe, in full view of the absurdity of doing so, that God will show him the best way in an unexpected manner. As an example of this suspension of the ethical category in the interests of the higher category of religion he refers to Abraham in the Old Testament, who as a result of his faith in God was willing to sacrifice his son Isaac, despite the fact that his ethical consciousness rebelled at the thought of killing his own son. But Abraham was a true man among men, he was a "knight of faith," and therefore he agreed to go through with it. He agreed to obey God. In an unexpected way God then sent the ram into the thicket to save Isaac's life. God had proved the worth of Abraham by testing him to see if he would in an actual situation place obedience to God above human ethical demands.[10]

Unfortunately, Kierkegaard found that in his own day it was extremely difficult to become a true Christian. Few men were willing to choose a way of life which always involved suffering, which required their constant dependence upon a transcendent God, and which might subject them to abuse and ridicule at the hands of society. Yet it was Kierkegaard's conviction that only by becoming a Christian could one become fully a man. If we are to come to grips with Kierkegaard we must take a careful look at his writings on becoming a Christian in a supposedly Christian land.

An Existential Choice—Becoming a Christian   Kierkegaard maintained, as
we have seen, that for one
to really be a man he should commit himself to a way of life which he
himself had freely chosen. Unfortunately, as he noted in his *Journal* in
1837: "There are many people who reach their conclusions about life like
schoolboys; they cheat their master by copying the answer out of a book
without having worked out the sum for themselves." [11] Precisely was this
the case, in his judgment, concerning most of the so-called Christians in
Denmark.

Although Kierkegaard frequently stressed that one ought to choose his
own way of life, rather than imitating others, he did not believe that
all life styles were equally desirable. He claimed that the most significant life style for any man was to choose to become a Christian.
In his own view all of his writings were essentially religious; they were all
concerned, either directly or indirectly, with making the existential choice
of becoming a Christian. His edifying discourses (he refused to call them
sermons since he said he lacked the authority to preach) and his last
attacks upon Christendom were put forth in his own name, but most of
his writings were credited to pseudonyms. In *The Point of View for My
Work as an Author* he explained that he adopted the indirect method
of communication in his aesthetic and philosophical works, claiming to
be the editor of the books rather than their author, in order to make the
people who think they are Christians take notice. If he appealed to
them directly, he would quickly lose them, but by indirect communication their interest may be so aroused by the aesthetic character of the
works that they themselves might become more inward about their own
existences.[12]

To Kierkegaard, we have said, the hardest task in the world is to
become a Christian. There is no *being* a Christian in the full sense, only
becoming a Christian. It is a task which requires constant moment-by-
moment decisions, and which is beset by dangers from aestheticism and
speculation (philosophy). The primary aesthetic danger is that in the
love of beauty and the desire for pleasure and comfort, one may accept
Christianity as a cult of joy and material pleasure. On the other hand,
the speculative danger is that of looking down on Christianity from the
vantage point of "superior philosophical speculation." Kierkegaard believed that the churchmen of his day were captivated by both the
aesthetic and the speculative errors. Instead of facing the reality of suffering as expressed by Abraham and Job in the Bible, instead of bringing men to confront the moment-by-moment decision to become
Christians, they were extolling the beauties of Christianity and elaborating

philosophical explanations of Christian doctrines. Christianity, he maintained, was not a system of doctrines, but rather "an existential communication expressing an existential contradiction." [13] It was directed to each person as an individual in his own unique situation, but it could not be understood in terms of human intelligence since it confronted man with the absurd paradox of a God-man who as the eternal had nevertheless entered history. To become a Christian required that one fully accept the paradox of Christ as both God and man. Only in this way could one obtain eternal blessedness. In contrast with this, modern Christianity had become enmeshed in society; plainly it had become another form of world-affirmation and had lost its power to change men and remake the world. Under these circumstances, perhaps the best that one can do, Kierkegaard suggested, is to stay away from church, for then at least one will not be making a mockery of God.

Religion was a matter of great importance to Kierkegaard; it was his ultimate concern. Just as a lover is not actually in love if he can give objective rational judgments concerning his love, so a Christian is not a true believer if his faith is not an inward existential matter. Not through knowledge of the externals of religion, but through an inner conviction of faith does one become a Christian. It is for this reason that Kierkegaard's writings seem peculiarly related to his personal situation, for only thus was he able to believe truth could be found. Truth, for him, was not basically academic, rather it was achieved in a passionate search for one's own way of life.

Kierkegaard not only believed that religion was a personal matter for each individual, but also that it was only through subjective personal experience that one had genuine access to truth. Impersonal objective reflection about human beings and their problems is a distortion of reality. Objective knowledge is always by means of concepts which give us knowledge only of phenomena or appearances. Furthermore, objective knowledge is always static while reality is dynamic. The real, he maintained, can be known only in experience which is subjective, immediate, existential. He did not deny that the possible (or abstractly distinguished by the reason as idea) can be presented by objective knowledge. On the other hand, however, that which is actual (or immediately experienced as reality) can be caught only through personal existential thought. Only in action, in moments of decision, in actual subjective experience can the real be grasped. All the systematic philosophers' concepts are frozen experiences; the true is that which is experienced moment by moment.

In regarding subjectivity as truth, Kierkegaard also maintained that the truth known by any individual is in proportion to the sensitivity and suffering of that person. A person who has never suffered has never learned about life. All truths, being existential, involve risk. The degree of truth you possess depends upon the intensity of your living. To know the truth you must be passionately concerned about it. If you cannot get thoroughly interested, it is not true for you. Kierkegaard was here calling attention to one of his main concerns: to restore the individual person to the center of importance. And of course by truth he is referring to the existential reality of the individual himself, and not to knowledge about nature which he admitted is obtained in an objective way by the natural sciences. What was important to him was to stress the fact that each person is a uniquely existing individual, and no category of humanity in general can deal adequately with the reality of one's own experiences. Frequently, he made his view clear by interjecting humor into even serious discussions, as in the following passage:

> Two ways, in general, are open for an existing individual: *Either* he can do his utmost to forget that he is an existing individual, by which he becomes a comic figure, since existence has the remarkable trait of compelling an existing individual to exist whether he wills it or not. . . . *Or* he can concentrate his entire energy upon the fact that he is an existing individual. It is from this side, in the first instance, that objection must be made to modern philosophy; not that it has a mistaken presupposition, but that it has a comical presupposition, occasioned by its having forgotten, in a sort of world-historical absent-mindedness, what it means to be a human being. Not indeed, what it means to be a human being in general; for this is the sort of thing that one might even induce a speculative philosopher to agree to; but what it means that you and I and he are human beings, each one for himself.[14]

Kierkegaard's criticism of his age as one which ignored the uniqueness of each individual in favor of mass opinions is one aspect of his thought which seems particularly germane to our own century. His attack upon the crowd as representing untruth, upon people relying on the mass media for their opinions, was an essential aspect of his investigation into what it really meant to be a man. Part of the difficulty of the modern world Kierkegaard felt was awe of the crowd. In the sphere of ethical and religious matters each person must decide for himself; it is not true that the majority tips the scales in favor of one view of life or another. As Kierkegaard put it:

> Wherever there is a crowd there is untruth, so that (to consider for a moment the extreme case), even if every individual, each for himself in private, were to be in possession of the truth, yet in case they were all to get together in a crowd—a crowd to which any sort of *decisive* significance is attributed, a voting, noisy, audible crowd—untruth would at once be in evidence.[15]

But Kierkegaard was even more specific in his indictment of his age. Independently of Karl Marx, Kierkegaard came to similar conclusions concerning the effect of urban and industrial society upon the individual. In his *Works of Love*, written at the same time as the *Communist Manifesto*, Kierkegaard pointed out that in the industrialized cities man is a cipher, a fraction, of the truly human man.[16] The modern man is "lost" in the crowd and "at a loss" apart from the crowd. He is an empty, anonymous, dependent being, unable to be himself or to act distinctively. Though in agreement thus far, Kierkegaard differed from Marx in one radical respect: Marx proposed to solve the problem of man's "self-alienation" by a revolutionary take over of the capitalistic economic system by the working class; Kierkegaard reacted violently in the direction of calling man to become an individual passionately concerned with his own existence.

The individual who stresses his own existence will look frequently within his own life. Kierkegaard in many of his writings praised Socrates for being concerned with self-knowledge rather than with knowledge of the external world. Socrates' motto "Know Thyself" was to Kierkegaard far more true than the concern of his age with impersonality and objectivity. Self-reflection and deep probing into one's own life were required if one were to accept the challenge of becoming a real individual.

Kierkegaard in several of his books anticipated depth psychology. In *Fear and Trembling* and *Sickness Unto Death* he applied a method of self-analysis characterized by inwardness and intense self-examination— a method which resembles to some extent the method of psychoanalysis. This method had radical results for Kierkegaard. He found that the intellect, in its thirst for truth concerning existence, is unable to transcend the realm of essences (abstractions, ideas) with which it is characteristically concerned. This inability causes a crisis of despair, in which it realizes its own limitations, and at the same time finds the heart rebelling against it in the name of real existence. At first it seems as though the surrender of the pride of the intellect means the surrender of all hope, but this is not so. The wonder of life is that when the intellect in despair surrenders itself, there follows suddenly the disclosure of existence. Something like this happens: there is a sickness unto death, a terrible anguish (*angst*) and even a paralysis of fear, lest an abyss of nothing be about to swallow up all that has seemed certain and clear. In despair the question is asked: If the intellect is adrift and lost, is not all lost? But no, the paradox of the situation is just this, that the final collapse of intellect issues in the freedom to *be*. By a "leap," the individual commits himself to real existence; henceforth he lives in reality, in God, in subjectivity, in real selfhood.

This seemed to Kierkegaard to be true in the Christian life. The Christian individual must be intensely concerned about his religion and his destiny, otherwise he is not really religious. As Kierkegaard put it in one of his summarizing sentences: "Christianity is spirit, spirit is inwardness, inwardness is subjectivity, subjectivity is essentially passion, and in its maximum an infinite, personal, passionate interest in one's eternal happiness." [17]

Subjectivity and inwardness characterize existentialism to such a degree that systematic philosophy, with its objective contemplation of essences, is rendered suspect by it. The speculations of the philosophers, Kierkegaard declared, are several degrees removed from reality. Philosophers fall into the error of accepting their own experiences as standard and then seeking to universalize them for others; but in the very act of seeking to capture the subjective in objective impersonal terms they lose reality and describe what is purely artificial and illusory. There is no possible rational guide to existence, therefore, and this is what Kierkegaard means by saying that our existence is irrational. There is an unbridgeable gap between the universal essence (with which the philosophers have been concerned) and the particular existence of each person. There can be no eternal or universal answers given to particular problems.

It is one of Kierkegaard's most radical convictions that there is a complete gulf between the eternal and the temporal, the infinite and the finite, God and man. There is an essential contradiction between being (eternity) and becoming (time) which no individual can grasp by mental activity. All that an individual can do is to choose that which is of tremendous interest or importance to him, and hope that he has made the right decision. This aspect of life fills it with terrifying dread, and yet not to act is to fail to become anything—it is to decide to be nothing. The twentieth-century theologians who have taken their inspiration from Kierkegaard (Karl Barth and Emil Brunner especially) have stressed this aspect of his thought: there is a complete gap between God and man, eternity and time, and nothing can be done by man to bridge this gap.

In the light of this emphasis upon existential decisions, we can better understand Kierkegaard's interpretation of Christianity. The Christian faith is a scandal to philosophy; it is totally absurd that God should be incarnate in a man, that there should be a God-man. The paradox of Christ's nature cannot be resolved by reason, and it cannot be translated into an ethic universally applicable. As Kierkegaard saw it, the Hegelian philosophers had erred in trying to resolve the paradox of Christianity, while the humanists had misread Christ as an ethical teacher. Kierkegaard often remarked that in an age in which everyone else was making things easier, his task was to make something harder. Clearly he stressed time and time again how difficult it was to become a Christian in an age when Christianity had been watered down so as to be unoffensive to modern man. To become a Christian is extremely hard because it means to accept the paradox of Christ as an unexplainable enigma to the reason, a scandalous exception to all usual preconceptions and attitudes our modern age has toward life. In terms we use in the twentieth century we might suggest that Kierkegaard would fully agree that you cannot really get to know another person by means of the objective reports given by psychological tests and sociological investigations, but you can know him through personal encounter. So it is, said Kierkegaard, with our knowledge of Christ. Not by studying objective history, nor by listening to the clergy, but through personal encounter with Christ does one become a Christian. This experience is of necessity individual, existential, inward, and can never be shared with anyone else. Moreover, stressed Kierkegaard, this experience must be constantly repeated for each man; there must be a moment-by-moment experience of the eternal reality of Christ, for it can never be expressed in objective terms. It was this that Kierkegaard meant when he said that to become a Christian one must become contemporaneous with Christ.

Toward an Evaluation of Kierkegaard   Kierkegaard has influenced contemporary existentialists by his deep analysis of the predicament of man, although not all of them have been willing to follow him in the direction of Christianity. Thus, Heidegger, Jaspers and Sartre have stressed the existential aspects of his thought which give primacy to subjectivity, to inwardness, to moment-by-moment decisions. On the other hand, theologians, such as Barth, Brunner, Niebuhr and Tillich, owe much to Kierkegaard's religious emphasis. They have often referred to Kierkegaard in developing their views that only in the spiritual life can man hope to find his life meaningful; otherwise man continues to founder in the poverty and falseness of his intellectual and moral life. But it may well be said that in a sense these theologians are putting new clothes on the old emperor. Tillich, for one, has admitted that while existentialism is a correct portrait of the nature of man, it does not give man the religious answer to his life. The theological answer of God as the ultimate redeemer of sinful man is therefore not new; what is new is that it is restated in existentialist terms. Clearly many of the contemporary theologians are attempting to use the existentialist categories of Kierkegaard to show the relevance to the existing individual of the age-old Christian faith.

Before noting possible weaknesses in Kierkegaard, we do well to note the emphases in his writings which may be regarded as elements of strength in his position. For example, he put man, the individual, back in the center of life. Life is more than logic, he insisted. Reason is not the surest key to reality or being-itself. Kierkegaard effectively rebelled against the excessive rationalism of the systematic philosophers of his time. Man, he said, is not being treated fairly or truly if he is merely objectively viewed by the reason, looked at from the outside, turned into an object among other objects; he is subjectively very much an individual and has the inalienable right to be himself. The Hegelian philosophers, who assimilated man into their all inclusive rational systems as a part of the Absolute, especially revolted him. In reasserting the independence and truth of the subjectivity of the individual, he brought back into view aspects of human experience which the philosophers and theologians of his day were ashamed to admit to the sphere of their discussions: fear and trembling, dread, despair, crisis, the collapse of reason, the leap of faith. Kierkegaard at least made it possible to consider man as emotionally alive and free to choose the kind of life he wished to live.

But here the weaknesses begin to appear. Most of them are a result of an over-emphasis by Kierkegaard on the subjectivity of man, with the accompanying neglect of objectivity and reason. Kierkegaard denied that truth concerning man can be found by an objective examination of events, the study and analysis by reason of the facts thus obtained, their classification and systematization—in short, he repudiated knowledge about man and society in the form of impersonal scientific truth. Against Kierkegaard's either/or, one might well suggest that if we are going to understand man we need the objective findings of psychology, sociology and history just as much as we need to encourage each individual to introspect about the nature of his own life. But clearly Kierkegaard's preoccupation with the meaning of his own existence, his endless attempts to explain his engagement to Regina and his relationship to his father, suggests a morbid affectation on his part for melancholy and unhappiness. An excessive introspection, such as he practiced, need not bring one the truth about oneself, especially if one also fails to take account of what is actually happening in the world around one. It certainly seems unrealistic that Kierkegaard continued to hope that Regina would be restored to him, even after she was happily married for many years.

Similarly, he underrated logic and consistency in favor of contradiction and paradox. In matters of ultimate religious concern, where logic and consistency are transcended, and only what looks like absurdity remains, contradiction and paradox may be what the finite human understanding must settle for; at least so the mystics of every religious tradition have told us. But to repudiate logic and consistency as a part of one's way of life is another matter altogether. Kierkegaard is essentially correct in maintaining that the individual must choose his own way of life, or else his society will choose the prevalent fashionable one for him. But is he correct in maintaining that no reasons can be given for preferring the ethical life to the aesthetic life, or for making the religious leap of faith? One might not change his way of life purely on the basis of facts and reasons, but to repudiate them altogether is to open oneself to self-deception and irrational fanaticism.

Yet Kierkegaard constantly uses logic and reason to substantiate his position. Perhaps this is a part of his self-contradiction in the search for certainty, a use of reason to confound reason. Kierkegaard makes this claim himself, but anyone who reads his works with care will find him trying hard to use reason *to convince* the reader, not to discourage the reader concerning the effectiveness of reason. It is only fair to add, however, that he recognized the paradox of his own position: we cannot neglect reason, yet reason cannot acquaint us with the innermost nature of our own existences.

While Kierkegaard restored the sense of the difference of the individual from every other person, he emphasized this difference to the point of distortion. It is perhaps his gravest weakness that he ruled out the communal or social quest for truth in the moral and religious spheres. To Kierkegaard an individual is only really himself when he is before God; but he is before God only when he is most alone, and even then he is conscious of his human emptiness and nothingness and of his infinite distance from God. Is it true that only in turning from others to total isolation that one finds out who he really is? Must one forsake all causes and all friends to find himself? May it not rather be the case that in working with and for other men one might find his individuality and his meaning for life?

Even more disturbing, however, is Kierkegaard's view of the religious life as forever pervaded by suffering. There can be little doubt that his emphasis upon the demands that Christianity places upon one's life was a needed corrective of the view of the institutional church of his day with its stress upon belonging and fellowship. But his appeal to Job and Abraham of the Old Testament sounds too much like a rationalization for his own unhappy life. It is true that he claimed he was not himself a Christian, but he also said that he alone knew what Christianity really was. His appeal to the Bible itself rather than to theology has been followed by many of our present theologians. But even here Kierkegaard's position seems to be one-sided. The Bible also stresses the joy and fulfillment that one finds in his relationship with God, but this is a leitmotif that Kierkegaard rarely mentions.

Indeed there is even a paradox in Kierkegaard's own interpretation of Christianity. While in his early writings, and especially in the *Concluding Unscientific Postscript*, he stresses the passion with which one holds a belief, and the intensely subjective and private nature of the religious life, in *The Book on Adler* and in his *Attack upon "Christendom"* he stresses the necessity of obedience to the truths revealed by the Apostles. It appears that while Kierkegaard wanted the individual to appropriate religion inwardly, he also wished this religion to be orthodox Christianity as he interpreted it. But suppose orthodox Christianity is not subjectively true for a particular individual. To such a person Kierkegaard would presumably reply, as he did in *The Book on Adler*, "it is not doubt of religious truth but insubordination against religious authority which is the fault in our misfortune and the cause of it." [18] In this guise Kierkegaard appears as another champion of authoritarian religion, not of the right of each man to find his own truth.

One of the most obvious difficulties with Kierkegaard's position is his defense of the suspension of ethics for the higher purpose of obedience to God. The argument, it may be recalled, is that since religion is man's absolute and highest concern, and ethics his relatively lower task, therefore ethics may be suspended at the demand of religion. In fairness to Kierkegaard, one should point out that he did not believe that God might often make such a demand upon a man, but if He did, then the man should obey God. But precisely how can one tell that an apparent command to kill another person is a command from God rather than a demonic order from a deeply hidden part of one's own psychic nature? In fact, if God is love, as Christianity maintains, is it not clear that an order to do violence to another human being would clearly not be a divine command? If one takes biblical religion seriously, as Kierkegaard seems to ask his readers to do, then the ethical principles of justice, forgiveness, and love certainly seem to be what God wants man to obey. In fact, one can even read the Genesis story of Abraham and Isaac quite differently than did Kierkegaard. One could with just as much plausibility argue that God's providing the ram in the thicket to substitute for the sacrifice of Isaac was God's way of saying that He did not want human beings to be sacrificed to Him.

The reader himself may find other areas of disagreement or agreement with Kierkegaard's position. Clearly Kierkegaard is not a model for all men, nor did he intend to be one. His main concern was to recall man to his most important task, namely, of learning how he ought to live. In accomplishing this task Kierkegaard may shock us out of our complacency. We may be forced to reexamine our own convictions. Do we really believe them? What does it mean to really be a man? Is one really religious unless one is passionately devoted to its practice? Are we really individuals or are we but carbon copies produced by the mass media? If we come to grips with Kierkegaard then questions such as these cry for honest reflection on our part. Walter Kaufmann has aptly said concerning Kierkegaard: "One can hardly be satisfied with him or pleased; but his greatest value may well be that he does not allow us to be satisfied or pleased with ourselves." [19] More than anything else Kierkegaard's stress upon the individual, upon each man's own existential concerns, and upon ultimately committing oneself to a way of life with passionate devotion, represent his great contribution to one seeking guidance for living in our modern world.

Nietzsche: Man as the Creator of Values   Twentieth-century existentialists refer as much to the writings of Friedrich Nietzsche as they do to those of Søren Kierkegaard. We should be clear at the outset that Nietzsche did not call himself an existentialist, and that there are many facets to his thought which would not place him squarely in harmony with contemporary existentialist thinkers. Nevertheless, it is undoubtedly true that Jaspers, Heidegger and Sartre build upon insights which they have received from Nietzsche, and in this sense we may consider Nietzsche as a forerunner of existentialism.

Friedrich Nietzsche (1844–1900), the son of a Lutheran pastor, studied philology at the Universities of Bonn and Leipzig, and began his professorial career at the University of Basel in 1869.[20] He taught at Basel for ten years, during which time he became very friendly with Richard Wagner, the composer of music-dramas, and began publishing his books. *The Birth of Tragedy*, his first book, foreshadowed themes to which he returned throughout his life, especially his view that creation involves a struggle between two opposing forces, which in this book he called Dionysian (the strong passions) and Apollonian (the controlling reason). Tragedy, Nietzsche tells us, was born when the unbridled orgiastic passions of Dionysus were tamed by the rational powers of Apollo in the creation of Greek drama. Part of this first book was devoted to praising Richard Wagner who was in Nietzsche's opinion producing truly revolutionary music-dramas which heralded a new German art. Later on, when Wagner seemed in Nietzsche's judgment to be composing operas for the delight of the public, Nietzsche bitterly and unhesitatingly broke his friendship with him.

When Nietzsche resigned from the University of Basel in 1879 he was in very poor health. But despite severe headaches and very poor eyesight the next decade proved to be the one in which his most influential works were written. The method and direction in which Nietzsche's thinking tended can be found in an interesting book, *The Joyful Wisdom* (sometimes translated *The Gay Science*). He added a fifth book to this volume in 1886, and it is especially in this last section that Nietzsche develops the notion of the death of God and the tremendous responsibility faced by having to again find new values by which to live. *Thus Spoke Zarathustra*, the book which almost everyone associates with Nietzsche, was written in spurts of inspirational intensity. In order to explain some of the concepts he had in mind in this work of poetry-philosophy, he wrote *Beyond Good and Evil* and the *Genealogy of Morals*. In our discussion of Nietzsche's influential ideas for our own age these are the four works to which we shall most often refer.

In 1889 Nietzsche became insane, and although he had periods of lucidity he never recovered fully. Some writers who have found the lack of certainty and nihilism of our own age to stem from the writings of Nietzsche are fond of pointing out that this kind of thinking can only lead logically to insanity, as it did in the case of Nietzsche.[21] This kind of argument does not really refute Nietzsche's views, and ignores the general conclusion reached by scholars that Nietzsche's illness was an atypical paralysis probably caused by syphilis.

His sister, Elizabeth, took charge of Nietzsche during his last illness and upon his death edited *The Will to Power* from his unpublished manuscripts. The charge that Nietzsche was a proto-Nazi was based largely on this book, which modern scholars find to have been heavily tampered with by his sister to make him into an antisemite. At any rate, Hitler did use or misuse Nietzsche to help justify his cause, although the preponderance of Nietzsche's writings during his most creative and lucid decade are filled with attacks on German racialism and remarks against antisemitism. Nevertheless, here and there, one could find aphorisms which, especially when taken out of context, seemed to extoll the "blond beasts" as the new supermen to whom Nietzsche looked forward.

The existentialists turn to Nietzsche because they see in him that individual thinker who dared to question all the presuppositions of his age in his own struggle to find whether or not there was a meaning to life which could be found after the pious myths, illusions and so-called truths of the nineteenth century were destroyed. In the way in which Nietzsche lived through the problems which he examined he showed many of the twentieth-century existentialists the importance of being actively involved in the struggle to discover the truth for oneself.

Those who have read some of the writings of Nietzsche have probably been baffled by his short aphorisms, by his poetical-prose, by his jumping from one problem to another, and by his apparent lack of systematic and sustained development of one theme. One of the reasons some of the existentialists like Nietzsche is precisely because they find this unsystematic treatment of issues to be the sign of his active involvement with the problems he was considering; none of his problems were purely academic to him, but they threatened, as it were, his very life. Any brief summary statement, therefore, such as the one given here can't hope to do justice to the manifold richness of a direct confrontation with Nietzsche's writings. They may infuriate you, you may find them obscure, but on the other hand, you may also find help through his discussion of many of the issues which directly involve you in your present situation. Nietzsche's remarks on the failure of all educators might very well be a starting point for your serious consideration of his thought:

> *There are no educators.* As a thinker, one should speak only of self-education. The education of youth by others is either an experiment, conducted on one as yet unknown and unknowable, or a leveling on principle, to make the new character, whatever it may be, conform to the habits and customs that prevail: in both cases, therefore, something unworthy of the thinker. . . .[22]

Self-discovery is for Nietzsche the only way to learning.

Nietzsche's Method: The Destruction of Idols   Nietzsche's main concern was to examine all pre-suppositions which lay behind philosophical systems and customary moralities. His method was well summed up in the sub-title of his book *Twilight of the Idols: How One Philosophizes with a Hammer*. Nietzsche's philosophical hammer was used to destroy all the customary beliefs which were in fact idols, in order that one might be free to attempt to construct beliefs by which he could live. This was an existential concern with living truths for the individual, but before one could attempt to forge his own way ot life he had to, first of all, break free from the myths and customs of his age.

Nietzsche thus explored the beliefs and customary morality of the Germany of his day, of traditional Christianity, of the ancient Hebrews and of the golden age of Greece in order to show upon what presuppositions they were based. They were not based on "objective truth," he held, for in his view there was absolutely no way for any man to discover "truth." Neither facts nor philosophical truth could ever be found; in this sense, he said everything is falsehood. What we call facts depends upon the interpretation which we give to events, and there is no way by which we can say that any interpretation matches with reality. It is impossible for any man to really get outside of the conceptual scheme which he has adopted to see if it squares with what is given to him in experience. For what he experiences is conditioned by the concepts and the language which he has acquired from his society. Nietzsche maintained that the term "truth" really meant no more than the adoption by a particular people of certain values and ideas which aided them in their survival. One of his radical insights was that world-views are not based on objective facts or truths; rather they are interpretations which are of value to a people so long as they help to support and enhance their lives.

Nietzsche was philosophizing with a hammer, therefore, because he believed that the other philosophers of his age were merely rationalizing in their vain attempt to justify the status quo. For him, the values of Germany and Europe were no longer life-promoting; they were instead life-stultifying. Hence, his task was to reveal that they had outlived their usefulness; they had become idols rather than living values.) One must destroy them, and the presuppositions upon which they rested, before one could seek for a better way of life more appropriate to the modern world.

The most important aspect of Nietzsche's method of doing philosophy was his constant attempt to uncover the value or the usefulness of a belief. Since there were an infinite number of possible interpretations which could be made of the world, he attempted by means of what he described as "thought experiments" to try out as many possible alternative world-views as he could imagine. It is therefore sometimes difficult for the reader to know what Nietzsche himself defended, and what was rather but a plausible interpretation which he followed for a time and then dropped. But even then he has served his purpose, for he has provided his reader with another possible world-view. And if this possible interpretation does not make a difference in the life of the reader, then it is clearly one which has no value for him. Nietzsche will then have made one of his great points: only if a world-view, an interpretation, makes a difference for you should you adopt it. For, as Nietzsche remarks, "our duty is and remains first of all, not to get into confusion about ourselves." [23]

Nietzsche in *Beyond Good and Evil* contrasts the tasks of philosophical laborers and philosophers proper. The former he finds to be represented by Kant and Hegel who systematized and justified the beliefs of their time—a no mean feat, he admits. It might be necessary, he suggests, for the philosophers proper to begin as historians, critics, skeptics and free spirits "in order to pass through the whole range of human values and value feelings and to be *able* to see with many different eyes and consciences, from a height and into every distance, from the depths into every height, from a nook into every expanse." [24] But this is just the preparatory stage—the stage of broadening one's outlook, of becoming aware of presuppositions in one's thinking and in the thinking of those around one, of doubting the accepted and traditional answers given in the terms of one's own culture. Finally, the philosopher proper, who will always find himself in opposition to the prevailing values of his day, will create new values. Nietzsche portrays the philosophers proper as "applying the knife vivisectionally to the chest of the very *virtues of their time*." [25] But Nietzsche can't help asking, "Are there such philosophers today? Have there been such philosophers yet? *Must* there not be such philosophers?" [26]

Nietzsche was thus not interested in constructing a system, and in this the existentialists join him. For Nietzsche what was needed was a destruction of the old philosophies and moralities, but not just those that are easily the whipping boys of intellectual men because no one seriously entertains them as live options. Rather, when he speaks in his dramatic metaphor of "applying the knife vivisectionally. . . to the very virtues of their time" he refers to the philosopher attacking his own darling beliefs, his own presuppositions, the morality to which he is attracted. Thus Nietzsche in his own day attacked the notion of evolutionary progress as developed by what he thought was Darwin's theory, while in our own day many of the existentialist writers attack our reliance on science as the method to truth. To dare to attack that belief which makes me comfortable, to ask what is the presupposition of my pet theory, that is to philosophize in the sense which Nietzsche recommended. For Nietzsche there is no presuppositionless thinking. His method of doing philosophy was an attempt to unveil the perspectives, the vantage points, from which we view the world.

The Two Moralities: Master and Slave In Nietzsche's attempt to find a world-view for himself he was struck by how much all of our thinking is influenced by our moral prejudices. Some of you may have found it difficult to accept anything of value in the writings of Karl Marx because our present society is so determinedly anti-Communist that it is hard to conceive of anything the founder of Communism said as being worthwhile. On the other hand, those of you who are basically rebellious against our present society may find Nietzsche's nihilism and his extolling of the will to power as right down your alley. Both of these positions are hiding behind moral prejudices, and it was these which Nietzsche was striving to overcome. Nietzsche suggests that only if one is able to cut himself loose from his own or his society's moral prejudices will he be enabled to see morality itself as a problem. For Nietzsche all moralities are really cases of special pleading based on the prevailing customs of a group of people and the philosophical beliefs which have grown up to justify these customs.

It is very important to note that Nietzsche is not interested in simply looking at morality dispassionately. Rather, in true existentialist fashion, he insisted that his concern with morality was his own personal problem. The difference between an "objective" examination of values and the personal involvement of the thinker in seeking his own morality was put by Nietzsche as follows:

> It makes the most material difference whether a thinker stands personally related to his problems, having his fate, his need, and even his highest happiness therein; or merely impersonally, that is to say, if he can only feel and grasp them with the tentacles of cold, prying thought. In the latter case I warrant that nothing comes of it. . . .[27]

The usual error which he found in previous philosophical treatments of morality was that of assuming a consensus among civilized human beings as to what exactly the highest values ought to be, and then insisting that these values ought to be accepted by everyone, regardless of whether or not they fitted one's own needs. Or, some philosophers have made the reverse error, of assuming that since among different peoples values are necessarily different, that therefore no morality whatsoever can be binding upon anyone.

Nietzsche claimed, therefore, to be the first thinker to question the worthwhileness of morality itself. What purpose is served by a morality?

> How is it that I have not yet met with any one, not even in books, who seems to have stood to morality in this position, as one who knew morality as a problem, and this problem as *his own* personal need,

affliction, pleasure and passion? It is obvious that up to the present morality has not been a problem at all; it has rather been the very ground on which people have met after all distrust, dissension and contradiction, the hallowed place of peace, where thinkers could obtain rest even from themselves, could recover breath and revive. I see no one who has ventured to *criticise* the estimates of moral worth.[28]

Nietzsche's task, thus, was to question the worth of morality as such.

One of Nietzsche's great concerns was to uncover the presuppositions of all previous moralities, and then to show that the morality of his own age rested on presuppositions also. The goals which men have followed in different lands in different historical eras have been extremely varied; there have been a "thousand and one goals," as he poetically puts it. But in each case the world-view which has been followed by a culture has been chosen because it has aided the people of that culture to enhance their lives. Nietzsche has his spokesman Zarathustra show how four different cultures rose to greatness by following four quite different moral codes:

> "You shall always be the first and excel all others: your jealous soul shall love no one, unless it be the friend"—that made the soul of the Greek quiver: thus he walked the path of his greatness.
> "To speak the truth and to handle bow and arrow well"—that seemed both dear and difficult to the people who gave me my name —the name which is both dear and difficult to me. [Zoroastrians]
> "To honor father and mother and to follow their will to the root of one's soul"—this was the tablet of overcoming that another people hung up over themselves and became powerful and eternal thereby. [The Hebrews]
> "To practice loyalty and, for the sake of loyalty, to risk honor and blood even for evil and dangerous things"—with this teaching another people conquered themselves; and through this self-conquest they became pregnant and heavy with great hopes. [The Germans] [29]

Each of these four different moralities served a useful purpose for the people who adopted them, but our needs may be so different today that none of them may prove adequate for our own choice of a way of life.

What was the purpose which Nietzsche found that any morality served for its people? In brief he maintained that the function of any morality was to discipline and tame man's passions. The whole course of the development of any society was motivated by disciplining the passions of its members, as was represented in ancient Greece by the rational forces of Apollo taming the frenzied antics of the wild Dionysus. There is no eternal or absolute morality, therefore, for what is called morality within a particular society consists of those customs which have proved useful in harnessing man's passions for the benefit of the society's overall aims.

Nietzsche distinguished between two general types of morality: (a) one which harnessed the passions in such a way that productive and creative activities were encouraged by a kind of sublimation of the initial direction of the passions, and (b) the other which denied that the passions really ruled man and hence repressed them below the surface of consciousness, where they would emerge in ways destructive to the society or to the individual. The latter morality Nietzsche tended to identify with Christianity (the slave morality), while the former he identified with ancient Greece (the master morality).

It is important to recall that for Nietzsche moralities are not merely socially useful customs, but that more importantly they influence the way we look at the world and at ourselves. Hence, for him the majesty of the master morality involved a more life-affirming world-view as well as a nobler conception of human nature. In the master morality the more aristocratic members of the society who had attained power imposed their values on the world. These values differentiated between "the good" and "the bad"; the good meant that which was noble, exalted, proud, while the bad meant all that which was contemptible, such as liars, the petty, the narrow seekers of utility, and the flatterers. Nietzsche insists that the values of "good" and "bad" were first applied to different kinds of men, and only later and derivatively to actions. He thus describes the master morality as the self-legislation of values by the noble:

> The noble type of man experiences *itself* as determining values; it does not need approval; it judges, "what is harmful to me is harmful in itself"; it knows itself to be that which first accords honor to things; it is *value-creating*.[30]

The noble human being is primarily a person who has power, that is, control over himself. He helps the more unfortunate human beings, but not out of pity, but rather out of an overflowing of his excess power. Furthermore, the noble moral legislator honors tradition and age, and does not look forward to progress in the future. The stability of an order is based on law and tradition, and it is this which the noble aristocratic morality honors.

The obverse of this noble morality was that it was predicated on a huge group of common men who, herdlike, needed a noble to guide them. To the aristocratic master these common men were vile, un-cultured, and if necessary, could be punished or executed in order to fulfill the nobility's drive for complete mastery. The common men were looked at as human beings who had not quite made it; they were "also rans," and hence they were not to be blamed morally. They were simply *bad* human beings because they had not developed their will to power, and for this they could not be condemned. In ancient Greece these common men were slaves, and even for Aristotle, the Greek philosopher, slaves were not quite human beings, and hence it was justifiable to treat them as things. For Nietzsche, the masters could always act "beyond good and evil" in their treatment of the common herd of men.

On the other hand, the slave morality tries to make a virtue out of necessity. The slaves have no strong will to power, they do not possess strong drives or passions, and they call "evil" those very strong passions which the noble morality calls "good." As Nietzsche views it, the slave morality is based on a utilitarian justification of those acts which ease the lives of the suffering herd of humanity: pity, patience, humility, forgiveness, and industry are extolled as "good." The slave cannot be "evil" in his terms since he lacks the strong passional drives, but he calls the masters "evil" and seeks subtly to subdue the masters to the mediocre morality of the herd. This trick is accomplished by making the love of one's neighbor, pity, and forgiveness into virtues which all men, including the noble masters, ought to obey. The slave morality denies that men really have strong drives, and hence it inflicts men with a bad conscience whenever their strong passional urges seek to issue forth in action. This morality, for Nietzsche, then is one which represses man's will to power, and this can only result in these subterranean forces emerging in strong individuals as destructive actions taken either against others in the society or against themselves. And strangely enough this transvaluation of values is exactly what has taken place through the triumph of Christianity which, though it began as a morality of the slaves of the Roman Empire by justifying their lowly status in this world, has gained such strength that it has now become the morality of all men and is recommended to every man, without exception.

It is only fair to point out that Nietzsche makes it quite clear that he is discussing ideal types in his contrast of the master and slave moralities. He finds that in modern moralities much trouble is caused by the fact that they are mixtures, not only in the society, but even within each individual. Hence, for example, while we might on the one hand profess love for all mankind, we might on the other hand seek to justify a war against people who think differently than we do. It might be an interesting game for the reader to jot down some of his own contradictory moral principles; at least, it might help the reader to understand why Nietzsche believed so fervently that the traditional Christian morality has outlived its usefulness for the modern man. Nietzsche recognized that as conditions change within a society and within the world, a new morality is also needed. In this respect he is echoed today not only by the existentialists, but also by the Christian situation ethicists, and many others. Undoubtedly in our day when we face the threat of nuclear warfare, we feel even more deeply the inadequacy of a parochial morality, and should also feel the extreme need of finding a new morality which can deal with our being citizens in a global world.

Nietzsche, along with Kierkegaard, was one of the first in the modern world to cry out against conformity to mass mediocrity. He realized the intense loneliness and anxiety which all existentialists have stressed come to the man who finds that he is not in harmony with the values of his age. If he could accept the prevailing culture, if he could conform, he would not face the inner turmoil, the search for values to which he can fully commit himself. Nietzsche recognized how easy it was to be average, common, herdlike, normal—for society itself bestows the blessing of value upon those who do not stand out from the crowd. But for him the noble man resists these common hypercritical values of the crowd. Nietzsche and Kierkegaard also agreed that the depth of a man's insight into himself and his times is in direct proportion to the intensity of his suffering. The non-conformist must suffer alone, and this suffering and his psychological awareness of the masks worn by others, separates him from the rest of mankind. The task of the noble individual in the modern world for Nietzsche involves assuming complete responsibility for one's actions. As he puts it: "Signs of nobility: never thinking of degrading our duties into duties for everybody; not wanting to delegate, to share, one's own responsibility; counting one's privileges and their exercise among one's *duties*." [31]

But Nietzsche also seems to cling to the belief that any association in a community is bound to be common, plebeian, and therefore "bad." If the slaves made a virtue of necessity in stressing the value of forgiving love, Nietzsche also tried to make a virtue of the necessity of solitude for the man born out of his age:

> For solitude is a virtue for us, as a sublime bent and urge for cleanliness which guesses how all contact between man and man—"in society"—involves inevitable uncleanliness. All community makes men—somehow, somewhere, sometime "common." [32]

The Death of God and the Overman One of the great merits of Nietzsche in his search for the underlying presuppositions of the morality and philosophy of his day was that he was willing to dig way below the surface in order to read the signs of the breakdown of the Christian world-view. He was not one who gladly called himself an atheist, who was delighted that now that God was dead, all things were allowed. Rather he saw the great extent to which civilization itself was formed by artists, philosophers and saints who in the Christian world-view had found a meaning for life. There were many fashionable intellectual atheists in his day, but they thought they were merely rejecting belief in the supernatural in favor of a better human life on this planet. Nietzsche, however, saw that our view of man, our morality, even our belief in truth itself, also goes with the death of the Christian God. For with the death of God, there is no fixed and eternal truth. There is nothing higher than ourselves, and, as we have already seen, this leaves us with the common herd—hardly something in which to rejoice.

Nietzsche's parable of the Madman from his book *The Joyful Wisdom* is a masterpiece of literature and philosophy. When the madman entered the market place crying "I seek God" he was greeted by laughter from the atheists there gathered. They asked him such foolish questions as "Did he get lost?" "Has he emigrated?" etc. But the madman had a much deeper understanding of the loss of God than the sane rational atheists, as he cried, " 'Whither is God?' I shall tell you. *We have killed him*—you and I. All of us are his murderers." And then in poetical prose, the madman by asking questions of his audience shows that the killing of the Christian world-view was brought about on the one hand by the advance of science which destroyed the belief in the old Ptolemaic astronomy, and on the other hand by an increasing callousness and coldness in men's hearts. Upon reading the following passage one can't help but feel the shock which came upon the loss of belief in the stable world-view which had been connected with belief in the Christian God:

> What did we do when we unchained this earth from its sun? Whither is it moving now? Whither are we moving now? Away from all suns? Are we not plunging continually? Backward, sideward, forward, in all directions? Is there any up or down left? Are we not straying as through an infinite nothing? Do we not feel the breath of empty space?. . . God is dead. God remains dead. And we have killed him. How shall we, the murderers of all murderers, comfort ourselves? What was holiest and most powerful of all that the world has yet owned has bled to death under our knives. . . . What festivals of atonement, what sacred games shall we have to invent? Is not the greatness of this deed too great for us? [33]

Nietzsche's Madman continues that his prophecy has not yet been fulfilled, he comes too early: this great deed is still not known to men, despite the fact that they themselves have killed God.

Recently a small number of American theologians have popularized their position as a "Death of God theology." [34] Essentially what they say is a contemporary restatement of Nietzsche's position: in our modern scientific world-view we can no longer believe in the idea of God of the Christian tradition. This idea of God has been outgrown and it is irrelevant. They tell us we need therefore to construct a post-Christian theology. If many men in Nietzsche's day did not see all that was involved in the death of the idea of God, a stable belief which has permeated our culture for several thousand years, clearly some men of the twentieth century do see it. Of course, the theologians would not agree with Nietzsche's position that now we must ourselves become like gods in fashioning a new philosophy and a new morality for the new age, but they do recognize the tremendous changes and problems which are posed for a culture which has lost its moorings and is in desperate need of new bed-rock upon which to build its faith. Most of these contemporary theologians of the Death of God movement stress the life and teachings of Jesus as the way of finding a spiritual and moral guide to life. For Nietzsche, however, the answer to the death of God must be sought in going beyond man who was human, all too human, to the overman.

Zarathustra is the persona in whose mouth Nietzsche puts most of his insights concerning the overman. The overman is to be first of all the man who overcomes human nature, the man who again legislates new values as he rises above the mass of humanity. He is to be a creator, but first of all he must learn to control and master his own desires. After he has learned to control his drives he will be able to make something of himself as a result of free choice. He will accept the earth and will not despise his body. Beyond this Nietzsche does not specify very much about the nature of the overman who is to come. His only comparisons are with artists, saints and philosophers, with those men who have been productive and creative in an uncommon way. Clearly the overman is not meant to apply to the Aryan race, for he constantly reminds us that the overman is an exception who can appear in any society and at any time. Very specifically, Nietzsche attacks the notion that man is improving as the result of evolution—this kind of improving of the race will lead to what he calls the "last man"—the man who is content with small trifles and loves the happiness of the crowd. The overman is always the exception, he is the one who goes beyond the ordinary men of his day, the person who fully understands himself and who creates new ideals and values.

Perhaps the instructions which Zarathustra gave to his disciples sum up Nietzsche's view that the overman must educate himself, must overcome his own drives by self mastery, and only then will he be able to be joyously creative and productive. Zarathustra tells his disciples to go away and to resist his teachings; they must first find themselves before they can move toward becoming the overman:

> You say you believe in Zarathustra? But what matters Zarathustra? You are my believers—but what matter all believers? You had not yet sought yourselves: and you found me. Thus do all believers; therefore all faith amounts to so little.

> Now I bid you lose me and find yourselves; and only when you have all denied me will I return to you.[35]

One of Nietzsche's most elusive ideas in connection with the formation of a new morality for the modern world is that of eternal recurrence. The overman will be the man who will be able to bear the thought that the actions he chooses to perform may have to be performed an infinite number of times through an infinite future. In the ethical use of eternal recurrence Nietzsche suggests this most sobering thought: the choice I now make and the consequences which follow upon it, might have to be repeated over and over again. Only an overman in his view would be able to bear this kind of a scrutiny of his choices. To be able to say concerning all that one has done, and in fact about all that has happened in the world, that it be repeated eternally is the "Yea-saying" of Nietzsche's overman. While very few men would be able to realize Nietzsche's ideal of the overman, yet each man should be able to achieve that which he says is the one thing needful: "to 'give style' to one's character." [36]

Nietzsche looked into the abyss and found no eternal truths or absolute morality. The world is without significance in itself, it has no inherent meaning—this is Nietzsche's nihilism. But he does not wallow in despair, nor is he sick unto death as was Kierkegaard. Rather the absence of an eternal God to give a meaning to the world permits man to be really free and creative. Nietzsche's will to power then is the will to impose an order upon the world and to invent a meaning for our lives. He is calling for philosophers not to be mere critics and logicians, but to use all the means they can find to forge new values for our age which has shattered the idols of the past but does not yet have new goals toward which to strive. Nietzsche's doctrine of the overman is a poetic call for a more humane, more creative individual, who will confer joy and dignity upon this human life. As Nietzsche put it, "All truly noble morality grows out of triumphant self-affirmation." [37] Whatever else the overman might be, he must at least fully affirm his own nature and create his own values. He must live the philosophy which he professes.

Toward an Evaluation of Nietzsche   The reader has no doubt detected that there are a good many similarities between the thought of Kierkegaard and that of Nietzsche. Despite the fact that the former considered himself a theist, and the latter considered himself an atheist, they both stressed the primacy of the individual. Both of them insisted that each person had to find his own truth through wrestling with those problems which actually threatened his very existence. Only through suffering, through passionate concern, through maintaining one's own integrity despite the pull of the crowd toward conformity and mediocrity, only by seeking to become a real individual human being could one find meaning for his life. These refrains occur in the writings of Kierkegaard and Nietzsche, and are often cited by contemporary existentialists as well. Karl Jaspers, a contemporary German existentialist, suggests that both Kierkegaard and Nietzsche radically questioned traditional reliance upon reason from the depths of their existential concerns and from the perspective of an awareness of the death of the nineteenth-century world-view. But Jaspers also suggests that each man realized that he was an exception, not only to his own age, but to mankind in general. This is precisely the problem which we face in trying to provide an evaluation of Nietzsche's thought: what shall those of us who do not find ourselves so radically out of gear with our age say about Nietzsche's philosophy? [38]

Nietzsche's attempt to find the truth for himself, his refusal to accept blindly the presuppositions of his age, his attempt to subject all presuppositions to ruthless examination, and his constant concern with integrity and self-affirmation are admirable qualities in any thinker. At times Nietzsche seems to have restored the honest search for truth and values which characterized Socrates in ancient Greece. In his outright admission that the post-Christian era required new values he anticipated the major moral crisis of our own age.

But now some of the difficulties with Nietzsche's position come to the foreground. While he sought to discover what the presuppositions of his age actually were, he tended at times to become overly vindictive in his treatment of Christian values as "slave morality," and in his disdain for the common ordinary man. The ordinary man, for Nietzsche, was abandoned to being a herd animal; what he needed was a leader who could show him the way. It was only the rare exception who could be an artist, a philosopher, a scientist or a saint, and Nietzsche does say that these few great men are worth the destruction of a whole flock of ordinary men. Nietzsche, of course, often used metaphors and wrote in aphorisms and poetical-prose so that it is hard to tell when we should take him seriously. Nevertheless, his general drift is clearly to despise the ordinary, the common, and to identify it with the vulgar and "the bad." If he has been misused by the Nazis in order to justify their Aryan superiority, it is fair to say that there are passages in Nietzsche to which they could justifiably appeal.

On the one hand, it is refreshing to find Nietzsche extolling the virtues of a strong individual who achieves his own self-affirmation apart from the stereotyped morality of his own age; on the other hand, it is infuriating to find him extolling all the actions of noble and aristocratic men as "good" simply because they were done by these strong men of power. It is no doubt a misreading of Nietzsche to quote him in support of an anti-morality which claims that "anything is all right, if you are smart enough to get away with it." Nevertheless, there are some passages in Nietzsche where he calls for the strong man to be his own value legislator, and then extolls Napoleon and Cesare Borgia as examples of what he has in mind, which could lead one to draw precisely such a conclusion.

Kierkegaard seemed to believe that no one could really become a Christian in the modern world, or, perhaps more moderately, that becoming a Christian was such a terribly difficult thing that few would dare to even make the attempt. Still for Kierkegaard the irrational leap of faith toward belief in a wholly-other God was the only possible way that an individual could find any meaning or value to his existence. Nietzsche would have agreed with Kierkegaard that Christianity was absurd, but he insisted that one could not find a meaning for his life in the Christian faith, or in any blindly accepted faith. For him the great spirits were skeptics, they did not need convictions. And yet he seems to want us to accept his condemnation of Christianity as a slave morality for weak and impotent men, and to accept his challenge to venture forth and form new values which will satisfy our own will to power. The vision of the over-man is also a faith, and perhaps equally as irrational as the Christian faith which he so readily condemned. Perhaps Nietzsche fell into his own trap, and did not really question seriously his own drive to power, his own yearning for a pristine age of noble skeptics who could act again in a grand manner unfettered by cultural restrictions. If Nietzsche is correct that there can be no presuppositionless philosophy, then that holds for his own world-view as well.

We are again faced with a serious difficulty in our attempt to come to grips with Nietzsche. Precisely when are we to take him seriously, and when is he being ironical? Nietzsche scholars are by no means in agree-ment on this question. Some suggest that only his published writings before his insanity reveal the real Nietzsche, while others hold that only in terms of the unpublished manuscripts written during the last decade of his life can his total philosophy be seen in perspective. Crane Brinton finds that the Nazis had good warrant for using Nietzsche's views to support their claims of being the supermen, while Walter Kaufmann stresses that Nietzsche was not antisemitic and that the "overman" was to be a rare individual and not a racial group.[39] Again, just as in the case of Marx, proof texts can be found to support either of these positions. However, the proof-text method is not very satisfactory, for a thinker such as Nietzsche admitted that he was making experiments with his thought, he was exploring ways of thinking anew. The result is that some-times his thought breaks off in his books, and he turns to another topic which seems radically unrelated to what he had been previously develop-ing. Certainly, if there is a system in Nietzsche's works it is not overt.

At any rate, the great value of Nietzsche's work is not merely in being one of the forerunners of contemporary existentialism. Rather, here we find a writer who is a delight to read, whose aphorisms require our pon-dering, and sometimes our smiles. We cannot be his disciples in toto, but then he tells us that he did not want disciples. He wanted people to think for themselves, to get behind the presuppositions of their age, and to find out how much their view of the world and of life was clouded by their own moral prejudices. In Nietzsche's attempt to understand his own cen-tury, he clearly saw the crisis of intellect and morality which would follow hard upon the death of the traditional Christian idea of God. But he also saw that with the death of God man becomes spiritually free, and is therefore obligated to find for himself a satisfactory way of life. The existentialists, to whom we shall now turn, take up this challenge of Nietzsche's and attempt to find meaning for living in a godless world.

NOTES FOR CHAPTER IV

1 For the biographical data in this section I am indebted to Walter Lowrie, *Kierkegaard* (2 vols.; New York: Harper Torchbooks, 1962).
2 Søren Kierkegaard, *The Journals*, trans. and ed. by Alexander Dru (New York: Harper Torchbooks, 1959), pp. 39–41.
3 *Ibid.*, p. 44.
4 Søren Kierkegaard, *Either/Or*, trans. by Walter Lowrie, rev. and foreword by Howard A. Johnson (Garden City, N. Y.: Anchor Books, Doubleday & Co., Inc., 1959), II, 173.
5 Søren Kierkegaard, *Concluding Unscientific Postscript*, trans. by David F. Swenson, introd. and notes by Walter Lowrie (Princeton, N. J.: Princeton University Press, 1944), p. 284.
6 Quoted in Walter Lowrie's Introduction to Søren Kierkegaard, *Stages on Life's Way*, trans. by Walter Lowrie (Princeton, N. J.: Princeton University Press, 1945), p. 9.
7 Kierkegaard, *Either/Or*, II, 343.
8 Kierkegaard, *Concluding Unscientific Postscript*, p. 261.
9 Søren Kierkegaard, *Sickness Unto Death* in *Fear and Trembling and The Sickness Unto Death*, trans., introd. and notes by Walter Lowrie (Garden City, N. Y.: Anchor Books, Doubleday & Co., Inc., 1955), *passim.*
10 Kierkegaard, *Fear and Trembling* in *Fear and Trembling and The Sickness Unto Death, passim.*
11 Kierkegaard, *The Journals*, p. 53.
12 Søren Kierkegaard, *The Point of View for My Work as an Author: A Report to History and Related Writings*, trans., introd. and notes by Walter Lowrie (New York: Harper Torchbooks, 1962), *passim.*
13 Kierkegaard, *Concluding Unscientific Postscript*, p. 339.
14 Søren Kierkegaard, *Concluding Unscientific Postscript* in *A Kierkegaard Anthology*, ed. by Robert Bretall (New York: The Modern Library, 1938), pp. 202–203.
15 Kierkegaard, *The Point of View for My Work as an Author*, p. 110.
16 Søren Kierkegaard, *Works of Love*, trans. by Howard and Edna Hong (New York: Harper and Brothers, 1962), *passim.*
17 Kierkegaard, *Concluding Unscientific Postscript*, p. 33.
18 Søren Kierkegaard, *On Authority and Revelation: The Book on Adler, or a Cycle of Ethico-Religious Essays*, introd. by Frederick Sontag, trans., introd. and notes by Walter Lowrie (New York: Harper Torchbooks, 1966), liv.
19 Walter Kaufmann, *From Shakespeare to Existentialism* (New ed., Garden City, N. Y.: Anchor Books, Doubleday & Co., Inc., 1960), p. 203.
20 For the biographical data in this section I am indebted to Walter Kaufmann, *Nietzsche—Philosopher, Psychologist, Antichrist* (New York: Meridian Books, 1956).
21 Paul Roubiczek, *Existentialism: For and Against* (Cambridge, England: Cambridge University Press, 1964), pp. 51–52.

22 Friedrich Nietzsche, *The Wanderer and His Shadow* in *The Portable Nietzsche*, trans. and ed. by Walter Kaufmann (New York: The Viking Press, Inc., 1959), p. 70.
23 Friedrich Nietzsche, *Joyful Wisdom*, trans. by Thomas Common, introd. by Kurt F. Reinhardt (New York: Frederick Ungar Publishing Co., 1964), p. 350.
24 Friedrich Nietzsche, *Beyond Good and Evil—A Prelude to a Philosophy of the Future*, trans. by Walter Kaufmann (New York: Vintage Books, Inc., Random House, 1966), p. 136.
25 *Ibid.*, p. 137.
26 *Ibid.*, p. 136.
27 Nietzsche, *Joyful Wisdom*, p. 280.
28 *Ibid.*, pp. 280–281.
29 Nietzsche, *Thus Spoke Zarathustra* in *The Portable Nietzsche*, pp. 170–171.
30 Nietzsche, *Beyond Good and Evil*, p. 205.
31 *Ibid.*, p. 221.
32 *Ibid.*, p. 226.
33 Nietzsche, *The Gay Science* in *The Portable Nietzsche*, pp. 95–96.
34 "The Death of God theologians" are considered in greater detail in chapter six of this book.
35 Nietzsche, *Thus Spoke Zarathustra* in *The Portable Nietzsche*, p. 190.
36 Nietzsche, *Joyful Wisdom*, p. 223.
37 Friedrich Nietzsche, *The Birth of Tragedy and The Genealogy of Morals*, trans. by Francis Golffing (Garden City, N. Y.: Anchor Books, Doubleday & Co., 1956), p. 170.
38 Karl Jaspers, *Kierkegaard and Nietzsche* in *Existentialism: From Dostoevsky to Sartre*, trans. and ed. by Walter Kaufmann (New York: Meridian Books, 1957), pp. 158–184.
39 These contrasting interpretations of Nietzsche are found in Crane Brinton, *Nietzsche* (New York: Harper Torchbooks, 1965); Arthur C. Danto, *Nietzsche As Philosopher* (New York: The Macmillan Co., 1965); Kaufmann, *Nietzsche—Philosopher, Psychologist, Antichrist*.

SELECTED READINGS

* Available in paperback edition.

* Barrett, William. *Irrational Man: A Study in Existential Philosophy*. Garden City, N. Y.: Anchor Books, Doubleday & Co., Inc., 1958. Especially chapters 7 and 8.

Bretall, Robert, ed. *A Kierkegaard Anthology*. New York: The Modern Library, 1948. An excellent selection from all of the major writings of Kierkegaard, with useful introductory notes by the editor.

Danto, Arthur C. *Nietzsche As Philosopher*. New York: The Macmillan Co., 1965.

* Kaufmann, Walter, ed. and trans. *Existentialism: From Dostoevsky to Sartre*. New York: Meridian Books, 1957. Selections from all the major existentialists.

* ———. *Nietzsche: Philosopher, Psychologist, Antichrist*. New York: Meridian Books, 1956.

* ———, ed. and trans. *The Portable Nietzsche*. New York: The Viking Press, Inc., 1959. Includes complete text of *Twilight of the Idols*, *The Antichrist*, *Nietzsche Contra Wagner*, *Thus Spoke Zarathustra*.

Kierkegaard, Søren. *Concluding Unscientific Postscript*. Translated by David F. Swenson, completed after his death and introduction and notes by Walter Lowrie. Princeton, N. J.: Princeton University Press, 1944.

* ———. *Either/Or: Volume I*. Translated by David F. and Lillian Marvin Swenson. Garden City, N. Y.: Anchor Books, Doubleday & Co., Inc., 1959.

* ———. *Either/Or: Volume II*. Translated by Walter Lowrie with revisions and foreword by Howard A. Johnson. Garden City, N. Y.: Anchor Books, Doubleday & Co., Inc., 1959.

* ———. *Fear and Trembling and The Sickness Unto Death*. Translated, introduction, and notes by Walter Lowrie. Garden City, N. Y.: Anchor Books, Doubleday & Co., Inc., 1955.

* Lowrie, Walter. *Kierkegaard: Volume One* (I. Childhood, 1813–1830; II, Youth, 1830–1838; III. Early Manhood, 1838–1844). New York: Harper Torchbooks, 1962.

* ———. *Kierkegaard: Volume Two* (IV. Intellectual Maturity, 1844–1847; V. Becoming A Christian, 1848–1852; VI. The Corrective: The Sacrifice, 1852–1855). New York: Harper Torchbooks, 1962.

* Nietzsche, Friedrich. *Beyond Good and Evil: A Prelude to a Philosophy of the Future*. Translated by Walter Kaufmann. New York: Vintage Books, Inc., Random House, 1966.

* ———. *The Birth of Tragedy and The Genealogy of Morals*. Translated by Francis Golffing. Garden City, N. Y.: Anchor Books, Doubleday & Co., Inc., 1956.

* ———. *Joyful Wisdom*. Translated by Thomas Common. Introduction by Kurt F. Reinhardt. New York: Frederick Ungar Publishing Co., 1964.

* ———. *Thus Spoke Zarathustra: A Book for All and None*. Translated by Walter Kaufmann. New York: The Viking Press, Inc., 1966.

V

Humanistic Existentialism:
Jean-Paul Sartre

Jean-Paul Sartre is undoubtedly the best known of the contemporary existentialists. The general reader may not have read any of his difficult philosophical works, such as *Being and Nothingness*, but he has more than likely read some of Sartre's plays, short stories or novels. Perhaps the reader also knows that Sartre was one of the leaders of the French Resistance movement while Paris was occupied by the Nazis, or he may have a dim awareness that in recent years Sartre has become more sympathetic to Marxism. In many respects Sartre represents a man who has moved from his own analysis of the human predicament to an active involvement in trying to improve the political nature of the world. Fully convinced that there are no absolute values, he has sought for something to which he could commit his own life, as well as for a way of waking all of us from our contented middle-class slumbers. In our attempt to create our own life styles, we should examine very carefully Sartre's philosophy, for probably no other thinker of our century has been so often quoted and so little understood.

Jean-Paul Sartre was born in Paris in 1905. He never knew his father, who died while he was an infant, and was reared in the home of his maternal grandfather, Charles Schweitzer, an uncle of the famous missionary physician and philosopher, Albert Schweitzer. Sartre describes his development as a child in the first volume of his autobiography, *The Words*. Not being physically strong, he developed an early interest in reading and writing. He tells us in his autobiography that by the age of nine he was firmly committed to becoming a writer. He was obsessed by the earthly immortality of the printed word, which would live long after the physical death of its author. Unable to accept either the Protestant or Catholic Christianity of his parents and grandparents, he viewed writing as a secular means of achieving an identity in the world, of discovering who he was, of achieving salvation. Sartre describes that while waiting for some schoolmates one day in 1917, he decided to occupy his mind by thinking about God:

> Immediately He tumbled into the blue and disappeared without giving any explanation. He doesn't exist, I said to myself with polite surprise, and I thought the matter was settled. In a way, it was, since never have I had the slightest temptation to bring Him back to life.[1]

Thus, was born Sartre's atheism.

Even in his early childhood Sartre reveals that he was obsessed with the feeling of boredom and with an overbearing desire to create his own life. His grandfather attempted to get him to follow an academic career, and Sartre followed his advice to the extent of getting a degree in philosophy at the Ecole Normale Superieure in 1929. Still wishing to become a novelist, he taught philosophy for the next ten years in various *lycées*, except for the academic year 1933–1934, which he spent studying philosophy in Berlin.

Sartre was bored with orthodox philosophizing for it seemed to be so concerned with abstractions that it lost sight of the concrete details of ordinary life. His life-long friend, Simone de Beauvoir, has described how it came about that Sartre went to Germany to study philosophy. Raymond Aron, having just returned from Germany, was extolling to Sartre the new method of philosophizing upon the concrete being developed by the German philosopher Husserl. Philosophy was to become a disclosure of the concrete, of the way in which the things themselves reveal themselves to us. Husserl called the method by which philosophy was to get back to the things themselves, phenomenology. Aron pointed to his drink, and said, " 'You see, my dear fellow, if you are a phenomenologist, you can talk about this cocktail and make philosophy out of it!' "[2] Although Sartre had never heard of Husserl before, he was so intrigued with Aron's description of this new method of doing philosophy that he spent a year studying with Husserl in Berlin. When he returned to France he developed his own version of this method of philosophy, one which is known as existential phenomenology.

We shall examine Sartre's existential phenomenological method later on, as well as the respects in which this differs from the method of Husserl. It is important for us to note at this point, however, that it was this new way of looking at man and the world which was responsible not only for Sartre's massive philosophical work, *Being and Nothingness* (1943), but also for his achieving his early desire to become a novelist. *Nausea*, his first novel, was published in 1938. The following year a collection of his short stories was published. *Nausea* and his short stories are literary examples of his basic philosophical posture, but they cannot be taken by themselves as complete expositions of Sartre's philosophy. At about the same time as the publication of these literary works, Sartre issued four philosophical treatises applying his new method to the imagination, the emotions and the ego. In one of these treatises, *The Transcendence of the Ego* (1936–1937), Sartre shows his disagreements with Husserl's method and presents in outline the theory which was to be developed at great lengths later on in *Being and Nothingness*. Thus, Sartre's position was already well developed before the outbreak of the Second World War; hence, those attempts by some critics to dismiss *Being and Nothingness* as a philosophy written merely to justify the French opposition to the Nazis are inaccurate.

While Sartre's basic philosophical position had been formulated before the Second World War, there is nevertheless some justification for linking his philosophy with the French Resistance movement. Sartre was drafted into the French army in 1939, was captured by the Germans, and spent nine months in a German prisoner of war camp. He was returned to Paris because of ill health, and became one of the writer-leaders, along with Albert Camus, of the French Resistance movement.

During the Nazi occupation of Paris, Sartre wrote two plays, *No Exit* and *The Flies*, which were actually produced under the eyes of the Nazi authorities. *The Flies* was generally understood by the French as a portrayal of the French Resistance movement, which to pass German censorship was presented in the form of an old Greek myth. These two plays brought Sartre to the attention of the general public who found in them a philosophical presentation of their historical predicament. Not only for the French in occupied Paris, but also for many readers in all countries since that time, Sartre seemed to present the substance of the existentialist philosophy in *The Flies*. Man has no God and no determined being; he must himself choose what he will become. In response to Zeus' offer to forgive Orestes if he repents of his freedom, Orestes says:

> Foreign to myself—I know it. Outside nature, against nature, without excuse, beyond remedy, except what remedy I find within myself. But I shall not return under your law; I am doomed to have no other law but mine. Nor shall I come back to nature, the nature you found good; in it are a thousand beaten paths all leading up to you—but I must blaze my trail. For I, Zeus, am a man, and every man must find out his own way. Nature abhors man, and you too, god of gods, abhor mankind.[3]

We may for convenience in our discussion suggest that thus far there have been three main periods in Sartre's life. We have already mentioned the first one, which was primarily concerned with finding a philosophical method by which man could be studied in the concrete reality of the life he actually lives. The outcome of this study was to suggest to Sartre that man was radically free to choose the being he wished to become. Until the Second World War he was primarily concerned with showing man his individuality, his aloneness, and with challenging each man to find his own way of salvation.

The second stage in Sartre's career began during the War when he stressed the importance of a man committing himself to a group or to an image of what man ought to become. After the War he united with Raymond Aron, Merleau-Ponty, and Simone de Beauvoir to found *Les Temps Modernes*, a review which was to be concerned with social and political issues, as well as with literature. This monthly publication sought to apply Sartre's existentialist view of man to the actual political and social crises of the post-war world. It was his method of becoming involved in the life of his fellow men. Not considering himself fitted for an active political life, Sartre became the advocate of an "engaged literature." For a brief period Sartre seemed to think that a unified humanity was possible, that all men might be able to accept their freedom only if all other men were free as well. According to his view in 1947 the prose writer should have only one basic topic: the freedom of all mankind. Hence on whatever hand freedom was threatened, the prose writer had an obligation to raise his voice in protest. As Sartre put it: "One is always responsible for what one does not try to prevent." [4]

This second stage of Sartre's career in which he stressed commitment to the freedom of all mankind is also represented by his brief address, *Existentialism Is a Humanism* (1946). But his optimistic hope that all men would unite in seeking each other's freedom was short lived. Instead of one human world at peace, he found two power blocs of nations opposing each other across an Iron Curtain. The cold war, the conflicts in Algeria, Korea, and Viet Nam, suggested to him that he could no longer remain committed to a vague ideal of human freedom for all men. He considered it his responsibility to affiliate himself with one movement which he thought offered the last best hope for mankind. This movement was Marxism.

It is important to bear in mind that while Sartre today considers himself a Marxist, he has not formally joined the Communist Party. Rather he considers Marxism to be the only philosophy of the twentieth century. When Marx's original concern with the plight of the individual is restored to present-day Marxist thought, Sartre believes existentialism will justifiably disappear. He says that he has lost all his old illusions about writing as a way to his individual salvation. His only function now is to serve to revitalize Marxism so that it may again have a revolutionary appeal for the working class. This is the Sartre of the third stage. In many respects it appears that he has undergone a radical conversion from his early views of *Being and Nothingness;* clearly he stresses the importance of collective action in organized groups in a way that he did not even then envision as possible for man. We shall look closely later on at his recent opus, *Critique de la raison dialectique,* published in 1960. For in this volume, which is even longer than *Being and Nothingness,* he presents his critique of Marxism in the light of his existentialism. Sartre thus considers himself a fellow-traveler and has sworn to hate the bourgeoisie until the day he dies. His conversion, as he describes it, came when he realized the futility of neutrality in the present struggles of the East and the West. Therefore, he committed himself, by saying, "I would stand on the side of the Communists and I would proclaim it." [5]

But perhaps Sartre has not yet reached the end of the line. Clearly his truce with Marxism seems to be an uneasy one, and he himself admits that he is somewhat at loose ends as to where his new position will take him. Near the end of *The Words* he writes:

> For the last ten years or so I've been a man who's been waking up, cured of a long, bitter-sweet madness, and who can't get over the fact, a man who can't think of his old ways without laughing and who doesn't know what to do with himself. [6]

Despite this statement of Sartre's there are some common threads which run through his entire work. Let us turn now to an investigation in detail of Sartre's views during each of these three stages which we have sketched.

The Human Condition: Being and Nothingness   The subtitle of *Being and Nothingness* is *An Essay on Phenomenological Ontology.* This rather forbidding phrase indicates that Sartre's objective in this book is to describe the basic structures of the world and of man in terms of the way these structures actually appear to us in our experience. We have seen that Sartre spent a year studying with the founder of phenomenology in Germany, and it is now time for us to present more clearly the nature of this radically new method of philosophical investigation.

The phenomenologist attempts to observe phenomena (that which actually appears to us) as they actually disclose themselves rather than to categorize phenomena on the basis of the traditional subject-object theory of knowledge. Edmund Husserl (1859–1938) developed his method of phenomenological analysis by means of what he called a "psychological-phenomenological reduction." [7] In this reduction the observer puts the world in brackets so as to exclude the distinction of subject and object as well as any value judgment about the phenomenon. He wished to allow the actual things of experience to disclose themselves to him, much as they do to a small child who has not yet learned to differentiate itself from the things around it. What he was bracketing was the question concerning the nature of that which appears. Is it real, or an image? Is it outside the mind or within my consciousness? These questions Husserl put to one side; he might return to them later, but not until he had allowed the things as they actually appeared to consciousness to reveal themselves. What he claimed to have discovered by his method was the essential contact between consciousness and the world which rests on what he called the transcendental Ego. Thus, instead of having only a subject which then had to justify the world, as in the case of Descartes, Husserl posited the basic relation of awareness as a consciousness-of-the-world. In other words, I do not apprehend myself, but rather I apprehend my being conscious of something. The world presents itself to my consciousness in my primitive awareness and I then confer a meaning upon the world. By Husserl's method one concentrates upon what phenomenologists call the intentional act. We take a new attitude to the world; we view it in regard to our intentions, and this opens up the possibility of apprehending the basic structures in terms of which human beings constitute their world by their desires, needs, projections, etc.

There is, however, a real difference between the phenomenological method of reduction as practiced by Husserl, and the existential phenomenological method as practiced by Sartre and Heidegger, the German existentialist. Husserl believed that existence itself could be bracketed and ignored for the sake of pure phenomenological description. All the existentialists believe that this is a mistake for they insist that one cannot ignore the actual finite concrete existence of the philosopher who is thinking. The actual existence of the concrete man precedes his dealing in terms of theoretical essences; it is this which at least partly explains the emphasis upon existence preceding essence.

The existential phenomenologists are therefore interested in describing the concrete data of experience as immediately given. While Sartre first learned of the phenomenological method from Husserl, his own use of the method is closer to the methods of Hegel and Heidegger.

Hegel in his first major book, *The Phenomenology of Spirit*, sought to describe human experience in its broadest aspects. In his description he found that experience was never static, and that the present can only be viewed as a coming from the past and a moving toward the future. Neither Heidegger nor Sartre follow Hegel into his abstract realms of speculation, but they do agree with him that man's experience is a constant movement toward a future. Rather than study man as an abstraction, however, they attempt to study the concrete life of the individual as he actually lives it. Both Heidegger and Sartre discover that behind scientific knowledge and reflective self-awareness there is a more basic *Lebenswelt* (life-world) in which we human beings always live, and which gives us our first awareness of ourselves and the world around us.

Heidegger has stressed that man understands himself with his entire being, not merely with his reflective consciousness. Hence, Heidegger maintains man is thrown into a world in which he must work out his own destiny. His philosophy is an attempt to reveal the human life-world as it actually appears to man. Heidegger thus maintains that my awareness of the world is disclosed first of all by mood and feeling, rather than by concepts. This existential mode of mood and feeling is prior to any subject-object distinction and reveals to me the fact of my being-in-the-world in concrete situations which press upon me and call me to solve or escape from them. Heidegger with his great interest in the etymologies of words tells us that "phenomenon" means in Greek "that which shows itself in itself." [8] If we let the thing reveal itself to us we shall see it in a new light, the light of truth, of revelation. This method permits us therefore to observe a great deal which our predilection for objectivity would hide from us. We are encouraged to deal with our acts from the inside as we actually live them, and by so doing we are told that we shall discover structures as they are actually found in the concrete contexts of our lives. By this method the individual's mode of existing is disclosed and then amazingly enough he can discover analogies with other persons' modes of existing.

But what exactly does Heidegger mean by a life-world? It will be important for us to clarify this conception, since Sartre himself holds a similar position. A concrete illustration will make our task easier. We are all aware of clock-time, so that if I ask you what time it is you will glance at your watch and respond by saying the hour and minutes which you read off the face of your watch. But this is an agreed upon social convention by which we human beings measure the passage of time, and is not the same as "lived time." At the end of a boring lecture, you may say, "That hour passed slowly. I thought it would never end." Or, after a pleasant week of vacation, you may say, "Time went so fast; it seems as though we just came and now we must go home." In these last two instances you are dealing with "lived time," time as you have actually experienced it, and not with clock-time. In terms of clock-time, the hour's lecture was filled with sixty minutes—no more and no less, but it seemed like an eternity to you, because you were bored. On the other hand, there were seven full days in your vacation, but you enjoyed them so thoroughly that it seems as though the week had just begun when it had ended. It will prove interesting for the reader to contrast for himself his lived space with physical space; Russia may be closer to his concern than the little town a few miles away. Your world is constituted by your concerns, your interests, and your projects for the future—it is these which the existential phenomenologists wish to study for these, they maintain, are the really basic human structures of life.

Sartre has formulated his own method of existential phenomenology which while in general agreement with the method used by Heidegger seeks to avoid some of the mystical overtones and metaphysical obscurities into which the latter has sometimes fallen. Sartre is concerned with giving a general description of the world and of human reality. He agrees with Heidegger that we possess a pre-reflective awareness, and therefore disagrees with Freud's theory of our having an unconscious. We act in the world, and adopt emotional reactions in the light of this pre-reflective awareness, and only in moments of reflection do we try to analyze ourselves. He agrees with Husserl that consciousness is always of something: we can never catch our pure consciousness in itself. But he offers an apparently astonishing reason why we can never find our pure consciousness. It is because consciousness in itself is completely empty; it is literally a nothingness. The entire world exists outside consciousness and constitutes being; my consciousness then is merely a lack of being, it itself is nothing desiring to become something. What exists for consciousness is being-in-itself, which is solid, completely filled. But a man is not a being-in-itself, at least not completely, for his consciousness is that emptiness, that lacking, that desiring, which forces him to choose the kind of person he wishes to become. But he also must choose what he wishes to know; he must choose how he will see the world. Sartre is concerned with revealing to man that he has no fixed determinate nature, such as a stone has, and that therefore man is condemned to choose his being by his every act, thought and emotion.

While Sartre maintains that man has no essence, no fixed determinate nature, the reader should not conclude that therefore nothing can be said other than that each man must choose what he shall become. While man cannot be discussed as a concept or as an abstraction, Sartre attempts to analyze man as he actually lives in various concrete situations in the world. In *Being and Nothingness* Sartre, therefore, was concerned with understanding the general structure of what he calls human reality. The massive world with which an individual is confronted he called "being-in-itself," while the individual's own consciousness he characterized as "being-for-itself." But in addition to these two structures, he found that there were also two derivative ones, "being-for-others" and "being-with-others." Since so much of Sartre's philosophy depends upon understanding the distinctions he makes between these four modes of being we shall examine them in some detail.

(1) *Being-in-itself.* When Sartre reflects upon being as it must appear when considered purely in itself, before human consciousness has named and classified it, he concludes that about all we can say is that: "Being is. Being is in-itself. Being is what it is." [9] All that we can attribute to being-

in-itself is that it is massive, undifferentiated, amorphous, and senseless existence. It is a plenum, completely filled. Nothing more can be said about it. Being simply is. It is everything except the human consciousness. It is what is there to confront the human consciousness when it arrives upon the scene.

Being-in-itself is not to be identified with what we call objects or things. It is true that objects have being-in-itself, there is something about them that presents them to us as outside ourselves, as obstacles to be overcome, or tools to be used, etc. But the moment that we are able to mention stones, pens, paper, and so on, the human consciousness has already been at work bestowing upon these areas of being-in-itself specific characteristics.

To human consciousness, being-in-itself is absurd, disgusting, nauseating! In his novel *Nausea* Sartre pictures the hero, Roquentin, on a bench in a city park, near an old chestnut tree whose ugly black roots plunge down into the ground; the man on the bench senses suddenly that the crowding roots groping about unseen under the earth are symbolic of the nauseating senselessness and absurdity of the ground of being, being-in-itself. As Roquentin remarks:

> This root, in contrast, existed in such a way that I could not explain it. Knotty, inert, nameless, it fascinated me, filled my eyes, brought me back unceasingly to its own existence. In vain I repeated, "This is a root"—it didn't take hold any more. . . . That root, with its color, shape, its congealed movement, was—beneath all explanation. . . . That black there, amorphous, weakly presence, overflowed sight, smell, and taste. But this exuberance became confusion and finally it was no longer anything because it was too much. . . . But the images, forewarned, leaped up and filled my closed eyes with existences: existence is a fullness from which man can never get away.[10]

This is about as close as one can come to conveying what Sartre means by being-in-itself. To say any more, or indeed even this much, is to be put into contact with the other primal mode of being, being-for-itself.

(2) *Being-for-itself*. If being-in-itself is just what it is, inert and unintelligible, and can be nothing other than what it is, being-for-itself never *is* but continuously *has to become*. It fundamentally contrasts with being-in-itself which already is and which has no becoming. Man, alone of all the beings in the universe, is characterized as a being-for-itself. There is always some gap between man's consciousness of himself and any attempt to describe him as an object with a completely determinate nature. But if being-in-itself completely exhausts substantial existing being, then being-for-itself must be a nothingness. Sartre does not shrink from making this claim; man as a being-for-himself has no essence. He will become only what he makes of himself. Pure being-for-itself is a lack, an emptiness, a

nothingness. It is through man that Sartre finds that nothingness appears in the world. Man is the being who can question, who can negate, and who can conceive of that which is not. When Sartre considers the human self (being-for-itself) he maintains that "existence precedes essence," that is, an individual's pre-reflective awareness exists before he has a nature or character. No man is born with a character but acquires one by the choices which he makes. Sartre puts the matter clearly enough:

> What do we mean by saying that existence precedes essence? We mean that man first of all exists, encounters himself, surges up in the world—and defines himself afterwards. If man as the existentialist sees him is not definable, it is because to begin with he is nothing. He will not be anything until later, and then he will be what he makes of himself. Thus, there is no human nature, because there is no God to have a conception of it. Man simply is. Not that he is simply what he conceives himself to be, but he is what he wills, and as he conceives himself after already existing—as he wills to be after that leap towards existence.[11]

It is important to keep in mind that Sartre does not claim that man is a pure being-for-itself. Just as being-in-itself was not to be literally equated with determinate objects in the world, but was rather the ground of all being, present in all objects, so being-for-itself is a limiting concept and is not to be equated with human reality. However, it is only in the case of man that being-for-itself appears at all in the world, and no man can continue to be human and become merely an object in the world. A particular individual always unites in his person being-for-itself and being-in-itself. A man always finds himself in a particular situation; he has a particular perspective because of his body, because of the occupation he is engaged in, because of where he lives, and so on. These aspects of human reality Sartre calls "facticity." But no individual can characterize himself purely in terms of facticity, for he also has his own projects for the future, his own ideas of what he wishes to do and become, and he always has the possibility of even radically altering his perspective on the world and his character. It is in these respects that man is a being-for-himself; he creates his own nature by acting on the world outside of himself.

Sartre uses some excellent illustrations to explain his views of man as a being-for-himself. One of the most frequently quoted is his description of the polished café waiter who by his every move appears to others to be almost an automaton. But as Sartre remarks, "From within, the waiter in the café can not be immediately a café waiter in the sense that this inkwell *is* an inkwell, or the glass *is* a glass."[12] The inkwell has no choice as to whether or not it will be an inkwell, but the waiter has chosen to play the role of a waiter. It is true that in a sense he is a waiter, but he is also a man who transcends his position. In a radical move he could choose to be late for work so often that finally he would be fired. He would then not be a waiter any longer. But, according to Sartre, he never really has been a waiter in the mode of being-in-itself. He has been a man who has assumed being a waiter as one of the roles which he plays in his world. But he plays other roles as well; he may play the roles of father and husband, of being a Communist or a Christian, and so on. But, as Sartre concludes, "We are dealing with more than mere social positions; I am never any one of my attitudes, any one of my actions." [13] Each individual recognizes himself as more than his attitudes, more than his body, and more than the roles which he plays. Sartre's method has been an attempt to remind us that this ability to question our own existence, to change our character, is at the root of what it means to be a man. It is that which he means by being-for-itself.

But Sartre attempts to describe being-for-itself even more precisely. Man's self viewed as a being-for-itself is nothingness, it has to become, but as yet it is a "hole" in the density of being-in-itself. Being-for-itself, therefore, is also characterized as a lack or a desire to fill this void, to actually become something. One of the ways which Sartre suggests that a being-for-itself seeks to overcome this lack of being is by seeking satisfaction through the accumulation of possessions, or through the human activities of art, science and play. These modes of human action are all viewed by Sartre as forms of appropriation, not only of the particular objects desired, but more basically of being-in-itself. He describes the "lived" existential meaning of the desire to possess something as at root a yearning to be united with the object itself:

> Thus the desire of a particular object is not the simple desire of this object; it is the desire to be united with the object in an internal relation, in the mode of constituting with it the unity "possessor-possessed." The desire to have is at bottom reducible to the desire to be related to a certain object in a certain relation of being. [14]

It is obvious that to possess something means to have it for myself. Thus, one of the means whereby being-for-itself seeks to overcome its lack of being is by constituting itself by the accumulation of objects. But these objects are not purely external to me; rather they constitute myself. It is this which he means when he speaks of being related to one's possessions by an internal relation. My books, my car, my phonograph records are part of my own personality. I care for these objects in a way in which no one else does, for they are one mode of my obtaining substantial reality in the world. If my only mode of choosing myself were to consist in appropriating objects, then these objects would be myself:

> Thus to the extent that I appear to myself as *creating* objects by the sole relation of appropriation, these objects are *myself*. The pen and the pipe, the clothing, the desk, the house—are myself. The totality

of my possessions reflects the totality of my being. I *am* what I have.[15]

There is an instability in constituting oneself only by the accumulation of objects, however, for despite the fact that my books reflect myself, they nevertheless are outside myself in the external world and they remain beings-in-themselves despite my possession of them. Hence, appropriation of objects represents what Sartre calls a "magical relation," a transference of myself by my intentions to those objects which exist in the outside world. It is an attempt to fill the void in my being-for-itself:

> In the relation of possession the dominant term is the object possessed; without it I am nothing save a nothingness which possesses, nothing other than pure and simple possession, an incompleteness, an insufficiency, whose sufficiency and completion are there in that object. In possession, I am my own foundation in so far as I exist in an in-itself.[16]

But, this relation of appropriation is always an ideal and symbolic one, for I can never satisfy my desire to be my own foundation for my being simply by accumulating possessions. Possession of objects is therefore only part of the solution to my quest for a substantial reality, for my being-for-itself always stands apart from the objects themselves.

One of the most important characteristics of being-for-itself is precisely this ability to stand apart from objects, to transcend them. In fact, Sartre stresses the capacity to transcend itself, or to project states of affairs different from those now in existence, as one of the defining characteristics of being-for-itself. This is what he means when he says that, "I am not the self which I will be." [17] I can never identify myself with my past achievements, nor with what I am doing in the present. For I am always looking toward a future, and projecting what I wish to do, how I wish to change myself, and what I wish to become. In fact, I even decide how I am going to interpret what has happened to me in the past; that is, I decide what meaning to give to my past and how I am going to appropriate it in building my own life. It is the for-itself that confers value upon the world. We should recall that Sartre insists that man is not a pure being-for-itself; man is limited by what has been, what kind of a body he has, and so on. But, and this is the important point, man can decide what he is to make of the facts, such as how he is going to view his physical deficiencies. Let us consider an example to make clearer what Sartre means by the ability of man to transcend himself. Suppose that one is crippled, and no operations are known which will correct the deformity. Then that is a part of what Sartre calls one's facticity—it is a fact in the world. However, if one is crippled one has the ability to interpret what "being a cripple" means to him. He can pity himself, ask for and feel entitled to charity from others, and blame his sadness upon his being crippled. He may even form his own self-image so that he consciously describes his essential nature by saying, "I am a cripple." But to respond in this way is an instance of what Sartre calls "bad faith." The cripple is lying to himself, but he is not really deceiving himself. He knows, to the extent that he is a being-for-itself, that he is not a cripple in the way that the inkwell is an inkwell. The inkwell can do nothing whatsoever about its being an inkwell; it has a substantial being-in-itself. But no man while he is still alive is ever completely describable, not even to himself, as a being-in-itself. The very nature of what being crippled means depends upon how the person who is crippled interprets this fact about his life. Despite his physical infirmity, his whole nature is not summed up by saying, "I am a cripple." He can accept his physical infirmity as part of the facts which he cannot change, but he can also view himself as a man who can decide how he should view his life, what he ought to do and become. Thus, instead of seeking pity and asking for charity, the man who is crippled may choose to work hard at accomplishing some task or goal which he has set for himself in order that other people will view him as a man and not as a cripple. He may choose to become independent and self-supporting, for he too is a man. Thus, a man transcends his present and past existence by choosing what meaning he will place upon what has happened to him in the world.

We have in our discussion of man's capacity to transcend himself already touched upon what is for Sartre the most significant characteristic of man as a being-for-itself, namely freedom. For if man is to choose the kind of person he is to become, he must be free to both make such a choice, and to act in such a way as to realize his choice. More than anything else, it is this freedom which Sartre finds differentiates human reality from all other beings in the world; it is freedom which permits man to make his own essence:

> Human freedom precedes essence in man and makes it possible; the essence of the human being is suspended in his freedom. What we call freedom is impossible to distinguish from the being of "human reality." [18]

Hence, man is condemned to freedom. He cannot escape, although he may try by many ways to mask his freedom or to surrender it. Even in such disguised forms, however, man has chosen and his freedom will keep haunting him.

The human situation in which man is thrown into a world, surrounded by being-in-itself, and condemned to choose his own nature has both its heartening and disheartening sides. On the heartening side, we have these conditions: (1) Since being-in-itself and being-for-itself exhaust all the possibilities of reality, there can be no God. The idea of God is merely

an ideal hope of a union of the in-itself with the for-itself in a final unchanging synthesis. But the for-itself never is, it is always in the process
of becoming; furthermore, it could never be completely incarnated in an
in-itself for then it would no longer be for-itself. Hence, Sartre finds the
traditional idea of God to be self-contradictory. But rather than find the
absence of God disheartening, man should realize fully that he cannot be
predetermined, and that therefore he can really make himself by his own
choices. (2) Since there is no standard given to man from on high by a
God there is no objective Good, no ultimate value. Man therefore, must
make his own life-plan. This offers him creative possibilities. As Sartre
puts it:

> Freedom is precisely the nothingness which is made-to-be at the
> heart of man and which forces human-reality to make itself instead
> of to be. . . . For human reality, to be is to choose oneself; nothing
> comes to it either from the outside or from within which it can
> receive or accept. Without any help whatsoever, it is entirely
> abandoned to the intolerable necessity of making itself be—down to
> the slightest detail. Thus freedom is not a being; it is the being of
> man. . . .[19]

We have already seen in the last quotation some of the disheartening
aspects of man's freedom: we are abandoned to choose our being, down
to the very last detail. Furthermore, neither within our own nature, nor
from outside ourselves can we gain any definitive help for our quest.
Freedom is therefore apprehended by anguish and dread. "I am condemned to be free. This means that no limits to my freedom can be found
except freedom itself or, if you prefer, that we are not free to cease being
free."[20] Let the reader note that Sartre is not merely saying that I must
choose my destiny at some time or other, and then I can rest content.
Rather, he is maintaining that I must constantly choose each moment of
my life, by all my actions, thoughts, feelings and hopes the kind of a man
I want to become. Furthermore, I cannot blame my heredity nor my
environment for the kind of a person I am and become, for the simple
reason that I am free to determine what to make of my heredity and
environment. Hence, in a sense I am fully responsible for myself. No
wonder that Sartre tells us that we usually apprehend this radical freedom
in anguish and dread. All my acts and gestures refer to my world-view;
they reflect my choice of my self constantly being renewed. The fundamental act of freedom which I constantly renew is "a choice of myself
in the world and by the same token it is a discovery of the world."[21]
    One might object that Sartre has ignored the possibility of one follow-
ing the advice of another in constructing his own life-plan, or of simply
falling in line with the prevailing trends within his society. One has not
chosen in such a situation; he has instead allowed others to make the

choice for him. Not so fast, for Sartre even in these possibilities insists upon man's radical freedom. "Freedom is the freedom of choosing but not the freedom of not choosing. Not to choose is, in fact, to choose not to choose." [22]

(3) *Being-for-others*. While it is true that the two limiting concepts for Sartre are being-in-itself (filled massive being) and being-for-itself (nothingness, becoming), nevertheless, in his analysis of the human situation he discusses a third possible mode—being-for-others. When I am thrown into a world I find myself not only surrounded by objects but also by other people. Other selves are a very present reality for us. As Sartre sees it, the process by which I become aware of them is precisely like that by which I become aware of myself—an immediate and direct experience; in this case it is a slightly enlarged awareness which takes some such form as this: I am sitting on a park bench and another person, a stranger, walks by and raises his eyes to look at me; immediately, I become, and *know* I have become, an object, a thing, a body, to him. He annihilates my subjectivity in making me his object. Suddenly fear and shame engulf me and I make a valiant struggle to regain my selfhood and my freedom. This experience has such indubitable reality that I am as sure of his existence as I am of my own. By experiences such as these, men know they live in a world of other selves with whose existences they are involved.

We have noted in the above illustration, that when the other person looks at me, he makes me an object (an in-itself) for his own consciousness. Annoyed at becoming a mere object, like the park bench upon which I am sitting, I in turn stare at the other person in such a way as to see him as an object. Only in this way can I keep from being reduced to a thing in the eyes of the other; but by my glance I have reduced the other to a thing for me. This illustration represents Sartre's version in *Being and Nothingness* of the only possibilities open in any human relationship between two people: one of them must become a thing, a being-in-itself, for the other, who is being-for-itself. Sartre sees no possibility of an inter-subjective awareness, of what Martin Buber has called an I-Thou relationship. Instead Sartre acknowledges that, like Karl Marx, he finds that Hegel was profoundly correct when he recognized the basis of all human relationships as that of Master to Slave. When the other person who looks at me makes me into an object for his glance, I have become his slave. Only when I can reduce him to an object for my glance, do I become master of the situation. Thus, for Sartre: "Opposite the Other and confronting the Other, each one asserts his right of being individual." [23]

Yet, paradoxical as it may at first appear, the other is not merely a thing, a being-in-itself, and my relationships with him are doomed to frustration for "the Other is on principle that which can not be an object." [24] Hence, when the other glances at me and I feel shame at being reduced to an object, I am immediately aware of the other's subjectivity. But beyond this I cannot go, for I cannot know the total organization of the world as the other has constituted it for himself. He has the power to have his own point of view, which is not mine. Furthermore, I cannot think his thoughts, but by acting upon his thoughts the other may constitute a real danger to me. I can recognize him as a being-for-itself, but I cannot exhaust his being no matter how hard I try. For even when I successfully reduce him to an object for my purposes, he always has the possibility of reversing the relationship. The other also transcends himself. Hence, as Sartre sees it, there are two authentic attitudes possible in any relationship I have with another person:

> That by which I recognize the Other as subject through whom I get my object-ness—this is shame; and that by which I apprehend myself as the free object by which the Other gets his being-other— this is arrogance or the affirmation of my freedom confronting the Other-as-object.[25]

Since I can never capture the self of the other, since his being-for-itself always eludes my grasp, inevitably I view the other as a permanent threat to my own existence as a free subject. At least, that is what Sartre's analysis implies:

> The Other-as-object is an explosive instrument which I handle with care because I foresee around him the permanent possibility that *they* are going to make it explode and that with this explosion I shall suddenly experience the flight of the world away from me and the alienation of my being. Therefore my constant concern is to contain the Other within his objectivity, and my relations with the Other-as-object are essentially made up of ruses designed to make him remain an object. But one look on the part of the Other is sufficient to make all these schemes collapse and to make me experience once more the transfiguration of the Other [into a subject].[26]

With this belief concerning the threat which other people pose to one, it is little wonder that a character in *No Exit* aptly sums up the theme of Sartre's play in his remark: "Hell is—other people!" [27]

Furthermore, other persons can say the same things about their relations with me, as I can say about them. I constitute a threat to their subjective being. As Sartre states:

> While I attempt to free myself from the hold of the Other, the Other is trying to free himself from mine; while I seek to enslave the Other, the Other seeks to enslave me. We are by no means dealing with unilateral relations with an object-in-itself, but with reciprocal and moving relations. . . .[28]

Hence, Sartre concludes, "Conflict is the original meaning of being-for-others." [29]

As we have seen Sartre denies that it is ever possible for two persons to have an I-Thou relationship so that each preserves his own subjectivity. Even in his analysis of love, Sartre insists that one of the persons involved must become an object to the subjectivity of the other. The analysis would seem to indicate that love amounts to mutual self-frustration, for as in all other human relationships Sartre finds conflict to be dominant. In the first place, love is the wish to be loved; but this means that I want to be the object of another's devotion, the source of the other's values. Consequently, I tend to *seduce* the other by making myself a fascinating object. But if this succeeds, I do not become the object by which the other's subjective freedom is achieved; the other loves me to the degree of surrendering the subjectivity of the subject and incarnating it in me, thus becoming object in relation to me as subject. If, in seeking to avoid the frustration of such a reversal, I choose *masochism* and reduce myself to nothing but the object of the other's total freedom, this would fill me with deep shame and the other with a sense of guilt at robbing me of my freedom. I could regain my freedom by consciously trying to reduce the other to object, either by retreating into indifference (reducing the other to no more than a thing among other things) or by exciting in myself and the other sexual *desire* and thus ensnaring the other's freedom in a purely fleshly encounter. By such means I could practice *sadism*, the attempt to produce a lasting reduction of the other to self-conscious fleshiness and self-disgust; but this frustrates me too, because I fail to capture the other as subject in reducing the other to mere object. And so on. Love turns out to be an endless battle in which each person is seeking to annihilate the subjectivity of the other.

This description of the nature of love represents, for Sartre, the inevitable nature of all human relationships. As he puts it:

> Thus ceaselessly tossed from being-a-look to being-looked-at, falling from one to the other in alternate revolutions, we are always, no matter what attitude is adopted, in a state of instability in relation to the Other. We pursue the impossible ideal of the simultaneous apprehension of his freedom and of his objectivity. . . . But . . . we shall never place ourselves concretely on a plane of equality; that is, on the plane where the recognition of the Other's freedom would involve the Other's recognition of our freedom.[30]

Lest one thinks that Sartre's analysis is meant to apply only to human life in the twentieth century, he makes it clear that it is impossible for me to respect the freedom of any other person. Even if I show tolerance to others, I restrict their freedom simply by turning up in the world which they apprehend. I limit their possibilities and hence restrict their freedom:

> To realize tolerance with respect to the Other is to cause the Other to be thrown forcefully into a tolerant world. It is to remove from him on principle those free possibilities of courageous resistance, of perseverance, of self-assertion which he would have had the opportunity to develop in a world of intolerance.[31]

In fact, even education compels a child to accept certain values. Whether the educator enforces his values upon the child by a direct use of force, or by gentle persuasion makes little real difference. He does not in either case respect the child's freedom.

Thus respect for the Other's freedom is an empty word; even if we could assume the project of respecting this freedom, each attitude which we adopted with respect to the Other would be a violation of that freedom which we claimed to respect.[32]

(4) *Being-with-others.* Sartre devotes only twenty pages of *Being and Nothingness* to a discussion of being-with-others, and in most discussions of his philosophy this part of his analysis is ignored. However, in light of his recent turn toward Marxism, it will help us greatly in our later analysis of his present position if we examine his earlier view of the relations of people in groups.

One of the reasons for Sartre's discussion of being-with-others usually being ignored is that he insists that it is only a special relation of being-for-others. He finds that there are two radically different forms of the experience of being-with-others: (a) The Us-object, which corresponds to being-looked-at in the relation of a For-itself with the Other; and (b) The We-subject, which corresponds with being-in-the-act-of-looking in the relation of a For-itself with the Other.

It is in Sartre's analysis of the Us-object that he shows great affinities with the views of Karl Marx. In the "Us" experience we undergo shame as a community alienation. When two of us who are walking together are looked at by a third person, we experience a collective shame. Certain situations in human experience, such as participating in communal work, are likely to precipitate the experience of being an Us-object. "The one who experiences himself as constituting an Us with other men feels himself trapped among an infinity of strange existences; he is alienated radically and without recourse." [33] Class consciousness describes the assumption of a particular "Us" when the collective situation is more structured than is usually the case. Thus, the members of the working class experience the capitalists as Thirds; "that is, as those who are outside the oppressed community and for whom this community exists." [34] It is through the capitalists that the working class experiences itself as constituting a group of men who are collectively alienated, who are collectively reduced to objects for the benefit of others. Because each worker shares this alienation with all other workers, it is no longer merely a case of each individual struggling to recapture his subjective freedom. Rather, in Sartre's terms: "The oppressed class can, in fact, affirm itself as a We-subject only in relation to the oppressing class and at the latter's expense; that is, by transforming it in turn into 'they-as-objects' or 'Them'." [35]

An important corollary of Sartre's discussion of the nature of an Us-object is that it can be constituted only in terms of a concrete situation in which one part of humanity is immersed to the exclusion of another part. In other words, there can be no universal community of all mankind, "although everyone keeps the illusion of being able to succeed in it by progressively enlarging the circle of communities to which he does belong. This humanistic 'Us' remains an empty concept. . . ." [36]

While Sartre finds that the Us-object reflects a dimension of real experience with the world, he insists that the We-subject is merely a subjective psychological experience possible only in societies of a certain economic type such as capitalism. In such societies, one has the feeling that he unites with others in such a fashion that "we" use the subways, "we" elect the President, and so on. But actually the "we" in these cases is simply a short-hand way of saying that each individual uses the subways, that each individual votes for the President, and so on. There is no collective way of my being united with other subjects so that we could act mutually together as for-ourselves. Indeed, our analysis of being-for-others should have made this clear. For, if it is impossible for two lovers to achieve mutual self-fulfillment in their love for each other; if they always remain separate consciousnesses; then clearly there can be no legitimate "we" experience. To dream of a totality of all humanity functioning as "we" to subdue the world for human purposes is, alas, but to dream.

Sartre's analysis of the Us-object and the We-subject did not at all change his conclusion about the nature of the relations of human beings. In reality, there can be no being-with-others, except in the experience of an intensified and oppressive alienation inflicted upon a group by other men. Thus Sartre reiterates:

> It is therefore useless for human-reality to seek to get out of this dilemma: one must either transcend the Other or allow oneself to be transcended by him. The essence of the relations between consciousnesses is not the *Mitsein* [being-with]; it is conflict. [37]

Our long discussion of Sartre's view of the human situation as presented in *Being and Nothingness* may have served to fill the reader with existentialist despair. Man is not a being-in-itself but rather a nothingness which seeks to become something by his choices. But he cannot avoid being an object-for-others, and he cannot help but use others as objects for his own purposes. There is no God to unify the world and human experience, and there is no blueprint anywhere to tell man what kind of a life he ought to lead. He is condemned to be free. He is condemned to attempt the impossible task of achieving a substantial nature in the world while retaining his own being-for-itself. But he is doomed to fail before he starts, because man as a being-for-itself is always a project for the future and can never be incarnated into an objective being-in-itself. He cannot achieve "a synthetic fusion of the in-itself with the for-itself," although it is his passion to make this attempt.[38] The man who is fully aware of his human situation realizes that:

> All human activities are equivalent (for they all tend to sacrifice man in order that the self-cause may arise) and that all are on principle doomed to failure. Thus it amounts to the same thing whether one gets drunk alone or is a leader of nations.[39]

The self-cause in the above quotation refers to the limiting concept of a being-for-itself-in-itself, that which traditional religion has called God. Man desires to become God, to unite both being and nothingness in his own person, but he yearns in vain since the idea of God is self-contradictory. Hence, Sartre concludes at the very end of Part IV of *Being and Nothingness:* "Man is a useless passion." [40]

Man: The Creator of Values In his analysis of the nature of values in
Being and Nothingness, Sartre agrees
with Nietzsche that man is himself the creator of his values. We have already seen that for Sartre it is man who confers meaning and significance upon the experiences which he has in and of the world. The reader may recall that Sartre stresses that while I can't prevent my physical deficiencies, I can decide how I shall interpret them. Clearly no man is a cripple in the way in which a stone is a stone, for each person who is crippled chooses what meaning he shall give to this fact of his being. The stone, on the other hand, has no choice but to be a stone. Thus, Sartre concludes that "human reality is that by which value arrives in the world." [41]

On the surface, this does not appear to be a very radical assertion for many people would agree that it is mankind, or society, which places valuations upon objects and upon certain kinds of behavior. Each individual is born into a society, and very early in his life he learns that certain ways of acting are approved and called "good," while other forms of behavior are disapproved and called "bad." Thus, each one of us has been taught that lying is wrong; that truthfulness is good. Sartre admits that each person is thrown into a world where he finds that values have already been conferred upon experiences and objects by others. Furthermore, if I follow what he calls everyday morality, I respond automatically in conformity with the socially accepted mores; the status of these approved values is not questioned. When I obey the existing tabus, I recognize that they in fact exist in my culture. I am not their creator; although they have been created in the first place by other men. Sartre remarks:

> The bourgeois who call themselves "respectable citizens" do not become respectable as the result of contemplating moral values. Rather from the moment of their arising in the world they are thrown into a pattern of behavior the meaning of which is respectability. Thus respectability acquires a being; it is not put into question. Values are sown on my path as thousands of little real demands, like the signs which order us to keep off the grass.[42]

In other words, each individual always finds himself in a situation in the world with other people who press upon him demands and obligations. But to the extent that the individual simply accepts these demands as facts, as what one does, he has not freely chosen them as values and he has not been the creator of his own values.

Sartre has frequently been criticized for being apparently obsessed with the deviant in human behavior, with abnormal sexual patterns, such as the homosexuality of Jean Genet. His novels and short stories are filled with traitors, sexual deviants, prostitutes, impotent men and women, and so on. He can be justified in his use of the apparently abnormal person to exemplify his view of human reality, however, for he agrees with Freud that the abnormal represents the so-called normal person with his eccentricities exaggerated. While in our observances of common everyday morality we tend to follow the approved conventions of our society, what do we do when we find a conflict between the principles approved by our society with no specific guidance as to how we should choose between them? The situation of occupied France during the Second World War provided ample illustrations for Sartre to establish his view of the nature of value judgments. The French had been taught to obey the state. What should one do, however, when the existing state was that of the conquering Nazis? The French had been taught that it was wrong to lie and that one should be loyal to one's friends. What should one do if he were asked by the Nazi authorities to reveal the presence of some Jewish friends? If he told the truth, his friends would be sent to a concentration camp and probably be killed. If he lied, he would be violating the moral imperative to speak the truth as well as tacitly refusing to obey the state. Whatever decision an individual reached, there were no existing universal moral principles to which he could appeal in confident justification of his decision. In a similar manner, the abnormal person in a society is often faced with choices for which he alone must be responsible, choices which he can rarely justify by an appeal to customary morality. Thus, Sartre's use of the abnormal in his novels and plays, of extreme life situations, highlights what he believes to be the real situation with regard to any reflective man concerning the values he adopts. When we are reflective, we realize, he insists, that each one of us creates his own values, even if these values of ours happen to be those of the majority of the people in our culture.

We can clarify his position on each man choosing his own values even more. When one views himself as a person, a being-for-itself, then he understands himself as one who is projecting what he wishes to become into the future. He is not already what he will become; his decisions and acts reflect the image of himself which he is attempting to achieve in the world. Even when I adopt the conventional values of my group, I am the one who denominates them as *values for me*. Sartre himself expresses this clearly enough:

> As soon as the enterprise is held at a distance from me, as soon as I am referred to myself because I must await myself in the future, then I discover myself suddenly as the one who gives its meaning to the alarm clock, the one who by a signboard forbids himself to walk on a flower bed or on the lawn, the one from whom the boss's order borrows its urgency, the one who decides the interest of the book which he is writing, the one finally who makes the values exist in order to determine his action by their demands.[43]

I am filled with anguish when I realize that ultimately I am my own maker; that in the last analysis even such a decision as not to walk on the lawn is one which I have made and which reflects my own choice of values. My consciousness of my own ultimate freedom assures me that I alone sustain values in being, and that there is always the possibility for me to question the values I have so far adopted and to choose new ones in their place. This is not a realization over which I would ordinarily rejoice; in fact, Sartre maintains that most men would rather be born into a world where values are predetermined, where they need not choose them. I am filled with anguish when I realize that I create my own values, because I see then how unjustifiable any of my value choices are. I can no longer say that God gave me a moral code, nor even that my society has presented me with ready-made values which I must adopt. The full realization of my responsibility for my own values comes to me as a consequence of my freedom:

> It follows that my freedom is the unique foundation of values and that *nothing*, absolutely nothing, justifies me in adopting this or that particular value, this or that particular scale of values. . . . I do not have nor can I have recourse to any value against the fact that it is

I who sustain values in being. Nothing can ensure me against myself, cut off from the world and from my essence by this nothingness which I *am*. I have to realize the meaning of the world and of my essence; I make my decision concerning them—without justification and without excuse. . . . In anguish I apprehend myself at once as totally free and as not being able to derive the meaning of the world except as coming from myself.[44]

With this forceful insistence upon the absolute freedom of each individual to confer his own values upon the world and upon human behavior, it appears that Sartre is really defending an extreme form of moral relativism. All values are relative to myself, not the person who I am, but the person whom I am on the way toward becoming! It is this latter aspect of Sartre's position which makes the individual fully responsible for whatever values he adopts. Sartre is not defending a position which would claim that because I am the kind of person I am, therefore I cannot help but act in the ways in which I do act. The delinquent, the criminal, and the homosexual are held by Sartre to be fully responsible for adopting their ways of behavior. In fact, each person is fully responsible for his own life pattern, whether or not it follows conventional middle-class morality. Sartre's view, therefore, rules out any possibility of a person claiming that his values are different from others because of the nature of his heredity or his environment. He is not defending a relativism which would hold that since people are not all alike, therefore, we cannot expect that they will all have the same values. No excuse at all is given to the individual for the values he happens to hold. He has chosen them, and he is fully responsible for his choice. No man is born a criminal; he makes himself become a criminal by the choices which he makes and continues making. No person is born a homosexual; he makes himself into one by the patterns of sexual behavior which he freely chooses. Any man, according to Sartre, can choose at any time in his life to alter radically the values he has adopted in the past. The criminal and the homosexual can choose not to follow their old ways of life; again we are reminded that no man is a fixed being with a determinate nature in the way in which objects in the world, such as stones, are fixed and determined natures. Sartre's version of moral relativism, therefore, is one in which each person is alone responsible for his values since he has chosen them. His values are relative to his choice of the image he has adopted of the kind of man he wishes to become.

With Sartre's great insistence upon each individual recognizing that he is the person who chooses his own values, the reader might expect that Sartre would defend an ethic of authenticity. Heidegger, from whom Sartre learned a great deal, insists that each man ought to choose to exist authentically rather than inauthentically. In fact, because some people have tended to confuse Heidegger's position concerning authentic existence with Sartre's viewpoint, it will be most useful for us to glance briefly at Heidegger's stance in order to contrast it with Sartre's.

Heidegger's contrast between unauthentic and authentic existence bears striking resemblances to Erich Fromm's distinction between nonproductive and productive character orientations which we have discussed in a previous chapter. Heidegger maintains that it is very easy to exist unauthentically: it is to lose oneself in the It-world. It is to become a thing used and manipulated by others, while at the same time you use others as things. In Heidegger's description of the everyday world of *das Man* he shows how we are predisposed in unauthentic existence to judge ourselves in terms of the functions which we perform. The point here is that others might perform these functions; in fact, it does not matter who performs them. If I view myself primarily as a person doing a certain job, wearing certain styles of clothing, living in a particular apartment—all these do not by any means refer to my particularity as an existing unique human being. In unauthentic existence I become my social security number, a mark on the bell-shaped curve of distribution in intelligence, and a spot on a graph depicting life expectancy of males of my age and profession. In short, I escape into the anonymous safety of the masses and gain reassurance from doing what everybody else is doing. Now in a certain sense there is comfort in unauthentic existence, for I can rest content without making decisions of my own. I can find support in adopting views which are the popular opinion. I can always become one among billions of others, and all of us are interchangeable with each other. One does what is expected of one: one is successful, one is loyal to one's country, one respects one's friends, one worships one's God, and so on. But this one could be any one! It need not be me. This impersonal mode of existence is not distinctly human, therefore, but is rather a confusion of a human being with an object or a thing.

But what does it mean to exist authentically? Here it is not possible to be as clear as in the analysis of unauthentic existence. Heidegger stresses that each individual can choose to protest against unauthentic existence since each person has the possibility of being himself, i.e., of being human rather than a thing. Authentic existence will accept certain "boundary situations" as involved in human life and not try to escape from them. These "boundary situations" are the inescapable limits which restrict me, and while I can push back the boundaries in some cases, I cannot ultimately overcome them. I am a being thrown into a world situation which I have not chosen and from which there is no escape. Furthermore, I face an uncertain future which in the very end will defeat all my projects. I did not choose the present international conflicts, but I cannot escape from living in the world constituted by these and other crises. The plans I make for myself may be defeated by having to go to war, and even if peace returns my life will eventually end in failure: for I shall die. Thus, Heidegger makes a great deal of guilt, suffering and death as among those situations which are an inevitable part of any human life. To deny their presence, to seek to evade them, is simply to seek existence at the level of things rather than on the level of conscious human responsibility. As an example, Heidegger makes a great deal of the authentic man as a person who faces up to the inevitability of his own death as the end in the light of which he will project his life. The authentic man does not try to deny that he will die, nor does he try to evade the full significance of death. Recognizing the ambiguity concerning when and how he may die, and the eventual inevitability of death, he chooses to live now so that if death should soon strike, his life would have had some meaning. If I am to exist authentically I must realize that nothing can save me from myself; I cannot really lose myself in the crowd or become a complete organization man. I must rather choose in moment-by-moment decisions to be that which I most supremely want to be. John Wild has described authentic existence in this manner:

> The authentic person has really decided. He is sure of the whole of himself as revealed in the light of his last possibilities. He knows that his being is not circumscribed like that of a thing, nor locked up inside a mind container. He knows that this being is stretched out ahead of himself, and is aware of its relational structure. Hence he is sure of the human world that he inhabits. But he also knows that there are broader horizons beyond in the ultimate world of reality, which he does not confuse with the human island. This, he recognizes, is ordered to an apex determined by human choice, and he is aware of its varying forms and manifestations. He has decided the structure of his own world, and is aware of the risks he has taken in so deciding. Whether this world is at peace or at odds with that of his friends and neighbors, he is ready to bear the responsibility and to defend it. If occasion should demand, he is ready to change it, and even retract it. But the last decision rests with him.[45]

It should be obvious that Heidegger's description of authentic existence bears striking similarities to Sartre's description of man as a being-for-himself. Both stress the individual fully choosing his own way of life, and accepting full responsibility for his choices. Sartre's discussion of bad-faith and sincerity echoes Heidegger's analysis, but there are significant differences as we shall see.

Sartre's description of a man in bad faith parallels very closely Heidegger's discussion of unauthentic existence. In bad faith I hide the truth from myself. When I lie, I know the truth, but I am attempting to deceive another person. In bad faith, however, I am attempting to hide the truth from myself. I cannot hide the truth from myself, unless in one sense I already know the truth. Hence, Sartre vigorously attacks

Freud's division of man's psyche into an ego, which is my consciousness, and an id, which stands for the unconscious urges at the basis of my personality. If I am going to repress some aspects of my personality, I must already be aware of those urges which I attempt to repress. Otherwise, I could not repress them. It is not necessary to postulate an ego, id, and super-ego to account for man repressing certain desires. In fact, Sartre suggests that without a man being conscious of repressing, the task could never be accomplished:

> How can the repressed drive "disguise itself" if it does not include (1) the consciousness of being repressed, (2) the consciousness of having been pushed back because it is what it is, (3) a project of disguise? [46]

Sartre then proposes that the phenomenon of repression can better be understood in terms of the distinction which he has drawn between man as an unstable union of being-in-itself and being-for-itself. Bad faith represents many patterns of behavior by which men seek to avoid full responsibility for choosing their own destinies. A man is in bad faith, however, only if he has chosen it for himself; he must be at least partly aware of what he has done.

One form of bad faith arises when I tend to view myself purely in terms of facticity; I think of myself wholly as a being-in-itself. It is one mode by which I consciously seek to escape from being responsible for myself by claiming that things couldn't be otherwise than they are. I claim that I am bound to one way of life, and that I cannot escape from it. I attempt to constitute myself as a wholly determinate being, with a fixed essence like a stone. Thus, to revert to an illustration we have used previously, the cripple may be in bad faith by claiming that he is a cripple and that nothing can be done about it. He can refuse to recognize that it is in his power to decide exactly what his being crippled shall mean in his own life. He can, in short, view his being crippled as an objective fact which constitutes him exactly as a fountain pen is constituted. He might then try to describe himself by saying, "I am a cripple." Exactly the same mode of bad faith would be employed by anyone viewing himself as a fixed object in the world, and denying that he can do anything at all to escape being the kind of person he is. The waiter may view himself as merely a waiter; the homosexual may consider himself as one born that way. But as we have seen man also has the capacity to transcend his present mode of being, he can put it into question, and realize that he is not merely a waiter, not actually a homosexual, and so on. Is man in good faith in these cases?

One might immediately suppose that denying that one was a waiter or a homosexual would constitute good faith or sincerity. However, Sartre's analysis suggests that good faith is an impossible possibility, a goal toward which man ought to strive, but which he can never reach. Attaining good faith is impossible precisely because of the ambiguous nature of human existence: man is always both that which he has been and now is, and that which he is not now but desires to become. Thus, quite obviously, the waiter is a waiter—at least in the sense that he does perform the functions of being a waiter, and this is a part of the being he is. Likewise, the homosexual by his acts in the past and the present has been and is a homosexual, although his essence as a man could not be summed up this way since he always has the possibility to change. However, it would be another instance of bad faith if he insisted that he was in no respects at all homosexual. Man seems to be caught in an unstable attempt to either view himself as an object, or not as an object—it does not seem possible for man to be completely sincere to the point where he can preserve the balance between the being which he is, but is not, and the being which he is not but which he wishes to become. Man, we must repeat, is condemned to freedom.

Sartre has used the concept of bad faith in the mode of becoming thing-like to great advantage in his *Portrait of the Antisemite*. The antisemite holds that Jews are all alike, they are the incarnation of all the evil in the world. He describes Jews as though they were objects which could be readily identified by specific characteristics, just as we identify a metal by its chemical and physical properties. But the antisemite views himself as a thing as well; he considers himself as a common decent ordinary middle-class man. In fact, by hating the Jews he seeks to establish his own being as substantial, as good, as worthwhile, but he does this as a member of a mob, and not as an individual who assumes full responsibility for his convictions. It is not merely the case that hating Jews is one characteristic of the antisemite; rather it is his global attitude in terms of which he is choosing himself as a person. As Sartre so deftly remarks about the antisemite:

> He is choosing the permanence and the impenetrability of rock, the total irresponsibility of the warrior who obeys his leaders—and he has no leader. . . . He chooses finally, that good be ready-made, not in question, out of reach; he dare not look at it for fear of being forced to contest it and seek another form of it.[47]

But the kind of person whom Sartre is describing uses the Jews merely as a pretext to justify him in considering himself as the solid embodiment of virtue. In other places and times the scapegoats may be the black or the yellow race. The structure of this form of bad faith will remain the same, however, for his prejudices permit him

> to nip his anxieties in the bud by persuading himself that his place has always been cut out in the world, that it was waiting for him and that by virtue of tradition he has the right to occupy it. Anti-

semitism, in a word, is fear of man's fate. The antisemite is the man who wants to be pitiless stone, furious torrent, devastating lightning: in short, everything but a man.[48]

Another form of bad faith is exhibited in those persons who constitute themselves completely as beings-for-others. These persons see themselves merely as what other people want them to be. The responsibility of choosing one's own destiny can be escaped by allowing one's life to be patterned in the way in which others desire. A son may avoid anguish and the terrible freedom of having to choose a profession or a wife by allowing his parents to do this for him. He may come to believe, despite being at least partially aware of his deception, that he is what others say he is. He may then decide to play the role which has been assigned to him. Sartre's analysis of Jean Genet is a good example of this type of bad faith in operation. Genet was an orphan and in the home of his foster-parents he started to steal. Apprehended in the act, he was labeled a thief. He then decided that he must be what he was said to be. Sartre perceptively comments:

> *Genet is a thief;* that is his truth, his eternal essence. And, if he *is* a thief, he must therefore always be one, everywhere, not only when he steals, but when he eats, when he sleeps, when he kisses his foster mother. Each of his gestures betrays him, reveals his vile nature in broad daylight.[49]

Since Genet was an orphan he was very lonely; he felt he did not belong to anyone—he had no self-identity. Hence, to be labeled a thief at least gave him an identity, and from that moment at the age of ten when he was first called a thief, he devoted himself to a life of crime. He had deliberately chosen to live as a criminal in order to play the role which society had given to him. He obtained his being by being wholly what others expected of him. In fact, he even betrayed fellow criminals to the police—he became the incarnation of what others called evil.

If Genet were nothing more than what others said he was, if he deliberately chose to be "as others see me," how then can Sartre justify the title of his book about him: *Saint Genet: Actor and Martyr?* How can a man so obviously in bad faith be considered a saint? In a recent interview granted to *Playboy* magazine, Sartre responded to the question concerning why he canonized Genet:

> It wasn't I. He canonized himself. When *I* say Saint Genet, of course, I'm being ironic. There once was a real Saint Genet, by the way, an actor who became a Christian and was put to death by the Romans. But Genet the writer always says in his books, "I'm a saint," or rather, "I'm a *girl* saint." This sums up what he wants, what he aims at. But it's not what he *is*, because one never *is*. We *tend* to be, but we don't achieve our intention.[50]

Genet was an actor in the sense that he played the role which others expected him to play, and he was also a martyr in the sense that society sent him to prison time and time again. Sartre devoted a long book to analyzing Genet's life, not merely for the reasons cited thus far, but more importantly because Genet fully accepted the responsibility in the last analysis for being and becoming the man he was. He alone was responsible for being "Genet the thief." As a result of this realization he was able to remake his life and find his salvation through literature. By his own efforts and choice he became "Genet the poet."

Could we then say that Genet overcame bad faith through sincerity? Has he realized "good faith"? Sartre's own judgment is that Genet has recently become a rather contented upper-class bourgeois citizen, and that as a result his springs of creativity have dried up. While this might be an unhoped for result of Genet's life project at the moment, does he not now represent a person who has achieved good faith? Is he not now existing authentically, is he not now a being-for-itself?

Sartre's answer appears implicit in the comment we have already cited, "We *tend* to be, but we don't achieve our intention." That is, despite our attempts to become sincere with ourselves, to live our lives in good faith, we cannot succeed. Even more explicitly Sartre in *Being and Nothingness* maintains that no matter how much one may try to choose his existence in sincerity, he is doomed to fail:

> In introspection I try to determine exactly what I am, to make up my mind to be my true self without delay—even though it means consequently to set about searching for ways to change myself. But what does this mean if not that I am constituting myself as a thing? [51]

> Thus the essential structure of sincerity does not differ from that of bad faith since the sincere man constitutes himself as what he is *in order not to be it*. This explains the truth recognized by all that one can fall into bad faith through being sincere.[52]

The ideals of sincerity and of good faith are unobtainable, because, as in the case of bad faith, they are ideals of being-in-itself. We are reminded again that the essence of a man can never be summed up while he is still alive, because of the fact that "the nature of consciousness simultaneously is to be what it is not and not to be what it is." [53] The ideal of authenticity then is one we might strive for, but we seem to be assured that we shall never fully achieve it.

Sartre even more specifically rejects Heidegger's analysis of what an authentic life would be like. He finds that death is absurd; it is the end of all my possibilities. Hence, he cannot agree with Heidegger that in an authentic existence I live my life as a project toward my own death. Since death is the end of life, it removes all meaning from life. Thus,

Sartre suggests that to live my life toward my death is to live my life from the viewpoint of others. I ask what will others make of me after I am dead, and choose to live in such a way that I shall be pleased with the image they will construct of me. But this is not to choose my own existence for myself, but to again allow others to choose my being for me.

What then does Sartre apparently value? What ought man to do? The most that can be said on the basis of *Being and Nothingness* is that one ought to choose one's own life style and accept full responsibility for this choice. No matter what choice one makes, however, he will not be able to achieve a synthesis of being-for-itself with being-in-itself. Could we suggest then that Sartre's ultimate value is freedom? Is he maintaining that every man should aim for his own freedom? But this would be a strange position to take, and it does not appear that it could be Sartre's for he reminds us time and time again that we are free no matter how much we try to disguise this fact from ourselves. Is he then maintaining that each man ought to realize that he is free and accept the full responsibility for his choices in his particular situation? Apparently this much can be said, but one must also add that Sartre does not give us any help in suggesting how this awareness of freedom could be pursued in good faith.

Let us suppose that I approach as nearly as possible to choosing my own life in full responsibility for my choice. What ought to be my behavior toward others? Should I act so as to enhance their own realization of freedom? Apparently not, since we have seen that Sartre maintains that the freedom of any other man is always a threat to my freedom. If I choose to realize my freedom, then I must zealously guard against the other person developing his freedom so that he reduces me to being an object in the world.

Is there no possibility of developing an ethic from the viewpoint of humanity? Could one not maintain that some types of conduct are better in the long run than some others? Sartre would not deny that one could indeed maintain that some forms of conduct are better than others, but he would deny that anyone could give any satisfactory justification for his preferences. They would be his preferences, his own choices, and he could not justify them. Clearly, Sartre maintained in *Being and Nothingness* that it was impossible to get a universal point of view on ethics, for the simple reason that each man views life through his own spectacles in his own particular situation in the world. Hence, there is no privileged position; your view has just as much justification, and as little, as mine. Sartre clearly tells us: "There is no absolute point of view which one can adopt so as to compare different situations; each person realizes only one situation—his own." [54] Sartre approvingly quotes a fable of Kafka's and then adds some comments of his own in illustrating this point:

A merchant comes to plead his case at the castle where a forbidding guard bars the entrance. The merchant does not dare to go further; he waits and dies still waiting. At the hour of death he asks the guardian, "How does it happen that I was the only one waiting?" And the guardian replies, "This gate was made only for you." Such is precisely the case with the for-itself if we may add in addition that *each man makes for himself his own gate.* The concreteness of the situation is expressed particularly by the fact that the for-itself never aims at ends which are fundamentally abstract and universal.[55]

Since each man always views events from his own perspective, it is impossible to ever adopt the point of view of an imagined whole of humanity. Hence, about all one can say is that in this first stage of Sartre's career he stressed the importance of the individual freely choosing and accepting responsibility for the person he now was and the person he was striving to become. Each man in that sense creates his own values. Beyond this, however, Sartre did not go. He did promise at the very end of *Being and Nothingness* that he would devote a later volume to ethics, but this work has not appeared. In fact, Sartre has said recently that he has given up any idea of writing the promised book on ethics. His interests have turned to other problems, as we shall see when we examine his most recent writings. But before we examine his present stance, we should look at the second stage in his development, the stage best represented by a lecture he gave in 1946 called *Existentialism Is a Humanism.*

Existential Humanism: An Ethic of Ambiguity   Sartre's existentialism, with its radical stress upon the complete freedom of the individual to choose the kind of person he wished to be and become, seemed to many critics to rule out the possibility of a positive ethics. In fact, many people linked existentialism with all forms of non-conformity and amoralism. If, as Sartre had said in *Being and Nothingness*, "Man is a useless passion," [56] and "Thus it amounts to the same thing whether one gets drunk alone or is a leader of nations," [57] then why should one not become irresponsible and live his own life in such a way that he gets the maximum fun and enjoyment? The Parisian post-war "beatniks" who hung around in the cafés, loved jazz, and adopted a uniform of black sweaters, black shirts and black trousers were dubbed "existentialists" by the newspapers and magazines. Sartre was annoyed that these youth were used by the mass media to discredit his philosophy. Simone de Beauvoir summed up the reaction which developed against Sartre as follows:

What confidence could one have in a philosopher whose teachings inspired orgies? How could one believe in the political sincerity of a "master thinker" whose disciples lived for nothing more than having a good time? [58]

A philosophy which extolls each man's freedom to choose his own life style can, of course, result in some people choosing sensual pleasure, orgies and irresponsibility. But this was not what Sartre intended, and in his writings immediately after the War he attempted to make clear that freedom involved responsibility. Sartre himself had been relatively uncommitted to anything but his own "salvation" before the Second World War. In his autobiography he tells us that he was Roquentin, the hero of *Nausea*. He attempted to create a meaning for his own life through writing; it was his means to achieve a secular salvation by means of works. He believed that he could achieve being, a substantiality, through the immortality of words. There are no social or ethical implications to be found in *Nausea;* it is a descriptive account of a man's awakening to the absurdity of being-in-itself and to the realization that it is only an individual man who confers any meaning upon life and the world. Sartre himself says it plainly enough:

> I *was* Roquentin; I used him to show, without complacency, the texture of my life. At the same time, I was *I*, the elect, chronicler of Hell, a glass and steel photomicroscope peering at my own protoplasmic juices. Later, I gaily demonstrated that man is impossible; I was impossible myself and differed from the others only by the mandate to give expression to that impossibility, which was thereby transfigured and became my most personal possibility, the object of my mission, the springboard of my glory.[59]

In *Being and Nothingness* Sartre had sought to demonstrate that man was impossible in the sense that he could never completely fuse his being-for-himself into a permanent solidified being-in-itself; that is, man could never become God. This was an inevitable part of every human situation. But each man could choose what kind of a being he wanted to become. He could always act so as to approach more nearly the impossible goal of becoming what he really wished to be. Sartre made a great deal of the human situation: each man finds himself thrown into a world where there are other people, as well as things. Sartre's being thrown into a world at war undoubtedly helped him to modify his concern for his own self salvation to one of concern for the freedom of all other men as well.

Although Sartre's emphasis upon the freedom of the individual in *Being and Nothingness* is well known, it is often overlooked that he also stressed each man's responsibility as well. I am not only responsible for what I make of myself, but I am responsible for community events as well:

> Thus there are no *accidents* in a life; a community event which suddenly bursts forth and involves me in it does not come from the outside. If I am mobilized in a war, this war is *my* war; it is in my image

and I deserve it. I deserve it first because I could always get out
of it by suicide or by desertion. . . . For lack of getting out of it,
I have *chosen* it.[60]

Hence, all my actions inevitably involve me in a world of others for
whom I am responsible. I have chosen my world and I cannot avoid assuming full responsibility for the world which I have chosen.

Fighting in the French Resistance movement during the Second World
War deepened Sartre's sense of the awesome responsibility each man bore
for his fellow men. Each member of the underground resistance movement was working alone and in secret. If one of their members were
arrested, he might under torture disclose the names of others who were
also implicated in the movement. Here, for Sartre, was a human situation
which clearly revealed man's total freedom of choice as well as his
responsibility for the lives of others. In commenting upon the solitude of
each man in the resistance movement, Sartre adds:

Nevertheless, at the depth of this solitude, others were present, all
the comrades of the Resistance they were defending; a single word
was enough to trigger ten, a hundred arrests. This total responsibility in total solitude, is it not the revelation of our freedom? [61]

After the War, Sartre continued to stress each man's responsibility for
the world in which he lived. He still considered himself to be ineffective
as a politician, but did attempt to reveal how the writer of literature bore
a moral responsibility to use his prose to make this a better world. Sartre
clearly objected to "art for art's sake," for in his opinion this was a movement designed to isolate the artist from the real problems of the world.
Literature which was not *engaged*, committed, was not worth its salt.
The prose writer should use his words as a means to action: a way to
disclose something about the world so as to reveal what change he wishes
to bring into the world by this disclosure. The engaged writer is one who
has given up as impossible the dream of being impartial about human
events. Sartre in *What Is Literature?* (1947) found the moral imperative
at the heart of literature. The very act of writing presupposes not only
the author's freedom but also the freedom of his readers. Rather than
maintain, as he did in *Being and Nothingness*, that the freedom of the
other always poses a threat to my own freedom, Sartre now insisted that
the individual's freedom was secure only if all other men were also free.
Hence, he maintained that it was impossible for a good novel to be
written in praise of antisemitism:

For, the moment I feel that my freedom is indissolubly linked with
that of all other men, it can not be demanded of me that I use it to
approve the enslavement of a part of these men. Thus . . . the
writer, a free man addressing free men, has only one subject—
freedom.[62]

The very activity of writing presupposes the freedom of the citizen, and Sartre did not hesitate claiming that the only regime in which writing could realize itself fully would be a democracy. The extent to which he was now willing to commit himself to the freedom of all men was forcefully expressed as follows:

> One does not write for slaves. The art of prose is bound up with the only regime in which prose has meaning, democracy. When one is threatened, the other is too. And it is not enough to defend them with the pen. A day comes when the pen is forced to stop, and the writer must then take up arms. Thus, however you might have come to it, whatever the opinions you might have professed, literature throws you into battle. Writing is a certain way of wanting freedom; once you have begun, you are engaged, willy-nilly.[63]

The value orientation professed by Sartre in *What Is Literature?* is strikingly similar to Kant's insistence that each man ought to be viewed as an end in himself. Sartre held that the writer's duty is to secure the good will of his reader so as to "provoke his intention of treating men, in every case, as an absolute end and, by the *subject* of our writing, direct his intention upon his neighbors, that is, upon the oppressed of the world."[64] But the writer will have failed if he merely holds up this ethical ideal, and does not also show his reader that in contemporary society it is impossible to treat concrete men as ends in themselves. The writer who remains silent about the injustices of his age is guilty of committing these injustices himself, since he has done nothing to prevent them. The writer's duty is to lead his reader to see that, "in effect, what he wants is to eliminate the exploitation of man by man."[65]

Sartre's version of commitment today has taken the form of an attempted reconciliation of Marxism with existentialism. In 1947 it was already clear that he considered it to be part of the task of the committed writer to show that a socialist revolution could be reconciled with the freedom of each man:

> For, a whole section of the public which we wish to win over still consumes its good will in person to person relationships, and another whole section, because it belongs to the oppressed classes, has given itself the job of obtaining, by all possible means, the material improvement of its lot. Thus, we must at the same time teach one group that the reign of ends cannot be realized without revolution and the other group that revolution is conceivable only if it prepares the reign of ends. . . . In short, we must militate, in our writings, in favor of the freedom of the person *and* the socialist revolution. It has often been claimed that they are not reconcilable. It is our job to show tirelessly that they imply each other.[66]

Sartre maintained that the means being used to achieve a socialist state in Russia might be such as to alter the envisaged end. Can a regime of freedom ever emerge from a regime of oppression? The oppression by the capitalists may be changed to oppression by the Communist party. The writer has the obligation to examine each specific case critically to see if the means to achieve the desired goal of a united humanity are in fact the best which can be employed. Above all, while some men may have to be used merely as means today because they stand in the way of the freedom of all men, nevertheless, we must not become so obsessed with the means that we lose sight of the ultimate end, a totality of free people.

In his discussions of the task of the writer, Sartre frequently touched upon the central themes of his popular lecture *Existentialism Is a Humanism*, delivered in 1946. This address, which was designed to answer some of the objections which had been raised to atheistic existentialism, maintains that existentialism is a humanism because it stresses that each man must choose himself, and in so doing he chooses for all mankind. More than any of the other writings of Sartre this lecture presents his thought in clear and understandable prose. Sartre defended his basic thesis that the existentialist does not sanction irresponsibility, for he holds each man completely responsible for all his choices and actions. No man can choose himself in a vacuum, however, for he finds himself in a world where his every action, thought and gesture impinges upon other people. That is why the existentialist novel so often stresses anguish, despair and abandonment. If in choosing my being, I choose for myself alone and others are not involved, then I might choose a life in which I could obtain the maximum of pleasure. However, in reality, I can obtain my pleasure only in a world where there are other people, and I must, therefore, take into account, the effects of my actions upon them. Sartre the moralist puts the case for each person's responsibility for other men clearly enough:

> Certainly, many people think that in what they are doing they commit no one but themselves to anything: and if you ask them, "What would happen if everyone did so?" they shrug their shoulders and reply, "Everyone does not do so." But in truth, one ought always to ask oneself what would happen if everyone did as one is doing; nor can one escape from that disturbing thought except by a kind of self-deception.[67]

Immanuel Kant long ago had formulated the categorical imperative for moral action: "So act that you could will the maxim of your action to be a universal law." In 1946, Sartre seems to have agreed with Kant, for he insisted that each man ought to ask himself, "Am I really a man who has the right to act in such a manner that humanity regulates itself by what I do?"[68] Unlike Kant, however, Sartre does not find that there are absolute moral rules, such as always speaking the truth, never taking a life, etc., to which contemporary existentialist man can appeal. This is what fills man with the feeling that he is abandoned in the world with no God or absolute moral principles to guide him. Each man must make his own decisions, but he ought to make them with a view to all other men making similar decisions in similar situations. He can never achieve authenticity if he thinks of himself as an exception, rather than as a model, to the rest of mankind.

The Kantian ethic fails to give one guidance for specific decisions. It tells one to treat all people as ends and never as means merely, but we live in a world where this is an impossible ideal. It is this which Simone de Beauvoir has in mind when she calls the existentialist ethic, *The Ethic of Ambiguity*.[69] Sartre, by his characteristic use of an excellent illustration, shows the ambiguity involved in a radical ethical decision. During the German occupation of Paris, a former student came to Sartre for moral advice. The only brother of this young man had been killed by the Germans, and his father had become a German collaborator. He was living with his mother, and since her husband had separated from her, she found her only consolation in him. The young man had the desire to escape from the occupied territory and join the Free French Forces in England, but he also had a desire to remain in Paris and comfort his mother. Since either of his projected choices could be justified morally, his dilemma concerned which alternative he ought to choose:

> Consequently, he found himself confronted by two very different modes of action; the one concrete, immediate, but directed towards only one individual; and the other an action addressed to an end infinitely greater, a national collectivity, but for that very reason ambiguous—and it might be frustrated on the way. At the same time, he was hesitating between two kinds of morality; on the one side the morality of sympathy, of personal devotion and, on the other side, a morality of wider scope but of more debatable validity. He had to choose between those two. What could help him to choose? . . . The Kantian ethic says, Never regard another as a means, but always as an end. Very well; if I remain with my mother, I shall be regarding her as the end and not as a means: but by the same token I am in danger of treating as means those who are fighting on my behalf; and the converse is also true, that if I go to the aid of the combatants I shall be treating them as the end at the risk of treating my mother as a means.[70]

Even in seeking moral advice, Sartre suggests we know what advice the person we have gone to will give us. Obviously, Sartre refused to decide the issue for the young man, and the reader already knows what Sartre replied to him: "You are free, therefore choose—that is to say, invent. No rule of general morality can show you what you ought to do." [71]

While Sartre and de Beauvoir maintain that actual ethical choices in concrete situations are bound to be ambiguous, they caution us against confusing absurdity with ambiguity. Miss de Beauvoir explains the difference this way:

> To declare that existence is absurd is to deny that it can ever be given a meaning; to say that it is ambiguous is to assert that its meaning is never fixed, that it must be constantly won.[72]

In concrete situations, one may choose to treat some people as means rather than as ends. In fact, both Sartre and de Beauvoir stress that in the present world the idealism of the Kantian ethic must be tempered with realism. If we attempt to treat all men as ends then we are never justified in using violence or oppression toward any man. Yet we must restrict the free actions of the white supremacy advocates, if we are to free the Negro. Sometimes we may even have to use force to compel white supremacy advocates to conform to our decisions. The ambiguity of our choices and actions rests on the fact that in freeing some, we are preventing others from exercising their freedom. While each concrete situation will require the individual to choose his own path of action, Miss de Beauvoir does present some general guidelines:

> In any event, it is evident that we are not going to decide to fulfill the will of every man. There are cases where a man positively wants evil, that is, the enslavement of other men, and he must then be fought. . . . It is no more necessary to serve an abstract ethics obstinately than to yield without due consideration to impulses of pity or generosity; violence is justified only if it opens concrete possibilities to the freedom which I am trying to save; by practising it I am willy-nilly assuming an engagement in relation to others and to myself. . . .[73]

Sartre stressed that there is at least one absolute in this version of Existential Humanism: free commitment. How one exercises this free commitment, however, will depend upon the situation in which he finds himself. Upon closer examination, however, it appears that what Sartre describes is really a commitment to *freedom* itself as the one absolute value:

> For I declare that freedom, in respect of concrete circumstances, can have no other end and aim but itself; and when once a man has seen that values depend upon himself, in that state of forsakenness he can will only one thing, and that is freedom as the foundation of all values. . . . We will freedom for freedom's sake, in and through particular circumstances. And in thus willing freedom, we discover that it depends entirely upon the freedom of others and that the freedom of others depends upon our own. . . . I cannot make liberty my aim unless I make that of others equally my aim.[74]

If each man pursues the freedom of all other men he will be helping to create the possibility for a human community. However, there is no blueprint available for such an ideal society. Each man must choose himself in such a way that he works toward his own vision of a better world. The humanistic aspects of existentialism are summarized by Sartre as follows:

> This is humanism, because we remind man that there is no legislator but himself; that he himself, thus abandoned, must decide for himself; also because we show that it is not by turning back upon himself, but always by seeking, beyond himself, an aim which is one of liberation or of some particular realization, that man can realize himself as truly human.[75]

Unfortunately, any man's choice to pursue the aim of freedom for all men becomes ambiguous and difficult not only because he has no absolute aim except freedom itself, but even more so because he does not know to what extent he can rely upon the help of others. Despite the glowing admonitions to pursue freedom as an absolute goal for all men, Sartre maintained in this same lecture that one can rely upon others who are committed to the same common cause only if they are in a party or group "which I can more or less control—that is, in which I am enrolled as a militant and whose movements at every moment are known to me."[76] I cannot count upon those whom I do not know; nor am I sure that others will continue my work after I am dead. Despair at this realization should not drive one to quietism, however, but it should permit one to join a party or organized group without illusions. Whatever is in the individual's power to do, he can do; beyond that he can count upon nothing. The individual must choose to act out his commitment without hope. More than that he cannot do.

Many admirers of Sartre have been displeased by his failure to write his promised volume on ethics. In this second stage of Sartre's career, which we have been considering, he extolled existentialism as a humanistic ethic and insisted that the freedom of any one man depends upon the freedom of all other men. But he did not show why this should follow, and in the light of *Being and Nothingness* it seems to be a far more arbitrary value choice than Sartre admitted. If the other is always in conflict with me, always over against me, if he is always a threat to my freedom in the sense that he always tries to make me an object to his subjectivity, why should I regard my surge toward freedom as involving his freedom as well? Was Sartre not smuggling in a bourgeois value after all? Was he himself in good faith in the lecture *Existentialism Is a Humanism?* Admittedly it was a popular address delivered to dissociate existentialism from the "beatnik hangers-on." Nevertheless, it seems that

Sartre's humanism was at odds with his basic phenomenological description of man.

Sartre may have felt that existential humanism could be better portrayed through literature than by a philosophical treatise. At any rate, he began work upon a projected series of four novels, *The Roads to Freedom*, which were to deal with alternative ways by which individuals might choose their own existence. He abandoned the project after three of the novels had been written: *The Age of Reason, The Reprieve*, and *Troubled Sleep*.[77] Unfortunately, these novels are didactic and lengthy. Hence, one can find better literary exemplars of humanistic existentialism in the novels and plays of Albert Camus than in those of Sartre himself. In fact, many people have considered *The Plague* to be the best description of what an existential humanistic ethic would be like.

In *The Plague*, Camus portrays the reactions of people in the Algerian city of Oran when they are visited by the plague. Some seek as much pleasure as they can get, for they may die tomorrow. Others resort to the Church for the assurance of an eternal salvation. There are few persons in the novel who react authentically, that is who make the choice to do what they can to help their fellow men. Dr. Rieux and his friend Tarrou are two men who minister to the needs of the sick. Tarrou is seeking to discover if one can become a saint without believing in God, while Dr. Rieux maintains that his task is the more humble one of being a man. In the involvement of these two men in relieving the miseries of their fellow men, one can find a moving description of the existential choice to play one's part in making this a better world. Neither Tarrou nor Rieux believe in God, furthermore they do not have illusions about society being just. They fully recognize the ambiguity of human choices, and do not believe that the struggle to free man from oppressive physical and spiritual plagues can ever be concluded. For after a particular disaster has ended, people resume their existences just as though nothing had happened. But Dr. Rieux learned one thing from the plague he fought: "There are more things to admire in men than to despise." [78]

> None the less, he knew that the tale he had to tell could not be one of a final victory. It could be only the record of what had to be done, and what assuredly would have to be done again in the never ending fight against terror and its relentless onslaughts, despite their personal afflictions, by all who, while unable to be saints but refusing to bow down to pestilences, strive their utmost to be healers.[79]

In a common struggle with the plague men have learned their solidarity and have perhaps acquired compassion and sympathy. On this basis, one can choose to play his small part in delivering his fellow men from terror and oppression.

Sartre himself has apparently abandoned the position of existential humanism which he put forth in 1946–1947. In fact, he now claims that it is futile in our present world to construct any ethic whatsoever. Some of his admirers, however, have attempted to develop the implications for an ethic which they find in his early writings. Before we examine Sartre's present position, it may prove interesting to glance at one recent attempt by an American writer to construct an ethic of humanistic existentialism.

Hazel Barnes, translator of Sartre's major philosophical works into English, is admirably equipped with a thorough knowledge of his philosophy. She is probably as well prepared as anyone could be to try to fill the gap provided by Sartre's failure to write his own book on existentialist ethics. In *An Existentialist Ethics* (1967) Miss Barnes attempts to find what implications for developing an ethics can be drawn from Sartre's *Being and Nothingness*. In general, her position is a restatement of Sartre's lecture *Existentialism Is a Humanism*, and of Simone de Beauvoir's *Ethics of Ambiguity*. There are some important departures from the views of Sartre and de Beauvoir, however, and it is to only these aspects of Miss Barnes' work that we shall refer.

The most significant point at which Professor Barnes differs with Sartre is on the nature of human relationships. Sartre has claimed that all the descriptions he gives in *Being and Nothingness* are of bad faith; he suggested in a footnote, which is often overlooked, that authenticity and good faith would be discussed in a later work. But this promised discussion by Sartre has not appeared. Furthermore, Barnes claims that Sartre's analysis of human reality has neglected the *Thou*, the second person aspect of human relationships. She agrees with Sartre that there can never be a complete inter-subjectivity of two persons so that their every project becomes in fact one. I can never experience the life of another person as that person actually feels it and lives it: "To live the experience of another in its uniqueness and singularity would be to become the other. It would be also to cease being myself." [80] Nevertheless, the confrontation of myself with another need not necessarily result in an eternal conflict in which we each seek to reduce the other to an object. But what would it apparently be like to have a relationship in good faith? Miss Barnes maintains that, "Obviously any human relation in good faith will retain at its heart the awareness on the part of each one that the Other is a free subject and not an object." [81]

Professor Barnes claims that Sartre has erred in analyzing the look of the other at me as always a stare; it could also be a look of exchange or "a looking-together-at-the-world." [82] Now with this revised foundation, there are some looks from others which help me to constitute myself in a new light. My point of view does not become that of the other, but my attitude is modified by including the other person within my own area of concern. The other person reciprocally will include me within his point of view and concern. "Although our worlds have not merged, each one will henceforth include structures which the Other has led me to embrace." [83] On some occasions the other may become so significant to me, that I may even suppress my own concern with myself. I have become existentially involved with a "You" or a "Thou."

> In the existential "You," I affirm with equal certainty the "I" of the Other. If the "You" is reciprocal, there has been a joint affirmation of two I-subjects even though.   there is neither possession nor merging. [84]

When this kind of a human relationship occurs, a We-subject has been achieved. But this is extremely difficult to achieve, even in love, and is at best precarious. There can never be a perfect understanding between two persons; in this Miss Barnes admits that Sartre is right. But she is optimistic enough to maintain that in love it is possible to *approach* perfect communication and total apprehension of the other as a person. This can be achieved, however, only by honesty and mutual agreement by both of the persons as to what their commitments to each other really are. Miss Barnes, therefore, holds that Sartre's view of man must be corrected to allow for the possibility of authentic love between two people.

The existentialist humanism advocated by Hazel Barnes proposes one categorical imperative: "Everyone is a subject and must be valued as such." [85] This ideal does not appear to be other than that of democracy, although she makes it clear that she does not accept the laissez-faire capitalism of Ayn Rand as an appropriate interpretation of this imperative. Nor, because of its stress upon collectivism, does she think that this ideal can be found in Communism. The welfare state comes the closest in modern history to the ideal relationship she proposes between the individual and his society:

> The ideal would be a state providing for the maximum opportunity for the free development of the individual's creative possibilities and happiness which is consistent with protecting the same opportunity for all others. Existentialism would, of course, emphasize the active, responsible side of government; that is, it advocates our responsibility to correct inequities and to foster freedom, not merely to refrain from interfering with the projects of free individuals. [86]

But there are more specific implications which Professor Barnes draws from her interpretation of an existentialist ethics. She sees our present educational system as one which stresses conformity to accepted patterns of behavior rather than the individual uniqueness of each person. She sympathizes with the New Radicals in their attempts to create a society in which men actually practice the justice and fairness which they preach. Each person has three needs which are too often ignored by our society, especially are these needs frustrated in the case of children: "They are: the right to live the extreme choice, the right to change, and the right to spontaneous self-realization." [87] We are, instead of recognizing these needs, attempting to make each person resemble every other person; our goal too often is to adjust each person successfully to our present society. However, an existential commitment to the real freedom of each person requires recognition of the right of any person to choose a life style which may be at odds with his society:

> Living a passionate commitment inevitably takes one beyond the horizons of conventional social ethics, and one is obliged to chart one's own way. In this sense authenticity and the extreme choice have a certain affinity. The right to choose the intense one-sided rather than the balanced life is perfectly consistent with existentialist ethics. [88]

On one other point Miss Barnes is at variance with most existentialists. She maintains that they have made too much of absurdity, to the neglect of the simple joys and everyday pleasures of life. Furthermore, sometimes value might be found in acceptance rather than in revolt.

> He [the existentialist] may be right in declaring that an ecstatic, "Oh, the morning glory!" is an inadequate method of dealing with the evil and suffering of the world. But perhaps there is bad faith and evasion in spending too much time in the contemplation of our anguish. [89]

All ethical philosophies ask man to become different from what he now is. The precise nature of Miss Barnes' humanistic existentialism is brought out in her discussion of existentialist faith. Although she does not share the nineteenth-century belief in the inevitable progress of man, she does believe that man can be improved. In the light of her analysis of the human situation she maintains:

> Particularly as existentialists, we are all but compelled to follow up our fundamental premises with a commitment to further change. That man is free and self-transcending, and that there is no determining human nature are empty mouthings of dogma unless we believe that man has the possibility of becoming something quite different from what he has been—and this existentially, not just socially and technologically. To say that he *will* do so is to make a statement of faith, not merely to hazard a guess as to whether man will or will not live up to his potentialities. [90]

Her faith is in an unseen future; it does not yet appear what man will become. The confidence of existentialist faith "lies in the conviction that if it moves forward, it will discover points worth climbing to." [91] This extremely open future is restricted only by a commitment never to ignore the individual freedom and subjectivity of each person. Furthermore, we bear an ethical responsibility for helping to make the future by our own choices and actions. It is clear that Miss Barnes has great faith in the possibility of each individual achieving good faith and making authentic choices, while at the same time helping to create a society in which all other individuals also have the opportunity to realize their unique selves. In this respect, her existentialist humanism turns out to be a restatement of "the American ideal"—democracy.

Sartre, however, does not think that our present society can warrant this kind of an optimistic faith. In fact, he goes so far as to claim that in our present world it is impossible to construct an ethic. He has become more convinced of the necessity of direct involvement in the struggle of the workingman, and maintains that Marxism is the only philosophy for our age. To write a book on ethics as long as men are in need, would be to opt out of the human struggle—at least, so Sartre now claims. Has he changed his position completely? Is he now merely one more Marxist? Or is his interpretation of Marxism really consistent with *Being and Nothingness*? We shall try to answer these questions in the next section.

Existential Marxism: The Critique of Dialectical Reason   Sartre had been moving toward Marxism as early as 1946. His opening sentences in "Materialism and Revolution" revealed a different preoccupation from that which he displayed in his first and second stages:

> Young people of today are uneasy. They no longer recognize their right to be young. It is as though youth were not an age of life, but a class phenomenon, an unduly prolonged childhood, a spell of irresponsibility accorded to the children of the well-to-do. The workers go without transition from adolescence to manhood.[92]

The day in which youth could have its fling seems to have passed, and Sartre noted that it is not necessarily bad that students are asked to commit themselves quite early in their careers. This essay, however, is very critical of Stalinist Marxism, to which many French youth were attracted. Sartre tried to unmask Communism as a false revolutionary myth; human action cannot be explained completely by blind deterministic material forces. He clearly refused to accept this Communist myth, for in his opinion it destroyed thought itself. Although he was convinced that one should work for the liberation of the working class, he did not believe that one had to adhere to a false philosophy in so doing. He wrote:

> I know that man has no salvation other than the liberation of the working class; I know this *before* being a materialist and from a plain inspection of the facts. I know that our intellectual interest lies with the proletariat. Is that a reason for me to demand of my thinking, which has led me to this point, that it destroy itself?[93]

While Sartre took great pains to protest against Communist dogma, which tries to fit the facts into a preconceived materialist philosophy, nevertheless, he no longer stressed the possibility of each individual choosing his own freedom to become what he wished to be. Even more specifically than in *Being and Nothingness*, Sartre maintained that the worker, unlike the lonely rebel, realizes that only if his entire class is liberated will he gain liberty as an individual. The capitalists have reduced the workers to being mere things, but since the worker as a human being realizes that he is not just a thing, there is always the possibility of his uniting with other workers in revolting against his oppression. This revolution must be a movement of the working class itself, since the individual workers do not have the liberty to rebel as individuals. Sartre very clearly maintained that the individual worker does not have the radical freedom, which he discussed in *Being and Nothingness*, to choose his own existence. "It is not likely that the worker would have chosen to do *this* work under *these* conditions and within *this* length of time for *these* wages, had it not been forced upon him." [94] Only by a revolutionary overthrow of the established order can the worker gain his freedom; but paradoxically, this revolution itself would reflect the basic freedom of the worker in his rejection of his present plight in order to move toward a brighter future. In order to implement this workers' revolution, Sartre called "for a new philosophy, with a different view of man's relations with the world." [95] He became concerned with finding or creating a philosophy which would meet a real need by those who are suffering in our economy of scarcity, and abandoned his privileged position of seeking bourgeois salvation through his own writing.

When Sartre began working on his book *Saint Genet* in 1949, according to Simone de Beauvoir, he had moved much closer to Marxism and psychoanalysis. He now seemed to believe that the freedom open to any person was strictly limited by his situation in life, and that in some cases "the margin of choice left to him came very close to zero." [96]

It was also in 1949 that Sartre gave up his idea of writing the book on ethics which the last sentence of *Being and Nothingness* had promised would soon be forthcoming. He wrote in his unpublished notebooks:

> The moral attitude appears when technical and social conditions render positive forms of conduct impossible. Ethics is a collection of idealistic tricks intended to enable us to live the life imposed on us by the poverty of our resources and the insufficiency of our techniques. [97]

This passage is almost a recapitulation of the position of Marx to the effect that ethics in a capitalistic society is one mode used by those in power to justify and maintain their oppression over the working class. Sartre now seems to hold that it is inhumane to worry about what is good or bad as long as there are millions of people who do not have enough to eat. His earlier call to all men to realize that they are not born cowards, but become cowards by the choices they make, now seems to be a very middle-class attitude. At any rate, the worker who must struggle to eke out a scanty subsistence has more basic worries than whether or not the bourgeoisie consider him a coward; more likely they simply view him as a thing used to produce consumer goods! The worker is so radically alienated that a moral appeal would not reach him in the situation in which he is forced to exist. Sartre clearly holds that in our world today a book on ethics is a dispensable luxury.

Sartre had hoped to find a third-way which could mediate between the East and the West, but by 1952, world events had convinced him that he had to come down firmly on one side or the other. The arrest of some French Communists by the government on apparently contrived charges resulted in what Sartre calls his conversion to Marxism. He wrote in an article on Merleau-Ponty:

> These sordid, childish tricks turned my stomach. There may have been more ignoble ones, but none more revelatory. An anti-Communist is a rat. I couldn't see any way out of that one, and I never will. People may find me very naive, and for that matter, I had seen other examples of this kind of thing which hadn't affected me. But after ten years of ruminating, I had come to the breaking point, and only needed that one straw. In the language of the Church, this was my conversion.[98]

Sartre explained that he had now fully discovered the horror of his own class. In the name of the very humanism it had inculcated into him, he says, "I swore to the bourgeoisie a hatred which would only die with me." [99] He decided to become a fellow-traveler and thus play his part in reforming Marxism. As Simone de Beauvoir puts it: "He [Sartre] had been converted to the dialectical method and was attempting to reconcile it with his basic Existentialism." [100]

How radical was Sartre's conversion? Some scholars maintain that he has all but abandoned existentialism and is in effect writing lengthy footnotes to Marx's writings. Others, however, while they admit that he has changed his orientation, insist that in his recent philosophical work, *Critique of Dialectical Reason*, Sartre has not abandoned the principles of *Being and Nothingness* but has applied them to his study of man in society.[101] Let us turn now to an examination of the most recent writings by Sartre in order to find out precisely what this existential Marxism is which he is now advocating.

Sartre prefaces his *Critique of Dialectical Reason* with a long essay, *Search for a Method*, which he had originally written for a Polish journal in 1957. Here Sartre attempts to find a method by which man can be understood in his relationships with others in groups, institutions and history. He no longer calls for a new philosophy for our age, as he did in 1946. Instead, he conceives Marxism to be *the* philosophy of our age for it alone represents the interests of the rising class, the proletariat. Although Sartre tells us that he had read the writings of Marx during his own student days, he maintains that it was not the reading of Marx which precipitated his conversion. Rather he became more aware of the "sub-men conscious of their subhumanity" [102] who surrounded his own comfortable bourgeois life. As Sartre puts it:

> By contrast, what did begin to change me was the *reality* of Marxism, the heavy presence on my horizon of the masses of workers, an enormous, somber body which *lived* Marxism, which *practiced* it, and which at a distance exercised an irresistible attraction on petit bourgeois intellectuals.[103]

Unfortunately, Marxism itself had come to a dead end. It was proclaimed as a dogma of deterministic materialism in terms of which concrete events were all reduced to a stereotyped class conflict. The early Marx was aware of the reality of the individual man in his particular situation. As we have seen in our discussion of Marx, in a previous chapter, he was concerned with showing that man was alienated from his own human nature in a capitalistic system. Contemporary Marxism is not interested in the particular man in his situation, however, but instead seeks to distort all events so that they can be fitted into a preconceived philosophical mold.

Sartre's search, then, is for a method which will revitalize Marxism by restoring the individual man as he actually lives his life in his home, in his work, and in his community to the center of Marxism's attention. He believes that it is existentialism which can now play this ancillary role to Marxism, but after Marxism has recovered its original concern for the concrete man, existentialism itself will no longer have a reason for being. He does not believe that Marxism is the final development in philosophy, however, for if its purposes are ever achieved, it too will have outlived its usefulness:

> As soon as there will exist *for everyone* a margin of *real* freedom beyond the production of life, Marxism will have lived out its span; a philosophy of freedom will take its place. But we have no means, no intellectual instrument, no concrete experience which allows us to conceive of this freedom or of this philosophy.[104]

It should be clear to the reader that Sartre has not gone back on his early concern with the individual and the way he lives his life from the inside. He repeats that it is man who confers meaning upon the world; it is man who makes history by his own projects toward the future. Historical man is not the abstraction which contemporary Marxism tends to make him in its attempt to reduce him to a blind pawn of economic forces over which he has no control. Sartre uses a rather strange illustration to show that contemporary Marxism has in effect excluded man from its considerations. He cites posters which appeared in Poland proclaiming: "Tuberculosis slows down production." Despite the good intentions of the government, these posters completely ignored the tubercular man, as though it were tuberculosis itself which stopped the machines from running in the factories! The message of these posters "reveals a new and double alienation by totally eliminating the tubercular man, by refusing to him even the elementary role of *mediator* between the disease and the number of manufactured products." [105] Sartre claims that Marxists tend to make such a fetish of their knowledge by constantly describing the inherent deterministic workings of capitalism, that they fail to understand the individual worker who *exists* his alienation. Existentialism, therefore, is a much-needed corrective to Marxism. Even the basic concepts of Marxism, such as alienation and exploitation, as well as its dialectical method, can easily be incorporated into existentialism. What the existentialist must reject, however, is the mechanistic determinism which has been grafted onto Marxism. Existentialism, Sartre suggests, can thus be seen to be in basic agreement with Marxism:

> Existentialism, too, wants to situate man in his class and in the conflicts which oppose him to other classes, starting with the mode and the relations of production. But it can approach this "situation" in terms of *existence* . . . it wants to reintroduce the unsurpassable singularity of the human adventure.[106]

The *Critique of Dialectical Reason* itself is concerned with establishing a framework in terms of which men can be understood as acting together in society. Sartre's brief discussion in *Being and Nothingness* of *being-with-others* anticipates the direction which he follows here, although he now believes that man is capable of much more concerted group action than allowed to be possible in his earlier book. While Sartre uses a different vocabulary and employs a more dialectical method in the *Critique*, nevertheless, this work is in many respects much closer to *Being and Nothingness* than to Sartre's lecture *Existentialism Is a Humanism*. Just as Sartre sought to investigate how each individual structures his world in *Being and Nothingness*, so in the *Critique* he is concerned with understanding the structuring of individual men into practical group relationships.

Sartre holds that any effective analysis of group activity in our world today must begin with the fact of scarcity. He does not deny that another day might dawn when this condition would be changed, but that would be such a radical conversion of the human condition that we now have no way to imagine it. While Marx at times attempted to describe the nature of the ultimate classless society which he believed would arrive at the end of this present historical period, Sartre plants his feet firmly on an analysis of the present human situation.

In the *Critique*, Sartre proposes to examine the nature of the different social structures in which we now live by beginning with the individual man as he actually lives his life in and through these structures. His first basic claim is that it is the individual's need, his lack, which relates him to the surrounding world. He needs food and shelter, and this can only be obtained outside of himself. His activity, *praxis*, is thus, first of all, an attempt to preserve his life by obtaining the basic necessities for survival. Human history begins with the realization that there is a scarcity of food, a scarcity which is lived "as the real and perpetual tension between man and environment, man and man." [107] Because of this scarcity, men can live only through struggle, not only with their material environments, but also with other men. The nature of human life thus far has been conditioned by scarcity, not only of food, but of any other products which men lack:

> In actual fact scarcity . . . is the expression of a quantitative fact, more or less strictly defined: any natural substance or manufactured product exists, in a specific social field, in insufficent number, *given* the number of members of the groups, or that of the region's inhabitants: *there is not enough for everyone.* Thus for each person, everyone (the group) exists insofar as the consumption of a certain product there, by others, deprives him *here* of an opportunity to find and consume an object of the same order. [108]

Other people exist for each individual as a threat because of the possibility of their consuming something which he himself needs in order to live. Hell still seems to be other people; but now none of us can be delivered from this state of affairs because of the fact of scarcity. We are condemned to live in a world where there simply is not enough for everyone.

Each national group determines which among its inhabitants are expendable; that is, it determines the number of expendables, although each member of the group has the possibility of surviving or being disposed of. Not everyone can satisfy his needs in an economy of scarcity, so the others become "inhuman" men who may remove what I need in order to live. But I also treat the others inhumanly in order that I may live. Therefore, "each person *is* the inhuman man for all the Others; he considers all the Others as inhuman man; and he really treats the Other with inhumanity." [109] The threat posed to human existence by other men as described in the *Critique* is therefore considerably worse than being annihilated into an object by a look, as in *Being and Nothingness:*

Nothing, in fact—neither wild beasts nor microbes—can be more terrible for man than a species that is intelligent, flesh-eating, cruel, a species which would be able to understand and to thwart the human intelligence, a species whose goal would be precisely the destruction of man. That species is obviously ours, taking hold of every man among others in the environment of scarcity.[110]

In an economy of scarcity ethics develops as the command to destroy the counter-man, the man who is a threat, for he is an evil man. Violence thus arises, but it always claims to be counter-violence, "that is, retaliation to the violence of the Other." [111] But even if I claim to justify my counter-violence by maintaining that I am restoring my rights, I am forced to act inhumanly to the other. The other is a hostile force; unless I realize that the other poses a threat to my very existence I am deprived of the ability to maintain my own life. Mankind is united only by a single negative fact: "we are united by the fact that we all inhabit a world defined by scarcity." [112]

Social groups within a culture may realign themselves in the project of combating scarcity. Labor thus becomes in a context of scarcity an active means of satisfying man's needs. For example, at certain periods of history, there may be a shortage of engineers in which case the man who is an engineer is scarce and valued highly for his skill. While in the abstract sense, he is still expendable, his society is likely to reward him well for his labors, and allow others in over-crowded fields of labor to die. Once the shortage of engineers has been overcome, however, the surplus engineer may find himself very expendable. Sartre agrees with Marxism that labor is the real basis upon which society constitutes all its other social relations.

Sartre devoted the greater portion of the *Critique* to an examination of the basic types of social structures: (1) a serial order, (2) a group-in-fusion, (3) a group perpetuated by an oath, and (4) the solidified institution. In a serial ordering, the individuals are not unified in a common practice, but are merely individuals awaiting their turn, as in a line waiting for a bus. The solitariness of individuals may be overcome, however, if there is a real threat to their existences which can be eliminated only by all of the individuals acting together; this concerted action is that of a group-in-fusion. Sartre uses the storming of the Bastille by the workers during the French Revolution as his example of a group-in-fusion. Once the needed objective has been obtained, however, the group falls apart into the individuals of which it is composed, unless each member takes an oath to support a common project which is still in the future. As the group constituted by an oath attains a kind of permanency, others are born into the group for whom the oath was taken by their parents or grandparents. Thus, the groups to which most of us belong have been passed on to us; we belong to them, despite the fact that we may never have pledged our allegiance to them. We are born into our social classes, our nation, our religion, etc. Finally, a group may become so solidified that it becomes an institution which claims its right to exist as an inert stable being. For institutions, individuals no longer count; for example, it is the institution which in an authoritarian state claims to be more important than the individuals of which it is composed. Nevertheless, Sartre maintains that even in a solidified institution a group never attains the status of an organism which can function independently of the individual members of which it is composed. His lengthy analysis of group relationships in the *Critique* does not reduce the individual to a cog in a machine; any group consists only of individual human beings who are cooperating to achieve some project they have chosen as individuals.

The *Critique* therefore seems in many respects far more consistent with the position which Sartre developed in *Being and Nothingness* than it does with his brief flirtation with existential humanism. We have seen that he is still interested in studying the individual man as, in this case, he lives his alienation. The other is still viewed as a threat to the individual; only now he is held to be such because we live in an economy of scarcity in which there are not enough consumer goods for everyone. The other, anyone, can at any time deprive me either directly or indirectly of my livelihood. The lived experience of becoming a surplus item on the labor market is an always present possibility to any man in today's world. Furthermore, while the *Critique* is devoted to the task of studying man's behavior in groups, Sartre still holds that it is only real concrete individuals who compose groups, and that groups never achieve any organic or metaphysical status apart from all the individuals who compose them.

There are some changes in Sartre's philosophy in the *Critique*, however, some of which have a crucial importance for our understanding of existentialist ethics. Many of these changes are inevitable in the light of his adoption of Marxism as the philosophy of our age. To what extent has he accepted Marxist philosophy? In order to form a reasonable opinion on this issue we should sketch the general areas of agreement between the views of Sartre in the *Critique* and those of Marx.

Sartre agrees with Marx that man's existence is directly conditioned by the mode and relations of economic production, and the social and moral structures which have been built upon them. Under all existing historical societies, these social relations have been developed in the form of classes of people, some of whom are the exploiters, and others of whom are exploited. Furthermore, he admits that the prevailing ideas and ideals of any historical period are those of the dominant class. The individual cannot help but express the viewpoint of his class by his behavior and attitudes. The struggles between the classes can be viewed only in terms of a dialectic of historical materialism which is working toward an ultimate synthesis of a classless society. Sartre also agrees with Marx that the

worker is alienated from himself and from his fellow men by the capitalistic system.

In the light of this quite general acceptance of the basic philosophy of
Karl Marx, it should be obvious that Sartre can no longer profess the
radical freedom of all men to choose their own existences. We have already seen that Sartre in 1949, had moved away from his belief in an
almost unrestricted freedom by maintaining that the worker was forced to
work in order to survive. In the *Critique* Sartre maintains that the individual worker is compelled to live a life of alienation which takes away
from him his basic liberty. Society imposes his alienation upon him, even
though it claims that he has the freedom of choice concerning whether
or not he will work, for whom he will work, and for what wages. The
language which suggests that the worker enters into a "free contract"
with his employer simply serves to mystify the real nature of this relationship. Sartre maintains that there is no really free choice; one must
work or starve. For the great majority of human beings in our present
world Sartre now holds that real freedom is but illusory. Or, as he puts it,
"freedom, here, does not mean the possibility of choice, but the necessity
of living the constraint." [113] Of course, it is still true that this worker, if
he were not completely exhausted by his labor, could choose to internalize
his acceptance of his fate, and in that sense choose what he will make
of his destiny. But even then, this will not be a radically free constituting of
his own essence for himself, for he must view his fate as a member of the
working class into which he has been born. Even his attitudes and convictions are not his own in any significant sense; they are rather those of his
class! Sartre seems to maintain that his earlier discussion of radical freedom
in *Being and Nothingness* is nonsense for the alienated worker. It is
foolish to talk of the freedom of choice when a person's only alternative
is to exist on a subhuman scale or die. Clearly, the Sartre who has become
committed to Marxism is concerned with practical freedom rather than
with his earlier notion of psychological freedom.

Sartre's commitment to Marxism, therefore, does not involve his surrendering the primacy of the individual. His new aim is restoring the
individual to the center of attention of contemporary Marxism. His
knowledge of world affairs, however, has led him to see that unless he
actually involves himself in the efforts to set men free, to change the
fate of the working class, that his philosophy will be but one more
middle-class justification of the status quo. While the readers of *Being
and Nothingness* presumably might be able to accept a radical freedom
of choice for their own lives, the sons of the working class cannot by any
means do this. Therefore, Sartre now fully agrees with Marx that it is not
enough to understand the world, philosophy must change the world. Only
if man is delivered from an economy of scarcity, only if all men become
fully human will the radical freedom of *Being and Nothingness* be possi-

ble. In this sense Sartre, like Marx, is committed to the future—to the society which is not now, but which might become. A man who is fully aware of his own existence will work to achieve this society and surrender his illusions of obtaining his own salvation by his philosophy and literature. This clearly seems to be Sartre's present value orientation.

It is not only Sartre's present stress upon the importance of practical activity which has caused him to give up his book on ethics, although this has played a part in his decision. Of more importance is his agreement with Marx that a system of ethics simply reflects the social class to which the man who writes it belongs. To extoll the hedonistic virtues of an upper-class writer would be meaningless to the worker, who is exhausted after working an eight-hour day on the assembly line. Sartre very specifically states why he does not believe that any meaningful moral system exists today:

> No true moral system exists today, because the conditions of a moral code worthy of the name are not present. Men are not visible to one another. Too many machines and social structures . . . block the view. It's impossible to speak of any true moral system today; only of moral codes applying to certain classes and reflecting specific habits and interests. . . . In a society such as ours, it's inevitable that the mass of social structures—not to mention the personal compulsions, private destinies—form barriers to mutual understanding.[114]

Sartre is convinced that before fellowship among men can be established, we have to first destroy the rule over men by things. What freedom will be like in an era when men are no longer alienated he does not venture to predict, but he does insist that as a matter of principle in any future society a man should always be treated as a human being, never as an object. In this respect, at least, he seems to be fully in accord with his views in *Existentialism Is a Humanism*. However, it is a position which is also fully consistent with the philosophy of the early Marx, who was most concerned with creating a world in which it would be possible for men for the first time to be fully creative and human. Sartre's new humanism is indeed, an existentialist interpretation of Marxism.

Toward an Evaluation of Humanistic Existentialism   Humanistic existentialism has made a vital contribution by recalling us to the more basic ethical and moral aspects of our lives as we actually live them. In this respect it can be considered as "a new name for some old ways of thinking." [115] Many of the treatises on ethics in our century are so technical and abstract that they seem to have little, if any, relevance for life itself. G. E. Moore, one of the great British philosophers of this century, clearly indicated that he did not find the basis for philosophical problems in life itself. He remarked:

I do not think that the world or the sciences would ever have suggested to me any philosophical problems. What has suggested philosophical problems to me is things which other philosophers have said about the world or the sciences.[116]

As long as the problems of ethics are purely philosophers' problems, divorced from the life of the ordinary man who must constantly make moral choices, we shall likely be dealing with an analysis of concepts purely for the sake of clarity and consistency, without realizing that life as it is actually lived by the ordinary man is filled with problems which threaten his very existence in the world. The emphasis by humanistic existentialism upon the moral problems and the viewpoints of individual human beings who live in the actual everyday world is undoubtedly a needed corrective to a sometimes one-sided tendency by philosophers to engage in a rarefied semantic analysis of concepts.

Furthermore, the humanistic existentialists deal with what might be called the basic spiritual character of man. Again this is an emphasis which modern philosophy has often neglected. It may seem strange to claim, however, that the non-theistic existentialists are primarily interested in man's spiritual existence. The reader will recall that the humanistic existentialists stress the importance of becoming engaged in the world, of becoming totally committed, of responsibly choosing one's own existence —these emphases can only be understood as key insights concerning man as a spiritual being. The theologian Paul Tillich has indicated that the existentialists raise the basic questions concerning human existence; they recall man to a fundamental awareness of his estrangement in the world, and they can help to point man toward an ultimate concern.[117]

Another valuable feature of humanistic existentialism is its stress upon the importance of choice in order to live an authentic existence. In fact, a man can only be fully understood if one has some idea of how he has chosen to view himself and the world. Binswanger, the Swiss existential analyst, claimed that many cases of mental illness could only be understood in the light of the world chosen by the patient in his relationships to nature, to others, and to himself. Those psychiatrists who have been influenced by existentialism all maintain that the individual cannot be understood adequately in terms of the traditional Freudian categories; instead they insist that to help a patient it is necessary to understand how he interprets his life and what his own goals are for the future. The values of each individual must be understood as he lives them and not in terms of objective presuppositions about his sexual and destructive impulses.[118] The reader will recall that Sartre and the other humanistic existentialists have all insisted upon the importance of each man choosing his own life style. Even to evade a problem, to accept the solution of the crowd, to live as a thing manipulated by others, is to choose a way of life, albeit a life not filled with significant meaning. But even then, in moments of anxiety and dread, in the fear of being alone, in the consuming necessity of getting busier, the individual may find his conscience recalling him to himself, to the person he can and must be if he is to achieve well-being.

The humanistic existentialists with their great stress upon each man choosing his own existence generally support a relativistic attitude toward values. If there is no God, or human nature, then it appears that each man is free to choose his own life style. The existentialists, however, do not shrink from recognizing that free choice implies responsibility for the choice made. Again, this seems to be a needed corrective for today since we tend to make so much of heredity and environment conditioning people to respond in ways for which they should not be held accountable. That each man is held responsible for the kind of person he now is, and the person he will become, helps to prevent existentialism from degenerating into a philosophy of moral anarchy.

With this extreme emphasis upon each person choosing his own values, some of the defects of humanistic existentialism begin to appear. One should strive to avoid bad faith; one should not become a phony by accepting the stereotyped values of his society. However, beyond these general suggestions no positive content is given by humanistic existentialism to man's basic choice. Is it not the case, however, that there are some modes of conduct which are better than others? Cannot at least some summary rules be given as guidelines for human behavior? Is a stress upon seeking for authenticity enough? An emphasis upon authentic commitment does not seem to make sense unless one is committed not only sincerely and by his own choice, but also to a goal or purpose which leads to human well-being. Furthermore, one should be able to give good reasons for choosing his particular goals rather than others which he might have chosen. Few of us would deny that in the flux of life one must sometimes make choices without clearly seeing which possibility is the best. But these choices can be made in the light of an over-arching philosophy of life, such as a dedication to expressing Christian love, or a love of humanity and a desire to add to human welfare. It is in this respect that the humanistic existentialists are probably most lacking in their ethics— even their very condemnation of some types of action as committed in bad faith, or as expressing unauthentic existence, implies that they have some idea, vague and unclear though it may be, of what is good for man. It seems obvious that the content of what is chosen is equally as important as that the choice be an authentic one. It is not difficult to realize that fanatics have often with complete commitment and personal choice embarked upon schemes which have been destructive to other men. In terms of any kind of humanism, such conduct simply cannot be condoned; yet, the humanistic existentialists do not seem to have any clear way of condemning such behavior if it were chosen in good faith.

We have seen that Sartre seems to have realized that one needs more than a vague goal of commitment to one's own authentic choices. In his second stage, he was willing to commit himself to the freedom of all mankind, despite the fact that his own analysis in *Being and Nothingness* did not provide a basis for this decision. Today, Sartre holds that to extoll free choice may be meaningful to the upper middle class, but it does not seem to have any real meaning to the radically alienated poor and underprivileged. His own present commitment, therefore, has been made to Marxism—so that, paradoxically, Sartre now is committed to an absolute hatred of the bourgeoisie and to a revolution which will overthrow the present society. Perhaps Tillich was right when he said that while existentialism provided an adequate diagnosis of the human predicament, it did not itself have any answer to propose. The value orientations adopted by existentialists, when they do in fact commit themselves to some future goals, are not new. Humanism, theism, and Marxism may be reinterpreted in existentialist thought-forms, but there is no basis within existentialism itself for choosing between them.

An existentialist's commitment to humanism or to Marxism seems in a sense to be paradoxical because both of these positions hold that man has a basic essence. In fact, Sartre and Heidegger could well be accused of having smuggled in an essence for man in their earlier descriptions of the human situation. Tillich, for one, has claimed that Heidegger's authentic existence, and Sartre's humanism actually involved a much more structured view of human nature than either of these philosophers recognized. Tillich's comment deserves serious reflection:

> Sartre says man's essence is his existence. In saying this he makes it impossible for man to be saved or to be healed. Sartre knows this, and every one of his plays shows this too. But here also we have a happy inconsistency. He calls his existentialism humanism. But if he calls it humanism, that means he has an idea of what man essentially is, and he must consider the possibility that the essential being of man, his freedom, might be lost. And if this is a possibility, then he makes, against his own will, a distinction between man as he essentially is and man as he can be lost: man is to be free and to create himself.

> We have the same problem in Heidegger. Heidegger talks also as if there were no norms whatsoever, no essential man, as if man makes himself. On the other hand, he speaks of the difference between authentic existence and unauthentic existence, falling into the average existence of conventional thought and nonsense—into an existence where he has lost himself. This is very interesting, because it shows that even the most radical existentialist, if he wants to say something, necessarily falls back to some essentialist statements because without them he cannot even speak.[119]

The point which Tillich tried to make was that existence and essence go together in the case of man, and therefore a complete account of the human situation cannot ignore the one at the expense of the other. It is, however, somewhat misleading to accuse Sartre and Heidegger of having smuggled in an essence for man. Clearly, the existentialists meant to reject the traditional philosophical belief that man had a fixed end or nature. The humanistic existentialists have called our attention to the difference between human existence and the existence of objects. The end of the acorn is to become an oak tree, but there is no fixed determinate end for man. It was in this sense that the existentialists denied that man had an essence: man's nature was not predetermined. They did realize, however, that human reality could be discussed in terms of dynamic structures and modes of existence, such as freedom and authenticity. Perhaps the issue between Tillich and the existentialists on this point is largely terminological. At any rate, it is an open question as to whether or not one is correct in claiming that man is totally free. As we have seen, Sartre himself has rejected this position in his later philosophical writings.

In his present stage of development, Sartre has adopted a Marxist philosophy which believes that man's true nature is alienated in our society, but will achieve its full humanity and freedom only when an economy of scarcity has been surpassed. It does not seem that Sartre could now maintain that man does not have an essence. If he did so, then he should have to abandon Marxism.

An evaluation of Sartre's present position would inevitably involve our reconsidering Marxism itself. We should certainly ask ourselves whether or not Sartre is correct in maintaining that Marxism is *the* philosophy of our age. In a welfare state it may well be that Marxism does not provide any guidance for the individual's own choice of values. Sartre's present discussions of the plight of the alienated worker seem rather outmoded. Erich Fromm and others have suggested that the consumers in our super-capitalist state are far more alienated than the workers. While Sartre attempts to study the worker as he lives his alienation, it is surprising that he always finds the individual enmeshed and determined by his membership in the working class. It would appear that from the point of view of an existential analysis, the worker is no more completely determined in his every thought and deed by his belonging to the working class than was the café waiter whom Sartre discussed in *Being and Nothingness* merely constituted as a waiter. *The worker* is itself an abstract category, which should be suspect to an existentialist. More specifically, one would expect an existentialist to hold that an individual constitutes his own life by his work, his hobbies, his family, his home, his interests, his religion, and so on. In choosing an essence for man, it appears that Sartre could have done better than to have chosen man as defined by his class membership.

That Sartre himself has abandoned his projected book on ethics and committed himself to Marxism may, on a deeper level than we have suggested thus far, imply that an existentialist ethic is an impossibility. If the basic relation between others is conflict or violence, how could an ethic of mutual relationships between men be constructed? We have seen that Hazel Barnes attempts to construct an ethic for humanistic existentialism by modifying Sartre's position so that I-Thou relationships become possible. The reader will have to decide for himself whether or not Sartre is correct in holding that in our present world the other is always a threat, or if the other may sometimes become a helper to one in one's own search for a meaningful life. On the social scale, is violence the only method we have for solving disputes? It is unfortunately true that mankind has and still is resorting to violence; wars and riots remind us that man does not always act as a reasonable loving creature. But is it not also true that sometimes reason and cooperation have brought about an improvement of some aspects of our lives?

Sartre's own refusal to write a book on ethics, and his maintaining that in our present world truly moral values are impossible may be based on a fundamental confusion in his own thinking. He believes that all present value systems are merely rationalizations and justifications of one's economic and social class consciousness. Undoubtedly, there is much truth in this contention. However, should not a philosopher then become in Nietzsche's terms, "a value legislator"? Or perhaps more moderately, does not the philosopher have an obligation to attempt to show exactly which of our values are class conditioned in order to seek for some basic values upon which all mankind could unite? Could one not find some basic rules for human action which would fully respect the freedom of all men? Freud and Fromm, among many other writers, recognized that many of our values were but socially accepted excuses for our conduct, but they went on to try to suggest how through reason and cooperation man might overcome conflict and violence. Sartre now holds that a humanistic ethic is impossible until the ultimate classless society is reached, and that only then can each human being be treated as a man rather than as a thing. Until the new society appears, conflict, alienation, exploitation and violence are the only ways open for human action. Violence, however, tends to breed more violence, as Sartre himself admits. Is it not possible to find some interim steps for an ethic, such as working for racial equality, or for more tolerance and understanding for those individuals who seem to differ radically with the conventional norms? Sartre still seems to yearn for the absolute God, only now he calls it the ultimate society which shall appear at some indefinite future time. But how can an ultimate day of peace, cooperation and good-will ever dawn if men are encouraged to commit themselves to a Marxist philosophy which even Sartre admits has tended to ignore the individual? Sartre has perhaps become too obsessed with a violent *praxis,* and he may, as a result, lose sight of the goal of human freedom to which he has always been committed. Simone de

Beauvoir states that while Sartre was visiting Castro in Cuba he realized that "it is only in violence that the oppressed can attain their human status." [120] One may with good reason wonder what kind of a human status would emerge, unless the violence itself were undertaken only after all peaceful ways to obtain redress had been exhausted. Sartre's preoccupation with the extreme case in both his studies of individuals, such as Genet, and of societies, such as Cuba, appears to have blinded him to the more common instances in which individuals and societies work out their destinies, no less authentically, by the use of reason, cooperation and brotherly love rather than by conflict and violence. Even if Sartre is basically correct, there would still be the need for some interim ethic to move from a revolutionary take over of the present society toward a truly humane future. For this interim period, Sartre gives us no guidance.

Nevertheless, Sartre may in one very important sense be right. He claims that existentialism is only ancillary to Marxism; that is, existentialism can restore an emphasis upon the human individual to a philosophy which has tended in recent years to forget the individual as it strove for a future classless society. If existentialism itself has no independent function or reason for existence, then each man can use an existentialist approach to his own basic value commitment, whether it be to theism, to humanism, or even to Marxism. Existentialism is a stance or a basic attitude toward life, and not a specific ethical theory. By itself, existentialism seems not to go beyond urging one to choose his own existence in good faith. To actually make such a choice, however, will put one in a realm of over-belief which has already left existentialism behind. Sartre never ruled out "the possibility of an ethics of deliverance and salvation." [121] However, he suggested that before this possibility could be achieved one would first of all have to experience "a radical conversion." [122] His own radical conversion has been to his own interpretation of Marxism. Nevertheless, others who have agreed with his basic analysis of man have found their "radical conversion" to take other forms. Hazel Barnes, as we have seen, extolls a humanistic democratic ethic of freedom for each man. In our next chapter, we shall see that existentialism has also led some men to embrace a theistic religion.

NOTES FOR CHAPTER V

1 Jean-Paul Sartre, *The Words*, trans. by Bernard Frechtman (New York: George Braziller, Inc., 1964), p. 251.
2 Simone de Beauvoir, *The Prime of Life*, trans. by Peter Green (Cleveland: The World Publishing Co., 1962), p. 112.
3 Jean-Paul Sartre, *The Flies* in *No Exit and Three Other Plays*, trans. by Stuart Gilbert (New York: Vintage Books, Random House, Inc., 1955), p. 122.

4 Jean-Paul Sartre, *What Is Literature?* trans. by Bernard Frechtman (New York: Philosophical Library, Inc., 1949), p. 289.
5 Jean-Paul Sartre, *Situations,* trans. by Benita Eisler (Greenwich, Conn.: Fawcett World Library, 1966), p. 200.
6 Sartre, *The Words,* p. 253.
7 See Pierre Thevenaz, *What Is Phenomenology? and Other Essays,* ed. and introd. by James M. Edie, preface by John Wild, trans. by James M. Edie, Charles Courtney, Paul Brockelman (Chicago: Quadrangle Books, Inc., 1962); Quentin Lauer, *Phenomenology: Its Genesis and Prospect* (New York: Harper Torchbooks, 1965); Edmund Husserl, *Ideas: General Introduction to Pure Phenomenology,* trans. by W. R. Boyce Gibson (New York: Collier Books, 1962).
8 Martin Heidegger, *Being and Time,* trans. by John Macquarrie and Edward Robinson (New York: Harper & Row, Publishers, 1962), p. 51.
9 Jean-Paul Sartre, *Being and Nothingness: An Essay on Phenomenological Ontology,* trans. and introd. by Hazel E. Barnes (New York: Philosophical Library, Inc., 1956), p. lxvi.
10 Jean-Paul Sartre, *Nausea,* in *The Philosophy of Jean-Paul Sartre,* ed. by Robert Denoon Cumming (New York: Random House, Inc., 1965), pp. 62, 63, 64, 67.
11 Jean-Paul Sartre, "Existentialism Is a Humanism," in *Existentialism from Dostoevsky to Sartre,* ed., trans., introd., and preface by Walter Kaufmann (New York: Meridian Books, 1957), pp. 290–291.
12 Sartre, *Being and Nothingness,* p. 59.
13 *Ibid.,* p. 60.
14 *Ibid.,* pp. 588–589.
15 *Ibid.,* pp. 590–591.
16 *Ibid.,* pp. 591–592.
17 *Ibid.,* p. 31.
18 *Ibid.,* p. 25.
19 *Ibid.,* pp. 440–441.
20 *Ibid.,* p. 439.
21 *Ibid.,* p. 461.
22 *Ibid.,* p. 481.
23 *Ibid.,* p. 236.
24 *Ibid.,* p. 268.
25 *Ibid.,* p. 290.
26 *Ibid.,* p. 297.
27 Sartre, *No Exit* in *No Exit and Three Other Plays,* p. 47.
28 Sartre, *Being and Nothingness,* p. 364.
29 *Ibid.,* p. 364.
30 *Ibid.,* p. 408.
31 *Ibid.,* p. 409.
32 *Ibid.,* p. 409.
33 *Ibid.,* p. 419.
34 *Ibid.,* p. 421.
35 *Ibid.,* p. 422.
36 *Ibid.,* p. 423.
37 *Ibid.,* p. 429.
38 *Ibid.,* p. 626.
39 *Ibid.,* p. 627.
40 *Ibid.,* p. 615.

41 *Ibid.*, p. 93.
42 *Ibid.*, p. 38.
43 *Ibid.*, p. 39.
44 *Ibid.*, pp. 38, 39, 40.
45 John Wild, *The Challenge of Existentialism* (Bloomington: Indiana University Press, 1955), p. 129.
46 Sartre, *Being and Nothingness*, p. 53.
47 Sartre, "Portrait of the Antisemite" in *Existentialism from Dostoevsky to Sartre*, pp. 286–287.
48 *Ibid.*, p. 287.
49 Jean-Paul Sartre, *Saint Genet: Actor and Martyr*, trans. by Bernard Frechtman (New York: The New American Library of World Literature, Inc., 1963), pp. 27–28.
50 Sartre quoted in "Playboy Interview: Jean-Paul Sartre—A Candid Conversation," *Playboy*, XII (May, 1965), p. 72.
51 Sartre, *Being and Nothingness*, p. 63.
52 *Ibid.*, p. 65.
53 *Ibid.*, p. 70.
54 *Ibid.*, p. 550.
55 *Ibid.*, p. 550.
56 *Ibid.*, p. 615.
57 *Ibid.*, p. 627.
58 Simone de Beauvoir, *Force of Circumstance*, trans. by Richard Howard (New York: G. P. Putnam's Sons, 1965), p. 142.
59 Sartre, *The Words*, pp. 251–252.
60 Sartre, *Being and Nothingness*, p. 554.
61 Jean-Paul Sartre, "The Republic of Silence" in *The Philosophy of Jean-Paul Sartre*, p. 234.
62 Sartre, *What Is Literature?* p. 64.
63 *Ibid.*, p. 65.
64 *Ibid.*, p. 275.
65 *Ibid.*, pp. 275–276.
66 *Ibid.*, p. 276.
67 Sartre, "Existentialism Is a Humanism" in *Existentialism from Dostoevsky to Sartre*, p. 292.
68 *Ibid.*, p. 293.
69 Simone de Beauvoir, *The Ethics of Ambiguity*, trans. by Bernard Frechtman (New York: The Citadel Press, 1948), *passim.*
70 Sartre, "Existentialism Is a Humanism" in *Existentialism from Dostoevsky to Sartre*, p. 296.
71 *Ibid.*, pp. 297–298.
72 de Beauvoir, *The Ethics of Ambiguity*, p. 129.
73 *Ibid.*, pp. 136–137.
74 Sartre, "Existentialism Is a Humanism" in *Existentialism from Dostoevsky to Sartre*, pp. 307–308.
75 *Ibid.*, p. 310.
76 *Ibid.*, p. 299.
77 Jean-Paul Sartre, *The Age of Reason*, trans. by Eric Sutton (New York: Bantam Books, Inc., 1964); Jean-Paul Sartre, *The Reprieve*, trans. by Eric Sutton (New York: Bantam Books, Inc., 1964); Jean-Paul Sartre, *Troubled Sleep*, trans. by Gerard Hopkins (New York: Bantam Books, Inc., 1964).

78 Albert Camus, *The Plague*, trans. by Stuart Gilbert (New York: The Modern Library, 1948), p. 278.
79 *Ibid.*, p. 278.
80 Hazel E. Barnes, *An Existentialist Ethics* (New York: Alfred A. Knopf, Inc., 1967), p. 330.
81 *Ibid.*, p. 332.
82 *Ibid.*, p. 333.
83 *Ibid.*, p. 333.
84 *Ibid.*, p. 339.
85 *Ibid.*, p. 362.
86 *Ibid.*, p. 283.
87 *Ibid.*, p. 296.
88 *Ibid.*, p. 297.
89 *Ibid.*, p. 272.
90 *Ibid.*, p. 445.
91 *Ibid.*, p. 446.
92 Jean-Paul Sartre, "Materialism and Revolution," in *Literary and Philosophical Essays*, trans. by Annette Michelson (New York: Collier Books, 1962), p. 198.
93 *Ibid.*, p. 221.
94 *Ibid.*, p. 237.
95 *Ibid.*, p. 251.
96 Sartre quoted in de Beauvoir, *Force of Circumstance*, p. 199.
97 *Ibid.*, p. 199.
98 Sartre, *Situations*, p. 198.
99 *Ibid.*, p. 198.
100 de Beauvoir, *Force of Circumstance*, p. 346.
101 See Mary Warnock, *The Philosophy of Sartre* (London: Hutchinson & Co., Ltd., 1965); Wilfrid Desan, *The Marxism of Jean-Paul Sartre* (Garden City, N. Y.: Anchor Books, Doubleday & Co., Inc., 1965); William Leon McBride, "Jean-Paul Sartre: Man, Freedom, and Praxis," in *Existential Philosophers: Kierkegaard to Merleau-Ponty*, ed. by George Alfred Schrader (New York: McGraw-Hill Book Co., 1967).
102 Jean-Paul Sartre, *Search for a Method*, trans. by Hazel E. Barnes (New York: Alfred A. Knopf, Inc., 1963), p. 19.
103 *Ibid.*, p. 18.
104 *Ibid.*, p. 34.
105 *Ibid.*, p. 178.
106 *Ibid.*, pp. 175–176.
107 Jean-Paul Sartre, "Critique of Dialectical Reason," in *The Philosophy of Jean-Paul Sartre*, p. 435.
108 *Ibid.*, pp. 435–436.
109 *Ibid.*, p. 438.
110 *Ibid.*, p. 440.
111 *Ibid.*, p. 441.
112 *Ibid.*, p. 445.
113 *Ibid.*, p. 463.
114 Sartre, "Playboy Interview," p. 72.
115 Although this was the subtitle of William James, *Pragmatism* (1907), it applies equally well to existentialism.
116 G. E. Moore, "An Autobiography" in *The Philosophy of G. E. Moore*, ed. by Paul Arthur Schilpp (New York: Tudor Publishing Co., 1952), p. 14.

117 Paul Tillich, *Theology of Culture*, ed. by Robert C. Kimball (New York: Oxford University Press, 1959), chs. 7 and 8, *passim.*
118 See Hendrik M. Ruitenbeek, ed., *Psychoanalysis and Existential Philosophy* (New York: E. P. Dutton & Co., Inc., 1962). Contains articles by Ludwig Binswanger, Rollo May, Paul Tillich, and others.
119 Tillich, *Theology of Culture*, p. 121.
120 de Beauvoir, *Force of Circumstance*, p. 591.
121 Sartre, *Being and Nothingness*, footnote, p. 412.
122 *Ibid.*, footnote, p. 412.

SELECTED READINGS

* Available in paperback edition.

Barnes, Hazel E. *An Existentialist Ethics.* New York: Alfred A. Knopf, Inc., 1967.

* Beauvoir, Simone de. *The Ethics of Ambiguity.* Translated by Bernard Frechtman. New York: The Citadel Press, 1948.

* Camus, Albert. *The Myth of Sisyphus and Other Essays.* Translated by Justin O'Brien. New York: Vintage Books, Inc., Random House, 1959.

* ———. *The Plague.* Translated by Stuart Gilbert. New York: The Modern Library, 1948.

* ———. *The Rebel: An Essay on Man in Revolt.* Foreword by Herbert Read. Revised and translated by Anthony Bower. New York: Vintage Books, Inc., Random House, 1956.

* ———. *The Stranger.* Translated by Stuart Gilbert. New York: Vintage Books, Inc., Random House, 1946.

Cumming, Robert Denoon, ed. *The Philosophy of Jean-Paul Sartre.* Introduction by Robert Denoon Cumming. New York: Random House, Inc., 1965. Also in Modern Library. Selections from all of Sartre's major works.

* Desan, Wilfrid. *The Marxism of Jean-Paul Sartre.* Garden City, N. Y.: Doubleday & Co., Inc., 1965.

* Heidegger, Martin. *Existence and Being.* Introduction by Werner Brock. Chicago: Henry Regnery Co., 1965. Four essays by Heidegger, including "What Is Metaphysics?" and Brock's summary account of *Being and Time.*

* Jaspers, Karl. *Tragedy Is Not Enough.* Translated by Harald A. T. Reiche, Harry T. Moore, and Karl W. Deutsch. Boston: Beacon Press, 1952.

* Kaufmann, Walter, ed. *Existentialism from Dostoevsky to Sartre.* Translated, introduction, and preface by Walter Kaufmann. New York: Meridian Books, 1957. Selections from Sartre include "The Wall" (a short story), "Self-Deception" from *Being and Nothingness*, "Portrait of the Antisemite," and "Existentialism Is a Humanism," pp. 222–311.

Laing, R. D. and D. G. Cooper. *Reason & Violence: A Decade of Sartre's Philosophy, 1950–1960.* New York: Humanities Press Inc., 1964.

* Molina, Fernando. *Existentialism As Philosophy.* Englewood Cliffs, N. J.: Prentice-Hall, Inc., 1962. An excellent introduction.

* Sartre, Jean-Paul. *Being and Nothingness: An Essay on Phenomenological Ontology.* Translated and introduction by Hazel E. Barnes. New York: Washington Square Press, Inc., 1966.

* ———. *Intimacy and Other Stories.* Translated by Lloyd Alexander. New York: Berkley Publishing Corp., 1966.

* ———. *Nausea.* Translated by Lloyd Alexander. Norfolk, Conn.: New Directions Books, 1959.

* ———. *No Exit and Three Other Plays (The Flies, Dirty Hands,* and *The Respectful Prostitute).* Translated by Stuart Gilbert and Lionel Abel. New York: Vintage Books, Inc., Random House, 1955.

* ———. *Saint Genet: Actor and Martyr.* Translated by Bernard Frechtman. New York: The New American Library of World Literature, Inc., 1963.

———. *Search for a Method.* Translated by Hazel E. Barnes. New York: Alfred A. Knopf, Inc., 1963.

———. *What Is Literature?* Translated by Bernard Frechtman. New York: Philosophical Library, Inc., 1949.

* ———. *The Words.* Translated by Bernard Frechtman. New York: George Braziller, Inc., 1964.

* Schrader, George Alfred, Jr., ed. *Existential Philosophers: Kierkegaard to Merleau-Ponty.* New York: McGraw-Hill Book Co., 1967. Contains excellent scholarly articles on all major existentialists.

Warnock, Mary. *The Philosophy of Sartre.* London: Hutchinson & Co. (Publishers) Ltd., 1965.

VI

Religious Existentialism, Radical Theology and the New Morality

One of the tasks of theology has always been to reinterpret the meaning of religion in terms of the prevailing philosophical and moral climate of opinion. St. Paul and St. Augustine interpreted the significance of Jesus in terms of the Greek philosophy of their own times. Thomas Aquinas in the thirteenth century adapted the Christian faith to the philosophy of Aristotle. It seems only natural, therefore, that many of the theologians of our century have used the perspectives of Marx, Freud, Kierkegaard, Nietzsche and even Sartre in their interpretations of the significance of the Christian message for man living in the modern world. It is of course true that many traditional Christians have resisted these attempts for they have claimed that after the "new theologians" are finished with their tasks of reinterpretation what is left has little relationship to the faith professed through the ages. While those who are called the "new theologians" do not agree on their specific programs for reconstructing the appeal of religion to meet the needs of our own age, it is fair to say that all of them recognize that the traditional religion cannot be preached in the same old way, unless it is assumed that religion has had its day and will soon cease to be of more than historical interest. There is a sense in which these new theologians are all religious existentialists. In one way or another they all stress that if religion is to be of any value to contemporary man it must meet him where he lives. Only if religion can be shown to be relevant to man's existential concerns with his own identity, with his labors to eliminate racial and social injustice, will it be able to continue as a transforming force for human life. The answers which these theologians propose are, however, very diverse indeed. Let us turn to an examination of some of the more important new theologians in order to see what relevance they find for religion in one's attempt to find a way of life.

Karl Barth: Neo-Orthodoxy Søren Kierkegaard pointed the way for the first significant contemporary reinterpretation of Christianity. The Swiss-German theologian Karl Barth agrees completely with Kierkegaard's stress upon the infinite qualitative distinction between God and man. He holds that the attempts of the liberal theologians early in the twentieth century to turn Christianity into a "social gospel" by applying the teachings of Jesus directly to life in a capitalistic civilization were doomed to fail. The optimism of the proclaimers of the social gospel led them to believe that the Kingdom of God could be brought into existence in the present century. All we needed to do was to roll up our sleeves and work with the inspiration and example of our elder brother, Jesus, and the world would for the first time become a realm of peace in which all men could dwell securely. Two world wars, economic depressions, and man's inhumanity to man as shown in the Nazi concentration camps, tended to expose the shallowness of this optimistic hope. Barth, however, maintains that it was not only events in history which dispelled this pious hope for a Kingdom of God on earth. Even more significant was the false accommodation of the wholly other God to this world. The liberal theologians had not heeded Kierkegaard's reminder that there is no way from man to God, that man before God is always a woeful sinner whose vaunted "progress" is really in the wrong direction. Man, according to Barth, is never more in error than when he believes that he can save himself by his own reason and goodness. Man can never find God; God must reveal Himself or man could never know Him. Barth rejected utterly the confidence of the liberals that both God *and* Man would deliver the world from sin and evil; the case was far otherwise; it was *either-or*: either man and sin or God and salvation. Toward the end of the First World War Barth, influenced alike by Kierkegaard and his own mountainous homeland, began to speak of man as standing on the edge of a precipice, compelled if he would know God to launch out into the bottomless gulf, where alone he might be grasped and saved by God's hand.

Barth's position was first clearly expressed in his intensive study of Paul's *Epistle to the Romans* (1918). It was his first statement of a "theology of crisis"; its message was that only when man stands in desperate weakness before the judgment bar of God, naked and alone, can he expect salvation. There is no possibility of man saving himself. Only when he feels himself totally condemned before God, a mass of sinfulness, a being totally lost, can he receive the word of God in truth or know the true God. Modern man must recall what Kierkegaard had claimed: God is wholly other than man. God, however, has chosen to enter history in one point only, in Jesus Christ. As Barth put it, Jesus Christ is the only "point where the unknown world cuts the known world." [1] God still remains "the great unknown," however, for only by a leap of faith into the void can God penetrate through man's self-sufficiency to show his condemnation of all human achievements.

The existential despair of modern man was clearly reflected in Barth's description of man without God. His answer to this despair was not the atheistic humanism of Sartre, however, but was a new presentation of theological Calvinist orthodoxy. In his systematic writings he has developed what he calls a "theology of the Word." In Barth's view God speaks to us in our time and with a direct message. But since God is the author of His own message its apprehension by man is itself a divine gift. When in all its givenness it comes to man, it authenticates itself, it proves to be the criterion of reasonableness and not the other way around; reasonableness from the human point of view is never the criterion of the Word of God. Barth maintains that "every science knows well that there is a minus sign in front of its parenthesis" [2]; our human efforts to build society on human morality and self-reliance lead only to the negation of life—war and other "atrocities of life." [3] The too-easy rationalism and fatuously confident humanism of modern man produce only crisis and despair, disillusionment and human hopelessness and helplessness.

Like Kierkegaard, Barth holds that we are capable of being delivered from our despair only by means of a paradox: in our crisis, while perhaps we wait in utter despair and hopelessness, God speaks to us, if we accept His point of view. But what is God's point of view? Barth holds that it has been revealed to us, once for all, in Jesus Christ. This divine disclosure is not presented in the Jesus of history, for he is by now only a construct of the historians, but in the Christ who is the living Word of God and who reconciles God and man, time and eternity, death and resurrection in a revelation that is "compelling and exclusive"—that is, *if* a man gives himself up to Him in the hour of self-despair and listens, in faith and surrender. God's point of view comes to man through the Word of God. Modern man can prepare himself for receiving God's Word through reading the Bible which is the record of God's revelation. Barth accepts liberal historical criticism of the biblical books and therefore holds that the Bible as a collection of writings is not literally word for word to be equated with the Word of God. Nevertheless, what one reads in the Bible may produce in one the spiritual experience of hearing God speak to one directly in a living Word that may be only suggested by the written words. Barth agrees with Kierkegaard in believing that Christ (as distinguished from Jesus) is not found in time, really, for he is an eternal figure; in him time and eternity meet. The Jesus of history is bound to and all but lost in time; but the Christ of faith is eternally contemporaneous: in his living presence a man is confronted by the incarnate Word of God.

We have considered the writings of the early Barth, which are far more other-worldly than that of the position he now holds. In fact, Barth himself has modified his original point of view so that one can find in his more recent writings penetrating insights into contemporary social and ethical issues. As a consequence of Barth's modified theological stance, many American theologians have been profoundly influenced by him. However, Barth's rejection of human reason operating independently of divine revelation, his insistence that only in Jesus Christ does God penetrate to our world, does not make much of an appeal to the unbelievers. They have all along known that religion is absurd and irrational; furthermore, they are firmly committed to human action in this world which they do not find to be a vale of tears but rather a place for happiness and success. Barth's theology may be comforting to those already secure within the Church, but it is not likely to win any converts from the ranks of the secularists. One might in a state of ultimate despair, leap into the void and find God; but, he might also, like Sartre, leap and find nothing, absolutely nothing. And if he does find what he calls God, how does he know that this experience is not the fulfilling of a subconscious wish, or a rationalization, or a reversion to primitive religious fantasy?

Paul Tillich: God as the Unconditioned Being Paul Tillich is the theologian who has made much more of an impression upon the contemporary American scene than has Karl Barth. Tillich recognizes that Barth spoke to people who were already in the churches and that he attempted to save them from a too-easy identification of Christianity with liberal secular progress. In this respect, he professes admiration for the work of Barth. Tillich's own concern, however, is with the educated doubters and with those who have already rejected traditional religion. He finds in the depth psychology of Freud, in the existential analysis of the human predicament in Heidegger and Sartre, and in the philosophical quest for metaphysics contact points between Christianity and the unbeliever. Tillich stresses that it is the obligation of the theologian to think critically and carefully. He said, "The intellect is also a God-given function, and I resent it very much when somebody accuses the theologian of sin when he thinks. This is his job. He is not a nurse. . . ." [4] Tillich has often described his work as being on the borderline between philosophy and theology. Certainly his understanding of the history of philosophy, his own commitment to truth, and his perceptive analysis of our cultural situation require any serious thinker to evaluate Tillich's religious philosophy.

The life of Paul Tillich (1886–1965) reflects his concern with philosophy and theology, and prepared him well to be a mediator between culture and religion. He taught philosophy in German universities until his outspokenness against Hitler forced him to flee the country. Reinhold Niebuhr, the distinguished American theologian, invited Tillich to Union Theological Seminary in New York City. Tillich taught there from 1933 to 1955, when he moved to Harvard as a University Professor, a position which allowed him to teach any subject he wished. Tillich was able to unite both the old German world and the new American world in his writings; he was able to bring to the American experience his European training and background, but as he himself remarks it was the openness and freedom of America which inspired his own mature critical investigation into the foundations of human existence and the relevance of theology to the modern world. He was not only impressed by the lack of authoritarianism in America, but also by the courage to engage in new and untried ventures. As he put it in his "Autobiographical Reflections":

> I saw the American courage to go ahead, to try, to risk failures, to begin again after defeat, to lead an experimental life both in knowledge and in action, to be open toward the future, to participate in the creative process of nature and history. . . . Finally, I saw the point at which elements of anxiety have entered this courage and at which the existential problems have made an inroad among the younger generation in this country. Although this fact constitutes one of the new dangers, it also means openness for the fundamental question of human existence: "What am I?" the question which theology and philosophy both try to answer.[5]

Tillich begins his theological inquiry at the spot where he finds modern man, and he attempts to show him by the use of the categories of existentialism that his life in order to have meaning must manifest some ultimate commitment. He admits that he is a Christian theologian, and that therefore his work stands within the theological circle of the Protestant Church. In order to show the relevance of Christianity to the modern age he insists that it is necessary and proper to use the categories of existentialism, of metaphysics, of depth psychology, and of the arts to reinterpret the age-old message of Christianity for the modern man. He does not shrink therefore from using new terms in his theology, if they are more revealing today than the old ones which have lost their forcefulness. Of even more significance, he often maintains that what Christianity really affirms can only be fully understood in terms of new categories which have now become available to us in the modern world. Let us first look at his analysis of the human predicament, before we turn to his solution.

Tillich begins where all the existentialists begin, with an analysis of the human predicament. As he puts it: "Our present situation is characterized by a profound and desperate feeling of meaninglessness."[6] Man realizes that he is estranged, separated, from his true human nature and he is overwhelmed by anxiety. He defines anxiety as "the state in which a being is aware of its possible nonbeing."[7] It is part of the inevitable human situation that we all realize that we are finite; we shall die. This realization of one's finitude is inescapable; it cannot be cured as can pathological anxiety, but it can be accepted. Tillich finds that there are three basic types of existential anxiety: (1) the anxiety of fate and death, (2) the anxiety of emptiness and meaninglessness, and (3) the anxiety of guilt and condemnation. Which type is dominant at any particular period of time depends largely upon historical cultural factors. One thing is clear for Tillich. No man can completely escape from existential anxiety. Although a man may seek to evade anxiety, he is haunted by it unless he has the courage to accept his anxiety as part of his inevitable human situation in the world. If he accepts his anxiety he can achieve the courage to be; otherwise, he will be plunged into despair unless he follows one of the escape routes offered by pathological anxiety.

Depth psychology has tended to view all anxiety as pathological, but Tillich believes that a philosophical analysis can show that, although pathological and existential anxiety cannot be completely separated from each other, they can be clearly differentiated. If a person does not succeed in accepting anxiety as part of his fate, he can seek to escape extreme despair by adopting a neurosis. He still affirms his personality, but on such a limited and restricted scale that the threat of non-being is avoided. For example, one may avoid the threat to oneself provided by other people by retreating into oneself, or by associating only with a few carefully chosen friends. Or one may amuse himself with the pursuit of available pleasures and refuse to read a newspaper, so that the threat of his being involved in a war or riot is hidden from him. Tillich does not shrink from admitting that most retreats to religion in the modern world bear the marks of a pathological anxiety; the church is sought as a safe haven from the pressures of the world, and one is assured of heaven despite his ineffectiveness in the temporal world. Unfortunately these limited attempts to achieve self-security are bound to fail. The security purchased is too limited and unrealistic; the real world inevitably breaks in upon one. Even one's friends may become threats; one may be drafted no matter how much he has sought to evade the news of the world; and even one's narrow religious certitude may be punctured by doubt. Pathological anxiety calls for healing, but existential anxiety cannot be cured. It must be honestly and realistically accepted as an inevitable part of what it means to be human. The acceptance of existential anxiety is by means of what Tillich calls courage.

Man must affirm himself, despite his awareness of his finitude and despite his existential anxiety. But even man's self-affirmation has two sides, as Tillich sees it. One may affirm himself as a unique, free, self-centered individual; or one may affirm himself as a part of a world or of a specific social group. Actually both these poles are involved in all self-affirmation, but one may be stressed far more than the other. As Tillich so aptly remarks: "Both sides of the polarity are lost if either side is lost. The self without a world is empty; the world without a self is dead." [8] Self-affirmation must therefore include participating in a world. Tillich refers to this aspect of self-affirmation as the "courage to be as a part." [9] One affirms one's self by viewing himself as a part of the community in which he participates. "His self-affirmation is a part of the self-affirmation of the social groups which constitute the society to which he belongs." [10] In the real existential world this affirmation of the self as a part may take such precedence over one's own self-affirmation as a unique individual that it becomes destructive. Tillich finds this to be the case in neo-collectivist movements such as Fascism, Nazism and Communism. These movements function like religions for in them "we find the willingness to sacrifice any individual fulfillment to the self-affirmation of the group and to the goal of the movement." [11] An outstanding example of the affirmation of oneself as a part is clearly found, Tillich maintains, in a loyal Communist. Here the individual's anxiety about fate and death is overcome by his participation in the collective movement; his courage to be is derived from his loyalty to an historical movement which will itself fulfill his destiny. He finds his meaning for life in the Communist program, and hence he overcomes the anxiety of meaninglessness. His ethical values are likewise derived from the collective movement, thus making it possible for him to eliminate the anxiety of guilt by striving to fulfill the goals of a Communist world order.

Tillich, like Erich Fromm, finds the same tendencies at work in democratic conformism. In the pattern of daily life and thought, democratic conformism might approximate the neo-collectivistic ideologies against which it has protested. Whether or not this occurs, will depend "on the power of resistance in those who represent the opposite pole of the courage to be, the courage to be as oneself." [12] The danger of an exclusive stress upon loyalty to the group in which one participates is the loss of the uniqueness of the individual self.

The other pole of self-affirmation is represented in its extreme form by the self-affirmation of the individual without regard to its participation in the world. Existentialism is the most radical of the modern affirmations of the individual at the price of the group. The nineteenth-century existentialist revolt was led by individuals who protested against transforming persons into things which could be manipulated. Twentieth-century existentialism recognizes that modern man has experienced meaninglessness and absurdity and is hence driven to despair. Its solution is an "attempt to take the anxiety of meaninglessness into the courage to be as oneself." [13] Tillich refers to "the essence of man is his existence" as "the most despairing and the most courageous sentence in all Existentialist literature. What it says is that there is no essential nature of man, except in the one point that he can make of himself what he wants." [14] This radical self-affirmation is courageous in its affirmation of the uniqueness of the individual self, but it is despairing because of its inability to suggest what man ought to become. The self it affirms is what the self chooses to make itself, but the existentialist *qua* existentialist cannot give any guidance concerning what the contents of the self which one chooses should be. Tillich very perceptively comments:

> The self, cut off from participation in its world, is an empty shell, a mere possibility. It must act because it lives, but it must redo every action because acting involves him who acts in that upon which he acts. It gives content and for this reason it restricts his freedom to make of himself what he wants. . . . The nonparticipating hero in Sartre's *The Age of Reason* is caught in a net of contingencies, coming partly from the subconscious levels of his own self, partly from the environment from which he cannot withdraw. The assuredly empty self is filled with contents which enslave it just because it does not know or accept them as contents. . . . He cannot escape the forces of his self which may drive him into complete loss of the freedom that he wants to preserve. [15]

The radical self-affirmation of the unique individual leads to the loss of the world in Existentialism.

Tillich's analysis has sought to show that if one stresses his self-affirmation as a part of a group, he tends to lose his unique individuality; while, on the other hand, if he affirms the uniqueness of his own self, he tends to lose the world. Are we to be buffeted from one extreme to the other, or is there an answer to this predicament? Tillich proposes an answer to this apparent dichotomy in terms of his understanding of religion. Every affirmation of the courage to be contains an implicit or explicit religious element. Tillich can make this claim because of his own definition of religion: "Religion is the state of being grasped by an ultimate concern, a concern which qualifies all other concerns as preliminary and which itself contains the answer to the question of the meaning of our life." [16] In this respect, one who is committed to Communism views it as his ultimate concern; it is what gives meaning to his life. In like manner, the radical existentialist's dedication to achieving his own unique freedom and to achieving his projects for his life is motivated by "an ultimate concern." One's dedication to democracy as a way of life, or to the American dream of success and happiness, or to the cause of racial justice can also be viewed as ultimate concerns, and therefore as at least "quasi-religions." Tillich explained that what he meant by ultimate concern was "taking something with ultimate seriousness, unconditional seriousness." [17] Tillich even maintains that "therefore if a painter has, let's say, artistic expression as his ultimate concern, this then is his religion." [18] That which grasps one in the center of his personality, that for which one is willing to suffer and if need be to die, that is one's ultimate concern—one's religion. According to this definition of religion every man, even the cynic, has a religion. The remaining question which Tillich asks is whether or not one's ultimate concern is adequate or partial; is it really directed to something which has the right to be an ultimate concern, or is it an idolatrous lifting of a particular concern to a falsely higher level?

From the subjective side every person then has a religion; for every man has an ultimate concern, whether it be himself, his loved ones, his nation, his vocation, or his God. Tillich, however, also maintains that there is an objective side to man's ultimate concern, which can only be fulfilled by a transcending faith. Let us examine how Tillich tries to show that a more sophisticated view of God than that usually presented in the churches is the only adequate objective component for an ultimate concern.

Tillich often refers to God as the "ground of being" and not as a being alongside other beings. What he means by this is that in much traditional theology God is pictured as a supreme being, as a Lord or as a Father, or in more philosophical theology, as the principle of explanation for the universe itself. But then God either becomes a person in addition to the other persons in the world, or a super-scientific causal agent in addition to the causes science itself employs in its explanations. It is therefore quite understandable, Tillich maintains, that many people have dispensed with the belief in this kind of a God. We are no longer prepared to accept God as a supernatural intruder into nature or history; God is no longer needed as a causal factor in our scientific explanations. A too literal identification of God as a Father or as the Lord is also untenable to many people in the modern world. While we can encounter other persons in the flesh, we do not have this kind of an encounter with God. Much so-called atheism is therefore a needed corrective to naive theology. However, in throwing out the traditional symbols for God, symbols which no longer live in our experience, we may have also thrown out a vital truth which traditional religious symbols sought to portray. Symbols are finite means for pointing to the ultimate; they themselves become idolatrous when they are substituted for the ultimate to which they should point. Tillich is therefore very sympathetic with those who are unable to accept the traditional literal interpretation of the God of the Judaic-Christian tradition, but he hopes to show them in terms of his philosophical theology that these traditional symbols when correctly understood served to direct man toward the truly ultimate. Tillich maintains that in a faith in the truly ultimate the distinction between subject and object is overcome:

> The finite which claims infinity without having it (as, e.g., a nation or success) is not able to transcend the subject-object scheme. It remains an object which the believer looks at as a subject. He can approach it with ordinary knowledge and subject it to ordinary

handling. . . . The more idolatrous a faith the less it is able to overcome the cleavage between subject and object. For that is the difference between true and idolatrous faith. In true faith the ultimate concern is a concern about the truly ultimate; while in idolatrous faith preliminary, finite realities are elevated to the rank of ultimacy. The inescapable consequence of idolatrous faith is "existential disappointment," a disappointment which penetrates into the very existence of man! [19]

Tillich, at times, describes the truly ultimate as the "God above God." [20] But what exactly does he mean by this phrase, or by "God as the ground of being"?

Tillich refers in his *Systematic Theology* to God as "being-itself." If God is viewed as a highest being, he is finite, for he is placed "on the level of other beings while elevating him above all of them." [21] It is therefore a mistake to speak of God as existing. Tillich holds that, "It is as atheistic to affirm the existence of God as it is to deny it. God is being-itself, not *a* being." [22] Everything finite participates in being-itself, for being-itself is the ground of all the beings that there are. In this respect, Tillich echoes Heidegger's concern with preparing man for the revelation of Being as the ground, source, and fulfillment of his finite life. Since God is the ground of being, it is Tillich's conviction that every courageous affirmation reveals the ground of being. "Every act of courage is a manifestation of the ground of being, however questionable the content of the act may be. The content may hide or distort true being, the courage in it reveals true being." [23] Thus, from still another angle, we see that for Tillich every man has a religion, a faith, and every man is rooted in the ultimate ground of being.

While every act of courage is rooted in the ground of being, and while every faith participates in this same ground, nevertheless, Tillich claims that there are some acts of courage and some faiths which are better than others. Traditional theism which holds that God is the subject and man the object must be rejected as less than the "absolute faith" which Tillich advocates. His exposition here reminds one of Sartre's discussion of the attempt of "the Other" to annihilate my subjectivity by a look:

God as a subject makes me into an object which is nothing more than an object. He deprives me of my subjectivity because he is all-powerful and all-knowing. I revolt and try to make *him* into an object, but the revolt fails and becomes desperate. God appears as the invincible tyrant, the being in contrast with whom all other beings are without freedom and subjectivity. . . . This is the God Nietzsche said had to be killed because nobody can tolerate being made into a mere object of absolute knowledge and absolute control. This is the deepest root of atheism. It is an atheism which is justified as the reaction against theological theism and its disturbing implications. It is also the deepest root of the Existentialist despair and the widespread anxiety of meaninglessness in our period.[24]

But Tillich holds that all forms of theism are transcended by what he calls "absolute faith." This absolute faith transcends the courage to be as oneself and the courage to be as a part, but also it transcends the Gods of mysticism and of personal encounter. Here it is perhaps best to let Tillich speak for himself in his attempt to explain what he means by being grasped in absolute faith by the God beyond God:

> The acceptance of the God above the God of theism makes us a part of that which is not also a part but is the ground of the whole. Therefore our self is not lost in a larger whole, which submerges it in the life of a limited group. If the self participates in the power of being-itself it receives itself back. For the power of being acts through the power of individual selves. It does not swallow them as every limited whole, every collectivism, and every conformism does.[25]

This ground of being, or God above God, is moving in the depth of all of a man's concerns. "It is the situation on the boundary of man's possibilities. It *is* this boundary." [26] Tillich concludes this discussion with the cryptic remark: "*The courage to be is rooted in the God who appears when God has disappeared in the anxiety of doubt.*" [27]

Tillich's exposition of God as the ground of being and of the God above God has often been interpreted as mysticism or pantheism in disguise. It has seemed difficult for many people to reconcile these statements of his with his sermons, or with the sections in his *Systematic Theology* in which he develops the meaning of many of the traditional Christian symbols applied to God. Tillich himself felt it necessary to reply to these objections. In the introduction to the second volume of his *Systematic Theology* he claims that the God above God was designed for those who are gripped by radical doubt; it was an attempt to show those who cannot even use the word "God" that they are gripped in the depths of their ultimate concern by the ultimate ground of all being. It was an answer designed for men who find themselves in an extreme situation of doubt and meaninglessness in the modern world. But Tillich continued his defense of this exposition of the God above God by saying:

> This is the answer to those who ask for a message in the nothingness of their situation and at the end of their courage to be. But such an extreme point is not a space within which one can live. The dialectics of an extreme situation are a criterion of truth but not the basis on which a whole structure of truth can be built.[28]

Tillich was apparently referring to his own defense of symbolic talk about God as not invalidated by the God beyond God. For he claimed that religious symbols could be used quite legitimately to point toward the true ultimate concern. What he wished to do was to speak to both those who could no longer accept the traditional "God talk" and to those who found the traditional symbols helpful for pointing them toward the true ground of being. As a result of this double stance, he was often attacked from both sides, both by the unbelievers and the believers.

Tillich described his theological method as one of correlation. It was an attempt to allow philosophy to ask the questions, and then to show that only theology could answer these questions. Philosophical categories were helpful up to a point, but after that religious symbols and the categories of theology had to take over. Philosophy could ask questions such as "Why is there anything at all?" but it could not answer them. Only a theologically informed use of categories such as the infinite, the unconditional and the ground of being, might be able to alert men to a fuller revelation of the nature of the divine in terms of the religious symbols found in the Bible. One must not forget that Tillich always insisted that he was working within the circle of the Christian faith; he was a Christian theologian trying to show the relevance of the Christ, the New Being, to modern man. Unlike Barth, however, who maintained that God touched the world only in Christ, Tillich firmly believed that unless God were in some sense present in all of life, He could not be found even in the Christ. Tillich's main concern, therefore, was not only to develop a systematic theology within the framework of the Christian Church but also to show how this theology had relevance to those men who were so alienated from the Church that they were forced to live their lives in the secular world. Even to these men, God was not wholly absent. He was present in them to the extent that they sincerely had ultimate concerns to which they were devoted in all seriousness. In many respects they were closer to God than the pious believers who mouthed the right theological language but who had substituted an orthodoxy of belief for existential commitment to the Christian God. Tillich steadfastly maintained that one should answer the questions one is asked to the best of one's ability, and one should never hide anything. Therefore, he always tried to show that faith involves doubt, that faith involves risk, and that to substitute beliefs for ultimate concerns is to destroy man's openness to new truth. Despite the difficulty of some of his philosophical and theological language, this attitude of his was stated very clearly in response to a question he was asked while lecturing at the University of California in Santa Barbara:

> The worst thing, and I censure them sincerely, is the reply of some Sunday-school teachers, when children ask questions: "You must not ask, you must believe." My reaction to that is very barbaric: I would say, "Throw those teachers out tomorrow morning! Forever!" [29]

When faith is understood as one's commitment to one's ultimate concern then Tillich holds one sees the necessity for talking about this faith in symbols and myths, unless one remains silent. Anything which can be completely described in terms of finite or scientific categories cannot be the object of anyone's ultimate concern. A symbol is taken from finite experience, but it points beyond itself and opens up levels of reality which are closed to a literal rendition of the symbol. Therefore, a picture, a poem or a play "gives us not only a new vision of the human scene, but it opens up hidden depths of our own being." [30] Symbols can die, however, when they no longer evoke a living response in the groups in which they are used. While nomads could well understand the symbol of God as "the good shepherd," this symbol, and others like it, may be dead for us today in our era of urban technological culture. Tillich puts the case for the use of symbols as follows:

> Whatever we say about that which concerns us ultimately, whether or not we call it God, has a symbolic meaning. It points beyond itself while participating in that to which it points. In no other way can faith express itself adequately.[31]

God thus becomes the fundamental symbol for one's ultimate concern, but not the only symbol:

> All the qualities we attribute to him, power, love, justice, are taken from finite experiences and applied symbolically to that which is beyond finitude and infinity. . . . They are symbols taken from our daily experience, and not information about what God did once upon a time or will do sometime in the future. Faith is not the belief in such stories, but it is the acceptance of symbols that express our ultimate concern in terms of divine actions.[32]

Likewise, ultimate concerns are expressed in terms of myths. Myths when taken literally are idolatrous, but when read correctly they point beyond themselves to the ultimate. Symbols and myths obtain their meaning within a community and maintain their power only within this community. In this sense, an outsider can never fully comprehend another faith, for he cannot experience the depth of the symbols and myths from the inside of the community.

An illustration of Tillich's use of the traditional symbols applied by the Christian religion to God may help to make clearer both his use of symbols and his attempt to balance his conception of God as both present in and transcendent from the world. Tillich holds that the Christian symbols of Father and Lord imply each other. Lord is primarily a symbol for the holy and unapproachable power of God, for the infinite distance which separates God from man. But if Christians refer to God only in terms of the symbol "Lord" then God easily becomes "a despotic ruler

who imposes laws on his subjects and demands . . . obedience and un-
questioned acceptance of his sayings." [33] The symbolic reference to God
as "Lord" needs to be balanced by the symbol of "Father," which refers
to the unity between man and God as expressed in terms of holy love.
But if Christians use the symbol of "Father" exclusively for their references to God, they tend to sentimentalize God and to create a God who
is expected to give men what they want and to forgive them whatever
they want to be forgiven. When men do not get what they want from
their Father in Heaven, they are radically disappointed, their "naive
confidence . . . . easily turns into disappointment." [34] "The Lord who is
not the Father is demonic; the Father who is not the Lord is sentimental." [35] But if the two symbols are taken together they complement one
another. "God must remain Lord and Judge in spite of the reuniting
power of his love. The symbol 'Lord' and the symbol 'Father' complete
each other. This is true theologically as well as psychologically." [36] These
basic symbols of "Lord" and "Father" express the I-Thou dimension of
man's relationship to God; they grow out of man's existential situation
and they point beyond it to a transcendent God. But there are other
symbols which express other dimensions of the divine; symbols which
more clearly refer to God as the ground of being: "Almighty God" and
"Eternal God" are two examples which Tillich cites. Just as one errs by
stressing God as either Lord or Father, so one ought not to concentrate
on God from the standpoint of divine-human encounter without making
adequate provision for reference to the ultimate mystery and transcendent
presence of God as the ground of all being.

Tillich maintains that we are justified in using personalistic language in
our symbolic references to God, for persons represent the highest beings
which we know. However, he cautions us that we ought not to consider
God as literally a person, for He is more than another person. God is
the cosmic ground of being. God is the ultimate, the unconditioned, the
fitting object for our ultimate concern, and we must guard against identifying the ultimate with any finite symbol or with any combination of
finite symbols.

Some of the symbols and concepts used in previous ages are no longer
relevant to us today. They have been so distorted by a legalistic or literal
usage that we must abandon them and seek for new thought forms in
which to convey the truth to which these symbols and concepts attempted
to point. While many people have identified "sin" with petty violations
of moralistic commandments, the reality which this term referred to can
be conveyed in terms of alienation or estrangement. Hence by reference
to "estrangement from oneself, from the other man, from the ground out
of which we come and to which we go" one may be able to make clear
what the old theologians meant by "original sin." [37] It is not the violation
of moral commandments which constitutes the reality of "sin," rather

it is treating another person as an object, as merely a thing among other things in the world. Likewise, "salvation" may have to be reinterpreted in terms of "healing," of "integrating," or "of making whole." Tillich therefore prefers to refer to Christ as the "New Being":

> There is a power from beyond existence which for us is verifiable by participation. . . . Christ is the place where the New Reality is completely manifest because in him in every moment, the anxiety of finitude and the existential conflicts are overcome. That is his divinity. . . . What he is, is healing power overcoming estrangement because he himself was not estranged.[38]

Tillich did not deny that many unbelievers might continue to fail to accept even his new interpretation of Christianity, but at least he would have attempted to communicate to them what the Christian faith was really about. He would at least have removed the old stumbling blocks of dogmatic beliefs and of dead symbols which could no longer speak to modern man. Finally, each person would have to make his own decision. Tillich's hope was that his reinterpretation of the Christian faith might make it a more viable faith for others who were now outside it. But he also believed that he was genuinely true to the spirit of the faith in his attempt to rephrase it into more contemporary language.

While Tillich devoted most of his writings to an elaboration of his philosophical theology in order to present Christianity as a live option for modern skeptics, he did towards the end of his career turn his attention more directly to the ethical aspect of human life. He was concerned with answering this question: "Can we point to something that transcends both graceless moralism and normless relativism in ethical theory and moral action?"[39] His attempt to answer this question presupposes that religious principles dwell within the principles of moral action. Indeed, this is what we would expect, for if God is the ground of being then there is no real separation between the religious and the secular, between religious ethics and secular ethics. Tillich rather conventionally maintains that "the moral imperative is the command to become what one potentially is, a *person* within a community of persons."[40] Morality is thus not obedience to an external law, whether it comes from the church or from the state, but it is rather a call to each man to be that which he is meant to be, namely, a fully free and responsible person. With Immanuel Kant, he holds that the form of the moral imperative is categorical or unconditional, although, unlike Kant, he maintains that the content of the imperative is always attended with the possibility of having made the wrong decision. Tillich believes that ethical values are grounded in being; they reflect the fulfillment of that which man essentially or potentially is. In this respect every moral imperative, even that of utilitarian happiness, reflects the dimension of an ultimate concern rooted in the ground of being itself. The religious quality of all morality is, for Tillich, the unconditional character of the moral imperative.

Tillich finds that the content of the moral imperative derives from natural law, for in all cultures, even if different specific codes of morality are professed each code is "rooted in man's essential nature and ultimately in the structure of being itself." [41]

Tillich thus opposes the main stream of contemporary philosophical investigations of the nature of ethics which maintain that an "ought" cannot be derived from an "is." G. E. Moore, the contemporary British author of *Principia Ethica*, had held that any ethic which attempts to derive its norms from sociological, psychological or metaphysical statements has committed "the naturalistic fallacy." Tillich does not accept this position for he clearly holds that values cannot be studied independently of their being grounded in the essential and ultimate nature of reality itself. Values are thus attempts to persuade man to recover that which he is basically or essentially, but if he did not already possess this basic nature, Tillich holds that he would be unable to change himself. Thus, although Tillich holds that there are universal norms grounded in the essential nature of man and the world, he does recognize that these norms must be flexible enough so that they can be adapted to meet the specific concrete needs of a changing world. Justice may be a universal norm, but what is just in a specific case may call for calculation and decision rather than simply obeying interpretations of justice put forth in traditional moral codes. In this respect, Tillich attempts to provide for an absolute standard of value, while also allowing this standard to be reinterpreted and adjusted according to the concrete requirements of a changing world order. Thus, he seeks to provide for both natural law and relativism in his theory of value.

Tillich holds that the ultimate moral principle is not justice but love, which contains justice within itself. Justice by itself may be detached and abstract, but if the other person is acknowledged as a person then one tends to get involved with that person so that love becomes the ultimate moral principle governing the relationship. Tillich interprets love as a desire for reunion with the separated, very much as Plato did in the *Symposium*. But Christian love viewed as *agapē* also expresses the religious element, the transcendent element of morality. Unlike some Christian theologians who have made a radical separation between *eros* (human love expressed as desire) and *agapē* (God's unconditional love of all persons), Tillich maintains that "Love is one." [42] *Agapē*, therefore, is never completely separated from the three other elements which Tillich distinguishes in love: *epithymia* (desire or *libido*), *eros* (aspiration toward value), and *philia* (friendship). None of these qualities of love is ever completely absent, although one quality may be more dominant than the others. Tillich therefore can claim: "There is an element of libido even in the most spiritualized friendship and in the most ascetic mysticism. A saint without libido would cease to be a creature. But there is no such saint." [43]

Agapē is not therefore a kind of love completely separated from all other kinds of love, but is instead the quality of depth in love. It is the way in which ultimate reality, or God, transforms life and love. The norm of *agapē* as presented in Christianity is Tillich's absolute norm, which while absolute is nevertheless changeable and adaptable to each specific situation. *Agapē* is the religious motivation within love and therefore never becomes codified into law itself. Tillich's very provocative discussion of the unity of love in all its various aspects has done much to destroy other-worldly asceticism, and to restore a divine quality to those types of love which some theologians had held to be "sinful."

Tillich's discussion of *agapē* as the objective norm for ethics will require close examination. It is this aspect of his thought which has been seized upon by the defenders of Christian situation ethics, whom we shall be examining later on in this chapter. As we have pointed out, Tillich holds that *agapē* is the unchanging principle of ethics, but he also insists that it always changes in its concrete applications. We will do well to quote him at some length on this matter:

> It [*agapē*] "listens" to the particular situation. Abstract justice cannot do this; but justice taken into love and becoming "creative justice" or *agapē* can do so. *Agapē* acts in relation to the concrete demands of the situation—its conditions, its possible consequences, the inner status of the people involved, their hidden motives, their limiting complexes, and their unconscious desires and anxieties. Love perceives all these—and more deeply the stronger the *agapē* element is.

> Tables of laws can never wholly apply to the unique situation. This is true of the Ten Commandments as well as of the demands of the Sermon on the Mount and the moral prescriptions in the Epistles of Paul. "The letter kills" not only because it judges him who cannot fulfill the law, but because it suppresses the creative potentialities of the unique moment which never was before and never will come again. . . . Therefore love liberates us from the bondage to absolute ethical traditions, to conventional morals, and to authorities that claim to know the right decision perhaps without having listened to the demand of the unique moment. . . . Love can reject as well as utilize every moral tradition, and it always scrutinizes the validity of a moral convention.[44]

Some people have read the above passages as though they defended the so-called "new morality." If by the "new morality" one means that persons are more important than moral conventions, that one ought to always act so as to display one's concern for justice and love in the specific situation unfettered by moral legalism, then Tillich's discussion of *agapē* does indeed defend the "new morality." If, however, one means by the "new morality" doing whatever one enjoys merely for the sheer pleasure one derives from one's actions, then Tillich's discussion would not support such a position by any means. He is not advocating irresponsible conduct, but is rather calling each man to the height of moral responsibility in which he treats all persons with the respect and love which they deserve as human beings.

While Tillich in the above passages justified setting aside traditional moral conventions for the sake of applying *agapē* in a concrete situation, he did not intend to throw out all the moral principles which our culture has acquired through the ages. Indeed, he continued his discussion of the basic nature of morality by suggesting that the moral principles formulated by a society represent practical wisdom:

> They represent the wisdom of the past about man, his relation to others and to himself, his predicament in temporal existence, and the *telos* or inner aim of his being. . . . As such, they are of tremendous weight, but do not possess unconditional validity. They guide the conscience in concrete situations, but none of them, taken as law, has absolute validity. Even the Ten Commandments express not only man's essential nature but also the wisdom and the limitations of an early feudal culture. Certainly there is risk in deviating from the wisdom embodied in a concrete tradition. But there is also risk in accepting a tradition without questioning it. . . . But accepting or trespassing traditional morals is spiritually justified only if done with self-scrutiny, often in the pain of a split conscience, and with the courage to decide even when the risk of error is involved.[45]

Out of courageous decisions to violate the traditional wisdom of the moral commandments of our culture, Tillich believed that new insights might develop. As a result we might find new and better principles which would be more morally adequate for our present situations than the inherited tables of the law. "Should this occur, love as the ultimate principle of the moral demands would be powerfully vindicated."[46]

The most important function of the religious element in morality, according to Tillich, is its ability to provide the motivation which men need to be moral. One cannot be commanded to be moral, or to obey the moral laws. Instead, Tillich, taking his cue from the findings of psychoanalysts, suggests that the individual needs the feeling of acceptance in spite of his specific moral deficiencies. The psychoanalyst accepts his patient as a person, and respects the center of the patient's integrity. Healing can then follow. Likewise, Tillich suggests, religion offers men the element of grace, the acceptance by God of a person in spite of his unacceptability with regard to his positive actions and desires. The motivation for morality itself is thus transmoral:

Where there is grace there is no command and no struggle to obey the command. This is true of all realms of life. He who has the grace of loving a thing, a task, a person, or an idea does not need to be asked to love, whatever quality of love may be predominant in his love. A reunion of something separated has already taken place, and with it a partial fulfillment of the moral imperative. As a gift of grace, it is not produced by one's will and one's endeavor. One simply receives it.[47]

Tillich did not make many concrete pronouncements concerning how a better world might be achieved through his Christian interpretation of the meaning of life. He was more concerned with providing the foundation of knowledge, faith, hope and love in terms of which each man could participate more creatively in the on-going historical tasks. While still in Germany he had been active in "religious socialism" which attempted to use religious principles as the foundation for a more humane social order, but as everyone knows the religious socialists lost out to the Nazis. Tillich never abandoned his belief in religious socialism, however, for although he always insisted that every solution of a problem in history creates new ambiguities, which must then be solved, he never advocated religious escapism. Knowledge must issue in action, and so must faith. The Christian believer should therefore work alongside all of those who are critically and rationally attempting to overcome those forces which are turning man into a thing, but he can, according to Tillich, work with greater conviction than the humanists because he knows that ultimately God must redeem history itself. There are no solutions to ultimate problems within history; nevertheless, the believer has an obligation to strive for as much reunion among men and nations as is possible under the exigencies of any particular historical period. Like Marx and Fromm, he believed that one should work to create a better community:

Christianity must declare that, in the next period of history, those political forms are right which are able to produce and maintain a community in which chronic fear of a miserable and meaningless life for the masses is abolished, and in which every man participates creatively in the self-realization of the community, whether local, national, regional, or international.[48]

It was extremely crucial for Tillich that faith, knowledge and action be creatively combined under the domination of Christian *agapē*.

It is important that we clearly understand that Tillich attempts to derive values and morality from the essential nature of man. For this reason, he often refers to the natural law as the basis of ethics and civil law, and speaks of love as reuniting, not as uniting. Man in his original state of innocence, before "the Fall," had not transgressed his essential unity with nature and the ground of being itself. The myth of "the Fall" in the

Judaic-Christian tradition stands for man's alienation or separation from his real essence. After this fall each man in his own life finds that he is a self separated from nature and from other selves, but he has the creative desire to seek for a reunion of his being with others and with nature itself. All attempts to achieve healing, integration, or salvation Tillich views as symbolic of man's desire to be reunited with the ground of all being, with God. But this reunion must not obliterate the unique individual selves; they must be affirmed but reunited through acts of love and creative justice. But even here Tillich finds that we have an ontological answer to our question of values, for what we ought to become has already appeared in the New Being, the Christ, and is visible in the activities of the manifest and the latent Church which is the beginning of the Kingdom of God. In the New Being man is reunited with nature, with his fellow men and with the ground of being itself. Man in his present state is alienated and separated from the ground of being, but to the extent that he opens himself to the New Being in Christ he can become reunited with his own essential nature.

Tillich devotes the second and third volumes of his *Systematic Theology* to developing the implications of this view of Christ, man, and the Kingdom of God. His method is largely dialectical, in the tradition of Hegel and Marx. Near the end of the third volume of his *Systematic Theology* he refers to the rhythm of both the Divine Life and of all creaturely life. He says:

> One could refer to this rhythm as the way from essence through existential estrangement to essentialization. It is the way from the merely potential through actual separation and reunion to fulfilment beyond the separation of potentiality and actuality.[49]

This is Tillich's philosophical reinterpretation of the myths of the creation, of Adam's fall in the Garden of Eden, of man's sinful existence on earth, and of his final salvation through eternal life. But in many respects it seems more philosophical than biblical. Tillich himself seems to recognize this strain in his thought, for in his discussion of Eternal Life he maintains that there can be only one "eternal One." Hence, eternal life can only mean life in God, who is the eternal One. He explains:

> This corresponds to the assertion that everything temporal comes from the eternal and returns to the eternal, and it agrees with the Pauline vision that in ultimate fulfilment God shall be everything in (or for) everything. One could call this symbol "eschatological pan-en-theism."[50]

This view of Tillich's surely seems like a gigantic speculation, but Tillich does not shrink from speculating. Tillich explained as follows:

> The word "speculate" has become a word of contempt, although it means to look carefully at something—*speculari* in Latin. It does not

mean flying up and over the clouds. It means looking carefully at the structure of reality. And in this sense I am willing to speculate.[51]

We should recall Tillich's reason for seeking to apply philosophical concepts and the insights of existentialism, art, and depth psychology to his interpretation of man's ultimate concern, God. Many of the traditional symbols were culture-bound; they simply do not live for us in our modern world. But symbols themselves are not sacred; they are valid only as ways of pointing beyond themselves. The American flag is not in itself a sacred object; but it is a symbol of what America stands for and hence patriots insist that it should be respected. A code for displaying the flag properly, and even for what one ought to do with a flag which is worn out, has been developed around this particular symbol. Many of the traditional Christian symbols have lost their usefulness, however, since they no longer reflect the nature of contemporary life or they have been so literally applied that they now fail to create a response. Tillich suggests that the traditional symbol of "original sin" has lost its meaning so that he would forbid, "under penalty of dismissal, any minister from using the word 'original sin' for the next thirty years, until this term regained some meaning." [52] He is doubtful, however, if it will ever regain viability, and suggests that perhaps it will have to be dropped completely. Tillich's theology is primarily an attempt to find new terms to deal with the realities which the worn-out symbols reflected. His criterion for the usefulness of a symbol, old or new, is that it should be immediately understandable. But we should let Tillich explain himself here, for on this matter he is most clear:

> When I speak in any college about estrangement, everybody knows what I mean, because they all feel estranged from their true being, from life, from themselves especially. But if I spoke of their all being sinners, they would not understand at all. They would think, "I haven't sinned; I haven't drunk or danced," as in some fundamentalist churches, or whatever they understand as sin. But estrangement is a reality for them. Yet estrangement is what sin means—the power of estrangement from God. And that is all it means.

> I believe that this is a possible solution to our problem, because the reality of Christian teaching about the human predicament is confirmed by every bit of writing, painting, or philosophizing of the entire twentieth century. And when we demonstrate this, and show how the great existential tragedies occur today, as in the past, we can make young people understand the human predicament. This is the point of my whole systematic theology.[53]

Tillich's philosophical theology is an attempt to answer the question, "How do I find meaning in a meaningless world?" [54] It is this question which he thinks has replaced in our day the traditional questions about the nature of God.

The Secular City and the Death of God The new young theologians in America today, although they have learned much from Tillich, tend to reject his existential basis for theology in behalf of a more radical secular pragmatic approach. This group of theologians, although they do not by any means agree completely in all aspects of their thought, begins from the belief that the secular has replaced the religious category in the contemporary world, and that therefore it is impossible to talk about God in either the traditional biblical or in new metaphysical ways. The more radical of these are the "Death of God theologians," while the others tend to still believe in God but shift their emphasis to ethics, or the importance of political action, rather than maintaining the priority of traditional theological "God talk."

The change in the emphasis of theology which has occurred recently is best documented by Harvey Cox's popular book, *The Secular City*, and by Bishop Robinson's *Honest to God*. Both of these men indicate their indebtedness to the German theologian Dietrich Bonhoeffer, who was killed by the Nazis just shortly before the end of the Second World War. Bonhoeffer wrote some letters and papers while in prison which upon their publication seemed to provide the new theologians with a novel relevant perspective. Despite the orthodoxy of many of his earlier writings, toward the end of his life Bonhoeffer thought about what would happen to Christianity in a world "come of age" in which men no longer could accept God as an explanatory hypothesis, and in which the traditional interpretations of religion were rejected by most men. Bonhoeffer concluded that we were now living in just such a world, of that he was convinced. Rather than evade the full force of the death blow applied to traditional religion, he believed that even the theologian must admit what has happened. In a letter from prison written on July 16, 1944, he wrote:

> So our coming of age forces us to a true recognition of our situation *vis à vis* God. God is teaching us that we must live as men who can get along very well without him. . . . The God who makes us live in this world without using him as a working hypothesis is the God before whom we are ever standing. . . . God allows himself to be edged out of the world and on to the cross. God is weak and powerless in the world, and that is exactly the way, the only way in which he can be with us and help us.[55]

Rather than decry the advance of science, technology and a secular society Bonhoeffer thought the Christian ought to accept these worldly events. In fact the world come of age could deliver us from an erroneous view of Christianity. As Bonhoeffer put it:

> To be a Christian does not mean to be religious in a particular way, to cultivate some particular form of asceticism (as a sinner, a penitent

or a saint), but to be a man. . . . Jesus does not call men to a new religion, but to life.[56]

Bonhoeffer's emphasis on the importance of living in the world as a man grew out of his own belief concerning the nature of Jesus. He returned many times to the question of what Christ is for us today in our godless world. It was his conviction that one should affirm this world fully, but that since persons were more important than things, the Christian should not hesitate to enjoy his personal intimate relationships. Jesus' concern for others suggests to Bonhoeffer that Jesus was the man for others, and that through all of his relationships he showed us the power of transcendent love. Thus, somewhat paradoxically, while God has been edged out of the world, he re-enters the world in Jesus and those who share the sufferings of others. This emphasis has been very strong in the American radical theologians, who, even though they may proclaim the death of God, affirm the reality and power of Jesus.

Bonhoeffer's ideas, all too briefly summarized above, were seminal; they were not well worked out by him. But many of the present American and British theologians have tried to develop the implications of his suggestions. Bishop Robinson elaborates upon the theme of Jesus as "the man for others" in order to suggest a new morality of situational ethics grounded in love, as well as to show that men can discover the nature of God only through the Christ.

The American radical theologians, Thomas J. J. Altizer and William Hamilton, unite Bonhoeffer's insights about Jesus as a man working alongside the neighbor with Nietzsche's announcement of the death of God. Unlike the secular existentialists, such as Sartre, who regret the death of God, Hamilton and Altizer not only gladly accept the death of God but they unite in "*willing* . . . the death of God." [57] They find Tillich and Bishop Robinson to be "far too confident about the possibility of God-language." [58] God does not appear in anxiety, nor as the ground of our being. Americans have never accepted these existentialist analyses of the human predicament. Harvey Cox unites with Hamilton and Altizer, at least in this respect, by maintaining that America is a land of optimism, of solving the next problem of society, and is not a nation of individuals who indulge in introspective probing of the so-called alienated human condition.

William Hamilton in speaking of his own belief in the death of God says:

I assert with Bonhoeffer the breakdown of the religious *a priori* and the coming of age of man.

The breakdown of the religious *a priori* means that there is no way, ontological, cultural or psychological, to locate a part of the self or a part of human experience that needs God. There is no God-shaped blank within man. Man's heart may or may not be restless until it rests in God. It is not necessarily so. God is not in the realm of the necessary at all; he is not necessary being, he is not necessary to avoid despair or self-righteousness. He is one of the possibles in a radically pluralistic spiritual and intellectual milieu.[59]

He explains that to be really secular is to not ask God to solve the world's problems. "Really to travel along this road means that we trust the world, not God, to be our need fulfiller and problem solver, and God, if he is to be for us at all, must come in some other role." [60] During the present period we have no way to speak about God; we must simply wait. But during this period of waiting, Hamilton suggests that the radical theologian knows what he is to do and where he is to be. "It is in the world, in the city, with both the needy neighbor and the enemy." [61] In effect, this means that the radical theologians turn from doing theology toward the practical problems of wars, riots, race relations, and so on. But their moves toward social action are not based on the traditional Christian belief that we ought to love each other because God first loved us. Rather they take their places with their needy neighbors out of a deep awareness of the loss of God and the belief that only man can solve the world's problems.

Nietzsche has often been called an atheist, and many who profess the views of these radical theologians have adopted the name of "humanists." Why then do these "theologians" still call themselves Christians? Hamilton responds that it is because their way to the neighbor is not only based on secular concerns, but "it is mapped out as well by Jesus Christ and his way to his neighbor." [62] There is a bit of mysticism in these theologians after all. For in working with the "unlovely" neighbor they find Christ there working alongside of them. Jesus for them is not the ground of being, or the meaning of life, but rather he represents a "place to be, a standpoint." [63] They have been drawn to work with the neighbor not through *agapē* (God's love) but through a broken love, more like *eros*, which they find has resemblances to the broken love displayed by Jesus on the Cross. Working alongside of, and for the neighbor, in attempting to solve particular social injustices, they find the meaning of Jesus' humanity, "and it may even be the meaning of his divinity, and thus of divinity itself." [64] Thus, although they affirm the death of God, of the transcendent God, or of Tillich's ground of being, they rejoice in affirming the gospel of Jesus as setting men free to be themselves.

We have already mentioned *The Secular City* by Harvey Cox. In many respects he does not wish to be associated with the "Death of God theologians," but he has in a more positive way tried to suggest the nature of the changes in the secular world which require a reinterpretation of Christianity if it is to be any value for contemporary man. Traditional Christianity has been too often identified with the cultures of the past, represented by the tribe and the small town. Hence, it tends to protest against the anonymous and depersonalizing aspects of modern urban technology. Cox suggests that this is a rear-guard action; the megapolis is here to stay, and preachers will not by sermons about a good shepherd do anything more than reveal their anachronism. However, and this is significant, Cox does not merely maintain that the urban technological civilization is here to stay; he positively rejoices in this new development as a liberation for men from the tyrannies of loyalty to a small tribe and from the gossiping parochialism of the small town. Men for the first time have the real opportunity to become themselves, to choose their friends for themselves, and to find that particular kind of life which best suits them among all the alternatives offered in a large modern city. Cox celebrates American pragmatism, secularization, and mobility as deliverances from the traditional cultural and ethical laws. Despite the fact that Tillich made a valiant attempt to make it possible for all men to have an ultimate concern, since all men could not help but be rooted in the ground of being, Cox finds that Tillich has absolutely no appeal to American people today who are fully content with the mass civilization in which they live. Cox makes his claim very clear:

> Tillich's approach has no place for pragmatic man. It is built on the assumption that man by his very nature *must* ask these "ultimate" or existential questions. . . . The difficulty, however, is that they are obviously *not* questions which occur to everyone, or indeed to the vast majority of people. They do not trouble the newly emergent urban-secular man. . . . Since to him the world has always appeared devoid of any built-in meaning, he tends to be puzzled by Tillich's fascination with "meaninglessness." . . . Urban-secular man came to town after the funeral for the religious world view had been held. He feels no sense of deprivation and has no interest in mourning.[65]

Cox attempts to justify his acceptance of the modern world by references to the scripture, and insists that the Gospel ("good news") is not a call to man to return to an historical stage he has abandoned. Cox claims:

> The Gospel does not call man to return to a previous stage of his development. It does not summon man back to dependency, awe, and religiousness. Rather it is a call to imaginative urbanity and mature secularity. It is not a call to man to abandon his interest in the problems of this world, but an invitation to accept the full weight of this world's problems as the gift of its Maker. It is a call to be a man of this technical age, with all that means, seeking to make it a human habitation for all who live within it.[66]

Cox faces the difficulty of speaking about God in a secular manner in the last chapter of *The Secular City.* He rejects metaphysics and traditional theology, and suggests that if we are to speak of God in the modern world we must do so in terms of sociological and political categories. We do not communicate when we speak of God in the ways of the past, and in fact we speak about God more adequately if we do not utter his name but reveal our concern by our actions.

> We speak of God politically whenever we give occasion to our neighbor to become the responsible, adult agent, the fully posttown and posttribal man God expects him to be today. . . . We speak to him of God whenever our words cause him to shed some of the blindness and prejudice of immaturity and to accept a larger and freer role in fashioning the instrumentalities of human justice and cultural vision. We do not speak to him of God by trying to make him religious but, on the contrary, by encouraging him to come fully of age, putting away childish things.[67]

Speaking of God thus becomes a political issue; it involves our discerning where God is at work in our world today and taking our stance there. "Standing in a picket line is a way of speaking. By doing it a Christian speaks of God." [68] Because of the traditional associations of the name "god," we may have to abandon it for the time being; perhaps we will be given a new name. "By what name shall we call the one we met both in the life of Jesus and in our present history as the liberator and the hidden one?" [69] We can't invent a name, and perhaps we may have to put a moratorium on "God talk." Moses was granted a name for the One in his experience; Cox suggests that if we also try to liberate the people in our present world we too may be given a name by which we can meaningfully refer to the One who is at work in urban-secular society. Cox, like Marx and Sartre, thus ultimately places his hope in the future, even though we do not see what the future will bring. The One of whom he tries to speak, thus becomes the One who keeps history and its possibilities open because he is ahead of and not "above" history. In this respect Cox attempts to preserve the transcendence of the biblical God.

The radical theologians thus reflect a basic American optimism. The Kingdom of God (or of Christ) is arriving in history, and the job of the Christian is to discern where it is appearing and to work in those concrete tasks to which the world calls him. The "Death of God" thus becomes the death of certain ideas about God, for these theologians all try to maintain the supremacy of Jesus. He is the "man for others." In working for and with those in need we are continuing his work. Americans are not filled with anxiety or despair; they have never lost a war and they have weathered economic depressions. Rejoice in the world; do not seek to escape from it. World-affirmation in a newly interpreted gospel of Jesus is their way of attempting to revitalize the dead faith of our fathers. One might summarize our discussion by saying that if God the Father is dead, the Son Jesus still lives!

Situation Ethics Versus Rule Ethics   The present trends in theology have tended to reflect a greater interest in ethics than in previous more theologically oriented periods of Christian history. Generally, almost all of the contemporary theologians stress Christian love, *agapē*, as the distinctive motivation for their ethical positions. They differ in the extent, however, to which they believe that *agapē* can be expressed in general rules or principles for human behavior. Bishop Robinson and Joseph Fletcher are the best known advocates of a situational approach to ethics; they claim that one ought always to ask what would be the loving thing to do in this situation for the persons involved. Emil Brunner, Reinhold Niebuhr and Paul Ramsey, while they do not deny that love may sometimes have to override traditional morality, firmly insist that *agapē* can be expressed in some general rules or principles which will give the Christian guidance for the specific situations he is likely to face in the world.

This difference of viewpoint concerning the place of love in Christian ethics is somewhat like the debate between the teleologists and deontologists in philosophical discussions of normative ethics. The teleologists maintain that acts are right if and only if their consequences are desirable, that is, if they produce the greatest amount of good possible for that particular situation. The deontologists, on the other hand, hold that there are some acts which are always right independently of the likely consequences of those acts in particular situations producing or not producing the greatest possible amount of good. The teleologists have often adopted some form of utilitarianism and have held that those acts are right which tend to produce the greatest amount of happiness for the greatest number of people. The deontologists have often appealed to some general principles, such as justice, or to general rules, such as one's obligation toward a benefactor, or the obligation not to harm another person, as providing *prima facie* moral rules which can be seen to be fitting or appropriate principles or rules for human behavior.

William Frankena in a very perceptive essay, "Love and Principle in Christian Ethics," tends to interpret Christian ethicists as usually holding to some form of teleological ethics. Christian love, or *agapē*, on this interpretation is concerned with advocating those acts which will produce the greatest possible amount of love-fulfillment or benevolence. Most of the writers whom we are discussing advocate a teleological ethic, although some, such as Paul Ramsey, seem to also stress a deontological aspect to the Christian ethic. In terms of a deontological interpretation, some acts are seen to be right because they always express *agapē*, while others are seen to be wrong because they never can express *agapē*. Many traditional interpretations of the Christian ethic which have literally identified it with obedience to the Ten Commandments and to the Sermon on the Mount would appear to be deontological.

In recent philosophical writing, there has not been quite the extreme disagreement between teleologists and deontologists which we have sketched. Instead, the debate has focused on two possible interpretations of utilitarianism: act-utilitarianism and rule-utilitarianism. The pure act-utilitarian maintains that in a specific situation one ought to explore·the likely consequences of one's actions and then choose to act so as to bring about the greatest amount of happiness possible. The important point here is that the pure act-utilitarian holds that one ought not to ask about the likely consequences which might ensue "if the same thing were done in similar situations (i.e., if it were made a rule to do that act in such situations)." [70] At issue for the act-utilitarian is only the specific contemplated act for a particular circumstance; it is held to be irrelevant to inquire as to whether one ought to act that way in future situations which might be similar. In contrast to the act-utilitarian, the rule-utilitarian maintains that in a particular situation one ought to appeal to some set of general rules, such as, "Tell the truth," "Do not commit murder," etc., rather than attempt to calculate the likely consequences of the contemplated action. The rule-utilitarian is not a deontologist, however, for he maintains that these general rules, such as, "Tell the truth," are justified because acting in accordance with these rules always produces the greatest good or the greatest happiness. In short, he is a utilitarian because his ultimate justification for the general rules he advocates is based on the greatest good for the greatest number of people, and not upon the rules simply being seen to be appropriate or fitting to the situation. For the rule-utilitarian it may be one's duty to follow the rule "Tell the truth" even if in a particular situation more good would apparently be produced by lying. Rule-utilitarians would justify the rule even in the exceptional case by pointing out that in the last analysis more good is achieved for everyone by always upholding the moral rules. While a lie in a specific situation might produce more immediate good for those directly concerned, it would tend to break down the moral fabric of our society and encourage lying in other situations which might be less justifiable. Therefore, the greatest amount of good in the long run for the greatest number of people would be obtained by an undeviating adherence to the moral rule.

There is, however, a third possibility: modified act-utilitarianism. This interpretation recognizes elements of strength in both rule- and act-utilitarianism. The modified act-utilitarian admits that rules can be formulated for moral action, but he insists that these rules are not absolute; they are only generally binding. Thus in most cases, "Tell the truth" will produce the greatest amount of good, but one is justified, for the sake of the ultimate principle of utility itself, in disobeying the rule in a particular situation where more good is likely to be achieved by such disobedience.

Frankena suggests that the debate concerning the status of rules or principles in Christian ethics parallels the above debate between the act and the rule utilitarians. The Christian ethic is often interpreted as asserting *agapē*, or the "law of love," as its highest and only ultimate principle. In the light of this ultimate commitment to *agapē*, however, the Christian ethic can be developed in terms of pure act-agapism, modified act-agapism, or pure rule-agapism. These distinctions are not sharply drawn in most of the writings on Christian ethics, but we shall attempt to suggest some ethicists of this century who seem to fit fairly well into this classificatory scheme.

Situation Ethics by Joseph Fletcher comes extremely close to being a perfect illustration of pure act-agapism; certainly the main drift of his position is toward the specific situation in which the person is acting and away from any general or summary rules for moral behavior. Fletcher holds that there are only three main approaches to the making of moral decisions: (1) the legalistic which always insists that the moral rules must be obeyed—they are absolute laws; (2) the antinomian or existentialist which maintains that there are no guidelines whatsoever for ethical choices since each situation is so unique that one must in each case make a new decision; and (3) the situational approach, which falls somewhere between these two other approaches, but comes down closer to the existentialist side than to the legalistic side. It is Christian situation ethics which Fletcher himself wishes to defend as the best approach to the making of moral decisions.

Fletcher maintains that a Christian practicing situation ethics approaches "every decision-making situation fully armed with the ethical maxims of his community and its heritage, and he treats them with respect as illuminators of his problems." [71] Nevertheless, in any particular situation Fletcher holds that it is best to set aside the inherited moral principles "if love seems better served by doing so." [72] He thus calls his version of the Christian ethic "principled relativism." [73] Rules or principles are valid only if they serve love in a particular situation. The most important factors in ethical decision-making would involve knowing the facts of the case, calculating the likely consequences of the alternative possibilities for action, and then choosing that act which will best serve love. In this preliminary discussion of the position Fletcher wishes to defend, he appears to be putting forth a version of modified act-agapism: principles are generally valid but one ought to set them aside in any instance in which love would be better served by not following them. In fact in one of his illustrations, he suggests that ethical rules are like the instructions in football, "Punt on fourth down. . . . The best players are those who know when to ignore them." [74] Fletcher holds that there is only one unexceptionable principle in Christian ethics—love. "Everything else without exception, all laws and rules and principles and ideals and norms, are only *contingent*, only valid *if they happen* to serve love in any situation." [75] The principles or rules of moral behavior then are, at best, cautious generalizations. In almost all of the illustrations which he uses throughout his book it is difficult to find him making any constructive use of the existing moral principles. Perhaps this is because all of his illustrations deal with exceptional cases, situations in which he believes love is best served by going against moral conventions. Despite his protest to the contrary, his ethics appears to be one of pure act-agapism, or act-agapism modified by rational calculation as to the likely consequences of a chosen action. In this respect he appears much closer to the radical existentialist ethic than he wishes to admit. Fletcher says *"only love and reason really count when the chips are down!"* [76] His extreme emphasis upon the uniqueness of each case, and the necessity for making a new decision in each case, undoubtedly derives from his conviction that Christian ethics has too often been identified with an unbending legalism.

Fletcher states the main propositions upon which his interpretation of Christian ethics rests as follows:

1. Only one "thing" is intrinsically good; namely, love: nothing else at all.
2. The ruling norm of Christian decision is love: nothing else.
3. Love and justice are the same, for justice is love distributed, nothing else.
4. Love wills the neighbor's good whether we like him or not.
5. Only the end justifies the means; nothing else.
6. Love's decisions are made situationally, not prescriptively.[77]

The opposite of love, according to Fletcher, is not hate but indifference, for even hate treats the other person as a "thou" while indifference reduces the other to a thing. To be filled with Christian love is to care for persons, and to do what one can for them in their specific situations. Fletcher adheres to a personalist interpretation of Christian ethics and hence asserts boldly: "There *are* no 'values' at all; there are only things (material and nonmaterial) which *happen* to be valued by persons." [78] Something becomes a value only if it becomes worth something to some person. Despite his initial exposition of his position, it thus appears that there are no principles or rules in Fletcher's ethic, except love in terms of which we are to do the greatest amount of good we can. That Fletcher does not shrink from this conclusion is evident in the following quotation from *Situation Ethics:*

> If a lie is told unlovingly it is wrong, evil; if it is told in love it is good, right. Kant's legalism produced a "universal"—that a lie is always wrong. But what if you have to tell a lie to keep a promised secret? Maybe you lie, and if so, good for you if you follow love's lead. . . . If love vetoes the truth, so be it. . . . *The situationist holds that whatever is the most loving thing in the situation is the right and good thing. It is not excusably evil, it is positively good.*[79]

Many Christian moralities, such as that of the Roman Catholic Church, have combined love with an ethic of natural law. In such positions justice is often used as an additional principle in determining one's actions. Fletcher not only rejects this approach, but even holds that the Ten Commandments and the injunctions in the Sermon on the Mount are not absolutely binding upon the Christian. In referring to the Ten Commandments Fletcher comments:

> Situation ethics has good reason to hold it as a *duty* in some situations to break them, *any or all of them.* We would be better advised and better off to drop the legalist's love of law, and accept only the law of love.[80]

Despite the fact that Fletcher, like most modern Protestant theologians, finds Bonhoeffer to be one of his forerunners, he objects to Bonhoeffer's belief that "all deliberate killing of innocent life is arbitrary," and therefore wrong, since Bonhoeffer believes that whatever is arbitrary is wrong. This for Fletcher is to put another norm alongside love; it is not to be fully situational. A situationist suggests Fletcher would protest "that, in principle, even killing 'innocent' people might be right." [81]

Tillich, as we have seen, found that there were aspects of all kinds of love present in every human instance of love. Fletcher disagrees with this analysis because he wants to separate *agapē* from all other kinds of love which have an aspect of desire in them:

> *Agapē* is giving love—non-reciprocal, neighbor-regarding—"neighbor" meaning "everybody," even an enemy. . . . Erotic and philic love are emotional, but the effective principle of Christian love is *will*, disposition; it is an *attitude*, not feeling.[82]

Fletcher's affinity with existentialist ethics comes through, even here, as he claims that each man must take the risk of making his own decisions in the light of his understanding of the facts of the case and his loving attitude: "Decision is a 'risk rooted in the courage of being' free." [83]

While Fletcher insists that there is only one principle in Christian ethics, namely love, he wants to make it very clear that the love he is talking about is not to be identified with sentimentality. Prudence and careful calculation are the ways by which Christian love works, so that justice is included within love and is not a separate principle from it. He admits that love including justice must give every man his due; since in most situations we are faced with a complex network of claims and duties, "love is compelled to be calculating, careful, prudent, distributive." [84] The Christian love ethic "needs to find *absolute love's relative course.* The what and the why are given but the how and the which must be found." [85] Fletcher insists that to separate justice from love tends to make love sentimental and justice impersonal and legalistic; furthermore, if they are separated neither *agapē* nor justice is satisfied. Hence, he maintains that "*agapē* is what is due to all others," and that "justice is nothing other than love working out its problems." [86] Even if it is maintained that justice is concerned with seeing to it that each man gets his rights, Fletcher claims that *agapē* is the only norm which can validate any human rights whatsoever:

> You have a right to anything that is loving; you have no right to anything that is unloving. All alleged rights and duties are as contingent and relative as all values. The right to religious freedom, free speech, public assembly, private property, sexual liberty, life itself, the vote—*all* are validated only by love.[87]

In the Christian's attempt to search for social policies he should unite with the utilitarian in seeking for the greatest good of the greatest number. The hedonistic calculus of the utilitarian thus becomes "the agapeic calculus, the greatest amount of neighbor welfare for the largest number of neighbors possible." [88] Fletcher does not shrink from admitting that the Christian seeks happiness as his end, indeed he insists that "all ethics are happiness ethics." There are different schools of ethics because not all men find happiness in the same things, but the Christian ethic *à la* Fletcher attempts to unite the best of naturalistic, self-realization and hedonistic positions. Thus Fletcher says:

> The Christian situationist's happiness is in doing God's will as it is expressed in Jesus' Summary. [Love God, and love your neighbor as yourself.] And his utility method sets him to seeking his happiness (pleasure, too, and self-realization!) by seeking his neighbors' good on the widest possible scale.[89]

If a particular situation arises in which the Christian finds himself confronted with a law which in all honesty he considers to be morally unjust, that is unloving, then he should not hesitate to disobey openly that particular law. Perhaps the situationist should do all that he can to get the law thrown out by the courts, or repealed by the legislature, but if he fails in these attempts then he decides to abide by the higher law of love and break the particular unjust law confronting him. This ought not to be a rash decision, for the Christian values civil law since it provides order within a society. Yet in the last analysis, "neither the state nor its laws is boss for the situationist; when there is a conflict, he decides for the higher law of love." [90]

We have already noted that Fletcher insists that *agapē* is not emotional love; it is not liking but it is an attitude of goodwill or benevolence toward all men, including those who are not likeable. It is not looking for reciprocity; it gives, expecting nothing in return, even if it hopes for a positive response. *Agapē* is not opposed to loving oneself in the right way; that is, in loving oneself for the sake of others. It seeks to do the most useful thing in any concrete situation. Its ultimate justification is that it loves the neighbor or oneself for the sake of God, not for the sake of the neighbor or for the sake of oneself. As Fletcher explains:

> To love is not necessarily to please. *Agapē* is not gratification. . . . For *agapē* is concerned for the neighbor, ultimately, for God's sake; certainly not for the self's, but not even for the neighbor's own sake only. Christian love, for example, cannot give heroin to an addict just because he wants it. Or, at least, if the heroin is given, it will be given as part of a cure. And the same with all pleas—sex, alms, food, anything.[91]

Fletcher uses a rather extreme case to illustrate the difference he finds between *philia* (love as liking each other) and *agapē:*

> A young unmarried couple might decide, if they make their decisions Christianly, to have intercourse (e.g., by getting pregnant to force a selfish parent to relent his over-bearing resistance to their marriage). But as Christians they would never merely say, "It's all right if we *like* each other!" Loving concern can make it all right, but mere liking cannot.[92]

Fletcher's radical commitment to the new morality, in which each situation differs radically from all other situations, is frankly admitted by him when he discusses the relationships of means to ends. After insisting that the means chosen should be as appropriate to the end as possible, for unloving means could well distort the loving end, he says:

> The new morality, situation ethics, declares that anything and every-thing is right or wrong, according to the situation. And this candid approach is indeed a revolution in morals! [93]

Love viewed as *agapē* is the only principle which makes any acts right or wrong. Thus, Fletcher continues:

> Theodore Roosevelt was either not altogether honest (candid) or altogether thoughtful when he said, "No man is justified in doing evil on the ground of expediency." He was mired down in intrinsicalist legalism. Love could justify anything. There is no justification other than love's expedients. What else? In a particular case, why should not a single woman who could not marry become a "bachelor mother" by natural means or artificial insemination, even though husbandless, as a widow is? [94]

Thus, although one ought to seek for appropriate means, one ought not to fail to realize that sometimes an evil means can bring about a good end. If this happens, then the evil means is fully justified by the end realized. Hence, even "paid sex" might be justified if a good result were achieved by it. Fletcher thus justifies the prostitute in the movie *Never on Sunday:*

We could, we might, decide that the whore in the Greek movie *Never on Sunday*, was right. In Piraeus near Athens she finds a young sailor who is afraid he cannot function sexually as an adult and virile man, and suffers as a prey to corrosive self-doubt and non-identity. She manages things deliberately (i.e., responsibly) so that he succeeds with her and gains his self-respect and psychic freedom from a potential fixation on sex itself.[95]

Fletcher in his discussion of the ethics of sex objects to the *Playboy* argument that anything sexual is all right if it is practiced by consenting adults and does not hurt anybody. Not hurting anybody is not a sufficient criterion for Fletcher, for "Christians say that nothing is right unless it *helps* somebody." [96] Thus, the prostitute in the movie *Never on Sunday* did the right thing—she did some good for the young man; she helped him to discover his sexual identity. Hence, the Christian is fully justified in doing "what would be evil in some contexts if in *this* circumstance love gains the balance. It is love's business to calculate gains and losses, and to act for the sake of its success." [97] Thus, if for the emotional and spiritual welfare of all the parties concerned, a divorce appears to be the best solution to an unhappy marriage, then "getting a divorce is sometimes like David's eating the reserved Sacrament; it is what Christ would recommend." [98] To will the end of loving welfare is to will whatever means are necessary to achieve that end.

Fletcher poses some interesting cases for his readers to think through for themselves, using his method of situation ethics. In one of these cases he describes a dilemma put to him by a young woman of about twenty-eight years of age who sat next to him on an airline flight. One of the American intelligence agencies had asked her to use her sex to lure an enemy spy into blackmail. When she protested that she couldn't violate her personal integrity in such a manner, they said, " 'We understand. It's like your brother risking his life or limb in Korea. We are sure this job can't be done any other way. It's bad if we have to turn to somebody less competent and discreet than you are.' " [99] The issue was "how was she to balance loyalty and gratitude as an American citizen over against her ideal of sexual integrity?" [100] Fletcher in a later essay indicates that he would have approved if the girl had said "Yes" to the intelligence agency. He flatly remarks, "Is the girl who gives her chastity for her country's sake any less approvable than the boy who gives his leg or his life? No!" [101] Again the existentialist emphasis in Fletcher's view comes to the foreground. Speaking of any sexual acts outside of marriage, he says:

The personal commitment, not the county clerk, sanctifies sex. . . .
In this kind of Christian sex ethic the essential ingredients are caring and commitment. Given these factors, the only reason for disapprov-

ing sexual relations would be situational, not legal or principled. . . .
There is nothing against extramarital sex as such, in this ethic, and in
some cases it is good.[102]

Only in a concrete situation, when the facts are known and the persons
involved are considered as persons can one give moral advice. Fletcher
rejects such questions as "Is adultery wrong?" They are too general to
call for a serious answer. He says:

One can only respond, "I don't know. Maybe. Give me a case.
Describe a real situation." Or perhaps somebody will ask if a man
should ever lie to his wife, or desert his family, or spy on a business
rival's design or market plans, or fail to report some income item in
his tax return. Again, the answer cannot be an answer, it can only
be another question. "Have you a *real* question, that is to say, a
concrete situation?" If it has to do with premarital sex or libel or
breach of contract or anything else ("you name it"), the reply is
always the same: "You are using words, abstractions. What you are
asking is without substance; it has no living reality. There is no way
to answer such questions." [103]

Although no prefabricated moral system can be offered, the situationist can tell people to make the best decisions in concrete situations
and then "sin bravely." [104] Love must decide in a concrete case and at a
specific moment of time. Legalistic moral codes simply do not fit our
present society, nor are they applicable to the real decisions most people
are called upon to make. The professed sexual code of most Americans
is so openly flouted in practice, that Fletcher holds we would be better
off to junk it rather than to pay lip service to it. Repressive legalism has
been most damaging to individuals precisely at this point of the ethics of
sexual behavior. Fletcher holds that rather than try to construct a network of moral rules regulating sexual behavior, we would be far more
ethical if we admitted that "whether any form of sex (hetero, homo, or
auto) is good or evil depends on whether love is fully served." [105] We are
moving into an age of honesty, Fletcher believes, and our age is allergic
to legalism. The time is ripe, therefore, for his tactical formula for making
moral decisions:

Love, in the imperative mood of neighbor-concern, examining the
relative facts of the situation in the indicative mood, discovers what it
is obliged to do, what it should do, in the normative mood. What is,
in the light of what love demands, shows what ought to be.[106]

Fletcher admits that many secular men who do not call themselves
Christians may actually advocate and practice the ethic he recommends
better than do many Christians. Why then does he call it a Christian
ethic? His answer is that "we understand love in terms of Jesus Christ.
This is the Christian faith ethic." [107]

Fletcher's interpretation of Christian ethics, despite his early insistence upon coming fully equipped with the moral baggage of our culture when we face an actual situation, turns out to be very close to the radical existential freedom of decision advocated by Sartre and other existentialists. In few, if any, of the actual cases which he discusses in his books and articles does he ever invoke a moral principle generally held to be correct by our society, unless it be to oppose it to what the right act would be for the particular situation he is discussing. In fact, his summary of what he understands situation ethics to be as he presented it in a paper called "Situation Ethics for Business Management" sounds like another American version of Sartre's position:

> Finally, in a situational approach, the decision must be made not only *in* the situation but also *by* the decider in the situation! It is an ethic of deliberate responsibility, based on the need for stoutly embracing "the burden of freedom" like men, not mice. The burden is only added to, not lightened, by the understanding that the decisions we make will rarely if ever be "correct." Its very relativism compels it to acknowledge that finite men will never fully foresee all of the consequences, never "objectively" assess all of the motives and means and ends at stake.[108]

It does not seem to bother Fletcher to admit that the decisions one makes by using situational ethics "will rarely if ever be 'correct.'" Instead, he concludes his advice to business managers by saying: "In all humility, knowing that he cannot escape the human margin of error, he will—to use Luther's phrase—'Sin bravely.'"[109] If, in Frankena's terminology, there is an exponent of pure act-agapism today it is Joseph Fletcher.

Bishop John A. T. Robinson prefers to link himself with the new morality or situation ethics, but it is clear from his presentations that he represents a modified act-agapism. He is just as opposed as is Joseph Fletcher to the old traditional ethic of prohibitions and legalism. Robinson holds that since people today no longer believe in the old supernatural God it is inevitable that they will not believe that the Ten Commandments or any other moral code represent God's absolute rules. As Robinson interprets the moral dilemma, he finds that:

> 'Why shouldn't I?' or 'What's wrong with it?' are questions which in our generation press for an answer. And supranaturalist reasons—that God or Christ has pronounced it a 'sin'—have force, and even meaning, for none but a diminishing religious remnant.[110]

Bishop Robinson, like Fletcher, maintains that Christian love is not only the one absolute principle in ethics, but also that it can be relied upon to find the right answer in a specific situation. He does, however, make much more of guiding rules for this love, and insists that without them, love could not even find its way:

Such an ethic cannot but rely, in deep humility, upon guiding rules, upon the cumulative experience of one's own and other people's obedience. It is this bank of experience which gives us our working rules of 'right' and 'wrong,' and without them we could not but flounder.[111]

Robinson, therefore, has much more respect for the moral rules and principles than does Fletcher, even though in the last analysis he suggests that they may be violated if love were better served.

The old morality, as Robinson calls it, tended to locate the unchanging element in Christian ethics in the contents of the moral commands, while the new morality finds in the attitude of "unselfregarding *agapē*" [112] the one unchanging element in Christian ethics. What the contents are of the Christian ethic will differ with every period of history, every group, and indeed even with every individual. Changing non-moral factors inevitably affect the moral scope of any generation. Thus in the modern world the new atomic and biological weapons which can be used in war profoundly affect any discussion of the morality of war. Sociological investigations which have shown the ineffectiveness of capital punishment as a deterrent to crime also suggest radical changes in the old moral commands. But, unlike Fletcher, he insists that there are some actions which are always wrong. We had better let him speak for himself here, so that we can see that he really represents a modified act-agapism:

I would, of course, be the first to agree that there are a whole class of actions—like stealing, lying, killing, committing adultery—which are so fundamentally destructive of human relationships that no differences of century or society can change their character. But this does not, of course, mean that stealing or lying can in certain circumstances never be right. All Christians would admit that they could be.[113]

If there are any absolutely unbreakable moral rules, however, they obtain their status because it is inconceivable how violating them could ever be an expression of love. He suggests that "cruelty to children or rape" are always wrong, but the reason they are wrong is because they never can be conceived to be commanded by love. In addition to these more absolute moral prohibitions, there are a whole host of "working rules" which can be laid down as practical guides to Christian conduct. But these working rules can be broken by love, if need be. This "moral net" of working rules is so important for the ordering of any society that Robinson is convinced that the Christian should be in the forefront to help repair the net when circumstances require that particular moral principles or rules be modified or replaced.

Robinson insists that his version of the Christian ethic begins with the primacy of persons and personal relationships. For this reason he holds that principles are not absolutely binding for men, "however much they may help them (and often, indeed, save them) in their moral choices." [114] Yet, he does admit that moral rules or principles are needed as guideposts for action, and that therefore the Christian is concerned with helping to create a just moral and legal code. Robinson remarks:

> The deeper one's concern for persons, the more effectively one wants to see love buttressed by law. But if law usurps the place of love because it is safer, that safety is the safety of death.[115]

Thus, the Christian should work to help create an ethos in his society which will support the development of human personality and eliminate exploitation and destructiveness. In this respect, Robinson insists Christian ethics is a form of humanism—the difference with most types of humanism is that Christianity has added to it an element of mystery.

Two other theologians, however, provide even better illustrations of the Christian ethic interpreted as a modified act-agapism. They are Emil Brunner and Reinhold Niebuhr. Both stress justice as a moral principle in addition to *agapē;* both attempt to avoid legalism in their concern to speak directly to our present human situation.

Emil Brunner, the Swiss theologian, has expressed his basic conviction concerning Christian ethics in *The Divine Imperative.* That which is good, that which we should do, is that which God wills. But God who is Love wills always that we should love the neighbor; only this is not a general commandment but a supremely personal existence communication (*à la* Kierkegaard) from God to the individual. As Brunner states it:

> The Good is simply what *God* wills that we should do, not that which we would do on the basis of a principle of love. God wills to do something quite definite and particular through us, here and now, something which no other person could do at any other time.[116]

In terms of this general statement Brunner's position does not seem to be far from that of situation ethics; even Fletcher himself says that Brunner almost made it to the situational approach, but then he backed away, since he admitted rules and principles to govern the social order. In fact, Brunner goes so far as to insist that the love God expects of us implies all the virtues of which the classical moralists spoke. "Each virtue, one might say, is a particular way in which the person who lives in love takes the other into account, and 'realizes' him as 'Thou.'" [117] Thus, although the Christian will reflect the virtues of honesty, justice, temperance, and wisdom in his actions he will do so because he is living a life of obedient love to God. Brunner insists that there can never be any inhuman commands in God's dealing with us; there can never be a suspension of ethics for a supposedly higher category as Kierkegaard had thought.

The basic difference between Brunner and Fletcher concerns the status of justice. Brunner would not agree that love and justice are the same. Brunner's discussion of *agapē* is basically in agreement with what Fletcher says about it. The love of God is *agapē*, that is, self-giving concern for others not limited by the worth of the person upon whom the love is bestowed. This kind of love is incomprehensible to human reason but is most clearly seen in Jesus Christ:

> This love is known only where God is revealed as He Who does not judge the sinner according to his deserts, but incomprehensibly forgives his sin and so heals the breach in communion. This love is therefore only to be comprehended and won by faith. For to possess this love is the same thing as to possess God—the God who "first loved us," and reveals Himself as that loving God in His acts of revelation and reconciliation.[118]

Justice for Brunner is an entirely different thing from Christian *agapē*. In justice we give the other person his due—no more and no less. He gets what he deserves, based on a sober, rational and realistic appraisal of the facts of the case. Justice is comprehensible to every one's reason and completely impersonal. It does not regard the person, but sees only what is right. As Brunner puts it:

> The just man recognizes in the other the same dignity which he finds in himself, the same quality as a person, the same general law of being. . . . Justice is never concerned with the human being as such, but only with the human being in relationships. Justice belongs to the world of systems, not to the world of persons.[119]

In its own sphere, justice is supreme. This has often led to misunderstanding, for it has been claimed that the Christian must cease to love in the realm of social relationships. Brunner insists that this cannot be true if the person is a true Christian.

How is this possible? How can one be just in his dealings in society and yet not relinquish his obligation to love? Brunner answers by saying that in the realm of systems love compels the Christian to be just. In other words, in the realm of impersonal relationships, the Christian must attempt to recoin love into justice. Thus, justice is not an inferior way of acting, but rather is as indispensable as love!

> This can be seen by the fact that the man of love, as soon as he has to act in the world of institutions, turns his love into justice. He knows that if he did otherwise, he would ruin, destroy, the world of institutions. Love which is not just in the world of institutions is sentimentality. And sentimentality, feeling for feeling's sake, is the poison, the solvent which destroys all just institutions.[120]

Does this mean that according to Brunner the Christian cannot display love in any of his relationships without recoining it into justice? No, in extremely close personal relationships, such as those of marriage, the Christian can show love directly to another person. Brunner proposes his law of the closeness of relationship to give a relative standard for determining when love is indeed possible: "The more closely an institution approaches the personal sphere, the smaller the number of human beings it embraces, and the less things in it predominate over persons, the greater is the scope it gives to love." [121] In the orders of life between marriage and the state one finds many social relationships in which one is involved. If in these relationships, persons predominate, then love rules; while if things are primary, justice holds sway. But even in the most impersonal institutions love can be shown indirectly in attitude and in criticism.

It is important to note that Brunner insists that while love transcends justice, it can never do less than justice demands. As Brunner points out in a pertinent example, "A citizen who falsifies his income-tax return in order to practise charity cannot appeal to love in exculpation; love of that kind is sheer sentimentality." [122] It is always the responsibility of love to see that justice is done, and then the real work of love actually begins. Justice can be achieved fully, but not love. "Only the love which is without measure fulfills itself—the love of God." [123] Love is always doing more; it is never finished, but in its eagerness to act it must be careful to fulfill the demands of justice lest, according to Brunner, it becomes irrational and sentimental.

Reinhold Niebuhr, one of the great Protestant ethicists of this century, stressed "the impossible possibility" of Christian love, particularly in the area of social ethics, and suggested that in the context of actions between groups or nations love must be recoined into justice. Love seeks to do more than justice, but it ought, according to Niebuhr, never to do less than, or other than, justice. The moral goals of the individual (love and unselfishness) cannot be applied to society. This is one of the themes running throughout Niebuhr's many books and articles.[124] We must get rid of the illusion which regards society as an "individual writ large." Action in society requires coercion, along with reason and cooperation among individuals, if we are to achieve a tolerable amount of justice. The religious fanatic and the moralistic idealist who attempt to apply love uncritically to social groups will either be destroyed by society or taken advantage of by others. We must be realistic; we must acquire some of the wisdom of the children of this world in our application of Christian love and moral ideals to social living. Niebuhr therefore calls for the Christian to work in and through the existing power structures in order to create justice within groups and between groups in society.

Thus, both Brunner and Reinhold Niebuhr introduce justice as an additional principle alongside of Christian *agapē*. If this interpretation of their thought is correct, then they represent modified act-agapism. Although they both stress *agapē* as the distinctive norm of Christian ethics, they insist that *agapē* cannot often be directly fulfilled in our world. Love must, therefore, serve as the motivating force for the Christian working in society to achieve justice for all mankind.

The best example of a Christian ethic which holds to general rules, and is therefore, largely an ethic of rule-agapism, or mixed agapism, is to be found in Paul Ramsey's recent treatment of ethics in *Deeds and Rules in Christian Ethics*. Indeed, Ramsey, who is Professor of Religion at Princeton University, is well acquainted with the writers in philosophical ethics, and is far more concerned with developing a Christian ethic which will meet the canons of consistency and validity than are either Fletcher or Robinson. His book also contains excellent criticisms of Fletcher's position, based partly on showing that Fletcher cannot avoid slipping into some summary or general rules even in what he directly says in *Situation Ethics*. This book by Ramsey will provide the reader with an excellent example of responsible ethical and philosophical thinking today by a Christian theologian, and is, therefore, well worth detailed study.

Ramsey takes his stand, along with Fletcher and Bishop Robinson, on the primacy of *agapē* as the basic norm of Christian ethics. Furthermore, he agrees with them that we begin with persons and take full cognizance of the facts which are applicable to any moral decision. Ramsey has, however, profited from his study of the philosopher John Rawls' provocative paper, "Two Concepts of Rules," and thus asks if Christian love should not also be concerned with evolving some general rules expressing what love requires to be practiced.[125] As he puts it: "The question is simply whether there *are* any general rules or principles or virtues or styles of life that embody love, and if so what these may be." [126] He agrees with the situation ethicists that the Christian ought to always seek to act so as to fulfill what love requires, but he objects to their belief that from the requirements of love no general rules for human behavior can be found. Let us see how Ramsey develops his position that *agapē* does in fact lead to general rules of practice for the Christian ethicist.

The interpretation which Ramsey gives of Christian ethics is primarily deontological. In this respect he differs with Frankena's identification of agapism with a teleological ethic.

> *Agapē* defines for the Christian what is right, righteous, obligatory to be done among men; it is not the Christian's definition of the good that better be done and much less is it a definition of the right way to be good.[127]

The Christian ethic is based on obedience to God as presented in Christ and the Kingdom of God. Hence, any teleological calculus, such as that advocated by Fletcher, must be subordinated to the Christian's "ready

obedience to the *present* reign of God, the alignment of the human will
with the Divine will that men should live together in covenant-love no
matter what the morrow brings. . . ." [128]

    While act-agapism may be adopted theoretically, Ramsey holds that
in practice it is almost impossible for the ethicist to avoid making some
general claims for human action which at least surreptitiously introduce
principles or rules into the ethical system. Thus, he finds that Fletcher
does make some general claims which would be wholly inconsistent with
a pure situation ethics. Despite his insistence that no two situations are
alike enough to allow for general statements of conduct, Fletcher himself
claims that "*no unwanted and unintended* baby should ever be born" [129]
is a general justification for abortion. In fact, Fletcher explicitly supports
Kant's second version of the categorical imperative:

> Kant's second maxim holds: Treat persons as ends, never as means.
> Even if in some situations a material thing is chosen rather than a
> person, it will be (if it is Christianly done) for the sake of the person,
> not for the sake of the thing itself. If a man prefers to keep his
> money invested instead of giving it to his son who needs it, it could
> only be because he believes his son will need it far more urgently
> later on. . . . Things are to be used; people are to be loved. It is
> "immoral" when people are used and things are loved. Loving actions
> are the *only* conduct permissible. [130]

Exploitation of persons is always wrong, according to Fletcher, because
it is unloving: hence, he condemns prostitution and the exploitation of
the laborer in the early nineteenth-century form of capitalism as "sins."
While his book is filled with extreme cases in which he can justify adultery, pre-marital sexual encounters, and so on, nevertheless, he insists
that sex is wrong unless love is present between the persons. He makes
clear in the context that he is referring to *agapē* and not to *eros:*

> The point is that, Christianly speaking, sex which does not have love
> as its partner, its *senior* partner, is wrong. If there is no responsible
> concern for the *other* one, for the partner as a subject rather than a
> mere object, as a person and not a *thing*, the act is immoral. [131]

It would appear clear, therefore, that *agapē*, even for Fletcher's radical
situational approach, does lead to at least some summary rules governing
human behavior. If Fletcher's above comment is interpreted as holding
that sex is always wrong unless it is done with love as its partner, then
he has even, although unwittingly, proposed a general ethical rule.

    We should clarify a distinction which Ramsey and Frankena make be-
tween summary rules and general rules in agapistic ethics. A summary
rule is one which holds that following the practice advocated is generally
best, or that avoiding the kind of behavior prohibited should prove in
the majority of cases to be the right way of acting. Thus, a summary rule

would have the form of "keeping promises is 'generally' love-fulfilling," while a general rule would maintain that "keeping-promises-always is love-fulfilling." [132] The difference is clarified by Frankena as follows:

> The difference is that on the latter view we may and sometimes must obey a rule in a particular situation even though the action it calls for is seen not to be what love itself would directly require. . . . "Summary rule" agapism . . . admits rules but regards them as summaries of past experience, useful, perhaps almost indispensable, but only as rules of thumb. It cannot allow that a rule may ever be followed in a situation when it is seen to conflict with what love dictates in that situation. [133]

Ramsey thinks that Frankena has drawn the distinction too sharply, for if Frankena's distinction is correct, then the most a Christian could follow in his moral decisions would be summary rules, "since he should always do what love requires." [134] Ramsey's proposal is that there may be some kinds of situations in which Christians can appeal to no more than summary rules, while there may be other kinds of situations in which they could appeal to general rules of universal validity. Beginning with persons, Ramsey believes that some rules of ethical conduct can be discerned which become more than summary rules. Asking what does love require, may lead to some rules of general validity. It is to cut off the investigation too soon, before it has gotten under way, if writers such as Fletcher simply deny that love can ever discern any general rules of universal validity. True to the spirit of much contemporary philosophical investigation, Ramsey suggests we must look and see whether or not love leads to any general rules embodying what love itself directly requires. He thus draws the following distinction between general and summary rules:

> If it could be shown that to act in accord with one of these love-formed principles of conduct is in a particular situation not what love itself directly requires, then that was not a general principle of conduct but a summary rule only. [135]

The Christian should be very careful, however, so that he does not confuse the demands of sentimental love with what *agapē* directly requires.

One of the dangers in situation ethics, as Ramsey sees it, is its attempt to limit the calculations of *agapē* to the direct consequences of the particular action under consideration. That is, it asks if it is the loving thing to lie, or to steal, or to engage in pre-marital sex, in this particular situation. How will it affect the other person? Will this action tend to bring more good into the lives of the people immediately concerned? Part of the difficulty encountered in any ethical calculus, including an agapistic one, lies in knowing exactly where to draw the line between those who are likely to be affected by the act, and those who will not be affected by it. Will the exceptional act which one believes justifiable for the two persons immediately involved really not have any affect upon others? Will it not affect one's parents or one's friends? How can one be sure? Furthermore, how can one tell how the act will really affect the other person? Ramsey makes this point even more strongly:

> But one way or another the Christian will know that an exceptional action of his (which may be the most loving thing to do in all its own *direct* consequences and probable consequences) may still as a side-effect tend to break down the social practice of a rule of behavior which "generally" embodies love, and thus lead in the end and on balance to a totality of less loving actions than if he had not made an exception of himself and his single action (which, however, it cannot be denied, *was* justified in terms of an individualistic act-calculus).[136]

The Christian should have a concern for the indirect effect of his actions upon the social order. Will his telling a justified lie tend to break down the fabric of truth-telling? If so, then this concern must also be taken into his calculations. As Ramsey puts it: "Order and justice are both 'values'; both are rules of love." [137] Order and justice are two of the social needs of men for which *agapē* should always strive. Ramsey suggests that a mixed agapism might be the best version of Christian ethics, that is, an ethic in which although love is the primary norm there are other norms such as man's natural sense of justice and order. Such an approach would stress the need for much careful thought before justifying the breaking of "unjust laws."

Following John Rawls' distinction of two concepts of rules, Ramsey proposes that some general rules in Christian ethics are based on the consequences of the acts, while the other type of general rules are rules of social practice. As examples of the first type he suggests that cruelty and rape are always wrong, because of the lovelessness that inheres in these acts, and breaking promises are always wrong, because they are never love-fulfilling in a personal sense. These general rules are justified because obeying them results in good consequences for persons. When love is not served by obeying these general rules, then the general rules should be modified and stated more precisely. Ramsey's interpretation of how general rules get revised is in agreement with the basic thesis of R. M. Hare, a contemporary British philosopher, whose ethical theory we shall examine in detail in the next chapter. Hare insists that on the basis of moral experience one formulates the general ethical rules more precisely, so that instead of "Never break a promise," one more correctly spells out the rule as, "Never break a promise except in cases where it is necessary to save a life, and so on." [138] This way of modifying general principles allows for both moral experience and for moral guidance.

Ramsey, however, is more interested in defending the general rules which are practices, a justification which is made independently of the consequences of observing the practice.

> *Rules of practices . . .* specify that to engage in a practice demands the performance of those actions required by the practice. *The practice* itself is to be justified by a direct application of Christian love. One asks *which practice* most embodies or fulfills love. But then one justifies an action falling under it by appeal to the practice.[139]

Ramsey, following Rawls' lead, explains what is meant by a practice by referring to the rules of games such as baseball and football. Thus, if while playing a football game, the captain of the team asked the officials if his team could not have five downs instead of four, he would be assumed to be joking. Among the rules of the game called football there is one which states that a team has four downs (tries) in which to make ten yards. If it does not make at least the required yardage it must surrender the ball to the other team. As long as the game of football is being played, this is among the rules of the game. One could attempt to reform the game by trying to get the officials of the league to change the rules, or one might even choose to construct a different ball game. But if he chose the latter course, he would have to specify some rules under which the new game were to be played. Now, according to Ramsey, rules of practice function in society very much like the rules of football function when that game is being played:

> Rules of practice necessarily involve the abdication of full liberty to guide one's actions case by case by making immediate appeals to what love (or utility) requires in each particular case. The point of a practice is to annul anyone's title to act, on his individual judgment, in accordance with ultimate utilitarian or prudential considerations, or from considerations of Christian love in that one instance alone.[140]

The practice itself, not a specific action falling under it, may be justified by an appeal to *agapē*. As long as the practice is part of the socially accepted and most love-fulfilling ethic, no individual has the right to claim to be an exception to the practice. He is only justified in trying to get the practice itself modified or replaced by one which he believes will more fully embody *agapē*.

Following a practice, however, does not mean that the individual may not have to deliberate in certain difficult cases which call upon him to make decisions. Ramsey is not defending the hard and fast legalism which situationist ethics criticizes. Instead he insists that in many instances the individual must ask what the practice really means, and try to understand the "qualifications and exceptions that should be understood to fall under the rules themselves." [141] We are born into a society in which there are certain moral practices, and part of our acquiring moral wisdom is our learning what these practices mean and in what circumstances qualifications are built into the practices themselves. Thus, to use a simple illustration, if someone under duress utters the words, "I promise," the simple uttering of the words does not in fact constitute a promise. If someone points a gun at you and forces you to promise to aid him in robbing a bank, no one would claim that you had made a promise which you were obligated to keep because it is an accepted social practice. Likewise if someone twists your arm, literally or figuratively, in order to get you to say that you promise to forgive him for what he has done, it seems clear that no genuine promise was made and that no real forgiveness was given. You must in the first place understand what it means to promise (a little baby cannot therefore promise anybody anything); you must make the decision freely (that is, not under compulsion); and you should be in a position to carry out your promise (you cannot promise to loan someone a thousand dollars if you do not have the money). Many moralists who defend a deontological ethic have maintained that there is a kind of hierarchy among the justified social practices, so that, for example, not taking a life is more binding than speaking the truth. W. D. Ross, a British moralist, has tried to establish some rough rules of preference among what he calls *prima facie* duties. [142] At any rate, a refinement of what exactly is meant by a moral rule, indicating the exceptions and qualifications which are built into the rule itself, might present a viable alternative to situation ethics.

Perhaps the case for general moral rules could be strengthened by continuing our comparison with the rules of games, such as football. Every year the Football Rules Committee of the National Collegiate Athletic Association approves the specific rules for that year. Hence, some years unlimited substitution has been allowed, while in other years limitations have been placed upon substitutions. Now there is no comparable body which decides the interpretation of and the specific moral rules for a society—there the parallel apparently ends. A study of the history of morals, however, shows that changes, even if they have been gradual, have occurred in both social mores and moral rules. An inspection of some of the accepted social rules for gracious behavior advocated by an etiquette book of fifty years ago would show that our patterns of acceptable etiquette are quite different today. Furthermore, both with respect to moral rules and the civil laws we now take far more cognizance of the psychological state of the person before we find him either morally or legally guilty of wrong-doing than was the case fifty years ago. Unofficially, but by a kind of general consensus, the moral rules get changed over the generations. The result of this may be a refinement of the moral rules, or a replacement of old rules by new rules which are more love-fulfilling, or which tend to produce greater good than the old ones. Ramsey has shown that this kind of an interpretation is a real alternative to a radical situation ethic which tends to treat the exceptional case as though it were the only type of case one ever encountered. The reader should recall that Ramsey is not denying that we may face some cases in which we must appeal to the general utility of the action to promote more good than any viable alternative. What he wishes to insist upon is that in addition to this type of example, there are a whole host of occasions for which our moral duty is more easily spelled out as acting in conformity with the accepted moral practice.

Toward an Evaluation of the New The attitude which one takes
Theology and the New Morality toward any theological position, or any version of the Christian ethic, is very likely influenced by one's own basic value commitments. If one has adopted a humanistic or a utilitarian ethical stance, then one is likely to reject any attempt to derive ethical norms from theological considerations. All of the theologians whom we have considered recognize that the traditional terminology, and perhaps even the traditional ideas of God, is not easily accepted by people living in the modern world. What they have attempted to do is to reinterpret their theological positions in terms of current philosophical and social thought in order to show that their beliefs are still relevant. Each individual will have to decide for himself to what extent they have succeeded. We shall, however, suggest some of the typical kinds of criticism which have been leveled at these reinterpretations of theology and Christian ethics.

We should recall that one of the main streams of Protestant theology moved from the neo-orthodoxy of Karl Barth, who maintains that God is wholly other than man, through the existential reinterpretation of religion as man's ultimate concern in Paul Tillich, to the present American radical theologians, who maintain that even the word "God" is meaningless for modern man. Tillich, it may be recalled, rejected Barth's position by holding that unless the ultimate were in some sense already present in nature and history, it would be impossible to apprehend the ultimate at all. Thus, for Tillich, even when we deny God with our lips, He is present in whatever concern we have to which we devote our lives with passionate and ultimate commitment. In this sense, Tillich claims that there are no atheists, although some people may profess their loyalty to a pseudo-ultimate rather than to the really ultimate or unconditioned reality he calls the God above God, or the ground of being.

One of the criticisms leveled against Tillich maintains that the triumph he apparently wins is at the price of emptying the Christian faith of its traditional content. The ground of being, or the God above the God of theism, is not what the Christian believer has meant by his appeal to God as Lord and Father. Tillich, you recall, tries to reinterpret the traditional Christian symbols and claims that God is indeed both Lord and Father, but it is very difficult to see how the philosophical conception of a ground of being could be described in such personalistic terms. The ground of being then seems to become *a* being, despite Tillich's protests to the contrary. It may very well be that Tillich himself found no difficulty in making this transition, but it has not been easy for others to follow him.

Indeed Tillich has been accused of being an atheist himself. The philosopher Alasdair MacIntyre in commenting upon Tillich's view of ultimate concern says:

> The conversion of the unbeliever is only so easy for Tillich because belief in God has been evacuated of all its traditional content. It consists now in moral seriousness and nothing more. Even if we were to concede Tillich a verbal triumph over the atheist, the substance of atheism has been conceded.[143]

We have noticed that Harvey Cox directs another criticism at Tillich's position, namely that his existential analysis of man's sense of meaninglessness is simply false for modern Americans. Cox denies that modern pragmatic man asks questions about an ultimate concern at all; he is more interested in solving the day to day problems of a modern technological civilization. Tillich thus is, according to this criticism, the theologian for those who still wistfully long for the religion of the past; he is "the indispensable comforter of those who grew up in a faith they can no longer believe." [144] The extent to which one accepts this criticism depends upon the degree to which one rejects existentialism as a correct probing of the human condition. Clearly not everyone in our society is quite as pragmatic and operational in his approach to life as Cox suggests.

Cox and the "Death of God theologians" do not try to reinterpret traditional religion for modern man; they rather rejoice in the death of the old legalistic and mythological idolatry which was falsely called "the true faith." They do not seek to persuade man that in addition to his particular specialized concerns, he will also find that he has an ultimate concern. They fully accept modern man in his independence and his reliance upon specialized science and technology for the answers to any of his problems. As Cox puts it:

> In former ages, man looked to muses, gods, or "values" for the answers to his problems. Secular man relies on himself and his colleagues for answers. He does not ask the church, the priest, or God.[145]

Cox suggests that we meet God in our work in the secular city, fully accepting the modern world. Altizer and Hamilton maintain that we meet Jesus in this work, but not God, for God has disappeared and we live in a time of the absence of God. But how does this differ from Nietzsche's atheism? Nietzsche, they admit, was the first man to see clearly all that was involved in the death of the Christian idea of God; what he predicted has now come to pass in our world. But unlike Nietzsche who suggested that men must now create their own values, men must become like gods, the "Death of God theologians" find the answers to their problems in serving Jesus by serving their neighbors. But if Jesus is viewed primarily as "the man for others" it is difficult to see how this evaluation would differ from that of many humanists. The only differences might be that the humanist would probably find other models to follow in addition to Jesus, and he would more honestly admit to complete atheism. The acceptance of the modern world by the radical theologians seems to be limited in one respect at least: they still believe that Jesus is the answer to the meaning of life.

All of these reinterpretations of Christianity for the modern day seem to fall under Professor MacIntyre's criticism:

> We can see the harsh dilemma of a would-be contemporary theology. The theologians begin from orthodoxy, but the orthodoxy which has learnt from Kierkegaard and Barth becomes too easily a closed circle, in which believer speaks only to believer, in which all human content is concealed. Turning aside from this arid in-group theology, the most perceptive theologians wish to translate what they have to say to an atheistic world. But they are doomed to one of two failures. Either they succeed in their translation: in which case what they find themselves saying has been transformed into the atheism of their hearers. Or they fail in their translation: in which case no one hears what they have to say but themselves.[146]

The readiness of many people to listen to these new theologians may arise from a kind of uneasy compromise which many people have adopted of professing complete acceptance of the pragmatic method for solving their immediate problems, while still keeping one eye partly alerted to the religious claims of salvation and deliverance from this world. In time of dire need, of crises, people still tend to turn toward the Church. Cox and the radical theologians may appeal to those who have not experienced crises in their lives, but to those who have, the claims of Tillich and the other existentialists do not go unheeded.

It is with respect to ethics, however, that the Christian theologians have made their greatest contribution. Frankena has pointed out that Reinhold Niebuhr and Emil Brunner have devoted their energies to honest and realistic appraisals of the place which ethics can play in the power structures of a complicated society. This concern with social ethics is not one which philosophers have paid much attention to in recent years. In addition to their theoretical writings, the actual work by many Christian theologians to improve the lot of the poor, of the Negro, and

274 Conflict of Ideals

of the underprivileged in our society has won respect from many who do not share their theological views. Here, however, we shall confine ourselves to an attempt to evaluate the major quarrel between situation ethics and an ethics based upon rules or principles.

Almost all of the writers on Christian situation ethics have, like Fletcher, tended to stress the exceptional case. Thus, they have been concerned with showing that under certain circumstances almost any action whatsoever might be what is demanded by Christian love. Fletcher has justified abortion, pre-marital sex, extra-marital sex, paid sex, and even the killing of innocent lives. Let us look more closely at what Fletcher said about certain of the cases he examined in order to evaluate his proposed ethic.

Fletcher is correct when he refuses to give general answers to such questions as "Is lying good?" "Can pre-marital sex be justified?" and so on. He insists that a specific case must be spelled out in detail in order to discover what the most loving thing would be for that particular situation. Unfortunately, very few, if any, of the cases which he discusses are presented in sufficient detail for one to make a careful calculation following Fletcher's own principles. In one of the examples which we have quoted from Fletcher, he maintained that the Christian would not give heroin to an addict just because he wanted it. If heroin were given to the addict it would be as part of a cure. But we should have to know much more about the specific case than this. Who was the addict? What was your relationship to him? What would he be likely to do if you did not give him money to purchase heroin? Was he so desperate that he would probably steal to get heroin? Or perhaps assault someone, or even kill to satisfy his craving? If some of these circumstances were indeed present it would seem completely justifiable on the basis of Fletcher's ethic to give the addict money for heroin. The evil which he might do otherwise would greatly offset gratifying his immediate want—this would be *agapē* in action, would it not?

Many Christian writers in stressing *agapē* as the distinctive principle in ethics, have tried to draw a hard and fast distinction between *eros* and *agapē*. Fletcher maintains that *agapē* is not liking; it is never sentimental and it does not seek for reciprocity in its actions. This distinction between *agapē* and *eros* can lead to some rather difficult questions. Apparently if liking, *eros*, is present *agapē* is absent. At least in one illustration Fletcher suggests that it would be acting in accordance with *agapē* for a young couple to have pre-marital sexual relations in order to force their parents to consent to their proposed marriage. But he adds that it would not be justifiable for them to engage in sexual relations just because they liked each other. Now, might not their act be justified as more loving if they did in fact like each other? Where does liking end and loving begin? Fletcher tends to hold that while any kind of sexual action may be good in a particular situation, the criterion for its being good is that it does good for someone. Thus, the prostitute in *Never on Sunday* did the loving thing when she helped the sailor to discover his sexual identity. In opposition to *Playboy*, Fletcher holds sexual acts must not only not harm anybody; they must do somebody some good. But is this not to view sex instrumentally, as a means to something else? Might not sexual activities be enjoyable in and for themselves without any good or bad consequences following from them?

The reader will find it very worthwhile to read Fletcher's book and to try to add to his meager descriptions other factors which would be needed to justify the decisions which he makes. One last case will be singled out for comment here. We have discussed one of the problem cases he presents near the end of *Situation Ethics* in which a young lady is asked to use her sex in counter-espionage by a member of the United States intelligence agency. The dilemma she faces, as Fletcher portrays it, is should she value her chastity more than service to her country. His answer is a clear "No." But again, Fletcher has oversimplified this case. It could well be that the young lady would agree that in fulfilling *agapē* there might be occasions which would fully justify her surrendering her chastity. But is patriotism itself a sufficient reason for her doing so? She might disapprove of espionage; she might maintain that her country ought not to rely upon sexual lures to get secret data from another country in peace time. In fact, she might claim that it was not only the loving thing to do to refuse the request of the intelligence agency, but that it was also the patriotic thing to do. Just because an agency of the government asks one to do something does not mean that the act therefore is above moral evaluation. Obeying the commands of a governmental agency could well become just as vicious a legalism as the one Fletcher rejects.

This last illustration we have considered can also help to make clear another feature of situation ethics. The young lady could also maintain that sacrificing her chastity under the circumstances suggested to her was the loving thing to do and the patriotic deed as well. This is the answer Fletcher apparently had in mind. However, the fact that she could by appealing to the same motives, love and patriotism, reject the proposition as unloving and unpatriotic shows that this ethic is radically existentialist, and that in its implementation almost every decision is left up to the individual. But it is extremely difficult to be aware of all one's own motives in a specific case, and it requires a great deal of fact finding and rational calculation to come up with serious answers to most of the dilemmas Fletcher presents. The rules and principles of Christian ethics, therefore, are attempts to present some guideposts for the individual, and while they may be set aside at times, they do provide for some minimal guidance. An appeal to let love and reason decide then and there does not seem to be sufficient for rational ethical choice. One might profess to be following *agapē*, but prejudice and *eros* or self-interest might be the real motivating forces.

The other Christian ethicists we have examined agree with Fletcher concerning the primacy of *agapē*, but they disagree with his elimination of all other norms, principles or rules. Justice, as we have seen, is often proposed as another norm which keeps Christian love from sentimental or irrelevant decisions. Likewise, these writers claim that the principles or rules of ethical behavior are not a hindrance to *agapē* but are rather constructive guides to it in various situations in which one may be called upon to make difficult decisions. The moral codes of a society reflect its collective experience as to which acts tend to produce the greatest good for the greatest number. Thus, one does not need to calculate each time he is faced with whether or not he should tell a lie; the general rule is "Tell the truth unless to do so would result in the killing of an innocent person, or in irreparable harm to a human personality, and so on." Now we all face situations in which it is not clear that obeying the general rule would produce the greatest amount of good; in such cases we usually modify the rule so as to make it more explicit. In this way one's action represents a creative union of received moral principles and responsible decision making.

It is of course true that Fletcher and the situation ethicists are not defending irresponsibility or amorality. Unfortunately, with their attention so concentrated upon the extreme cases they give us little guidance for the more ordinary situations which all of us face every day. Ramsey and other writers want to remind us that the typical case occurs far more frequently than the extreme ones, and that one of the jobs served by moral rules is to provide for the typical cases. If one combined Ramsey's stress upon moral rules with Fletcher's agapeic calculus, which could be invoked in unusual situations, one would have an interpretation of Christian ethics that was neither antinomian nor legalistic.

NOTES FOR CHAPTER VI

1. Karl Barth, *The Epistle to the Romans*, trans. by Edwyn C. Hoskyns (New York: Oxford University Press, 1963), p. 29.
2. Karl Barth, *The Word of God and the Word of Man*, trans. by Douglas Horton (Boston: The Pilgrim Press, 1928), p. 192.
3. *Ibid.*, p. 18.
4. Paul Tillich as quoted in D. Mackenzie Brown, ed., *Ultimate Concern: Tillich in Dialogue* (New York: Harper & Row, Publishers, 1965), p. 191.
5. Paul Tillich, "Autobiographical Reflections," in *The Theology of Paul Tillich*, ed. by Charles W. Kegley and Robert W. Bretall (New York: The Macmillan Co., 1961), pp. 20–21.
6. Paul Tillich, *Systematic Theology* (3 vols. in one; Chicago: University of Chicago Press, 1967), I, 201.

7 Paul Tillich, *The Courage To Be* (New Haven: Yale University Press, 1952), p. 35.
8 Tillich, *Systematic Theology*, I, 171.
9 Tillich, *The Courage To Be*, p. 89.
10 *Ibid.*, p. 91.
11 *Ibid.*, p. 99.
12 *Ibid.*, p. 112.
13 *Ibid.*, p. 140.
14 *Ibid.*, pp. 149–150.
15 *Ibid.*, pp. 151–152.
16 Paul Tillich, *Christianity and the Encounter of the World Religions* (New York: Columbia University Press, 1964), p. 4.
17 Tillich quoted in Brown, ed., *Ultimate Concern: Tillich in Dialogue*, p. 7.
18 *Ibid.*, p. 15.
19 Paul Tillich, *Dynamics of Faith* (New York: Harper Torchbooks, 1958), pp. 11–12.
20 Tillich, *The Courage To Be*, p. 182.
21 Tillich, *Systematic Theology*, I, 235.
22 *Ibid.*, p. 237.
23 Tillich, *The Courage To Be*, p. 181.
24 *Ibid.*, p. 185.
25 *Ibid.*, pp. 187–188.
26 *Ibid.*, pp. 188–189.
27 *Ibid.*, p. 190.
28 Tillich, *Systematic Theology*, II, 12.
29 Tillich quoted in Brown, ed., *Ultimate Concern: Tillich in Dialogue*, pp. 194–195.
30 Tillich, *Dynamics of Faith*, pp. 42–43.
31 *Ibid.*, p. 45.
32 *Ibid.*, pp. 47–48.
33 Tillich, *Systematic Theology*, I, 287.
34 *Ibid.*, I, 288.
35 *Ibid.*, I, 287.
36 *Ibid.*, I, 288.
37 Paul Tillich, *Theology of Culture*, ed. by Robert C. Kimball (New York: Oxford University Press, 1959), p. 210.
38 *Ibid.*, p. 212.
39 Paul Tillich, *Morality and Beyond* (New York: Harper & Row, Publishers, 1963), p. 14.
40 *Ibid.*, p. 19.
41 *Ibid.*, p. 34.
42 *Ibid.*, p. 42.
43 Paul Tillich, *Love, Power, and Justice: Ontological Analyses and Ethical Applications* (New York: Oxford University Press, 1960), p. 33.
44 Tillich, *Morality and Beyond*, pp. 42–43.
45 *Ibid.*, pp. 44–45.
46 *Ibid.*, p. 46.
47 *Ibid.*, pp. 61–62.
48 Paul Tillich, *The World Situation* (Philadelphia: Fortress Press, 1965), p. 27.
49 Tillich, *Systematic Theology*, III, 421.
50 *Ibid.*, III, 420–421.

51 Tillich quoted in Brown, ed., *Ultimate Concern: Tillich in Dialogue*, p. 192.
52 *Ibid.*, p. 89.
53 *Ibid.*, p. 98.
54 Tillich, *Systematic Theology*, III, 227.
55 Dietrich Bonhoeffer, *Letters and Papers From Prison*, ed. by Eberhard Bethge, trans. by Reginald H. Fuller (New York: The Macmillan Co., 1962), pp. 219–220.
56 *Ibid.*, pp. 222–224.
57 Thomas J. J. Altizer, "America and the Future of Theology" in Thomas J. J. Altizer and William Hamilton, *Radical Theology and the Death of God* (Indianapolis: The Bobbs-Merrill Co., Inc., 1966), p. 20.
58 William Hamilton, "The Death of God Theologies Today," in Altizer and Hamilton, *Radical Theology and the Death of God*, p. 24.
59 *Ibid.*, p. 40.
60 *Ibid.*, p. 40.
61 *Ibid.*, p. 41.
62 *Ibid.*, p. 48.
63 William Hamilton, "Thursday's Child," in Altizer and Hamilton, *Radical Theology and the Death of God*, p. 92.
64 *Ibid.*, p. 92.
65 Harvey Cox, *The Secular City: Secularization and Urbanization in Theological Perspective* (Rev. ed.; New York: The Macmillan Co., 1966), pp. 68–70.
66 *Ibid.*, pp. 72–73.
67 *Ibid.*, p. 223.
68 *Ibid.*, p. 224.
69 *Ibid.*, p. 232.
70 William K. Frankena, "Love and Principle in Christian Ethics," in *Faith and Philosophy: Philosophical Studies in Religion and Ethics*, ed. by Alvin Plantinga (Grand Rapids, Mich.: William B. Eerdmans Publishing Co., 1964), p. 207.
71 Joseph Fletcher, *Situation Ethics: The New Morality* (Philadelphia: The Westminster Press, 1966), p. 26.
72 *Ibid.*, p. 26.
73 *Ibid.*, p. 31.
74 *Ibid.*, p. 28.
75 *Ibid.*, p. 30.
76 *Ibid.*, p. 31.
77 *Ibid.*, Chapter headings for chs. III, IV, V, VI, VII, VIII.
78 *Ibid.*, p. 58.
79 *Ibid.*, p. 65.
80 *Ibid.*, p. 74.
81 *Ibid.*, p. 75.
82 *Ibid.*, p. 79.
83 *Ibid.*, p. 84.
84 *Ibid.*, p. 89.
85 *Ibid.*, p. 90.
86 *Ibid.*, p. 95.
87 *Ibid.*, p. 95.
88 *Ibid.*, p. 95.
89 *Ibid.*, p. 96.

90 *Ibid.*, p. 101.
91 *Ibid.*, p. 117.
92 *Ibid.*, p. 104.
93 *Ibid.*, p. 124.
94 *Ibid.*, pp. 125–126.
95 *Ibid.*, pp. 126–127.
96 Joseph Fletcher, *Moral Responsibility: Situation Ethics at Work* (Phila-delphia: The Westminster Press, 1967), p. 40.
97 Fletcher, *Situation Ethics*, p. 132.
98 *Ibid.*, p. 133.
99 *Ibid.*, p. 164.
100 *Ibid.*, p. 164.
101 Fletcher, *Moral Responsibility*, p. 39.
102 *Ibid.*, pp. 39–40.
103 Fletcher, *Situation Ethics*, pp. 142–143.
104 *Ibid.*, p. 135.
105 *Ibid.*, p. 139.
106 *Ibid.*, p. 151.
107 *Ibid.*, p. 157.
108 Fletcher, *Moral Responsibility*, p. 181.
109 *Ibid.*, p. 181.
110 John A. T. Robinson, *Honest to God* (London: SCM Press Ltd., 1963), pp. 109–110.
111 *Ibid.*, pp. 119–120.
112 John A. T. Robinson, *Christian Morals Today* (Philadelphia: The West-minster Press, 1964), p. 12.
113 *Ibid.*, p. 16.
114 *Ibid.*, p. 42.
115 *Ibid.*, p. 26.
116 Emil Brunner, *The Divine Imperative: A Study in Christian Ethics*, trans. by Olive Wyon (Philadelphia: The Westminster Press, 1947), p. 117.
117 *Ibid.*, p. 167.
118 Emil Brunner, *Justice and the Social Order*, trans. by Mary Hottinger (New York: Harper and Brothers, Publishers, 1945), pp. 126–127.
119 *Ibid.*, pp. 127–128.
120 *Ibid.*, pp. 128–129.
121 *Ibid.*, p. 129.
122 *Ibid.*, p. 129.
123 *Ibid.*, p. 130.
124 See Reinhold Niebuhr, *An Interpretation of Christian Ethics* (New York: Harper and Brothers, Publishers, 1935); Reinhold Niebuhr, *Moral Man and Immoral Society: A Study in Ethics and Politics* (New York: Charles Scribner's Sons, 1948); Reinhold Niebuhr, *The Nature and Destiny of Man: A Christian Interpretation*, One Volume Edition: I. Human Nature, II. Human Destiny (New York: Charles Scribner's Sons, 1946).
125 John Rawls, "Two Concepts of Rules," *The Philosophical Review*, LXIV (1955), 3–32. Also reprinted in many anthologies.
126 Paul Ramsey, *Deeds and Rules in Christian Ethics* (New York: Charles Scribner's Sons, 1967), p. 112.
127 *Ibid.*, p. 108.
128 *Ibid.*, pp. 108–109.

129 Fletcher, *Situation Ethics*, p. 39.
130 *Ibid.*, p. 51.
131 Fletcher, *Moral Responsibility*, p. 35.
132 Ramsey, *Deeds and Rules in Christian Ethics*, pp. 109–110.
133 Frankena, "Love and Principle in Christian Ethics," in *Faith and Philosophy*, p. 212.
134 Ramsey, *Deeds and Rules in Christian Ethics*, p. 111.
135 *Ibid.*, p. 112.
136 *Ibid.*, p. 115.
137 *Ibid.*, p. 116.
138 See R. M. Hare, *The Language of Morals* (Oxford: Clarendon Press, 1952), chs. 3 and 4; Luther J. Binkley, *Contemporary Ethical Theories* (New York: Philosophical Library, Inc., 1961), pp. 132–140.
139 Ramsey, *Deeds and Rules in Christian Ethics*, p. 134.
140 *Ibid.*, p. 135.
141 *Ibid.*, p. 136.
142 See W. D. Ross, *The Right and the Good* (Oxford: Clarendon Press, 1955), ch. 2; Binkley, *Contemporary Ethical Theories*, pp. 30–34.
143 Alasdair MacIntyre, "God and the Theologians," in *The Honest to God Debate*, ed. by David L. Edwards (Philadelphia: The Westminster Press, 1963), p. 220.
144 Cox, *The Secular City*, p. 69.
145 *Ibid.*, p. 70.
146 MacIntyre, "God and the Theologians," in *The Honest to God Debate*, pp. 222–223.

SELECTED READINGS

* Available in paperback edition.

* Altizer, Thomas J. J. and William Hamilton. *Radical Theology and the Death of God*. Indianapolis: The Bobbs-Merrill Co., Inc., 1966.

Barth, Karl. *The Epistle to the Romans*. Translated by Edwyn C. Hoskyns. New York: Oxford University Press, 1963.

* Bonhoeffer, Dietrich. *Ethics*. Translated by Eberhard Bethge. New York: The Macmillan Co., 1965.

* ———. *Letters and Papers from Prison*. Edited by Eberhard Bethge. Translated by Reginald H. Fuller. New York: The Macmillan Co., 1962.

Brown, D. Mackenzie, ed. *Ultimate Concern: Tillich in Dialogue*. New York: Harper & Row, Publishers, 1965. An excellent introduction to Tillich's views as presented in his exchanges with students in a seminar he gave at the University of California in Santa Barbara in 1963.

Brunner, Emil. *The Divine Imperative: A Study in Christian Ethics*. Translated by Olive Wyon. Philadelphia: The Westminster Press, 1947.

———. *Justice and the Social Order*. Translated by Mary Hottinger. New York: Harper and Brothers, Publishers, 1945.

* Buber, Martin. *I and Thou*. Translated by Ronald Gregor Smith. New York: Charles Scribner's Sons, 1958.

* Cox, Harvey. *The Secular City: Secularization and Urbanization in Theological Perspective*. Rev. ed. New York: The Macmillan Co., 1966.

* Fletcher, Joseph. *Moral Responsibility: Situation Ethics at Work.* Philadelphia: The Westminster Press, 1967.

* ———. *Situation Ethics: The New Morality.* Philadelphia: The Westminster Press, 1966.

Mehta, Ved. *The New Theologian.* New York: Harper & Row, Publishers, 1965. An excellent introduction to the new theology for those unacquainted with the movement.

Niebuhr, Reinhold. *An Interpretation of Christian Ethics.* New York: Harper & Brothers, Publishers, 1935.

* ———. *Moral Man and Immoral Society: A Study in Ethics and Politics.* New York: Charles Scribner's Sons, 1948.

* ———. *The Nature and Destiny of Man: A Christian Interpretation.* One vol. ed. New York: Charles Scribner's Sons, 1946.

Plantinga, Alvin, ed. *Faith and Philosophy: Philosophical Studies in Religion and Ethics.* Grand Rapids, Mich.: William B. Eerdmans Publishing Co., 1964.

* Ramsey, Paul. *Deeds and Rules in Christian Ethics.* New York: Charles Scribner's Sons, 1967.

* Robinson, John A. T. *Christian Morals Today.* Philadelphia: The Westminster Press, 1964.

* ———. *Honest to God.* London: SCM Press Ltd., 1963.

* Tillich, Paul. *Biblical Religion and the Search for Ultimate Reality.* Chicago: University of Chicago Press, 1955.

* ———. *The Courage To Be.* New Haven: Yale University Press, 1952.

* ———. *Dynamics of Faith.* New York: Harper Torchbooks, 1958.

* ———. *Love, Power, and Justice: Ontological Analyses and Ethical Applications.* New York: Oxford University Press, 1960.

———. *Morality and Beyond.* New York: Harper & Row, Publishers, 1963.

* ———. *Theology of Culture.* Edited by Robert C. Kimball. New York: Oxford University Press, 1959.

———. *Systematic Theology.* Three Volumes in One. Chicago: University of Chicago Press, 1967.

* ———. *The World Situation.* Philadelphia: Fortress Press, 1965.

VII

Meta-Ethics and Moral Decisions

We have been examining alternative moral ideals, or life styles, which are live options for one in the Western world. Each one of the positions we have presented maintains that there are some basic values which one ought to incorporate in his life plan; in this sense, we have been describing normative ethical theories. The reader may have noticed that very few of these value systems have been proposed by writers who are usually classified as philosophers. In fact, most twentieth-century British and American philosophers hold that the philosopher *qua* philosopher has no special insight into what our values ought to be. While he might speak out on moral issues as a *man*, they generally suggest that he should not claim that his professional competency in philosophy entitles him to any special consideration as an advisor on actual moral problems. Thus, we have suggested, in the preceding chapter, that in our present day it has been the theologians more than the philosophers who have sought to give moral advice. The reader may nevertheless ask, "Why is it that the professional philosopher today seems so unconcerned with presenting a philosophy of life in terms of which others could more rationally make their own personal decisions?" Surely the philosophers of past ages, such as Plato, Aristotle, Kant, Bentham and Mill attempted to develop philosophies which were concerned with telling men how they ought to live. What has happened to contemporary philosophers? Why do they refuse to propose normative theories of value?

The basic explanation for contemporary professional philosophers not advocating a particular value theory is that they have a new conception of what moral philosophy itself ought to do. Rather than propose a way of life, they suggest that the philosopher's task should be to analyze the meaning or use of basic value terms, examine the nature of what it is for a judgment to be a moral one, and to inquire into the ways in which moral arguments can be said to be justified. Thus, the philosopher is concerned with what he often calls meta-ethics rather than with ethics itself. Meta-ethics is often described as a second-order study of ethics; that is, it does not make normative pronouncements but inquires into the nature of morality itself. It does not tell us what we should value as good, but instead asks what is the meaning of the word "good" as it is usually used in moral statements. It does not tell us what decisions we should reach in moral crises, but instead seeks to examine what the nature of a moral argument is. Just as the philosopher of science is not actually proposing scientific theories and then testing them, so the philosopher who inquires into ethics is not making normative judgments. The philosopher of science can suggest canons of valid scientific reasoning; he can examine scientific arguments and make clear what it is that the scientist presupposes, etc. In a similar manner the philosopher who studies ethics can examine moral arguments; he can attempt to make clear what is presupposed in a particular moral dispute, etc. But in neither case does the philosopher engage in the first-order discipline; that is, he is not a scientist or a moralist. His analysis of scientific theories may show that some are well-founded, while others are not; his analysis of moral proposals may also show that some are capable of being rationally defended, while others are not. But it is the job of the scientist to discover which of the theories which meet the canons of scientific reasoning is most adequate to account for the largest range of facts. Likewise, each individual, who was searching for ideals to which he could commit his life, would have to make his own choice as to which of the alternative life styles he considered best. All the moral philosopher could do as a philosopher would be to provide certain minimal criteria as to what would count as acceptable reasons for justifying such a choice.

The study of meta-ethics is a much more technical inquiry than one finds in the writers who proposed the normative ideals which we have considered in previous chapters. There are exceptions to this claim, however, for in the case of Sartre we had to introduce a technical terminology in order to understand his method of existential phenomenology. We were willing to make this effort because we were promised a new theory of what it is to be a man when we reached the end of our painstaking inquiry. But why should we examine meta-ethics when its advocates tell us in advance that we shall not find them defending a particular normative theory of value when we reach the end of their investigations? The philosophers might be interested in what the word "good" means, but how will examining their works help the average man who has to make difficult moral decisions? We don't ordinarily ask people, what do you mean by "good"? Instead we ask ourselves what is the best course of conduct that we ought to follow in this particular situation, and the analytic philosophers tell us, even before we start examining their views, that they will not be concerned with answering this question for us.

We shall find, however, that an investigation of meta-ethical theories will be quite helpful to us in dealing with some of the following questions. How can we choose between the competing ideals of life presented by Marx, Freud, Fromm, Kierkegaard, Nietzsche, Sartre, Fletcher, and the other writers we have considered thus far? How should we go about making a difficult moral decision? Are there any methods by which we can show a Nazi that he ought not to persecute Jews? Can we show that the white segregationist is wrong in maintaining that the black man should be treated differently than the white man?

In addition, we may discover that the meta-ethicist's discussions concerning the meaning and use of evaluative terms, such as "good," may clarify the various contexts in which we use these terms. Evaluative terms are not always used in moral contexts; sometimes they are used in aesthetic, religious, prudential, and many other contexts. We shall see that there are some times when our arguments concerning what is really good could be settled, or at least shortened, if we paid attention to the way in which the word "good" was being used in that particular situation. Let us begin by examining several different kinds of disputes which involve evaluative expressions.

Consider, for example, a simple case of a dispute in a non-moral context. Suppose you have found a restaurant which serves very good hamburgers, and you invite a friend to go there with you for lunch. Your friend takes one bite of his hamburger and says, "This is terrible." You, however, having tasted your hamburger would have been inclined to say, "This is an excellent hamburger." Ordinarily, I suspect, you would ask your friend why he said the hamburger was terrible. His response might be that it was terrible because it was too rare. Now, the apparent disagreement ends, because when he tells you he likes his hamburgers well done, you recall that you had claimed the hamburgers in that restaurant were good because you liked them very rare. Both of you made different statements using value words, such as "good" and "terrible" because each of you had different criteria for what constituted good hamburgers. In such a simple case as this, value words are used to express each person's taste, and the tastes of your friend and yourself are not the same. At this point, you would simply recognize the difference in tastes, and perhaps apologize for not having realized that your friend did not like rare hamburgers. If you had realized it, you would not have told him that the hamburgers in that restaurant were excellent. It is not likely that you would insist that he ought to have the same tastes in food that you have.

Disputes concerning whether or not a particular painting is good might in some respects be very similar to the above example concerning tastes in food. If you can either "take art or leave it," you might be content to respond to a friend who did not like a certain painting, which you thought was very good, by saying that not all people have the same tastes. You like the painting; he does not. As far as you are concerned that is the end of the matter. But suppose you are an art critic, and your friend has had very little acquaintance with art. You might then, if he responded to your comment that the painting was very good by saying, "I don't like it," proceed in the following manner. You could say that you were making an aesthetic judgment when you said that it was a very good painting, and that such a judgment was not equivalent to your saying, "I like it." You might continue by saying, "Look at the way the lines are balanced, the colors shade into each other, the completely abstract character of the entire painting, etc." Your friend might reply that because it was so completely abstract was exactly why he said he did not like it. Further-more, he says that no abstract painting can be good art. If you cannot identify persons or scenes from a painting, he claims that you can be sure that it is not good art. As an art critic you believe that you can educate your friend's taste by explaining to him what abstract art tries to do. You might try to help him look at a painting as an object in itself rather than as a copy of a landscape. You might point out various features of the painting, call his attention to the balance of the composition, the rich hues of the colors, etc. This would take some time, to be sure, but you are willing to make this attempt because you believe that you have *good reasons* to justify your saying that it is a good painting, and that your friend does not have good reasons for maintaining that the painting is not good. In fact, in a strict sense, you could even say that he really did not have any reasons at all for his evaluation. Or perhaps, more cor-rectly, that your friend really was not making an aesthetic judgment but was expressing his personal taste. In the language of analytic philosophers, you were playing different games. Your game of aesthetic evaluation is one which requires that reasons be given for justifying an aesthetic judg-ment, but his game of expressing his personal tastes is not one in which reasons are normally expected. To show that the two of you were en-gaged in different activities, you could even say that while you thought that the painting was a good painting, nevertheless, in fact, you did not particularly like it. An art critic can sometimes clearly separate his personal tastes from his aesthetic judgments, although it is most likely that they will usually not conflict with each other.

Suppose that we vary our illustration so that the dispute as to whether or not the painting is a good one takes place between two art critics. Would the dispute then become one concerning merely the personal tastes of each art critic? If the reader examines books on art history and art criticism he will discover that not all experts on art always arrive at the same judgments concerning particular art objects. However, you will also discover that rarely do these experts really judge one painting to be a good one simply because they happen to like it. Art critics proceed to explain why they consider a particular painting to be a good one of its kind. They refer to aspects of the painting, the technique displayed in the painting, the handling of the subject matter, the use of color, line, shading, etc. Certain features which they find to be present in the painting provide the reasons for their aesthetic judgments. Not only would they consider personal likes and dislikes to be irrelevant to their task, but also they would usually rule out moral, prudential and religious considerations as well. Clearly, they would hold the facts that a particular artist had beaten his wife, left his family, and in general been what most people would call an immoral man, irrelevant to the aesthetic worth of one of his paintings. The art critic is evaluating a painting on aesthetic grounds; he is not evaluating the quality of life of the artist. He might, as a man, agree that a particular artist was an immoral man, but then he would be making a moral judgment about the man, and not an aesthetic judgment about a painting. The point which we should note here is that the art critic or the art historian would claim that the use of evaluative terms in aesthetic judgment is controlled by at least some minimal criteria of relevance to the painting itself as an art object. Not all art critics would adopt exactly the same criteria, but, at the very least, a disagreement between them could be carried on rationally, since there would be at least some reasons which they would rule out as irrelevant to the particular function which they were performing.

But what do these illustrations have to do with moral decisions? The reader might admit that he does not hold that moral disputes are merely about what the parties to the dispute like and dislike. Liking hamburgers is very different from liking to tell a lie. Calling rare hamburgers "good" is very different from saying, "Joe is a good man." And if I don't care for abstract art, why should I study it in order that I can understand why some people can say that one abstract painting is better than another? Objections like these are often raised, and they must be met. We have deliberately used illustrations of disputes involving the word "good" from non-moral contexts in order to make it clear that evaluative words do not occur in moral discourse only, as well as to show that in some contexts such disputes do involve giving reasons for the evaluation. Furthermore, it should appear obvious that most moral disputes resemble the model of an aesthetic dispute more than they do a dispute merely about tastes in food. But the reader may still claim that while he can learn more art if he wants to, and thus become able to distinguish acceptable reasons for an evaluative judgment about a painting from those which are not acceptable, he still does not see the relevance of this discussion to moral decisions or to his choice of a basic life style. A full answer to this kind of an objection can only emerge as we consider meta-ethics in more detail in the rest of this chapter. However, at this preliminary stage, we can perhaps say at least this much. If some person claims that the members of a certain minority group (Negroes, Jews, Chinese-Americans, Protestants, Christian Scientists, homosexuals, bachelors, widows, hippies, philosophy professors) *ought* to be persecuted because he does not like them, one can respond that such an *ought* judgment needs to be defended by reasons, if there are any, and not merely by a statement concerning one's personal likes and dislikes. If aesthetic evaluations, when sincerely made, need to be capable of being supported by good reasons, then it would appear that moral evaluations also should be capable of being rationally defended. Perhaps here a close study of the work of analytic philosophers may help to provide us with good reasons to use against those who think that they are justified in morally condemning or persecuting people just because they happen to be members of a minority group. Each one of us, no matter who he is, belongs to at least one minority group. Even if we make most of our decisions on the grounds of our own self-interest, some of the writers whom we shall consider will provide us with good reasons for rejecting all persecution of minority groups.

Part of our investigation will be concerned with an attempt to discover the central uses of evaluative language. We shall be more concerned, however, with attempting to find if there are any justifiable reasons which can be given for moral judgments, as well as with seeking to discover if there are any criteria for determining the validity of a moral argument. In a very significant sense we can refuse to make evaluative statements about art, either because we profess ignorance or because we are indifferent. We cannot, however, in the same manner refuse to make moral decisions, for as Sartre has told us, even if we prefer to let our choice be guided by someone else, we have made a choice nevertheless and are responsible for the choice we have made. Perhaps a brief study of contemporary meta-ethical theories may give us some help after all in making our choice of a life style a rationally defensible one. Let us see.

The Meaning of Ethical Terms   Philosophers in the early part of the twentieth century were concerned with the meaning of basic ethical terms such as "good," "right," and "ought." Their search was for an exact definition of these value words. We shall limit ourselves to their attempts to define "good," although many of them were concerned with other evaluative terms as well. According to their strict notion of definition, the word being defined (the *definiendum*) had to be completely analyzed and explicated by another expression which had the same meaning and significance (the *definiens*). If a definition for a particular term were correct, then that definition could be substituted in any instance in which that term was normally used. Thus, for example, we could substitute the expression "male sibling" for the word "brother," since "male sibling" is an analysis of what the term "brother" means or signifies. How did the philosophers fare in their attempt to find an exact equivalent definition for the word "good"? We shall mention the three leading positions which were taken by philosophers in their attempts to define "good," but in doing so we must eliminate the respects in which particular philosophers often differed with each other even though they could generally be said to fit into one of the three basic camps which we shall discuss.

Those philosophers who attempted to define "good" in terms of expressions which are not themselves evaluative expressions, but are rather descriptions of some biological, psychological or sociological properties are said to have held a naturalistic theory of value. Among the definitions of "good" proposed by the naturalists were the following: "that which is desired," "that which brings happiness," "that which is approved by most human beings," "that which is most evolved," and "that which satisfies basic human needs." It might be difficult to discover empirically what is desired, what brings happiness, what is approved by most human beings, and so on, but in principle each one of these proposals maintained that the various sciences could in time answer these questions quite satisfactorily. The point of their purported definitions was to claim that "good" could be fully explicated in terms of natural scientific categories. In previous chapters we have referred to a basic difference between facts and values. The naturalists denied this distinction and maintained that value terms such as "good" were really descriptive terms denoting some natural property of an object or characteristic of a person or society.

Erich Fromm is one of the writers we have studied who appears to be a naturalist. He maintains that the knowledge which we get from the sciences and from the great literature of the world shows us what would be good for man. Man, he claims, ought to be productive and creative, and he derives this claim from his objective knowledge about human nature. In terms of meta-ethics Fromm is then a naturalist, if he intends to claim that the sciences of man inform us about objective human needs whose satisfaction is really good for man.

There are at least two basic difficulties with all proposed naturalistic definitions of "good." One is based upon the fact that the proposed definitions are couched in such general terms that they seem to be of little help in clarifying the meaning of the value word being defined. Happiness, pleasure, more evolved, and so on, would also need to be explicated, and we might find that we would be engaged in an infinite regress.

A more basic criticism, however, is that proposed by G. E. Moore, a leading British philosopher of the first part of our century. He proposed a test which he thought destroyed all attempted definitions of "good," not only those of the naturalists. Moore's test, which is often called "the open question argument," consists in asking of any proposed definition of "good" whether that which is stated in the definiens is actually good. Now Moore's point is that it does not make sense if a student of mathematics were to ask, "Is a plane figure consisting of three noncollinear points and the line segments joining them really a triangle?" The only response one might make would be that the student asking the question didn't know what "triangle" meant, for if he did he would have known that "triangle" is defined in terms of "three noncollinear points and the line segments joining them." But Moore claimed concerning the proposed definitions of "good," that "whatever definition be offered, it may be always asked, with significance, of the complex so defined, whether it is itself good." [1] If this question can be asked with significance then the supposed equivalence required in a definition of the definiens and the definiendum has not been established, and the proposed definition must be rejected. Thus, to glance at some of the proposed naturalistic definitions of "good" which we have listed, it does make sense to ask about something which is desired, "But is it really good?" I might desire to become a thief, but is it good if I follow my desire? Is that which is approved by most human beings really good? If most people approved of war, would that make war good? Is that which promotes happiness really good? Would it be good for me to promote my happiness at the expense of injuring others?

It is important to note that Moore did not deny that most of the things we call good do bring us pleasure or happiness; nevertheless, there is not an exact equivalence in meaning of "good" and "pleasure" or "happiness." It surely seems obvious that while I might obtain pleasure by inflicting pain upon someone else, that I could still maintain that it was not good that I do so. We have already seen, in our evaluation of Fromm's position, that one could with significance ask if it really is good for him to develop his complete physical, intellectual and spiritual natures, or if it might not be better for him to become one-sided, stressing one aspect of his being to the neglect of the others. The decisions which one would reach in such cases would themselves be guided by his own basic moral ideals. Moore's point would be that the very fact that one could ask if one ought to seek self-realization of all his capacities, or only of one or several, simply shows that the proposed definition of "good" fails to meet the required test.

The second position developed in an attempt to define "good" was proposed by G. E. Moore himself. Moore held that not only the naturalistic definitions but also metaphysical or theological definitions failed to fulfill the conditions of his open question argument. He proposed an explanation for the failure of an attempted definition of "good" when he claimed that good was a simple, non-naturalistic, indefinable property. There are some words which are so basic that we do not define them; "good" Moore held functioned like "yellow" in at least this respect.

We learn to use the word "yellow" by having people point to certain objects and saying, "this is yellow," "this is not yellow," and so on. In this respect, "good" functions like "yellow" in that it is such a basic concept that we do not go to a dictionary to find out what it means. According to Moore, then, we simply intuit or see immediately how the word "good" is used. By calling good "non-natural" he means to stress that it is a value term which cannot be reduced to neutral words which do not themselves function as value expressions. Or, to put his thesis more generally, ethics is an autonomous study in that it cannot be explained without remainder by the natural or social sciences.[2]

Other British philosophers in Moore's day agreed that at least one value term must be taken as basic, as immediately understood, in terms of which other value terms could then be defined. W. D. Ross claimed that both "good" and "right" were simple indefinable concepts, while A. C. Ewing maintained that "ought" was the basic ethical concept in terms of which other value terms such as "good" and "right" could be defined.[3] The reader thus has already at his finger tips some of the arguments which could be given against this theory concerning the meaning of basic value terms. If even Moore's contemporary philosophers disagreed as to which of the value terms was simple, basic, and indefinable, it seems clear that not all men see that "good" is the basic indefinable concept in our ethical language. Furthermore, what is it to be a non-natural property? Yellow might be called a natural property of some colored objects, but is it not misleading to speak of a mysterious non-natural property of goodness? Is this not to multiply entities beyond necessity? If the naturalists failed to give an exact equivalent definition of "good," has Moore done much better by claiming that "good" is a non-natural, simple, indefinable property?

Those philosophers who held to the third position we shall examine concerning the attempt to define "good" agreed with G. E. Moore that "good" was indeed indefinable, although they gave different reasons for this conclusion than Moore did. This group of philosophers adopted what is called the *emotive theory of meaning*, which held that value terms were used to express or arouse emotions. They claimed that Moore was misguided by his thinking that "good" was a cognitive term, and that therefore he had to invent a non-natural property for goodness, since he was correct in not finding it equivalent to any natural property in the world. A. J. Ayer, one of the leading defenders of the emotive theory, maintained that "good" does not refer to any property whatsoever, natural or non-natural.[4] Basic value terms have no descriptive meaning, but only an emotive meaning. They are therefore non-cognitive.

According to Ayer's theory, if I say, "He shot his father!" or "He ought not to have shot his father," both sentences refer to the same facts. In this respect they have the same descriptive meaning since they both refer to a state of affairs which could be either true or false. That is, I might learn that I was mistaken in saying, "He shot his father!" His father may have shot himself, and I could be presented with evidence to confirm or disconfirm any factual claim about the event. The exclamation point at the end of my statement, "He shot his father!" functions, for Ayer, like the words "ought not" in my second sentence. In each case I am uttering my disapproval of his action, which could be done by certain punctuation marks, tones of voice, or facial expressions, just as well as by the introduction of value words such as "ought not." Thus, according to Ayer's analysis, the search for a definition of value words was misguided since they do not have a cognitive use. They are used merely to express our emotions of approval or disapproval, and to evoke similar emotions in our hearers. Thus, "good" functions more like an expletive, such as "Hurrah"; it has only an emotive meaning.

If our use of moral language simply expresses our own feelings, how then could there be any significant ethical disputes with others who have different feelings than we do? Ayer's point was that there could be no significant dispute about values, for we cannot rationally argue about our tastes and feelings. Descriptive statements could contradict one another in the sense that it cannot both be true, for example, that the cat is on the mat, and the cat is not on the mat. But if you and I have different basic feelings of approval, no contradiction could be involved. He insisted, however, that most so-called disputes about values turn out upon examination to be disputes about the facts of the case. Since we have been brought up in the same culture, we have been conditioned to share the same basic feelings about human actions. In general, unless there were extenuating circumstances, we should all feel that a son ought not to shoot his father. If the facts convinced us that the son actually did shoot his father, and if it can be shown that there were no extenuating circumstances, we should be inclined to say that the son ought not to have performed this action. Our moral disapproval would be withdrawn if someone could show that it was really an act of self-defense on the part of the son, but then we have accepted new facts, and have not revised our moral feelings. If someone said that "He ought to shoot his father" and maintained it seriously, Ayer claims that we would have no way of engaging in a rational dispute. We simply have different values, and our moral dispute turns out to be one about our tastes, much as our initial illustration referred to disagreements in taste concerning food.

The most sophisticated defense of the emotive theory of ethics was presented by Charles Stevenson.[5] He agreed with Ayer that the primary use of value expressions was to vent our approval or disapproval and to seek to arouse others to share our attitudes. Stevenson, however, met some of the objections to Ayer's bold thesis by admitting that value terms have both a descriptive and an emotive meaning. Thus, if I say, "That is a good sports car," my statement may be taken as referring to certain descriptive facts about sports cars: easily maneuverable, rapid in acceleration, fast, capable of holding the road at high speed, etc.—this would be the descriptive meaning of the word "good" in this context. However, in addition to this descriptive meaning, I would also be expressing my approval of this particular sports car and entreating you to share my approval as well. Stevenson thus held that the descriptive meaning of "good" varied according to the context in which it was used. In its primary evaluative use, however, "good" expressed my approval of that object, act or person to which I had applied the word.

Stevenson was also led to conclude that the most one could do logically in a moral argument would be to show that one's opponent was defending two inconsistent principles, but there was no logical or rational way for suggesting which of the two principles he should abandon. Thus, for example, if someone said that all human beings are entitled to equal treatment, but in the course of an argument went on to maintain that Negroes should not be allowed to live in certain restricted housing developments within a city, you could point out that he was maintaining two inconsistent principles. You could not, however, convince him by logic and reason alone as to which of his two conflicting principles he had to surrender. For this reason, Stevenson maintained that actual moral arguments do take place but they are not like rational arguments about the facts of the case, but rather they are persuasive arguments in which any means can be used to change the beliefs and attitudes of your opponent.

In a moral dispute one is always pleading a cause, according to Stevenson, and any kind of argument is allowable if it succeeds in converting your opponent. Thus, if I am arguing with a man who generally follows what I believe to be reason, I might try to get him to retract his proposal for restricted housing by getting him to see that Negroes are human beings, and that he was being irrational in his initial proposal. However, if that argument did not succeed, I might then say that if the Negroes are denied access to the new housing complex, there will undoubtedly be a riot in which my opponent's property might be damaged or destroyed. If I succeed by my second move, it is as justifiable an ethical argument, according to Stevenson, as my first more rational attempt. What counts, in short, in ethical arguments is success—they are justified only pragmatically, and if propaganda and appeals to fear work better than facts and reason then I am justified in using them. The connection between reasons and the conclusion in an ethical argument turns out to be psychological, then, and not logical.

The Use of Moral Terms   Contemporary philosophers are not concerned with providing an exact equivalent definition of moral terms, nor do they subscribe to the emotive theory of meaning. Instead of asking for the meaning of value terms, they have turned their attention to how value words are actually used. In what contexts, and on what occasions, do we use words such as "good," "right," and "ought." This approach to meta-ethics is influenced by the later work of Ludwig Wittgenstein and the current school of Oxford philosophy. The charge often made by these philosophers against previous ethical theorists is that instead of examining moral language as we actually use it, they legislated how it should be used. Perhaps our actual usage of moral language is far richer and more complex than either the naturalists, intuitionists, or emotivists thought. There may even be a kind of logic to moral arguments which would separate propaganda from moral reasoning in a way which Stevenson could not do in terms of his theory. Earlier theorists may have been misguided because they had too restricted an idea of meaning itself. Instead of deciding what we shall count as meaningful, let us look and see what we consider meaningful in our ordinary use of language. Here we shall have time for only a brief examination of this new approach to meta-ethics, although the reader should understand that this linguistic approach has been applied in other areas of philosophical investigation as well.

Wittgenstein had suggested in his *Philosophical Investigations* that for many cases we should ask not for the meaning of an expression, but for its use. Philosophers had often been misled, he said, because they had considered only one kind of example. Then they constructed their theories by creating artificial pigeon-holes, such as descriptive and emotive meaning, into which all the uses of expressions in our language were forced. In the case of meta-ethics, Stephen Toulmin suggests that some philosophers were misled by noticing some similarities of ethical sentences with the sentences of science (naturalists), while others were misled by noticing that some sentences using value words are similar to sentences expressing one's tastes (emotivists). On the other hand, another group of philosophers noticed that some ethical sentences were not at all like scientific statements or emotive utterances (non-naturalists). These philosophers were all correct in noticing various similarities and differences between ethical statements and other statements, and if we view their positions as presenting disguised comparisons, rather than literal descriptions of ethical sentences, then they are not necessarily incompatible with one another. We do not then have to choose between them.[6] If we actually look at the various occasions on which we use words such as "good," we will find that on some occasions we use the word almost as though it were a short-hand description, as in "This is a good pencil," while on other occasions we might merely be giving vent to our emotions, such as in "Gee, that's good." In short, we should actually examine the ways in which we use value expressions, and while some uses might approach very closely to descriptions and others to purely emotive assertions of our feelings, we shall probably find that there are many uses which fall in between these two neat categories. Toulmin has made this point very clearly in the following passage:

'What is wanted' (to adapt something John Wisdom wrote in another context), 'is some device for bringing out the relation between the manner in which ethical sentences are used and the manners in which others are used—so as to give their place on the language-map.' It will be from such a description, or 'language-map,' rather than from a one-sided and disguised comparison, that we shall obtain the understanding that we seek—whether of the generality of ethical judgments, their expressiveness and rhetorical force, the function and importance of moral principles, the place of the moralist, or the principles of the 'open society'; or, most important, what it is that makes an ethical argument a valid argument, and what things are *good reasons* for ethical judgments. Furthermore, such an account, free from the distractions of any particular beguiling analogy, will suggest to us all the comparisons we want: and enable us to display the distinctions between concepts of different kinds without falsifying our usage.[7]

There is at least one respect in which most of the linguistic analysts agree with G. E. Moore, although they do not support his defense for his position. Most of the analysts maintain that value judgments *cannot* be reduced without remainder to descriptions of psychological or sociological properties. They hold, in general, that to describe is to describe, to utter one's emotional feeling is to utter one's emotional feeling, and to give an evaluation is to give an evaluation. None of these activities can be reduced to any of the others. Thus, in order that we become clearer about what it is to express an evaluative judgment, they propose that we actually look and see how value words function in our ordinary use of language.

There is also at least one similarity between the defenders of the emotive theory and the linguistic meta-ethicists. They both agree that in their primary uses value words such as "good" do not have merely a descriptive or cognitive meaning. However, the linguistic analysts maintain that it is misleading on this account to say that therefore they have an emotive meaning, which becomes a kind of catchall category for all statements which are neither logical nor factual. Even more significantly, they maintain that the emotive force of an utterance is not actually part of the meaning of a sentence at all, and is a psychological rather than a linguistic category. Hence, most of the linguistic analysts maintain that while they adopt a non-cognitivist position on ethics, this does not mean that they are in accord with the emotive theory. Instead, they propose to examine the ways in which we actually use value terms in our everyday lives.

Rather than examine in a sketchy manner the positions of the most important recent writers on meta-ethics, we shall concentrate upon the writings of one of them, namely, R. M. Hare of Oxford University. While many other professional philosophers have contributed much to the present discussion of the nature of ethics, Hare has more directly addressed himself to the issues of moral choice with which this book has been concerned. An examination of Hare's ethical theory, therefore, will be extremely worthwhile for the reader who is seeking for a rational method to guide him in choosing his own life style.[8]

Hare's general conviction is that ethical language is primarily used prescriptively in order to guide human conduct. In developing this position Hare maintains that the primary function of value words is to commend or condemn. Thus he claims that the most general value word in our language is "good" and he accepts the *Oxford English Dictionary*'s statement on how this term is ordinarily used: Good is "the most general adjective of commendation, implying the existence in a high, or at least satisfactory, degree of characteristic qualities which are either admirable in themselves, or useful for some purpose. . . ."[9] Whenever the word "good" is used in an evaluative sense, we know that no matter what the word is being applied to, that, whatever it is, is characterized as an outstanding, or at least satisfactory, one of its kind. Surely in the sentence, "This is a very good wine," although you might not know the criteria I have used to characterize this wine as good, you do know that I am commending it as an outstanding wine. Rather than maintain that "good" is used in many different ways, and that therefore it has a different meaning in each case, Hare claims that in all evaluative uses of the word it has a common meaning of commendation, although the criteria (or the good-making characteristics) for the application of "good" vary according to the class of objects being discussed. Thus, for example, the criteria of a good steak are quite different from those of a good sports car, but in both cases the evaluative meaning of the word "good" is to commend the object referred to.

Hare does not deny that "good" has descriptive meaning, but he wants to insist that this is only a secondary meaning; the primary meaning of the word is evaluative. He suggests two main reasons for calling the evaluative meaning of "good" primary: (1) "the evaluative meaning is constant for every class of object for which the word is used,"[10] while its descriptive meaning varies according to the object to which one is referring; (2) "we can use the evaluative force of the word in order to *change* the descriptive meaning for any class of objects."[11] We might, for example, say that it is not really good to be a rugged individualist, despite the fact that this quality was once valued very highly in the past. Today, we might instead say that it is good to be sociable and cooperative with one's fellow men. We are still commending when we use "good" in this case, although our standards of commendation have changed from rugged individualism, which was approved in the frontier days, to cooperative behavior, which is praised in our present society.

Hare does suggest that there are some parasitic uses of the word "good" in which it is not used in an evaluative sense, but is used descriptively to refer to what the actual value judgments of my society happen to be. It may be necessary in such cases to inquire into what the speaker means if we are not certain whether or not he is expressing an evaluation by his use of this basic value term. If the speaker is really making an evaluation, then Hare maintains that it logically follows that he would choose those objects or kinds of actions which he is commending. Hare insists that the primary use of value words is to help guide our choices. We do not use them for things which individuals do not have to choose between; we do use them to help guide ourselves or others in making choices between things either now or in the future. If we never had to choose between which play to see, which auto to buy, which kind of man to emulate, we should never apply "good" to these kinds of things.

In addition to being used to guide our choices, Hare insists that value judgments are, at least implicitly, universal in character. When I say that something is good I imply something about other objects of the same class with similar characteristics, namely that they are good as well. Thus, in commending a particular object, I am implicitly commending other objects in the same class which are exactly like it in the relevant respects. It is in this sense that Hare claims that value judgments function like universal imperatives. Hence one might recast "This is a good apple" into "Choose apples with exactly these characteristics." The similarity in the functioning of universal imperatives and value judgments can be seen in the necessity to be consistent in using them. Clearly you would have a right to ask me what reasons I could give if, in the case of two apples which appeared to be as similar as any two apples could be, I said that one of them was good, while the other was bad.[12] Hare insists that this same type of logical consistency is called for when value words are used in moral as well as in non-moral contexts. While it is true that we are more concerned about what evaluations we receive as human beings, nevertheless, this is no reason for assuming that the logic applied to the use of evaluative words is different in moral contexts from what it is in non-moral contexts. If in two situations in which all the relevant facts are as similar as they can be, I call the one man "good" and the other man "bad," I may justifiably be accused of inconsistency. Hare holds that one of the basic characteristics of a moral judgment is its universalizability; that is, it would hold for all other persons under relevantly similar situations.

While Hare began his investigation by suggesting that he intended to search for the ways in which value words such as "good" are actually used in our language, it seems that he too may have been searching for one basic use. At any rate, other writers, who admit that the central use of moral language is to guide choices, claim that there are other uses of moral language which are not adequately accounted for by Hare. Thus, Nowell-Smith, another British philosopher, claims that if one actually looks at moral language as it is used, one will discover that value words play many different roles:

> They are used to express tastes and preferences, to express decisions and choices, to criticize, grade, and evaluate, to advise, admonish, warn, persuade and dissuade, to praise, encourage and reprove, to promulgate and draw attention to rules; and doubtless for other purposes also.[13]

According to Nowell-Smith, when we use "good" for a moral purpose we are taking a pro-attitude toward that which we call good. Furthermore, we are prepared to back up our pro-attitude with reasons. He finds, however, that there are other uses of "good," so that we might on some occasions say, "He is a good liar," by which we were not expressing a pro-attitude toward lying, but simply saying that a particular person was successful in performing a certain action. Yet, even here, there is at least an indirect connection with a pro-attitude. Nowell-Smith explains that "good" in this context "implies success, and 'success' is a pro-word. A man is not a good liar unless he fairly consistently achieves his aim." [14] At any rate, Nowell-Smith claims that there are other evaluative uses of "good" in addition to the central one of guiding moral choice.

Nowell-Smith's study of the uses of value expressions thus appears to be closer to the work of Wittgenstein than does that of Hare. Wittgenstein used the example of how we use the word "game" to refer to many different activities, such as card games, board games, ball games, Olympic games, etc. Now if you list all the ways in which you use the word "game," you will not be able to find that there is any one thing which they all have in common. Wittgenstein's remark here has become a slogan for those pursuing careful investigations into the uses of terms in our language: "Don't say: 'There *must* be something common, or they would not be called "games" '—but *look and see* whether there is anything that is common to all." [15] You might claim, however, that all games involve competition. Did you in arriving at that claim consider solitaire, or throwing a ball into the air and catching it yourself? It would be rather strange to say that one was competing against the cards, or against the ball. You might then suggest that all games involve skill. But what skill does one need to play solitaire? And if you call that skill, it is quite different from the skill needed to play baseball, which is in turn different from the skill needed to play chess. The reader might well continue to list the characteristics which he would apply to the various different games he can imagine. He should not fail to consider uses of the word in "war games," "the game of life," "the game of power politics," and so on. In comparing those things which we call games in this way Wittgenstein finds what he calls "family resemblances"—that is "similarities, relationships, and a whole series of them at that." [16] What we have not found is some defining characteristics which appear in every use of "game." Instead, games form a family in a way much like "the various resemblances between members of a family: build, features, colour of eyes, gait, temperament, etc. etc. overlap and criss-cross. . . ." [17] Nowell-Smith seems to have found that "good" is used in many different ways, and that while there is no one element, not even commending, which is common to all of them, these uses do have family resemblances.

Some philosophers have suggested that Hare was misled into identifying one central use of "good" because he paid too much attention to those instances in which moral judgments resembled commands. It is true that sometimes we do give moral advice to another person, and in such contexts our advice may function very much like a command. "You ought not to write in books which belong to the library," seems very similar to the command, "Don't write in books which belong to the library!" R. B. Braithwaite, a Cambridge philosopher, has suggested that the more primary use of moral language involves my own subscription to a moral policy, and that in this respect it resembles affirmations as to the truth of factual statements or beliefs about the world. When I utter my moral principles, I am declaring that I will play my part in attempting to follow these principles in my own life. And in this sense Braithwaite finds subscriptions to moral policy analogous to confessions of belief: "Just as I cannot tell anyone to believe something without knowing what it is to believe it myself, so I cannot tell anyone to do something (or play his part in doing something) without knowing what it is to do it myself (or to play my part in doing it)." [18] According to this position, it is erroneous to suggest that subscriptions to moral policies are like imperatives; rather, they function like declarations of intention or resolution.

There is still much work to be done in the investigation by philosophers of the uses and functions of moral language. For our purposes, however, we have said enough about the nature of this inquiry. We have on several occasions noted that these philosophers claim that moral judgments must be based on good reasons, and that they must be universalizable. But exactly what counts as a good reason for arriving at a particular moral judgment? How does one justify one's moral stance? Let us see how some of the analytic philosophers reply to these troublesome questions.

Toulmin's Good Reasons for Moral Judgments Recently analytic philosophers have turned from describing how value words are actually used to describing what is the nature of a moral argument. This development arises quite naturally from their concern to describe the use of value words, for one cannot describe the use of terms such as "good," "right," and "ought" unless one pays attention to the context in which these words are used. Hence, it becomes important to study not only isolated sentences in which value words appear, but to look at the whole context in which these sentences fit into actual discussions. Obviously, a complete contextual analysis of the use of value words would then include social and psychological aspects of human behavior, as well as linguistic performances. The reader may discover, therefore, that in the remainder of this chapter he is on more familiar ground, since in searching for good reasons to justify moral judgments, we shall find that we are in fact dealing with matters of great significance.

Stephen Toulmin was one of the first philosophers of our century to maintain that the central question in ethics is "What is a good reason for a particular ethical conclusion?"[19] The search for a definition, or even for a central use of ethical terms, was misguided because the main concern of ethics is not with the use of ethical language but rather with what should count as a justifiable reason for one ethical conclusion rather than another. Toulmin suggests that philosophers had failed to deal with this central issue largely because they were under the spell of regarding reasoning as confined to only logic, mathematics, and the sciences. Under the influence of the Cambridge philosopher John Wisdom, Toulmin proposed that if we actually look at the various contexts of human activity we shall find that in many circumstances, other than those of logic and science, we specify some reasons as good (or valid) and others as bad (or invalid). No teacher of mathematics would accept as a good reason for my giving a certain answer to a problem my saying that I copied it from the answer book. He would want to see what steps I used in accordance with mathematical procedure to get the answer. Likewise, we should not accept as a good reason from a football coach who drilled his men to the point of exhaustion that he just liked to see his men do this sort of thing. But we would be inclined to consider as a good reason his statement that his men would be in better physical condition when they played their first game as a result of this intensive training, and that therefore they would play to the best of their abilities when the season started. To use an illustration closer to our interest in ethics, we should not consider the following a good reason for opposing socialized medicine: "It is fashionable to oppose this kind of thing today." We should, however, consider a statement that socialized medicine tended to break down the personal relationship between a doctor and his patients to be a good reason. Of course, we might question whether in fact this belief itself is warranted, and we should ask for other reasons as well. It is a point of great significance, however, that in many contexts of ordinary life we consider some kinds of reasons worthy of acceptance and others not.

Are there any criteria for what count as good reasons in moral arguments? Toulmin insists that the study of ethics must begin by realizing that any community must have some rules of behavior, otherwise the community could not continue to exist. Our moral judgments function within a communal context, and if we bear this in mind, we shall discover that in our society we do consider some reasons as good reasons, while we consider others as bad reasons, for justifying particular moral actions. Toulmin finds, therefore, that there are in general two main types of reasoning within moral contexts: (1) that concerned with the rightness of a particular act, and (2) that concerned with the justice of an existing social practice. As an example of the first type he considers how one would justify the keeping of a promise, such as a promise made to Smith to repay the money I had previously borrowed from him. I could justify my keeping my promise in this particular case by citing that it was an instance of the general practice of promise-keeping, which is accepted by my society as a good social practice. Beyond that I could not go. Toulmin, thus, is in accord with the deontologists, whom we mentioned in the previous chapter, in holding that good reasons for performing a particular act are found by showing that it is an instance of an accepted practice.

What is one to do, however, when one faces a conflict between two accepted social practices? Toulmin suggests that in such cases we should have to estimate the probable consequences of our acting in one way rather than another. This kind of case then would be justified by an appeal to the arguments teleologists have offered. Thus, if I had promised to repay Smith the money I had borrowed from him by Saturday afternoon, but in the meantime circumstances arise which impose another duty upon me, such as my aiding an injured person at the scene of an accident, I would justify my aiding the injured person on the grounds that this act was likely to bring about the best consequences.

It is very likely that most of the moral decisions we have to make could be defended in the ways Toulmin has already sketched. But what am I to do if I defend my act by saying it is an instance of an accepted social practice, or in terms of the probable consequences, and someone still insists that these reasons are not adequate? What more can I do to answer such a skeptical person? Toulmin holds that within the limits of my moral code, the one accepted by my community, there is no more that I can do. I have given all the good reasons which I could give.

The reader could well protest at this point that sometimes one does question the accepted moral code of his community. One can ask, "Is this practice of promise-keeping really morally right?" Toulmin does not deny that such questions do in fact arise, but insists that there is no way of answering them within a particular moral code. What is at issue in these cases is the justice of an existing social practice or moral principle. Thus, this is an example of the second kind of moral reasoning which

Toulmin discusses. What I can do if promise-keeping as a practice is called into question is to offer a justification in terms of not inflicting avoidable suffering, of producing the least conflict of interests, of this practice being in the long run harmoniously satisfying, etc. Ultimately, the most that I could do would be to specify the whole way of life of which promise-keeping is a part. After I have done that, it is a personal decision for each individual as to whether or not he accepts this way of life as better than alternatives which could be proposed. At this point the giving of reasons would have come to an end.[20]

Toulmin maintains that there is a special kind of inference, "evaluative inference," which he finds justifies passing from ethically neutral facts to moral conclusions.[21] While Toulmin is not clear as to what exactly this evaluative principle of inference is, it appears that he does identify it with what he calls the function of ethics: "to correlate our feelings and behaviour in such a way as to make the fulfillment of everyone's aims and desires as far as possible compatible."[22] Thus, one would justify the practice of promise-keeping by pointing out that keeping promises is conducive to social welfare, and therefore this provides a good reason for the practice. But Toulmin himself explains what he has in mind:

> Of course, 'This practice would involve the least conflict of interests attainable under the circumstances' does not *mean* the same as 'This would be the right practice'; nor does 'This way of life would be more harmoniously satisfying' *mean* the same as 'This would be better.' But in each case, the first statement is *a good reason* for the second: the 'ethically neutral' fact is *a good reason* for the 'gerundive' moral judgement. If the adoption of the practice would genuinely reduce conflicts of interest, it is a practice *worthy of adoption*, and if the way of life would genuinely lead to deeper and more consistent happiness, it is one *worthy of pursuit*. And this seems so natural and intelligible, when one bears in mind the function of ethical judgements, that, if anyone asks me *why* they are 'good reasons,' I can only reply by asking in return, 'What better kinds of reason could you want?'[23]

There is little doubt that Toulmin's presentation of what count as good reasons in arriving at ethical decisions does reflect the way most of us would attempt to justify our moral decisions, if we are called upon to do so. Toulmin claimed to be doing meta-ethics, that is, he said he was exploring the logic of good reasons for ethical conclusions, and not actually advocating any specific normative ethical system. It appears, however, that he has presupposed a utilitarian normative ethical theory in his analysis. Toulmin's good reasons for adopting a practice are that the practice would involve the least conflict of interests and be harmoniously satisfying. But is this not to plead for a particular kind of normative ethics? One could indeed reject Toulmin's good reasons, and in doing so

Conflict of Ideals

would not be violating any rules of sound moral reasoning. R. M. Hare, in his review of Toulmin's book, suggests that the following debate might well ensue concerning Toulmin's good reasons for a practice:

> Suppose that someone were disputing this, by saying, 'Without conflict, the full development of manhood is impossible; therefore it is a bad reason for calling a practice right to say that it would involve the least conflict of interests.' We might reply, as Mr. Toulmin does here, 'This seems so natural and intelligible. . . . What better kinds of reason could you want?'. And if we said this, and the other man replied, 'I don't find it natural or intelligible at all; it seems to me that the development of manhood is a cause superior to all others, and provides the only good reason for any moral conclusion,' then it would be clear that what was dividing us was a moral difference.[24]

If Hare is correct, then Toulmin's rule of inference for ethical judgments is actually a moral judgment itself. The general rule which Toulmin uses to justify a moral practice seems at first glance to be adequate for most moral arguments, but perhaps it appears so because it is really a restatement of the general moral principle most of us accept: so act as to bring about the greatest happiness or welfare for the greatest number of people. This is, of course, the basic principle of utilitarianism—a normative ethical theory.

Hare is also concerned with investigating the nature of moral arguments, but, unlike Toulmin, he maintains that it is impossible to arrive at a moral conclusion unless one begins with at least one evaluative premise. In order to better understand Hare's contention as to what he thinks Toulmin is really doing let us put his argument in syllogistic form:

> *Major premise:* Practices worthy of adoption genuinely reduce conflicts of interest.
> *Minor premise:* This is a practice which genuinely reduces conflicts of interest.
> *Conclusion:* Therefore, this practice is worthy of adoption.[25]

Clearly nothing is wrong with the reasoning here, but one has not gone from ethically neutral facts to an evaluative conclusion, but has instead clearly stated his normative principle in his major premise. Hence, in Toulmin's case, it seems justifiable to conclude that his analysis of metaethics is actually not a neutral one, but is rather based upon assuming that the normative ethical theory of utilitarianism is correct. Rejection of Toulmin's good reasons for an ethical decision might then be based upon rejecting the normative ethical theory he is assuming to be the correct one. W. D. Ross had maintained that utilitarianism is an inadequate moral theory since it does not take account of the various obligations which we may have to other people because of some previous acts, such as the prima facie duties of fidelity and gratitude.[26] John Rawls and

David Lyons have also suggested that utilitarianism does not adequately account for our moral principle of justice as fair play.[27] Justice involves a fundamental respect for persons, and it is not at all clear that we would morally approve satisfying Toulmin's criterion of reducing the conflict of interests if in doing so we had to, for example, imprison or execute a small dissident minority group. The very fact that these suggestions give us pause, would seem to show that Toulmin has not given the only criteria which we could accept for good reasons in moral arguments.

Hare's Analysis of a Moral Argument   We have been concerned throughout this book with the various ideals which compete for acceptance in our present Western world. We are now ready to ask how a professional analytic philosopher would want to deal with the basic issues which we have examined in the previous chapters. In order to stress the kind of approach used by contemporary professional philosophers, we shall concentrate upon that method developed by R. M. Hare, who has devoted much of his recent writing to those issues of moral ideals which we have been considering.

R. M. Hare in his recent book, *Freedom and Reason*, has presented the most sustained treatment of the nature of moral argument by any of the analytic philosophers. In addition, he shows how this kind of an argument would actually function in debates with a Nazi or with a white segregationist. In this respect his treatment of the roles which the facts and the logic of moral reasoning play in such debates may be of considerable practical importance to the reader in his own attempts to choose between competing moral principles or life styles. Let us see to what extent Hare's analysis will be of help to us.

Hare maintains that there are two basic rules of moral reasoning. In a particular case in which I am trying to decide what I ought to do, I am looking for an action to which I could commit myself; that is, in Hare's view, I am looking for a *prescription* to which I could subscribe in this particular situation. If I am really engaged in moral reasoning, however, I realize that more is involved than just considering myself in my own unique situation at the time. Hence, I should also ask whether or not I am prepared to recognize the action which I have committed myself to as one which exemplifies a principle of moral action which could be prescribed for all other persons in relevantly similar situations. This is Hare's principle of *universalizability*, which he holds is a primary characteristic of moral reasoning. Hare makes this point very explicit:

If, when we consider some proposed action, we find that, when universalized, it yields prescriptions which we cannot accept, we reject this action as a solution to our moral problem—if we cannot universalize the prescription, it cannot become an 'ought.' [28]

These basic rules of moral reasoning, however, do not by themselves give one any definite answers to perplexing moral problems. Rather, Hare claims that they are the formal criteria which one ought to apply in order to discover whether or not his proposed action could be morally justified. One of the hallmarks of a decision really being a moral one, rather than one of personal preference or privilege, is whether you would be willing that anyone else, in a situation which was as similar to yours as it could possibly be, would be justified in acting the same way that you have decided to act. Hare's universalization principle of moral reasoning does not require that anyone ever be in exactly the same situation you are in, but it does require that if anyone ever were in a similar situation, then you should be willing to justify that person's acting in the same way you have chosen to act.

In using Hare's universalization principle there would be little difficulty in your justifying telling a lie in order to save a life. You could, for example, justify lying to a killer who was looking for his intended victim, because this is an action which could be universalized. You are not justifying lying under all and any circumstances, but rather are specifying the circumstances which in any case like the one you face would justify the telling of a lie. Or to put it another way, in such a situation you would have a good reason for lying, and this would be quite different from lying whenever you felt like it, or whenever you stood to gain from lying. If you sought to justify your lying in order to gain a promotion, and you specified that there were no unusual circumstances in the case, other than your desiring the promotion, then you would quite likely recognize that there was no moral justification available for your action. For if you applied the universalization principle, you would have to also commend anyone else who lied in order to obtain a promotion, and Hare does not think that this would yield a prescription which you could accept. Thus, if we give as complete a description of the situation as possible, and use Hare's method of universal prescriptivity, there will be some limitation placed upon what we would call moral justifications for our actions.

In our discussion we have already in using some brief illustrations touched upon the other elements which Hare finds in moral arguments: the facts of the case, our inclinations, and our use of imagination. In many instances, the moral argument may terminate when the persons in the dispute come to agree on the facts of the case. A. J. Ayer, you may recall, insisted that most so-called moral arguments were really about facts and were not disputes about ultimate value judgments at all. In some cases, we revise our previous condemnation of someone if we come to find that there were some relevant facts which we had not known or had not considered when we first made our moral judgment. Let us consider a simple illustration of this point. You may condemn a friend who was supposed to meet you on a street corner to go shopping because he did not arrive on time. Your justification is as follows: "He promised to be here at 10 o'clock, and he is already twenty minutes late. He ought to keep his promises. It is a bad trait not to be punctual." You decide to wait a few minutes longer, however, and finally your friend rushes up to you, out of breath, and says, "My car broke down on my way downtown, and I had a terrible time getting a garage to repair it. I am sorry I am so late." Although you might still be somewhat annoyed, you would most likely withdraw your initial condemnation of his failure to arrive on time. He couldn't help that his car broke down, and in most cases, you would accept this fact as a justifying excuse for his being late and as a reason for revising the moral judgment you had made previously.

The facts of the case and the logic of moral language will only go so far, however, in solving moral arguments, and in many cases this is not enough. Hare suggests that many perplexing moral arguments can reach satisfactory conclusions only if the persons in the dispute share similar inclinations. Hare, even though he claims to be doing meta-ethics, does not hesitate to build his case for these moral arguments upon his supposition that human inclinations are roughly the same. His assumptions about human inclinations are rather minimal, however, and are likely correct. He maintains that very few people, if any, would want to be afflicted with avoidable pain or suffering. Hence, he holds that "people's inclinations about most of the important matters in life tend to be the same (very few people, for example, like being starved or run over by motorcars). . . ." [29] Assuming that he has good warrant for holding that our inclinations about most of the important things in life are the same, the only other relevant factor to a moral argument is the use of a cultivated imagination. We can with practice build up our powers of sympathy and imagination so that we can imagine what it would be like to be the other person. We could imagine what it would be like to be a member of a minority group, and this might aid us in making better value judgments. It is a point of great significance that many of our moral arguments could be more clearly stated if we paid sufficient attention to all these four factors which Hare discusses. Whether or not they could all be solved satisfactorily, however, is another question.

The pattern of moral argument which Hare has sketched works best when we are faced with conflicts between interests when ideals are not involved. It is important to recall that Hare maintains that no moral argument ensues if one merely intends to follow his own inclinations without any consideration of the interests of others who might be affected by his action. The first step which takes such a self-seeking man toward moral reasoning at all is that he finds himself unwilling "to prescribe universally that people's likes and dislikes should be disregarded by other people, because this would entail prescribing that other people should disregard his own likes and dislikes." [30] Thus, when one is faced with a problem in which what he wants to do would interfere with the interests of other people, he would not ignore the desires and inclinations of the other persons if he were reasoning morally. Suppose, for example, you wanted to sing at the top of your lungs late at night while your wife, who is a light sleeper, was trying to fall asleep. In cases such as this, Hare suggests that a form of the golden-rule argument, "One ought to treat others as one would wish them to treat oneself," [31] or a reasoned application of the utilitarian principle which would consider the interests of all the persons involved, could adequately resolve the moral dispute.

Hare does not by any means suggest that the application of the utilitarian principle to moral disputes of this kind will always yield an easy answer. Rather, applying the utilitarian principle means "that everyone is entitled to equal consideration, and that if it is said that two people ought to be treated differently, some difference must be cited as the ground for these different moral judgements." [32] The major source of difficulty in actually solving a moral argument involving conflicting interests may lie in specifying what differences are to count as relevant and which are not relevant. This will require actually exploring in one's imagination what it would be like to have the roles reversed. To return to our simple illustration, how would you like it if you were trying to fall asleep, and your wife began singing as loudly as she could? This apparently trivial example could easily be complicated, however, if you were a professional singer and had to rehearse a difficult song. Supposing that you were the breadwinner of the family, and that you had no other time or place to practice, then you might claim that there was a relevant difference which could justify your singing while your wife was trying to sleep. You might then claim that the best interests of both your wife and yourself would be better served if you practiced your singing that night.

Hare admits that not all moral disputes could be solved by using the method which he proposes. It is especially with conflicting ideals of human excellence that Hare believes his four-fold pattern of moral argumentation would not succeed. We have been concerned in this book with describing alternative ideals which are live options for contemporary Western man, and it now appears as though even Hare's position will not give us any help in choosing between them. Beyond suggesting that many of the ideals of human excellence which we find in our culture, such as sincerity, honesty, etc., could be justified by their utilitarian or pragmatic consequences, Hare claims that we must recognize an inevitable pluralism in human ideals which is not likely to ever be eliminated. Hence, the moral philosopher ought not to try to find a method for solving disputes between upholders of different ideals in all cases. Hare makes this point in the following passage:

Suppose, for example, that one man has the ideals of an ascetic and another those of a *bon vivant*. Is it at all likely that moral arguments between them will be such as to compel one of them to adopt the other's point of view—assuming that neither is, by pursuing his own ideal, affecting one way or another the interests of other parties? The moral philosopher who thinks that he is failing his public if he does not provide a logic for settling such questions, would do well to ask almost any member of the public whether he *expects* them ever to be settled.[33]

Thus, Hare maintains that one could admit that there can be many life styles, all of which are good. The life of an athlete, a scholar, a monk, a devoted family man, a statesman, etc., all center upon somewhat differing ideals of what it is to be a good man. But there is no danger here, for these kinds of lives are not incompatible with the interests of other people. Thus, if we are faced with a conflict of personal ideals, where the interests of others are not involved, Hare does not think that much could be accomplished by moral argument. There are different ideals of what it is to be a good man, and Hare seems to agree with the existentialists that in this choice of a basic life style very little in the way of logical argument can be used. One must in the last analysis choose his own personal ideals; moral reasoning can only limit him to the extent of suggesting that he ought not to ride roughshod over the interests and desires of others in affirming his own ideal of a good life.

What happens, however, when there is a conflict between ideals and interests? Hare claims that "it would indeed be a scandal if no arguments could be brought against a person who, in pursuit of his own ideals, trampled ruthlessly on other people's interests, including that interest which consists in the freedom to pursue varying ideals." [34] Suppose someone seriously believed, "All people ought to be scholars. It is the only really justifiable way of being fully human." If this person actually tried to force his ideal upon others to the neglect of all persons' desires and interests, including his own, he would then become a fanatic, in the sense in which Hare uses this term. We could then bring into our debate with this fanatic his trampling upon the desires of other people who did not want to become scholars, and who held different personal ideals for their lives. In short, we would try to "reason" with him.

Conflicts of ideals rarely involve a scholar professing his ideal as the only worthy goal for all men in opposition to an athlete who claims that athletic prowess is the only worthy ideal at which anyone ought to aim. Instead, they are frequently concerned with very serious and basic beliefs as to what constitutes the preeminently best type of man, or what society would be preeminently best. Kierkegaard's conception of the best man as the religious man who was constantly choosing to become a Christian is radically in opposition to Fromm's belief that an ideal man should develop into being fully productive through realizing his potentialities. One who sought to defend Fromm's position against a Kierkegaardian might talk for a long time, but very likely he would not convert his opponent. However, it is not likely that either of these two individuals would try to force their ideals upon all mankind; clearly Kierkegaard himself did not try to do so, and Fromm is not trying to do so either. They both would agree that the individual must choose his own life style. Naturally, each would try to convince other persons that his way of life reflected the best ideal for them to pursue. Nevertheless, they both would firmly maintain that it would be wrong to forcefully compel anyone to become either a Christian or a humanist. In this sense, both positions hold to a more basic ideal of a liberal society in which the individual is given a great deal of freedom of choice concerning his personal ideals. Hence, one who held to Kierkegaard's image for man could live side by side with a humanist, very much as in our present society scholars and athletes both acknowledge other ideals for life than their own, although naturally they prefer the life they have themselves chosen to follow.

Not all conflicts of ideals take place within a liberal context where tolerance of the viewpoint of others is considered to be a paramount virtue. It is in these difficult cases that Hare finds his greatest challenge. Hare maintains that the chief cause of the Second World War was a conflict of ideals between the liberal democracies and Nazism. If the conflict had been merely between their different national interests, a reconciliation might have been achieved through bargaining and compromise. But the very basis of the conflict was "the fact that the Nazis' ideals of man and society were utterly different from those of, for example, liberal Englishmen or Americans." [35] At issue were irreconcilable ideals: "The Nazis thought a certain kind of society and a certain kind of man pre-eminently good—and it was a kind of man and of society which liberals, with their different ideals, could not but abhor." [36] In this case we were not faced with ideals which tolerated each other; instead we were faced with the ideals of the Nazis which because of the nature of their ideals were pursued in defiance of the interests and ideals of others. Is violence inevitable in such cases, or do we have any type of argument left with which we can combat ideals which are like those of the Nazis?

Granting that the Nazi and the liberal have conflicting ideals, Hare insists that we could carry on a moral argument with a Nazi since the Nazi's ideals conflicted with the desires and interests of other people. As long as the Nazi merely believed that the Jews were inferior, but did nothing in his actions to interfere with them, this line of argument would not be available. The moment, however, that the Nazi began systematically to exterminate the Jews we could show that in pursuing his own ideal he was riding roughshod over the interests of others. We could attempt to get him to see that if he is exterminating Jews on the basis of a professed ideal, that he must logically be willing to agree that anyone with the characteristics which he condemns in Jews should also be exterminated. If he is a real fanatic, an appeal to facts which would not confirm any significant difference between Jews and Aryans might not get us very far, for he would simply claim that he had other "facts" to show that the Jews were inferior and should be exterminated for the good of his country. Nevertheless, we should do our best to bring forth any factual evidence we could get. Our best move, according to Hare, would be to get him to admit that he was expressing a *universal prescriptive* judgment that anyone who had the characteristics of Jews should be exterminated. Then, according to the logical use of moral language, "it follows that, if he is sincere and clear-headed, he desires that he himself should be exterminated if he were to come to have the characteristics of Jews." [37] We then could trick the Nazi by claiming that we had in fact uncovered evidence to prove that he was adopted by the persons whom he now believes to be his parents, but that there is a birth certificate available to prove that he is the child of two pure Jews. We produce the birth certificate in question, and present him with other evidence to support our allegation that he himself is really a Jew. We also produce evidence to prove that his wife is a pure Jew. What then would his response be?

> Is he at all likely to say—as he logically can say—'All right then, send me and all my family to Buchenwald!'? And then let us imagine saying to him, 'That was only a deception; the evidence we produced was forged. But now, having really faced this possibility, do you still think as you used to about the extermination of Jews?' [38]

The basis for the success of Hare's maneuver in this example rests upon his assumption that the inclinations and interests of human beings about the major aspects of life are the same. Few, if any, people would want to be sent to a gas chamber. Therefore, if the Nazis could have really imagined themselves in the situation of the Jew, few of them would have been able to maintain their ideals as universal prescriptions. If some Nazi could still, after having gone through the above imaginary episode, have held to his ideals and said, "Let me be taken to the gas chamber," then he would really have been a fanatic, and no rational or moral argument would be able to get him to change his mind. Fortunately, as Hare points out, there appear to be very few persons in the world who would hold to such ideals even when they went against their own desires and interests. It is this fact about human nature which permits moral argument when one's pursuit of his ideals conflicts with the interests and desires of others.

Much of Hare's moral argument rests upon his defense of the liberal ideal of life as superior to other ideals, and in this sense, he is defending a particular normative ethical theory. Despite the fact that Hare is primarily interested in the logic and language of morals, he does not shrink from dealing with substantive issues of normative ethics. He does so, however, with great clarity because he has first of all tried to understand how ethical arguments function in the context of a community. The liberal is sometimes accused of not having any ideals, of simply adopting a live-and-let-live attitude. Hare maintains that this is unjust because although the liberal may profess some ideals as to what would be preeminently good in a man or in a society, "he *respects* the ideals of others as he does his own." [39] He need not share the ideals of others, but he recognizes their right to hold to them, and in fact to pursue them, unless in so doing they interfere with other people pursuing their own interests and ideals. Or to put the same point in another way, the liberal holds to the ideal of tolerance.

We shall never reach universal agreement upon all moral ideals and principles, if for no other reason than Hare believes there will always be some fanatics who by the use of propaganda and force will seek to propagate their views. The best weapon against such fanatics is clear thinking, and this it is the primary job of the philosopher to promote. The main task of the moral philosopher, according to Hare, is to help people recognize confused thinking, persuasive reasoning, and twisted facts when they encounter them. Hare puts the case for the study of meta-ethics as follows:

If a person understands clearly what he is doing when he is asking a moral question and answering it, and understands just how facts enter into moral arguments; if he is able to distinguish genuine facts from those 'facts' which are really concealed evaluations; if, in short, he is clear-headed enough to stick to the moral question that he is asking and to set about answering it in the way that its nature demands; then the propagandist will have little power over him. To arm people in this way against propaganda is the function of moral philosophy. [40]

Hare devoted the last chapter of his book to illustrating how his fourfold scheme of moral reasoning could be brought to bear upon the conflict between races, especially when one race claims that the other is not entitled to equal treatment simply because of the color of their skin. We can only summarize his general argument, and recommend that the reader study Hare's book itself in order to discover the wealth of insight which he brings to this issue. Hare uses the same technique which we have sketched him employing against the Nazi: (1) What are the facts? Does scientific evidence show that there are basic differences in the nature or abilities of persons who belong to different races? (2) If one is seriously maintaining a universal prescription to the effect that all the members of a certain race should be treated differently than the members of one's own race, does he realize that this principle would apply to him if he were a member of that race? (3) With one's desires and inclinations being what they are, could one want to be treated in the way that he wishes the members of the minority race to be treated? (4) Lastly, Hare suggests a means of appealing to the imagination of race baiters which should show them that they are entertaining a prejudice rather than a serious evaluative judgment in claiming that members of one race are not entitled to the same equal treatment as the members of other races. Suppose that you are arguing with a person who advocates white supremacy. If he is at all rational and imaginative, ask him to imagine that some scientist has discovered a bacillus which he plans to release into the air. The bacillus is harmless except that everyone who is infected by it finds that his skin color is changed from white to black, or vice versa. When the person with whom you are arguing has thought about the implications of this imaginary event, you might then ask if he still maintains that skin color is a sufficient criterion for moral discrimination. As Hare remarks:

> It is unlikely that he will go on saying that it is; for then he will have to say that if he catches the disease the former blacks who have also had it will have acquired the right to oppress *him*, and all his formerly white friends.[41]

Hare generalizes the principle which he is using here so that it would in fact apply to our maltreatment of animals as well as to racial discrimination:

> In all cases the principle is the same—am I prepared to accept a maxim which would allow this to be done to me, were I in the position of this man or animal, and capable of having only the experiences, desires, etc., of him or it? [42]

Of course, if the advocate of white supremacy is really fanatical, even this kind of reasoning will not move him to change his position. We have then, according to Hare, reached the end of moral reasoning, and may have to resort to persuasion and legislation in order that the interests of other people will not be trampled upon by such a fanatic. In the last analysis, just as we cannot prevent people from having eccentric desires, so we cannot rationally get them to abandon their fanatical ideals. But we can show them the price which they have to pay for adhering to their fanatical ideals—that they must be willing to sacrifice even their own basic desires and inclinations in order that their ideals will be fulfilled. Hare does not believe that many men would be willing to pay this high price. In the last analysis, however, Hare agrees with the existentialists in maintaining that the ultimate moral ideals we adopt are the result of our own free choices or decisions. Reason may help us eliminate some alternative ideals, but it cannot itself show us which of the remaining ones we should adopt.

Toward an Evaluation of Meta-ethics We have noticed that recent analytic philosophers have been concerned with examining the various different uses of value expressions, and have generally abandoned the search for an equivalent definition of such terms. However, there are still some philosophers who claim that value terms can be defined, and some of them even maintain that they can be defined naturalistically. Sometimes they justify this belief by claiming that G. E. Moore held far too restrictive a notion as to what a definition had to be. In the exact sense of equivalence it may be that only logical tautologies would qualify. Therefore, naturalists suggest that a correct analysis and explication of a value term should be considered a definition if it helps us to understand what the term being defined means. Naturalists, then, can continue their search for a definition of "good" which can be given in terms of psychological and sociological concepts. Whether any suggested naturalistic definition of "good" is adequate must then be determined by examining the definition itself. This would be a more empirical approach than to rule out all naturalistic definitions in advance as Moore did with his open question argument.

Under the influence of the later Wittgenstein and the Oxford philosophers, however, we have seen that most analytic treatments of ethics have been more concerned with discovering how value terms are actually used, than with attempting to frame adequate definitions for them. In this kind of an investigation we have been reminded that we should actually look and see how we use value terms, in what contexts and for what purposes. But there doesn't seem to be agreement among these philosophers either. Hare finds that the central use of "good" is to commend for the purpose of guiding our choices, while Nowell-Smith suggests that there are many other evaluative uses of the term which cannot be accommodated to this primary usage. This type of investigation is still continuing, however, and it may prove to be far more fruitful than it has been thus far. At any rate, it has already been very helpful in pointing out the many different ways in which we use value expressions. These analytic philosophers have provided analyses of the use of "good" in non-moral contexts which seem to be basically correct. We would agree, when we say that a pencil, a sports car, or a steak is good, that we are referring to certain descriptive characteristics of the objects cited as reasons for calling them good ones. When we come to moral uses of value terms, however, some philosophers have claimed that meta-ethicists were actually analyzing language in terms of a normative ethical theory which they had unconsciously presupposed. Their meta-ethical theories may not be as neutral as their defenders have claimed. We have seen, that in the case of Toulmin, the final reasons he gave for justifying a practice are utilitarian ones. Hare has, however, shown that one could reject these reasons if he held that certain ideals of manliness were to be placed higher in one's normative scale than utilitarian considerations.

Hare, however, has also been accused of identifying the language of morals with the normative ethical system of a liberal open society. He has replied to this charge that his analysis wrote into the nature of the logic of moral language features which reflected his own moral attitudes. In defending the neutrality of his meta-ethical theory, he said:

> But it is simply not true that the things which I have said about the logic of moral language are peculiarly tied to any particular moral standpoint. To say that moral and other value-judgements are prescriptive and universalizable is not, by that alone, to commit oneself to any particular moral opinion. By allowing that a sufficiently fanatical Nazi, who was really prepared to immolate himself in the service of his ideal, could not be touched by my arguments, I at least guarded myself against *this* allegation. Although I am a liberal and a protestant, what I have said about moral language could be accepted by somebody who was as illiberal and as counter-reformationary as could be. For example, the judgement that one ought always to do exactly what is said by a person in a clerical collar (or wearing a badge of superior military rank), no matter what it is, can be a prescriptive and universal judgement; yet it is not likely to be accepted by liberals or protestants.[43]

As he continues his defense, Hare maintains that there is absolutely no content for a moral prescription which is ruled out by the logic or language of morals. "What circumscribes the moral prescriptions that the non-fanatic can accept is, on my theory . . . the desires and inclinations of the human race."[44]

It is extremely important that we understand exactly what it is which Hare is claiming to do. In the first place, he wants to separate that which his study of meta-ethics has found to be characteristic of rational moral judgments, universal prescriptivity, from his own application of this principle to actual moral arguments. Anyone in applying the principle must put some content into it, based on psychological and normative assumptions, but that does not by any means show that the principle itself assumes a particular moral standpoint. If someone is seriously troubled by a moral issue, then Hare's method of universal prescriptivity gives him a minimal framework in terms of which he can explore alternative answers to his problem. If the person using Hare's method has different assumptions about human nature, if he is not committed to a liberal society which holds to the ideal of tolerance, then it is very likely that he will not get the same answers to moral problems as Hare would get. What Hare was mainly concerned with showing was that his principle of universal prescriptivity provides a very useful device by which one can determine if he is really holding to a moral judgment, or is engaged in special pleading.

The reader may, nevertheless, still be troubled. He may recall that the existentialists and the defenders of situation ethics appear to deny the relevance, in the last analysis, of any principles to moral decisions. They do so largely on the grounds that no two situations are ever exactly alike. The claim is made that relevant factors which should always be considered are that different persons are involved, that circumstances are never exactly the same, and so on. Therefore, the hallmark of an ethical decision for the existentialist seems to be that one has made an authentic or a free choice, while the Christian situation ethicists stress that one must apply love directly to the particular persons in the special circumstances in which he finds himself. Surely, the reader may conclude, Hare must have failed to consider existentialism when he proposed that the hallmark of a rational moral judgment was universal prescriptivity. It would appear, therefore, that Hare's proposal as to the formal conditions of a moral judgment must be unacceptable to one who has committed himself to existentialism or to situation ethics.

There are serious problems, however, for any ethic which insists that each situation is so unique that no comparisons can justifiably be made with any other situation. For how could one then distinguish between a moral question and a question of self-interest? Hare does not have to deny that each situation is unique. He could admit that no two situations ever were exactly alike in each and every last detail. The significant disagreement between a radical existentialist and Hare arises from Hare's claim that not all the details of a situation are relevant to a moral argument. The pattern of moral argument which Hare describes is designed to help one discover which factors of a particular situation one would be willing to claim were morally relevant. If a proposed action is specified in all the relevant details, then Hare claimed that one who committed himself to that action as morally right, should also have to recognize that he would have to commend the same action as right for anyone else who might ever be in a similar situation. Hare makes a great deal of the fact that it is irrelevant to his argument that one will never find himself on the receiving end of his proposed action. That is why he stresses the cultivation of a sympathetic imagination so that one could imagine what it would be like if one were in the other fellow's shoes. One who sub-scribes to Hare's principle of universal prescriptivity does not deny that circumstances alter cases, instead he insists that the circumstances must be spelled out in all the relevant aspects so that one can begin the task of seeking a solution to his particular moral problem. Thus, as we have noted in our discussion of Hare, one can justify lying in order to save a human life, not only in one particular case, but in all other cases which would be similar in the relevant respects.

We found that the existentialists stressed that we should make authentic choices, but gave us little guidance as to how we could determine what really was an authentic choice. The situation ethicists also reminded us that general rules of proverbial morality do not seem to really fit many of the moral problems which individuals face in their daily lives. But how can we decide whether we are following the lead of *agapē* or sentimentality? The reader may find that Hare's principle of prescriptive universality is exactly what he needs to supplement an existentialist ethic of responsible choice, or a Christian ethic of *agapē*.

One ought not to assume, however, that the application of Hare's principle of universal prescriptivity to moral problems will give one quick and easy answers. What it does provide is a useful method to sort out the aspects of a moral situation which one would be willing to consider relevant from those which are irrelevant. Part of the difficulty in applying Hare's principle, however, lies in specifying precisely which circumstances involved in a particular moral problem might make this case different from other cases in which one usually applied one's moral principles without thought. Thus, while most of us would subscribe to the general moral principle that persons ought to be accorded equal treatment, we would also claim that sometimes there are reasons which would justify our modifying this principle. Surely we might justify raising the salary of one secretary more than that of another, if the one secretary were more efficient and reliable than the other, but we would not justify such unequal treatment on the grounds that one was blonde and the other brunette. In this case, what makes efficiency a relevant ground for unequal treatment, and not the color of hair? The answer, if one applied Hare's method of moral reasoning, would be that one could will prescriptively to universalize salary increments based upon efficiency, but not those which were based merely upon the color of hair. Thus, Hare's method provides one with a way to determine which differences in a particular situation are relevant to a moral argument.

We have concentrated thus far upon Hare's principle of universal prescriptivity, but we should also glance at some of the other assumptions which he employs when he applied this principle in moral arguments. We have seen that the great forcefulness of Hare's argument against a Nazi or a white segregationist rests upon his assumption that the desires and inclinations of all men are basically the same. Hare admits that some men do have what he calls "eccentric desires," but maintains that fortunately there are very few men who desire to be starved, to be deprived of their liberty, or to be killed. Common sense would certainly agree with him. If one challenged the validity of this assumption, one would have to produce scientific evidence from the fields of psychology, sociology and anthropology to show that Hare was not warranted in making this claim. If one could show, for example, that many men have a Freudian death-wish, which overrides their desire for living, then Hare's assumption would be unfounded.

It appears that perhaps we have come full circle, for in order to justify Hare's psychological assumption we would have to deal with the questions which concerned many of the writers we considered earlier on: What is human nature? Indeed, is there such a thing as human nature? While a study of the logic and language of moral argument may help us in making our own moral decisions, we ought not neglect studying the nature of *the man* who is actually faced with moral problems. Language is after all a social instrument; it is used to achieve certain human purposes. In studying the language of morals, philosophers have perhaps tended to neglect too much the nature and motivations of the man who was using language. They should pay at least some attention to what the social sciences are discovering about man, otherwise they may find that their extremely detailed studies do not really reflect accurately the linguistic, let alone the moral, behavior of human beings.

In his actual application of his principles of moral reasoning, Hare does not hesitate to state quite frankly that he professes the ideals of a liberal open society. He claims that moral arguments which concern the conflicts of interests between persons within a liberal society can be solved by a reasoned application of utilitarianism or the golden rule. Toulmin's theory, the reader may recall, could also be employed in any moral argument which involved conflicts of interests. While there is an important theoretical difference between Toulmin and Hare concerning how one justifies passing from the facts of the case to an evaluative conclusion, their methods of moral reasoning in these cases both rely upon utilitarian considerations. Toulmin, however, claims that moral reasoning is appropriate only in those cases where one is concerned with a conflict of interests. Unless one is prepared to abandon a principle he now holds when he finds that it conflicts with the most important interests of other persons, he is not engaging in a moral argument on Toulmin's terms. Hare, however, in maintaining that some of the most fundamental disputes concern ways of life, suggests that his method of universal prescriptivity can help one to carry on a moral argument with a person who professes a different way of life, if the interests of other people are completely disregarded by this person. It thus appears that Hare's suggestions may be of more help to us than Toulmin's in our choosing a way of life. But of how much help is Hare's method?

Hare uses the term "fanatic" to refer to one who would hold to an ideal even though he clearly saw that carrying out this ideal would interfere with the interests and desires of people, including his own interests and desires. Thus, the Nazi who would still hold that all Jews ought to be exterminated, and acted in accordance with his belief, even after he realized that if he were Jewish he too would be sent to the gas chamber, would be a fanatic. Hare also suggests that one who held to an ideal of abstract justice so strongly that he would never bend this ideal, not even to prevent injury to himself, would be a fanatic. Hare believes that human nature is such that very few, if any, persons would sincerely be able to continue living by fanatical ideals if they really thought through the implications of their claims. But is this assumption warranted? For example, sometimes we praise a person as a man of principle, a good man, because he sticks to his ideals even when living by them interferes with his own desires. Might it be that we call "fanatics" those persons who profess ideals which are different than our own, while those who live up to the ideals which we profess, we call "idealists"?

It is important that we recall that Hare claims that in a liberal society the prime ideal is tolerance of the ideals of others. We may not like the ideals of others, but we do not attempt to force them to accept our own ideals of the good life. Yet, might not even a liberal profess adherence to an ideal in a particular situation? Indeed, is not one of the hallmarks of a moral decision that one intends to carry it out, even if it goes against his own inclinations and interests? Thus, for example, I might decide to speak the truth in a particular situation even though doing so makes me unpopular, or even causes me to lose my job. Suppose that in arriving at this decision I carefully considered the interests of all the people involved, and decided that I ought to tell the truth. I would not then be considered a fanatic by Hare, because I had considered the interests of all the people involved before I decided what I ought to do. I do not on that account become a fanatic, as Hare uses the term. If, however, I held very stubbornly to the abstract ideal that one ought always to speak the truth, and never even considered what the interests of people were in actual situations, and if I also tried to force others to accept the same ideal, then, according to Hare, I would become a fanatic. Depending upon one's moral beliefs, however, one might say that even then I had not by any means become a fanatic but that I was really a good man since I lived by the principles which I professed. It now seems to be the case that one determines the difference between an idealist and a fanatic on the basis of his own moral beliefs. It would then appear that Hare, as a proponent of a liberal open society, calls "fanatics" those who in carrying out their ideals interfere with the moral principle of toleration to which he subscribes. Hare would not deny that moral arguments use moral principles, and he clearly states his own commitment to the ideals of a liberal. But could we take his argument one step farther? Is there any way whereby we could more clearly differentiate those who as men of principle tried to live up to their ideals from those whom Hare has called fanatics?

Suppose we imagine an individual who holds strongly to the ideal that one ought never use alcoholic beverages. In our present society, this does not appear to be an ideal which most people share; nevertheless, we would agree that this individual not only has the right to hold to his ideal but also that he is at liberty to try to get others to accept his ideal. He may therefore join temperance organizations, help sponsor advertisements pointing out the dangers involved in the use of alcohol, and so on. Notice, however, that if he is successful in getting a sizable number of people to give up their use of alcoholic beverages, he has interfered with the interests of the owners of the local taverns and with the interests of the stockholders of liquor companies. Even if some taverns closed because of his campaign, we would not likely accuse him of having neglected to consider the interests of others. In fact, our defender of total abstinence would most likely claim that he was trying to get people to accept his ideal precisely because it was in their best interests to do so. He might cite medical facts and sociological statistics to show the bad effects upon individuals and society of the use of alcohol. Clearly on the basis of Hare's definition, this person would not be a fanatic. Yet, it cannot be denied, he has interfered with the interests of the tavern owners. What makes this situation different from that of the Nazi or the white segregationist?

Let us vary the tactics which one might use in order to get people to accept the ideal which one professes. Perhaps by doing this we might bring our defender of total abstinence closer to the case of the Nazi. We shall assume that the methods which were used above were not successful in converting anyone to the ideal of total abstinence. Our idealist, however, becomes even more convinced than before that all people should be made to give up the use of alcohol. If people could not be made to see what they ought to do for their own best interests, then, he concludes, they must be forced to do so. He might, therefore, stand outside the local tavern and use physical force to prevent people from entering. Let us suppose, however, that even this tactic does not work. The defender of the ideal of total abstinence might then set fire to the tavern. Clearly, most of us would agree that he had now become a fanatic in the pursuit of his ideal. But where exactly did he become a fanatic? In forcefully trying to restrain people from entering the tavern? Or not until he set fire to the building? Where would you draw the line separating the fanatic from the man of high moral principles?

Our imaginary case, with its variations, might help us to see more clearly how one could differentiate an idealist from a fanatic. It is not merely that one conflicts with the interests and ideals of others in pursuing one's own ideal that makes one a fanatic. Rather it is *how* one conflicts with the interests and ideals of others. This seems to have been the point which Hare wished to make in his discussion of the Nazi. The liberal need not tolerate behavior which forcefully denies others the right to follow their own interests and ideals. Hence, in our imaginary case, we could attempt to show the defender of total abstinence that he had gone too far when he began to ride roughshod over the interests of others. We might try to show him that in pursuing his own ideal he had violated the overriding moral principle of fair play. If, however, after we have been through a careful rational argument with this person, he still justified his action by claiming that the ideal of total abstinence ought to take precedence over all people's interests, including his own, then there is no more that we could do by reason alone. This person would then have shown that he was a hard core fanatic who would not be moved from pursuing his ideal, no matter what evidence or reasons would be presented to him.

There are, nevertheless, some thorny problems which arise in trying to differentiate the extent to which one is justified in interfering with the interests of others, or, even in some cases, ignoring their interests. Hare does not intend to suggest that one can use his formula as an automatic way of answering all these problems. It is surely very helpful in a dispute with a Nazi or a white segregationist, but there are borderline cases where one may have a hard time arriving at a decision which he can justify. We should recognize that sometimes in our liberal society we justify interfering with the inclinations and ideals of some people even though these people have not themselves interfered with others pursuing their own inclinations and ideals. Consider an example which Hare himself cites. Are we justified in forcefully hospitalizing a drug addict? Should we force him to be cured even if he does not desire to be cured? If we do so, are we not forcing our ideal of what a man ought to be upon someone who has a different ideal than ours? Hare in commenting upon this kind of case states that we defend our action because "we think that this is legitimate *in the interests of the addict*." [45] He continues by pointing out that the ideal which we have of the good man and the good society is such "that it cannot be realized by a man who is a drug addict or by a society which contains such men." [46] Unlike the Nazis, however, we do not then claim that drug addicts should be exterminated because they do not share our ideal of what a good man should be like. In Hare's language, we "put a curb on our ideal where it conflicts with another's interest." [47] While most of us would agree that we ought to help the drug addict overcome his addiction, we ought not to ignore that in making this claim we are making some value judgments. We are deciding what is really in the best interests of the drug addict himself. We are maintaining that because he is an addict he is not able to make rational decisions for himself. Therefore, we justify our forcefully hospitalizing him in order that he may be rehabilitated so that he can rejoin the ranks of free men in a liberal society. It is no doubt true that sometimes we must make decisions like these, but we should make them with great care.

There is great danger in relying upon what we believe to be the best interests of other persons as a justification for a moral judgment. In doing so, we may unwittingly have provided an opening for an argument which someone who defended racial discrimination might propose. Suppose such a person claimed that it was really in the best interests of the Negroes that they be segregated. While the argument concerning the best interests of the drug addict appears similar to this one concerning the best interests of the Negro, there is an essential difference between them. In the case of this purported defense of segregation, the argument rests upon prescribing the real interests of a whole group of people simply on the basis of the color of their skin, not on the basis of anything which they have done. In the drug addict case, however, we were concerned with an individual who by his actions had become incapable of following a normal life in our society. It might even be the case that the addict in his more rational moments might himself say that it would be for his best interests if he could be cured of his addiction. But if he does not make an admission of this sort, then it seems clear that in our trying to cure him of his addiction, we are prescribing for him that he *ought* to want to be cured. If this is the basis for our decision, then we are appealing to our own ideals concerning what a man ought to be, and are not relying merely on an assumption concerning the basic similarity of the desires and inclinations of all men.

We shall propose a few more complicated cases in which we sometimes justify interfering with the freedom of others to pursue their own inclinations and ideals. In these cases some readers might find this interference to be morally justified, while others might claim that it is not justified at all. Are we morally justified in taking the children of Christian Scientists to hospitals for medical treatment, even when their parents protest that this is a violation of their basic beliefs? Are we justified in requiring the children of the Amish sect in Pennsylvania to attend school during harvest time, when the parents hold that this interferes with their best interests? Are we morally justified in prosecuting a person who uses drugs as part of a religious ritual? Are we justified in restraining a person who occasionally smokes marijuana, but who is by no means a drug addict? If one believes that his country is engaged in an unjust war, are there any limitations which he ought to place upon his protests? Would such a person be morally justified in using force to prevent the delivery of troops to the war zone? The reader can continue this list of moral problems by supplying his own examples. The outcome of an argument concerning these cases would turn, most likely, upon the reader's own moral ideals. What kind of man and society the reader considers preeminently best would emerge when he carefully considered cases like these. It is quite likely that in dealing with some of these troublesome situations one would claim that his basic ideals ought to override the interests and inclinations of people. Perhaps one might even go further than Hare allowed, however, and claim that in some situations he could give good reasons why his ideals ought to take such precedence.

While there are undoubtedly difficult borderline cases where it is difficult to make a decision, we ought not to forget that if we grant Hare's psychological assumptions about human nature, accept his moral ideal of a liberal society as the preeminently best one, and use his method of universal prescriptivity, we shall find that his pattern for a moral argument can be of great help to us in arriving at moral decisions. What we have tried to suggest is that the principle of universal prescriptivity can function in Hare's desired way only if it is applied in a context of fairness, of not arbitrarily singling out just any characteristic for the basis of a moral judgment, but of trying to specify what shall count as relevant differences between persons. Alan Gewirth suggests that one basis for determining which characteristics of men are relevant or irrelevant to ethical judgments is "the difference between the goodness of traits which men have *qua* men, and those which men have in some more restricted capacity." [48] To make these distinctions, however, presupposes a normative ethical theory which holds that all men ought to be treated alike unless there are significant differences between them. It then becomes a matter of scientific fact to discover if the supposed differences really exist, and a matter of normative ethical theory as to whether or not these differences would constitute good grounds for supporting the proposed moral judgment.

Our study of meta-ethics has provided us with a better understanding of the nature of value judgments, and of the roles which facts and reasoning play in moral arguments. Armed with these tools we are better prepared to detect specious reasoning in moral disputes. In at least this respect our study of meta-ethics has been helpful in our search for a way of life.

NOTES FOR CHAPTER VII

1 George Edward Moore, *Principia Ethica* (Cambridge, England: Cambridge University Press), 1959, p. 15.
2 *Ibid.*, ch. 1.
3 W. D. Ross, *The Right and the Good* (Oxford: Clarendon Press, 1955), *passim*; A. C. Ewing, *The Definition of Good* (New York: The Macmillan Co., 1947), *passim*; A. C. Ewing, *Second Thoughts in Moral Philosophy* (London: Routledge & Kegan Paul Ltd., 1959), *passim*.
4 Alfred Jules Ayer, *Language, Truth and Logic* (2nd ed.; New York: Dover Publications, Inc., 1950), ch. 6.
5 Charles L. Stevenson, *Ethics and Language* (New Haven: Yale University Press, 1960), *passim*; Charles L. Stevenson, *Facts and Values: Studies in Ethical Analysis* (New Haven: Yale University Press, 1964), *passim*.
6 Stephen Toulmin, *The Place of Reason in Ethics* (Cambridge, Mass.: Cambridge University Press, 1950), pp. 61–64, 189–195.
7 *Ibid.*, pp. 194–195.
8 R. M. Hare, *The Language of Morals* (Oxford: Clarendon Press, 1952), part II.
9 Quoted in Hare, *The Language of Morals*, p. 79.
10 Hare, *The Language of Morals*, p. 118.
11 *Ibid.*, p. 119.

12 See also J. O. Urmson, "On Grading," *Mind*, LIX (1950), 145–169; reprinted in Antony Flew, ed., *Logic and Language* (1st and 2nd series; Garden City, N. Y.: Doubleday Anchor Books, 1965); and in Paul W. Taylor, ed., *The Moral Judgment: Readings in Contemporary Meta-Ethics* (Englewood Cliffs, N. J.: Prentice-Hall, Inc., 1963).

13 P. H. Nowell-Smith, *Ethics* (Baltimore: Penguin Books, Inc., 1954), p. 98.

14 *Ibid.*, p. 169.

15 Ludwig Wittgenstein, *Philosophical Investigations*, trans. by G. E. M. Anscombe (2nd ed.; Oxford: Basil Blackwell, 1958, and New York: The Macmillan Co., 1958), section 66.

16 *Ibid.*, sections 66 and 67.

17 *Ibid.*, section 67.

18 R. B. Braithwaite, "Critical Notice [Book Review] of *The Language of Morals* by R. M. Hare," *Mind*, LXIII (1954), 259.

19 Toulmin, *The Place of Reason in Ethics*, p. 4.

20 *Ibid.*, pp. 144–165.

21 *Ibid.*, p. 38.

22 *Ibid.*, p. 137.

23 *Ibid.*, p. 224.

24 R. M. Hare, "Book Review of Toulmin's *The Place of Reason in Ethics*," *The Philosophical Quarterly*, I (1951), 374.

25 Luther J. Binkley, *Contemporary Ethical Theories* (New York: Philosophical Library, Inc., 1961), pp. 115–116.

26 Ross, *The Right and the Good*, chs. 1 and 2.

27 John Rawls, "Two Concepts of Rules," *The Philosophical Review*, LXIV (1955), 3–32; John Rawls, "Justice As Fairness," *The Journal of Philosophy*, LIV (1957), 653–662; Both articles reprinted in Joseph Margolis, ed., *Contemporary Ethical Theory: A Book of Readings* (New York: Random House, Inc., 1966); David Lyons, *Forms and Limits of Utilitarianism* (Oxford: Clarendon Press, 1965), *passim*.

28 R. M. Hare, *Freedom and Reason* (Oxford: Clarendon Press, 1963), p. 90.

29 *Ibid.*, p. 97.

30 *Ibid.*, p. 113.

31 *Ibid.*, p. 34.

32 *Ibid.*, p. 118.

33 *Ibid.*, p. 151.

34 *Ibid.*, p. 157.

35 *Ibid.*, p. 159.

36 *Ibid.*, p. 159.

37 *Ibid.*, p. 170.

38 *Ibid.*, p. 171.

39 *Ibid.*, p. 178.

40 *Ibid.*, p. 185.

41 *Ibid.*, p. 218.

42 *Ibid.*, p. 223.

43 *Ibid.*, pp. 192–193.

44 *Ibid.*, p. 195.

45 *Ibid.*, p. 174.

46 *Ibid.*, p. 175.

47 *Ibid.*, p. 175.

48 Alan Gewirth, "Meta-Ethics and Normative Ethics," *Mind*, LXIX (1960), 191.

SELECTED READINGS

* *Available in paperback editions.*

ANALYTIC PHILOSOPHY: BASIC WORKS IN ANALYTIC PHILOSOPHY

* Austin, J. L. *How To Do Things With Words.* Edited by J. O. Urmson. New York: Oxford University Press, 1962.
———. *Philosophical Papers.* Edited by J. O. Urmson and G. J. Warnock. Oxford: Clarendon Press, 1961.
* Ayer, Alfred Jules. *Language, Truth and Logic.* 2nd ed. New York: Dover Publications, Inc., 1950.
* Flew, Antony, ed. *Logic and Language.* 1st and 2nd series. Garden City, N. Y.: Doubleday Anchor Books, 1965.
Wisdom, John. *Other Minds.* Oxford: Basil Blackwell, 1952.
———. *Philosophy and Psycho-Analysis.* Oxford: Basil Blackwell, 1957.
Wittgenstein, Ludwig. *The Blue and Brown Books.* New York: Harper Torchbooks, 1958.
———. *Philosophical Investigations.* Translated by G. E. M. Anscombe. 2nd ed. Oxford: Basil Blackwell, 1958. New York: The Macmillan Co., 1958.

INTERPRETATIONS OF ANALYTIC PHILOSOPHY

* Mehta, Ved. *Fly and the Fly-Bottle: Encounters with British Intellectuals.* Baltimore: Penguin Books, Inc., 1962.
Urmson, J. O. *Philosophical Analysis: Its Development Between the Two World Wars.* Oxford: Clarendon Press, 1958.
* Warnock, G. J. *English Philosophy Since 1900.* New York: Oxford University Press, 1959.
* White, Morton, ed. *The Age of Analysis: 20th Century Philosophers.* New York: The New American Library of World Literature, Inc., 1955.

ETHICAL THEORY: ANTHOLOGIES OF READINGS

* Castañeda, Hector-Neri and George Nakhnikian, eds. *Morality and the Language of Conduct.* Detroit: Wayne State University Press, 1965.
Katz, Joseph, Philip Nochlin, and Robert Stover, eds. *Writers on Ethics: Classical and Contemporary.* Princeton, N. J.: D. Van Nostrand Co., Inc., 1962.
* Margolis, Joseph, ed. *Contemporary Ethical Theory: A Book of Readings.* New York: Random House, Inc., 1966. An excellent anthology which includes most of the significant articles on meta-ethics.
* Taylor, Paul, ed. *The Moral Judgment: Readings in Contemporary Meta-Ethics.* Englewood Cliffs, N. J.: Prentice-Hall, Inc., 1963.

ETHICAL THEORY: PRIMARY SOURCES

Aiken, Henry David. *Reason and Conduct: New Bearings in Moral Philosophy.* New York: Alfred A. Knopf, 1962.
* Baier, Kurt. *The Moral Point of View: A Rational Basis of Ethics.* Abridged ed. New York: Random House, Inc., 1965.

D'Arcy, Eric. *Human Acts: An Essay in Their Moral Evaluation*. Oxford: Clarendon Press, 1963.

Ewing, A. C., *The Definition of Good*. New York: The Macmillan Co., 1947.

———. *Second Thoughts in Moral Philosophy*. London: Routledge & Kegan Paul Ltd., 1959.

* Hampshire, Stuart. *Thought and Action*. New York: The Viking Press, Inc., 1959.

* Hare, R. M. *Freedom and Reason*. Oxford: Clarendon Press, 1963.

* ———. *The Language of Morals*. Oxford: Clarendon Press, 1952.

Lyons, David. *Forms and Limits of Utilitarianism*. Oxford: Clarendon Press, 1965.

Moore, George Edward. *Principia Ethica*. Cambridge, England: Cambridge University Press, 1959.

* Nowell-Smith, P. H. *Ethics*. Baltimore: Penguin Books, Inc., 1954.

Ross, W. David. *Foundations of Ethics*. Oxford: Clarendon Press, 1949.

———. *The Right and the Good*. Oxford: Clarendon Press, 1955.

Singer, Marcus George. *Generalization in Ethics: An Essay in the Logic of Ethics with the Rudiments of a System of Moral Philosophy*. New York: Alfred A. Knopf, Inc., 1961.

* Stevenson, Charles L. *Ethics and Language*. New Haven: Yale University Press, 1960.

* ———. *Facts and Values: Studies in Ethical Analysis*. New Haven: Yale University Press, 1964.

Taylor, Paul W. *Normative Discourse*. Englewood Cliffs, N. J.: Prentice-Hall, Inc., 1961.

* Toulmin, Stephen. *The Place of Reason in Ethics*. Cambridge, England: Cambridge University Press, 1953.

Ziff, Paul. *Semantic Analysis*. Ithaca, N. Y.: Cornell University Press, 1960.

ETHICAL THEORY: SECONDARY SOURCES

Binkley, Luther J. *Contemporary Ethical Theories*. New York: Philosophical Library, Inc., 1961.

* Frankena, William K. *Ethics*. Englewood Cliffs, N. J.: Prentice-Hall, Inc., 1963.

Kerner, George C. *The Revolution in Ethical Theory*. New York: Oxford University Press, 1966.

Epilogue

A Basis for Decision

Suppose that after seriously considering the alternative ideals of life which compete for acceptance in our present Western world, the reader is still in doubt as to which of these values he should commit his life. Is there any defensible way of choosing between basic values? The reader will recall that we have seen in the last chapter that Toulmin and Hare suggest that the last line of defense for any proposed moral principle is a specification of the whole way of life of which this particular principle is a part. They do not, however, suggest that there are any principles which we can invoke in choosing between ways of life. They would no doubt encourage our examining the alternative ideals proposed by Ayn Rand, Hugh Hefner, Karl Marx, Søren Kierkegaard, Friedrich Nietzsche, Jean-Paul Sartre, Sigmund Freud, Erich Fromm, Joseph Fletcher, and the other writers we have considered, but how can we rationally choose between them? The analytic philosophers tell us we can explore in our imagination the implications of these ways of life and contrast them with the more or less unconsciously chosen ways of life we now follow. But, in the last analysis, the extent of their advice in helping us choose between alternative life styles is for them to agree with Sartre that each man must choose for himself and accept full responsibility for the choice he then makes. While we can justify a particular action because it falls under a particular rule, and we can in turn defend a particular rule because it fits in with a more general principle, how can we justify our basic principles? Are our basic ideals relative to our tastes after all? Are they ultimately arbitrary? I think not.

The reader who would decide to commit himself to a way of life after having explored alternative conceptions of the ideal life would not by any means be making an arbitrary decision. If he were to say that all the ways of life to which he might commit himself agree on all the basic ideals, therefore, it does not matter which he follows, he might indeed make an arbitrary choice. It would also be a foolish one, however, for it would be based upon a false premise. If the reader has gained anything from reading this book, it should be clear to him that not all the moralists we have studied affirm the same ideal goals for mankind. To commit oneself to Marxism, would imply working to achieve a classless society. This commitment would be radically different from devoting oneself to the society of free enterprise extolled by Ayn Rand. Neither goal would be consistent with R. M. Hare's commitment to a liberal open society. It is true that not all of the philosophies of life which we have considered disagree so radically, but that is far from saying that they are in basic agreement. Indeed, if they were in basic agreement concerning the best way of life for man, then we would face no conflict of ideals. We have seen, however, that there are alternative ideals of what a man ought to be. There is no scientific way of proving that one is correct, while the others are wrong. Indeed, since ideals deal with what ought to be, rather than with what is in fact the case, scientific information and logic cannot by themselves be used to generate a basic value commitment. We cannot avoid the fact that each man is faced with choosing his own life style. Again, however, to make such a decision after one has explored what the alternatives are is not to make an arbitrary choice, but is rather to make that decision upon the basis of the best evidence which one could find. Hare himself has expressed this point very well:

> To describe such ultimate decisions as arbitrary, because *ex hypothesi* everything which could be used to justify them has already been included in the decision, would be like saying that a complete description of the universe was utterly unfounded, because no further fact could be called upon in corroboration of it. This is not how we use the words 'arbitrary' and 'unfounded.' Far from being arbitrary, such a decision would be the most well-founded of decisions, because it would be based upon a consideration of everything upon which it could possibly be founded.[1]

If one is attempting to make a responsible moral commitment to a way of life, then a reflective consideration of alternative ways of life will be an extremely useful point from which to begin. We should be very clear, however, that such an investigation does not by itself prescribe what way of life one should choose. We have stressed many times that one's basic value commitments are influenced to a great extent by one's theory of human nature. What is man? What can he become? Indeed, is there a basic human nature which all men share? In answering these questions the findings of the natural and social sciences are extremely important, because any basic value commitment which would ask of man that which it is impossible for him to achieve would fail to satisfy our basic requirements of relevance and truth.

The thoughtful reader is now at the point of having to choose his own basic value commitments. While some ideals can be ruled out on the grounds of their failing to fit in with the beliefs about the nature of man which the reader holds, there are still many others which remain to compete for his acceptance. At this point we shall have to admit honestly that each person must make his own choice. If he is sensitive to the significance of ideals for his own conduct, he will make this choice in as responsible and rational a way as he can.

After one has made his own basic value commitments, he is committed to attempting to live by them. If he should find that the ideals he has chosen are not adequate to deal with the particular moral problems he faces, then he should reconsider his decision. In our changing world, it is quite likely that most of us will reexamine our ultimate commitments many times. The search for a way of life goes on as long as we live, for as Plato realized, "The matter is no chance trifle, but how we ought to live." [2]

We must disappoint the reader if he expected us to propose one ideal system of values to which all men would agree to commit themselves. What we can do, however, is perhaps of even more significance. We wish to stress that basic decisions about values should be made by examining the facts about man as they are made available to us by the sciences, and by a reflective consideration of the alternative ways of life which compete for our acceptance. This will provide us with a responsible basis for our own decisions concerning moral principles.

NOTES FOR EPILOGUE

1   R. M. Hare, *The Language of Morals* (Oxford: Clarendon Press, 1952), p. 69.
2   Plato, *The Republic* (352D), trans. by W. H. D. Rouse, in *Great Dialogues of Plato*, ed. by Eric H. Warmington and Philip G. Rouse (New York: The New American Library of World Literature, Inc., 1956), p. 152.

Acknowledgments

The author wishes to thank the publishers, or copyright holders, concerned for granting permission to quote from the following works:

Thomas J. J. Altizer and William Hamilton, *Radical Theology and the Death of God*, Bobbs-Merrill Co., Inc., copyright 1966.

Hazel E. Barnes, *An Existentialist Ethics*, © copyright 1967 by Hazel E. Barnes, reprinted by permission of Alfred A. Knopf, Inc.

Samuel Beckett, translated from his French original, *Waiting for Godot: A Tragi-Comedy in Two Acts*, Grove Press, Inc., copyright 1954.

Robert Bretall, ed., *A Kierkegaard Anthology*, Princeton University Press, copyright 1938.

D. Mackenzie Brown, ed., *Ultimate Concern: Tillich in Dialogue*, Harper & Row, Publishers, Inc., copyright 1965.

Emil Brunner, *Justice and the Social Order*, translated by Mary Hottinger, Harper & Row, Publishers, Inc., copyright 1945.

Harvey Cox, *The Secular City*, reprinted with permission of The Macmillan Company and SCM Press Ltd., London, © copyright 1965 by Harvey Cox.

Robert Denoon Cumming, ed., *The Philosophy of Jean-Paul Sartre*, reprinted by permission of Random House, Inc. and Alfred A. Knopf, Inc., © copyright 1965 by Random House, Inc.

Abraham Edel, *Ethical Judgment*, reprinted with permission of The Macmillan Company, copyright 1955 by The Free Press, a Corporation.

David L. Edwards, ed., *Honest to God Debate*, published in U.S.A. by the Westminster Press, 1963, © 1963 by the SCM Press Limited, London, used by permission of The Westminster Press and SCM Press Limited, London.

Frederick Engels, *Herr Eugen Dühring's Revolution in Science (Anti-Dühring)*, International Publishers Co., Inc., copyright 1939.

Joseph Fletcher, *Moral Responsibility*, The Westminster Press, © copyright 1967, used by permission of The Westminster Press and SCM Press Limited, London.

Joseph Fletcher, *Situation Ethics*, © copyright 1966 by W. L. Jenkins, used by permission of The Westminster Press and SCM Press, London.

Sigmund Freud, *Totem and Taboo* in *The Basic Writings of Sigmund Freud*, translated and edited by A. A. Brill, The Modern Library, 1938, by permission of Gioia Bernheim and Edmund Brill, holders of the copyright.

Sigmund Freud, *Civilization and Its Discontents*, translated and edited by James Strachey, W. W. Norton & Co., Inc., copyright 1961, by permission from the publisher for U.S.A. and dependencies only, world permission to quote from *Civilization and Its Discontents*, Volume 21 of the Standard Edition of *The Complete Psychological Works of Sigmund Freud* by Sigmund Freud Copyrights Ltd., The Institute of Psycho-Analysis and Mrs. Alix Strachey, and the Hogarth Press Ltd., London.

Sigmund Freud, *New Introductory Lectures on Psychoanalysis*, translated and edited by James Strachey, W. W. Norton & Co., Inc., copyright 1965, by permission of the publisher for U.S.A. and dependencies only, permission for the British Commonwealth by George Allen & Unwin Ltd., London.

Erich Fromm, *Man for Himself*, Holt, Rinehart and Winston, Inc., copyright 1947 by Erich Fromm, permission for U.S.A. and dependencies by Holt, Rinehart and Winston, Inc., permission for the British Commonwealth by Routledge & Kegan Paul Ltd., London.

Jean Genet, *The Balcony*, translated by Bernard Frechtman, Grove Press, Inc., copyright 1958.

R. M. Hare, *Freedom and Reason*, Clarendon Press, copyright 1963, by permission of the Clarendon Press, Oxford, England.

R. M. Hare, *The Language of Morals*, Clarendon Press, copyright 1952, by permission of the Clarendon Press, Oxford, England.

Hugh M. Hefner, *The Playboy Philosophy, Parts I, II, III, IV*, from *Playboy* Magazine, © copyright 1962, 1963, 1964, 1965 by HMH Publishing Co., Inc.

William James, *Pragmatism and Four Essays from the Meaning of Truth*, edited by Ralph Barton Perry, Longmans, Green & Co., Inc., copyright 1907, permission by David McKay Co.

Walter Kaufmann, trans. and ed., *The Portable Nietzsche*, The Viking Press, Inc., copyright 1954, reprinted by permission of The Viking Press, Inc.

Karl Marx, *Early Writings*, translated and edited by T. B. Bottomore, McGraw-Hill Book Co., Inc., copyright 1963, permission for world rights except British Commonwealth by McGraw-Hill Book Co., Inc., permission for British Commonwealth by C. A. Watts & Co., Ltd., London.

Karl Marx and Friedrich Engels, *The German Ideology, Parts I and III*, introduction and edited by R. Pascal, International Publishers Co., Inc., copyright 1947.

Arthur P. Mendel, ed., *Essential Works of Marxism*, Bantam Books, Inc., © copyright 1961.

Friedrich Nietzsche, *Beyond Good and Evil—A Prelude to a Philosophy of the Future*, translated by Walter Kaufmann, Random House, Inc., copyright 1966.

Friedrich Nietzsche, *Joyful Wisdom*, introduction by Kurt F. Reinhardt, translated by Thomas Common, Frederick Ungar Publishing Company, copyright 1960, permission by Frederick Ungar Publishing Company and George Allen & Unwin Ltd., London.

Paul Ramsey, *Deeds and Rules in Christian Ethics*, Charles Scribner's Sons, copyright 1967.

Ayn Rand, *The Virtue of Selfishness: A New Concept of Egoism*, The New American Library, Inc., copyright 1964.

Jean-Paul Sartre, *Being and Nothingness: An Essay in Phenomenological Ontology*, translated and introduction by Hazel E. Barnes, Philosophical Library, Inc., copyright 1956.

Jean-Paul Sartre, *Existentialism and Humanism*, translated by Philip Mairet, Methuen & Co., Ltd., London, copyright 1948. Reprinted as "Existentialism Is a Humanism" in Walter Kaufmann, ed., *Existentialism from Dostoevsky to Sartre*, Meridian Books, The World Publishing Company, © copyright 1956.

Jean-Paul Sartre, "Materialism and Revolution" in Jean-Paul Sartre, *Literary and Philosophical Essays*, translated by Annette Michelson, Collier Books, copyright 1962, permission for U.S.A. and open market throughout the world other than the British Empire by S. G. Phillips, Inc., holder of copyright, permission for British Commonwealth by Rider & Co., London, copyright 1955.

Jean-Paul Sartre, *No Exit and Three Other Plays*, translated by Stuart Gilbert, copyright 1946 by Stuart Gilbert, permission for U.S.A. by Alfred A. Knopf, Inc., permission for British Commonwealth by Hamish Hamilton Ltd., London.

Jean-Paul Sartre, *Search for a Method*, translated by Hazel E. Barnes, Alfred A. Knopf, Inc., copyright 1963, permission for the U.S.A. and Canada by Alfred A. Knopf, Inc., permission for the British Commonwealth under the title *The Problem of Method* by Methuen & Co., Ltd., London, permission for additional world rights by Editions Gallimard, Paris.

Jean-Paul Sartre, *What Is Literature?*, translated by Bernard Frechtman, Philosophical Library, Inc., copyright 1949.

Jean-Paul Sartre, *The Words*, translated by Bernard Frechtman, George Braziller, Inc., copyright 1964.

Mario Savio, "An End to History" in Paul Jacobs and Saul Landau, *The New Radicals: A Report with Documents*, Random House, Inc., copyright 1966.

Paul Tillich, *The Courage To Be*, Yale University Press, copyright 1952.

Paul Tillich, *Dynamics of Faith*, Harper & Row, Publishers, Inc., copyright 1957.

Paul Tillich, *Morality and Beyond*, Harper & Row, Publishers, Inc., copyright 1963.

Paul Tillich, *Systematic Theology (Three Volumes in One)*, University of Chicago Press, copyright Vol. I—1951, Vol. II—1957, Vol. III—1963.

Paul Tillich, *Theology of Culture*, Oxford University Press, copyright 1959.

Stephen Toulmin, *An Examination of the Place of Reason in Ethics*, Cambridge University Press, copyright 1950.

Peter Weiss, *The Investigation (A Play)*, English version by Jon Swan and Ulu Grosbard, Atheneum Publishers, © 1966 by Jon Swan and Ulu Grosbard.

John Wild, *The Challenge of Existentialism*, Indiana University Press, copyright 1955.

Index

Abraham and Isaac, Kierkegaard on, 135, 136, 143, 144
Absolute Spirit (Hegel), 48, 54
Absurd: all values viewed as, 4–7, 11, 37; Barnes on, 203; Beauvoir on, 198; theatre of the absurd, 5–7
Adler, Alfred, 105
Aesthetics, disputes about, 284–287
Agapē (Christian love), 314, 315; Brunner on, 251, 262–265; "Death of God theology" on, 247, 248; Fletcher on, 251, 253–260, 263, 266, 274–276; Niebuhr on, 251, 262–265; Ramsey on, 251, 265–269; Robinson on, 251, 260–262; Tillich on, 240–243
Agapism: act-agapism, 253, 254, 260, 266; mixed agapism, 265, 268; modified act-agapism, 253, 254, 260–265; rule-agapism, 253, 265
Alienation: African Communists on, 70; Camus on, 7; "Death of God theologians" on, 247; Fromm on, 76–79, 113–115, 120, 123, 217; Hegel on, 48, 50; Keniston on, 33, 34; Kierkegaard on, 139; Marx on, 34, 45, 48–56, 59–62, 72, 76–79, 113–115, 123, 207; of the New Radicals, 35–37; Niel on, 77–79; Sartre on, 177–180, 205–208, 211–213, 216–218; Tillich on, 214, 229, 230, 236–239, 244, 245; of youth, 1, 33, 34
Allport, Gordon, 106
Altizer, Thomas J. J., 247, 248, 272, 273
Altruism, Rand on, 25–27
Ambiguity, ethic of (Beauvoir), 197–201

Analytic philosophy and ethics, 213, 214, 282–327
Anguish: Kierkegaard on, 139; Sartre on, 175, 183, 184, 196
Antisemitism: and Nietzsche, 146, 158; Sartre on, 188, 189, 194
Anxiety, existential, 215, 247, 250; Freud on, 89, 99; Tillich on, 229–231, 235, 239, 241
Apollonian reason (Nietzsche), 145, 150
Aquinas, Thomas, 225
Aristotle, 26, 108, 116, 151, 225, 282
Aron, Raymond, 163, 165
Atheism, 111, 153–156, 233, 234, 271–273; of Sartre, 163, 164, 171, 174, 175, 181, 197, 215, 218
Augustine, St., 225
Authenticity, ethic of, 190, 214–219; Barnes on, 202–204; Heidegger on, 184–186, 190, 191, 216, 217; *see also* sincerity (Sartre)
Authoritarian ethics, 211, 229; Fromm on, 107–109, 117–119, 123
Ayer, A. J., 290, 291, 304

Bad faith (Sartre), 174, 186–191, 201, 215
Barnes, Hazel, 201–204, 218, 219
Barth, John, 5, 11
Barth, Karl, 140, 141, 226–228, 236, 271, 273
Bauer, Bruno, 49
Beauvoir, Simone de, 163, 165, 192, 197, 198, 201, 205, 206, 218, 219
Beckett, Samuel, 5, 6
Behavioral analysis of society, 36, 37, 74, 106; Dewey on, 18–22

333

334   *Index*

Being-for-itself (Sartre), 169–177, 181, 183, 186, 187, 190–193
Being-for-others (Sartre), 169, 176–179, 180, 189–191
Being-in-itself (Sartre), 169–174, 176, 180, 181, 187, 191, 193
Being-with-others (Sartre), 169, 179, 180, 208
Benedict, Ruth, 103
Bentham, Jeremy, 63, 76, 282
Bernstein, Eduard, 64
Binswanger, Ludwick, 121, 214
Bonhoeffer, Dietrich, 246, 247; Fletcher on, 255
Braithwaite, R. B., 298
Brinton, Crane, 158
Brunner, Emil, 140, 141, 251, 262–265, 273
Buber, Martin, 176

Camus, Albert, 7, 164, 200
Capitalism: Barnes on, 202; Barth on, 226; Fletcher on, 266; Fromm on, 113, 119, 120, 217; Hefner on, 130; Marx on, 45–67, 72–80, 139; Rand on, 25–32, 326; Sartre on, 179, 180, 196, 205–208, 211, 212
Carlyle, Thomas, 75
Carnegie, Dale, 17
Categorical imperative, 266; Barnes on, 202; Brunner on, 262; Kant on, 196, 197; Sartre on, 194, 196, 197; Tillich on, 239, 240, 243
Character orientations: Freud on, 112–116; Fromm on, 111–123
Chesterton, Gilbert K., 13
Choice, existential, *see* Existentialism
Christian love, *see* Agapē
Christian Science, 24, 320
Christianity, 34, 78, 79, 104, 111, 163, 215, 225–276; Freud on, 99; Kierkegaard on, 128–130, 134–144; Nietzsche on, 147, 151–153, 157, 158
Civil rights, movement for, 34–37
Civilization, Freud on, 85, 87, 93, 94, 96–106, 121
Class conflict, 208; Marx on, 51–60, 62, 63, 73–75; Sartre on, 207, 211–213
Classless society, 111, 209, 211, 213, 218, 219, 326; Lenin on, 67; Marx

Classless society (*Cont.*)
and Engels on, 44, 53–55, 57–62, 70, 75, 78–80
Communication, problem of, 6
Communism, 44–81, 139, 149; Barnes on, 202; Sartre on, 165, 166, 195, 196, 204–206, 217–219; Tillich on, 231, 232
Conditioning, cultural, 3, 8–10, 104–107, 112, 120, 123, 215, 291
Conformity to traditional values, 7, 10, 21, 24, 29, 32–38; Barnes on, 202, 203; Fromm on, 106, 107, 109, 120–122; Heidegger on, 185, 186, 216; Kierkegaard on, 128–130, 133, 136, 138, 142; Nietzsche on, 149, 153, 156, 157; Sartre on, 175, 181–184, 192, 215; Tillich on, 231, 235, 241
Conscience, 32, 215; Freud on, 87, 89, 98, 103; Fromm on, 109, 111, 117–119; Nietzsche on, 152; Tillich on, 242
Courage: Fletcher on, 255; Tillich on, 229–232, 234, 235, 242; *see also* Existentialism
Cox, Harvey, 22, 23, 32, 246–250, 272, 273
Crane, John, 31

Death: Heidegger on, 185, 186; Sartre on, 190, 191; Tillich on, 230, 231
Death of God, Nietzsche on, 145, 153–159, 234, 247, 273
"Death of God theology," 1, 23, 154, 155, 246–250, 271–273
Democracy, 232; Barnes on, 202, 204, 219; Bernstein on, 64; Dewey on, 21, 22, 24; Sartre on, 195
Descartes, Rene, 167
Despair, existentialist, 132–135, 139, 142, 143, 152, 153, 180, 196, 227–235, 248, 250
Dewey, John, 12, 18–22, 24, 108, 109; *see also* Pragmatism
Dictatorship of proletariat: Djilas on, 71; Lenin on, 66, 67; Mao on, 69; Marx on, 58, 59, 80; and Stalin, 67
Dionysian passions (Nietzsche), 145, 150
Djilas, Milovan, 70, 71

Dreams: Freud on, 85–87, 117; Fromm on, 117

Drives, basic, *see* Instincts

Drug addiction, 257, 274, 319, 320

Durkheim, Emile, 3

Edel, Abraham, 37, 38

Education, 34, 36; Barnes on, 202, 203; Dewey on, 19–22; Freud on, 101, 102; Fromm on, 114; Nietzsche on, 146, 155; Sartre on, 179

Ego: Adler on, 105; Freud on, 87–90, 93, 98, 100, 103, 104, 108; Fromm on, 108; Sartre on, 164, 187

Eichmann, Adolf, 115

Einstein, Albert, 1

Either/Or (Kierkegaard), 129–134, 138

Electra complex (Freud), 91

Empedocles, 92

Empiricists, 13, 14; Radical empiricism (James), 14–17

Ends-in-view (Dewey), 20, 24

Engels, Friedrich, 44, 60, 65, 68, 72; on class conflict, 55, 57; on classless society, 55, 62; life of, 46, 47; on peaceful means to achieve Communism, 63, 64; *see also* Karl Marx

Eros (love), 248, 255, 276; Fletcher on, 266, 274; Freud on, 90–93, 99–102; Tillich on, 240; *see also* Instincts, sexual

Estrangement, *see* Alienation

Eternal recurrence (Nietzsche), 155, 156

Ethical theory, 282–321; deontological contrasted with teleological, 251, 252, 265, 270, 300; emotive, 3, 290–294; meta-ethics contrasted with normative ethics, 282–284, 301–303, 309–313; naturalistic contrasted with non-naturalistic, 288–290, 293, 294, 312

Ewing, A. C., 290

Existentialism: and Freud, 93; and Fromm, 116, 120–122; and Hare, 307, 311, 314, 315; humanistic, 144–159, 162–219; and pragmatism, 16, 21, 23; and Rand, 25; religious, 127–144, 225–276

Existential phenomenology, 163–181, 200, 283

Existential psychoanalysis, 121, 214

Facticity (Sartre), 171–174, 187

Faith: Barnes on, 203, 204; Brunner on, 263; Fromm on, 118, 119; James on, 16, 17; Kierkegaard on, 134, 137, 140, 142; Tillich on, 233–238

Fanatic, 215, 264; contrasted with "idealist," 317–320; Hare on, 307–311, 313, 316–319; in moral arguments, 307–311

Father complex (Freud), 95–97

Feuerbach, Ludwig, 48–50, 72

Fletcher, Joseph, 251, 253–263, 265, 266, 274–276, 284, 325; Ramsey on, 265–267

Folkways, 4

Fosdick, Harry Emerson, 17

Frankel, Charles, 23

Frankena, William, 251–253, 260, 265–267, 273

Frazer, James, 94

Freedom, 34, 35, 72, 320; Barnes on, 201–204, 219; Camus on, 200; Engels on, 62; existentialists on, 127, 128; Fletcher on, 260; Fromm on, 107, 108, 116, 120; Hare on, 307; Hefner on, 29–33; Heidegger on, 184–186; Kierkegaard on, 131, 139; Marx on, 49, 50, 60, 68, 72, 76, 78; the New Radicals on, 35–37; Rand on, 25–29, 32; Sartre on, 164, 165, 169–184, 187–200, 205, 207, 212–218, 260, 325; Tillich on, 232, 234, 239, 242

Freud, Sigmund, 11, 31, 218, 225, 228, 284, 315, 316, 325; on civilization, 85–87, 93–106, 121; contrasted with Fromm, 106–108, 112–118, 121, 122; instinct theories of, 84–107, 115; life of, 84, 85; on morality and religion, 84–97, 100–105; on neurosis, 84–86, 89–97, 102–106; Sartre on, 169, 182, 187; on sexuality, 84–87, 90–92, 98, 101–105; on structure of mind, 85–94, 103, 104

Fromm, Erich, 11, 21, 29, 45, 72, 76–79, 104–106, 217, 218, 231, 243, 284, 288, 289, 307, 308, 325; on authoritarianism, 107–109, 117–119, 123;

Fromm (*Cont.*)
on character orientations, 111–123, 185; on çonscience, 109, 111, 117–119; contrasted with Freud, 106–108, 112–118, 121, 122; on faith, 118, 119; on normative humanism, 106–111, 116–119, 121–123; on relativism, 106, 108, 109, 118; on a sane society, 118–121; on our sick society, 106–109, 119

Genet, Jean, 5–7; Sartre on, 182, 189, 190, 205, 219
Gewirth, Alan, 321
God: Barth on, 226–228, 236, 271; Bonhoeffer on, 246, 247; Brunner on, 262–264; Cox on, 249, 250; "Death of God theologians" on, 247–250, 271, 272; Fletcher on, 256, 257; Hegel on, 48; Hegelians, left-wing on, 49; Kierkegaard on, 129, 130, 134–140; Ramsey on, 265, 266; Robinson on, 260; Sartre on, 163, 164, 171, 174, 175, 181, 193, 197, 218; Tillich on, 228, 233–245, 271, 272
Golden-rule, the, 306, 316
Good reasons in moral disputes, *see* Moral disputes, logic of
Growth, goal for Dewey, 20–22

Hamilton, William, 247, 248, 272, 273
Happiness as a value (Hedonism), 33, 228, 232, 239, 242, 288, 289; Fletcher on, 256; Freud on (pleasure principle), 88, 89, 95–98, 102; Fromm on, 115, 118; Hefner on, 30–32; Kierkegaard on, 130–133, 136; Rand on, 26–30; Sartre on, 196, 200, 213
Hare, R. M.: on language of morals, 295–298, 312, 313; on moral disputes, 268, 296, 302–321, 325, 326
Hebraic-Christian religion, 5, 118, 122, 147, 150, 233, 244; compared to Marxism, 54, 78, 79
Hefner, Hugh, 29–32, 37, 325
Hegel, G. W. F., 46–50, 54, 55, 63, 75, 79, 148, 167, 176, 244
Hegelianism, 45–50, 54; and Kierkegaard, 130, 134–142; and Marx, 45–50, 55

Heidegger, Martin, 141, 145, 167–169, 184–186, 190, 216, 217, 228, 234
Homosexuality: Fletcher on, 259; Sartre on, 182–184, 187–189
Hook, Sidney, 76
Horney, Karen, 105
Humanism, 34, 227, 243; and Christianity, 140, 248, 262, 271, 273; *see also* Existentialism, Freud, Fromm, Hare, Marx, the New Radicals, and Pragmatism
Husserl, Edmund, 163–169
Huxley, Julian, 117

Id: Freud on, 87–94, 98, 100, 103, 104, 108; Fromm on, 108; Sartre on, 187
Ideals, on choosing between, 325–327
Ideologies: Fromm on, 110, 111; Mannheim on, 4
Individual, primacy of, *see* Existentialism
Instincts, Freud on: aggressive and destructive, 84, 87, 90, 92–107, 115, 214, 315, 316; self-preservative, 88–92; sexual, 84–107, 214
Instrumentalism, Dewey's philosophy, 18–22
Intuitionists, *see* Ethical theory, non-naturalists
Ionesco, Eugène, 5–7
I-Thou relationships, 176, 178, 238; Barnes on, 201, 202, 218; Brunner on, 262–264; Fletcher on, 254

James, William, 12–18, 21, 22, 24
Jaspers, Karl, 141, 145, 156, 157
Jesus Christ, 76, 155, 225; Barth on, 227, 228, 236; Bonhoeffer on, 247; Brunner on, 263; Cox on, 250; "Death of God theologians" on, 247–250, 273; Fletcher on, 256, 259; Kierkegaard on, 129, 130, 135, 137, 140, 141; Ramsey on, 265; Tillich on, 236, 239, 244
Jung, Carl, 105
Justice: Fromm on, 115; and the New Radicals, 32–35; in philosophical ethics, 251, 300, 303, 317, 320; Rand on, 28, 29
Justice in Christian Ethics: Brunner on, 262–265; "Death of God theo-

Justice in Christian Ethics (*Cont.*) logians" on, 248, 250; Fletcher on, 254–256, 263; Niebuhr on, 262–265; Ramsey on, 268; Robinson on, 262; Tillich on, 225, 232, 237, 240, 241, 244

Kafka, Franz, 191, 192
Kant, Immanuel, 132, 148, 239, 282; compared with Sartre, 195–198; Fletcher on, 254, 266
Kardiner, Abram, 105, 107
Kaufmann, Walter, 144, 158
Kautsky, Karl, 65
Keniston, Kenneth, 33, 34
Keynes, John Maynard, 73
Kierkegaard, Søren, 11, 34, 77, 122, 225–227, 262, 273, 284, 307, 308, 325; on alienation, 139; on Christianity, 128–130, 134–144, 157, 158; on crisis of despair, 132–135, 139, 142, 143; on existential choice, 132–136, 140–144; on Hegelian philosophy, 130, 134–138, 140–142; life of, 128–130; and Nietzsche compared, 127, 128, 153, 156–158; on teleological suspension of ethics, 135, 144, 262; on three stages of life, 130–136, 142, 143
Kinsey reports on sexual behavior, 31

Law, civil, 115, 243, 256, 311; Fletcher on, 256; Ramsey on, 270; Robinson on, 262
Law, natural: in Christian ethics, 255; Tillich on, 240, 243
Legalism, moral, 76; Brunner on, 262; in Christian ethics, 272, 275, 276; Fletcher on, 253–257; Niebuhr on, 262; Ramsey on, 269; Robinson on, 260; Tillich on, 239, 241
Lenin, Nikolai, 58, 63–71
Libido: Freud on, 88, 106; Tillich on, 240, 241
Life-world (*Lebenswelt*), 168, 169, 214, 231
Linguistic analysis of value terms, 282–298
Lippmann, Walter, 2
Love: Barnes on, 202; Freud on, 91–93, 98–101, 104–107; Fromm on, 106, 107, 113–119; Hefner on, 31;

Love (*Cont.*) Kierkegaard on, 132, 137; the New Radicals on, 36, 37; Sartre on, 178, 180; Tillich on, 237–244, 255; *see also Agapē*
Lyons, David, 303

MacIntyre, Alasdair: on new theology, 272, 273
Madman, Parable of (Nietzsche), 154
Mannheim, Karl, 4
Mao Tse-tung, 69–71
Marcuse, Herbert, 106, 121
Marquand, John, 114
Marx, Karl, 11, 29, 106, 120–123, 149, 158, 225, 243, 250, 284, 325; on alienation, 34, 45, 48–56, 59–62, 72, 76–79, 113, 115, 138, 139, 244; on capitalism, 45–67, 72–80, 139; on class conflict and proletarian revolution, 46, 47, 51–60, 62–68, 73–75; on classless society, 44, 53–55, 57–62, 70, 75, 78–80; compared to Hebraic-Christian religion, 54, 78, 79; and dialectical (historical) materialism, 46–49, 54, 55, 59–62, 72–75, 79, 80, 102; on dictatorship of proletariat, 58, 59, 80; relation to Hegelians, 45, 46, 48–50, 55; as a humanist, 44, 45, 53–55, 59, 60, 69–73, 75–81; life of, 45–47
Marxism, 44, 45, 73, 74, 111, 326; classical, 54–63; ideological struggle within, 68–72; in Russia and China, 64–72; Sartre's relation to, 162, 165, 166, 176, 179, 195, 196, 204–213, 216–219
Maslow, Abraham, 106
Mass media, affect on values by, 8, 9, 77, 78, 120, 121, 138, 139, 144, 192
Materialism, dialectical (Marxian), 46–49, 54, 55, 59–62, 69, 72–77, 79, 80; Sartre on, 204–208, 211, 217
May, Rollo, 106, 121
Mead, Margaret, 103
Mental health: Freud on, 89, 94, 101–103; Fromm on, 107
Merleau-Ponty, 165, 206
Mill, John Stuart, 76, 282
Miller, Arthur, 25, 114
Minority group persecution, arguments against, 287, 303, 305

Money as a value, 266; Marx on, 52, 53, 77; Rand on, 29
Moore, G. E., 213, 214, 240, 288–290, 294, 312
Moral disputes, logic of, 283–287, 293–303; Ayer on, 291, 304; Hare on, 296, 302–321; Stevenson on, 292, 293; Toulmin on, 294, 298–303, 313, 316
Mores, 4

Naturalistic fallacy, 121, 122, 240, 288, 289, 312
Nazism, 162, 164, 182, 226, 231, 243, 246; and moral arguments (Hare), 284, 303, 308–310, 313–319; Nietzsche's relation to, 146, 157, 158
Neo-Freudians, 103–106, 107
Neo-Orthodox theology, 226–228, 271
Neurosis: Freud on, 84–86, 89–97, 102–106; Fromm on, 107, 118; Tillich on, 230
Newfield, Jack, 36
New morality, the, 11, 21, 32, 152–155, 225, 241, 242, 247, 257; see also Situation ethics
New Radicals, the, 34–38, 202
Niebuhr, Reinhold, 127, 141, 229, 251, 262–265, 273
Niel, Mathilde, 77–79
Nietzsche, Friedrich, 11, 34, 73, 122, 181, 218, 225, 234, 248, 273, 284, 325; on death of God, 145, 153–159, 247, 273; and existentialism, 144–148, 152, 153, 156–159; life of, 145, 146; on master and slave moralities, 149–153, 157, 158; on the overman, 146, 154–156, 158; view of philosophy of, 146–149, 153, 156
Normative humanism (Fromm), 106–111, 116–119, 121–123
Nowell-Smith, P. H., 297, 298, 312
Nuclear warfare, threat of, 115, 120, 121, 152

Objectivism (Rand), 25–30
Oedipus complex, 91, 92, 96, 103
One world, idea of, 1, 2
Open question argument, see Naturalistic fallacy

Open society, 14, 22, 24, 80, 229, 294; and Hare, 308–310, 313–321, 326
Organization man, the, 24, 25, 33, 37, 121, 186; and Rand, 25, 29
"The Other": Barnes on, 201, 202; Sartre on, 176–179, 191–196, 199, 201, 209–211, 218; Tillich on, 234, 235
Overman, Nietzsche on, 146, 154–156, 158
Oxford philosophy, 293, 312; see also R. M. Hare

Packard, Vance, 24, 25, 121
Patriotism, Fletcher on, 258, 275
Paul, St., 225, 226, 241, 244
Peale, Norman Vincent, 17
Peirce, Charles Sanders, 12
Phenomenology, 163, 166–169; see also Existential phenomenology
Philia (brotherly love), 240, 255–257; see also agapē, eros and love
Plato, 76, 108, 240, 282, 327
Playboy Philosophy, 29–33, 198; Cox on, 32; Crane on, 31; Fletcher on, 258, 275
Pleasure, see Happiness
Pluralism in ideals, Hare on, 306–308
Popper, Karl, 74, 75, 80
Power, will to, Nietzsche on, 146, 149–152, 156, 158
Pragmatism, 69, 246, 249, 250, 272, 273, 292, 306; Cox on, 22, 23; of Dewey, 12, 18–22, 24; of James, 12–18, 22, 24; popular, 12, 17, 22–24, 34, 36
Presuppositions, Nietzsche on, 146–150, 153, 157, 158
Prima facie duties, 251, 270, 302
Principles in ethics, see Rules in ethics
Propaganda, 292, 293; Hare on, 310
Property rights, Rand on, 27, 28
Psychoanalysis, 214; and Kierkegaard, 139; and Sartre, 205; and Tillich, 242; see also Freud and Fromm

Racial equality, 32, 34–47, 198, 218, 225, 232, 248, 273, 274, 292; Hare on, 303, 310–321
Ramsey, Paul, 251, 265–271, 276
Rand, Ayn, 25–30, 37, 202, 325, 326
Rank, Otto, 105

Rationalization: Freud on, 93, 100, 102; Nietzsche on, 147

Rawls, John, 265, 268, 269, 302, 303

Reason, basis for morality: Freud on, 84, 100–103; Fromm on, 108, 116–119

Relativism, moral, 2–12, 21, 24, 32, 37, 215, 325; Fletcher on, 253–260; Fromm on, 106–109, 118; Nietzsche on, 147–149, 156; Robinson on, 260–262; Sartre on, 175, 181–184, 191, 192, 196, 197, 215, 218; Tillich on, 239–241; two interpretations of, 4–11

Religion, 1, 2; Cox on, 22, 23; Dewey on, 19, 22; Freud on, 85, 94–97, 100–105; Fromm on, 112, 118; Hegelians on, 46, 49, 50; James on, 15–17; Marx on, 46, 49, 50; *see also* Christianity and God

Riesman, David, 121

Riots, 248, 292; causes of, 35

Robinson, John A. T., Bishop, 246, 247, 251, 260–262, 265

Rogers, Carl, 106

Roles, playing of, 25, 74; Genet on, 6, 7; Heidegger on, 185; Sartre on, 171, 172, 188–190

Ross, W. D., 270, 290, 302

Rousseau, Jean Jacques, 98

Rules in ethics, 251–254, 274–276, 325–327; Brunner on, 262, 263; Fletcher on, 259–262, 266; Frankena on, 266, 267; Hare on, 268; Ramsey on, 265–271, 276; Rawls on, 265, 268, 269; Robinson on, 260–262; summary rules distinguished from general rules, 266, 267; Tillich on, 242; Toulmin on, 300–302

Russell, Bertrand, 1, 2

Salinger, J. D., 33, 34

Sartre, Jean-Paul, 16, 141, 145, 225, 228, 232, 234, 247, 250, 260, 283, 284, 287, 325; on alienation, 177, 179, 180, 205–208, 211–213, 216–218; on bad faith and sincerity (good faith), 174, 186–191, 199, 201, 204, 215, 219; existential humanism of, 165, 166, 169, 181–201, 203–207, 211–219; on human condition (*Being and Nothingness*),

Sartre (*Cont.*) 166–181; life of, 162–166; on man as creator of values, 173, 181–192; and Marxism, 162, 165, 166, 176, 179, 195, 196, 204–213, 216–219; on values determined by social class, 205, 211–213, 217, 218; as a writer, 162–165, 193–196, 200

Savio, Mario, 36, 37

Scarcity, economy of, Sartre on, 205, 208–213, 217

Secularism and the new theology, 246–250, 272, 273

Self-interest, rational: Hefner on, 29–32; Rand on, 25–30

Self-realization, ethic of, 26, 27, 116, 117, 120, 289; Barnes on, 203; Fletcher on, 256; Nietzsche on, 146, 155–157; Tillich on, 230–232

Senghor, Léopold, 73, 74

Sex, ethics of: Fletcher on, 256–259, 266, 274, 275; Ramsey on, 267, 268

Sexuality, freedom advocated: Freud on, 84–87, 90–92, 98, 101–105, 112, 113, 116; by Hefner, 29–32; Sartre on, 178, 182; *see also* Instincts, sexual

Sin and salvation: Barth on, 226; Brunner on, 263; Fletcher on, 260, 266; Freud on, 97; Kierkegaard on, 134, 135; Marxism viewed in terms of, 77–79; Sartre on, 163–166, 193, 204–207, 213, 219; Tillich on, 238–245

Sincerity (good faith), Sartre on, 186–191, 197–201, 204, 219

Situation ethics, 21, 152, 241, 242, 247, 251–262, 265–271, 274–276, 314, 315

Skinner, B. F., 8–10

Social action, 226; of new theologians, 248, 250, 264

Social sciences and cultural relativism, 1–12, 21

Social structures, Sartre on, 209–213

Socialism, evolutionary, 64, 66, 78

Socialist Humanism, 45, 72, 76

Society, sane or sick, Fromm on, 106–109, 118–121

Socrates, 38, 102, 139, 157

Spinoza, Baruch, 108

Stalin, Joseph V., 63, 67–71, 115, 204

Status, as a value, 24, 25
Stevenson, Charles, 291–293
Subjectivity as truth, 127; Kierkegaard on, 130, 137–143
Sublimation: Freud on, 84, 88, 90, 94, 99–104; Nietzsche on, 151
Success as a value, 17, 30, 33, 34, 114, 228, 232
Sullivan, Harry Stack, 105, 107
Sumner, William Graham, 3, 4
Super-ego: Freud on, 87–94, 98–104; Sartre on, 187
Symbols and myths, Tillich on, 233–239, 243–245, 272

Technology, affect on values by, 1, 2, 12, 20, 23, 36, 37, 44, 62, 66, 68, 75–79, 111, 120, 139, 213, 237, 246–250, 261, 272, 273
Thanatos, *see* Instincts, aggressive and destructive
Tillich, Paul, on courage, 229–232, 234, 235, 242; on estrangement (alienation), 229, 230, 236, 238, 239, 244, 245; on ethics, 239–243; on God, 233–245, 271, 272; on humanistic existentialism, 141, 214–217; on Jesus, 236, 239, 244; on justice, 225, 232, 237, 240, 241, 244; life of, 228, 229; on love, 237, 238, 240–244, 255; on religion, 232–242, 271, 272; as a religious existentialist, 228–249, 271–273; on sin and salvation, 238, 239, 241, 243–245; on symbols and myths, 233–239, 243–245, 272; on transcending faith, 233–238
Tolerance, 84, 102, 103, 218; Hare on, 308–310, 313, 317, 318; Sartre on, 178, 179
Toulmin, Stephen, 293, 294, 298–303, 312, 316, 325
Transcendence: Barnes on, 203; Sartre on, 171–174, 177, 180, 183, 187
Truth: Nietzsche on, 146, 147, 153,

Truth (*Cont.*)
154; pragmatic test for, 14–17; *see also* Subjectivity as truth
Tucker, Robert C., 45, 76, 79

Ultimate concern, *see* Tillich on religion
Uncommitted, the, 33, 34, 36
Unconscious, the: Freud on, 84–93, 100–105; Sartre on, 169, 187
Utilitarianism, 239, 251–253, 256, 268–271, 276, 303; act- and rule-utilitarianism contrasted, 252, 253; Hare on, 306, 313, 316; Toulmin on, 301, 302, 312, 316
Utopian Socialists, 53, 76

Values: choosing between, 325–327; disputes about, *see* Moral disputes, logic of; facts contrasted with, 3, 8–10, 288–291, 301–305, 309, 310, 321, 326; as irrational and arbitrary, 4–7, 11, 37, 325, 326; theoretical basis for, 37, 38
Value judgment, nature of, 8–11
Value terms, meaning and use of, 282–303, 309, 312, 316
Violence: Beauvoir on, 198; Sartre on, 209, 210, 218, 219

Welfare state, 73, 78, 120; Barnes on, 202; and Marxism, 217; Rand on, 28
Westermarck, Edward, 2, 3
We-subject: Barnes on, 202; Sartre on, 179, 180
Whyte, William, 24, 25, 121
Wild, John, 186
Will to believe, James on, 16–18, 24
Wisdom, John, 294, 299
Wittgenstein, Ludwig, 293, 297, 298, 312

Zarathustra (Nietzsche), 145, 150, 155
Zen Buddhism, 24

This book is an introduction to, and an exploration in detail of, today's major Western value systems. These systems—Marxism, Psychoanalytic Humanism, Existentialism, New Morality, "Death of God" Theology, and Analytic Philosophy—deal with the search for satisfactory value commitments based on insights gleaned from the social sciences, the humanities, philosophy, and religion.

The first chapter surveys the moral climate of our century in order to show how the relativism and pragmatism of the early decades of the twentieth century have modified present day moral positions. The body of the book is then concerned with exploring in some detail the leading competing systems of values in the present Western world. In the final chapter the author shows how contemporary analytical philosophy can be relevant to one who is seeking to choose between conflicting ideals of life. Each chapter expounds the basic philosophies of the writers considered and raises central evaluative questions in order to help the reader think through the issues for himself.

Conflict of Ideals is intended to serve as a guide, not as a substitute, for the works of the most important thinkers who have influenced the present search for a satisfactory way of life. The text and suggested readings appended at the end of each chapter refer the reader to primary sources so that he may explore the works which interest him to better understand the consequences of the ideas examined. The book will be appropriate for a wide variety of introductory courses in Philosophy, Ethics, Religion, Social Sciences, and the Humanities, and can also be used in many courses dealing with the contemporary world. This volume, moreover, is equally helpful to the general reader who needs guidance in understanding the issues posed by competing values in our present world.

About the Author

LUTHER J. BINKLEY is Professor of Philosophy and Ethics and Chairman of the Department of Philosophy at Franklin and Marshall College. He received his Ph.D. from Harvard University, and has been a Visiting Fellow in Philosophy at Princeton University and Cambridge University, England. He has published two other books, including *Contemporary Ethical Theories*, and has contributed articles to several professional journals. Professor Binkley is a member of such groups as the American Philosophical Association, the American Society for Aesthetics, and the Society for the Scientific Study of Religion.

AMERICAN BOOK • VAN NOSTRAND • REINHOLD CO.
New York   Toronto   London   Melbourne

50446   140
              B51

50446   140

Binkley, Luther J.   B51

AUTHOR

Conflict of Ideals

TITLE

DATE DUE	BORROWER'S NAME	DATE RETURNED
FEB 6 '73	B. Macomber	
OCT 9 '73	Sharon Fedoruk	
JAN 29 '74	D. Westlund	SEP 25 '73
JAN 27 '76		JAN 25 '74
NOV 16 '76	Tim Bailey	MAR
MAY		